FROM THE BOOKS OF

Laurel Anne Cawrse

FABULOUS FRUIT DESSERTS

Also by Terence Janericco

The Book of Great Hors d'Oeuvre
The Book of Great Breakfasts and Brunches
The Book of Great Soups, Sandwiches and Breads

FABULOUS FRUIT DESSERTS

Their Preparation, Presentation & Creation

by Terence Janericco

A DIVISION OF YANKEE PUBLISHING INCORPORATED
DUBLIN, NEW HAMPSHIRE

Designed by Jill Shaffer
Color photographs by James Scherer
Line drawings by Anne Vadeboncoeur

First Edition
Copyright 1986 by Yankee Publishing Incorporated
Printed in the United States of America

Library of Congress Catalog Card Number: 85-51873
ISBN: 0-89909-092-3

To
David Blackmon
Susan Payne
Donna Thomas

Thank you.

Acknowledgments

My sincerest appreciation to Glenna Bradley and Jean Truitt for their patience and understanding. They are to be applauded for interpreting and retyping my original manuscript.

CONTENTS

Introduction 9

Fruit Preparation & Presentation 11

Simple Fruit Desserts 23

Macédoines, Mélanges, Cups & Compotes 73

Fools, Whips, Snows & Creams 87

Custards 99

Bavarian Creams 109

Charlottes 117

Mousses 131

Frozen Desserts 145

Puddings 161

Dessert Omelets 183

189   Crêpes

197   Fritters & Beignets

203   Soufflés

209   Tarts & Pies

235   Gâteaux, Torten & Fancy Cakes

259   Cookies, Plain Cakes & Confections

269   Sauces

277   Basic Recipes

287   Index

INTRODUCTION

APPLES and oranges, bananas, grapes, peaches and pears, raspberries, blueberries, any berries — the very thought of these fruits excites the palate. The mention of certain fruits evokes the seasons for us all as clearly as Proust's madeleines evoked memories for him. Berries and cherries hail the late spring and early summer. Peaches, nectarines, and plums remind us of summer full-blown, while apples and pears usher us into fall and winter. The dried fruits of summer and fall — the pears, apples, prunes, and apricots — not only get us through the winter, but also remind us of the joys to come with warmer weather.

Today, fresh fruits in great variety are available year-round. Although winter fruits are no match for those in season, most of us would agree that even winter strawberries can be delicious. And the rather too-green winter pears, which never ripen to out-of-hand eating perfection, work very well when carefully poached or baked. Apples, of course, are available in all seasons — from the world around. Then there are the ever-present citrus fruits: oranges, lemons, limes, and grapefruits. More markets are now stocking fruits from other lands than ever before, and in fact some once-exotic fruits, such as mangoes and papayas, are close to becoming staples. Even the more unusual fruits are no longer relegated to the gourmet shop:

carambolas, tamarinds, and prickly pears are often available in their season in many supermarkets as well as at luxury fruiterers. And now the darling of *nouvelle cuisine*, the kiwifruit, is found everywhere, too.

You can serve fruit as a dessert effortlessly. Most fruits need no more preparation than peeling, and are usually ready to eat when picked — presuming they were picked at the proper point of ripeness. But fruits also lend themselves to unlimited preparations, both hot and cold. Fruit desserts can range all the way from a simple bunch of grapes to elaborate torten, charlottes, and multi-flavored mousses.

Fruits, especially those in season, make economical dessert choices as well, although out-of-season fruits (winter raspberries, for example) can cost a fortune. And, of course, fruits that are highly perishable or require intensive labor to harvest cost more than those that are more easily and quickly harvested. Every fruit has its season and can usually be readily found at that time, though in certain areas the season may be quite short. Also, weather conditions may despoil a crop so that very little of a particular fruit appears in the markets. But neither high cost nor short supply need be a problem: fortunately, you can substitute fruits of similar types in most recipes. Most berries can be interchanged with delicious results, and apples, pears, and peaches can replace one another according to availability. (Naturally, though, if you have your heart set on a peach cobbler in January, an apple cobbler will not be the same!)

Besides being delicious and, when in season, economical, fruits are nutritious. They not only provide many vitamins but have the added benefit of being low in calories as well. With fruits, as with vegetables, it is what we do to them that is the problem. Many of the desserts in this book are low in calories, especially when compared to other desserts. There are, of course, a number of preparations that are sinfully and gloriously rich. But if you eat simple fruits for dessert most of the time, an occasional splurge won't harm your figure, and will most assuredly lift your spirits!

The majority of the recipes in this book call for fresh fruits. With the constant availability of wonderful fresh fruits year-round, there is little need to use frozen or canned fruits. (On occasion a frozen or canned fruit is acceptable: those instances are indicated in the recipes.) However, no self-respecting cook will use canned pears or frozen melon to prepare a dessert that specifically calls for the fresh ingredients. If the particular fresh fruit needed is not available, choose another dessert. With rare exceptions, only fresh fruits will make your desserts the best they can be.

The recipes in this book are arranged according to the various techniques of preparation, such as: Bavarian creams, soufflés, crêpes, etc. If you wish to know what to do with a surfeit of pears, check the Index for the many possibilities; if you would like to find a suitable type of dessert preparation, check the specific section.

As with all cookbooks, there are certain basic recipes that are used often. These are given, as are the various sauces, in a separate chapter at the end of the book for easy reference.

FRUIT PREPARATION & PRESENTATION

FRUITS may be served in many different — and inviting — ways. Serve them on their own as a snack, or to end a simple meal. Serve fruits hot, cold, raw, poached, or baked. Sprinkle them with sugar, top them with cream, or lace them with liqueurs — or use a combination of serving suggestions. For a more elaborate presentation, serve the fruit with a single sauce or perhaps two and in all manner of elegant desserts.

PROPER HANDLING

When you bring fruit home from the market, remove it from its package and go over it carefully. If you have not personally selected the fruits at the store, pick them over now and set aside any bruised fruits for immediate use. Damaged fruits or those that are overripe may need to be discarded. Spread berries on paper toweling and discard any stalks, leaves, twigs, or underripe berries, as well as berries that are not in fit condition.

Do not wash fruit until just before serving; fruit washed too long before serving will deteriorate rapidly. Return picked-over berries to their original container or to a colander so that air can pass around them. When you are ready to wash the berries, rinse them quickly under cold running water, drain them well, and dry them on paper toweling: porous berries such as strawberries will absorb water if left to soak. (In the past it was not uncommon for recipes to instruct the cook to rinse the berries in wine — champagne was usually specified — to clean them. The idea was only a little precious. The wine gives the berries an added dimension of flavor, and once any grit has settled, makes a delicious drink for the cook.) However you wish to prepare

them, always drain berries well and dry them on paper toweling; then keep them cool until ready to serve.

If you have your own berry patch, you know that fruits picked in the early morning with the coolness of the evening still on them are perfection. However, this opportunity is not available to most of us. Always let refrigerated fruit come to just below room temperature before serving: fruits served too cold have less flavor than those served at or just below room temperature. If needed immediately, serve just-purchased fruit that is still too warm on a bed of crushed ice. Or try the Italian method — place the fruit in a bowl half filled with cold water. The evaporation of the water helps to cool the fruit and keeps it at the proper temperature for eating. Do not use this method with porous fruits such as strawberries, however.

PREPARING THE INDIVIDUAL FRUITS

Many fruits are easy to prepare for serving, while others require special attention. The proper techniques for preparing the fruits used in this book follow here.

APPLES

Wash all apples to be eaten raw. For most preparations, apples should be peeled with a vegetable peeler. Core apples whole by inserting an apple corer through the center. If the apples are to be halved for stuffing, cut them in half from stem to blossom end; then, with a sharp knife or melon baller, scoop out the seed area. If the apples are to be sliced, cut them into quarters and remove the core, including the casings and seeds, with a knife; then cut into slices.

There is a star in every apple. To expose it to entice children to eat the fruit, cut the apple into slices horizontally. The seed casings form a star in the slice. In this way children can see where the seeds are and are less apt to bite into them.

APRICOTS
Wash before serving raw. Apricots are not usually peeled. To remove the pit from the apricot, cut around the apricot down to the pit. Twist the two halves, pull the fruit apart, and then pull out the pit.

AVOCADOS
Avocados are used in a few desserts. They are a surprising and interesting change from the usual fruits. With a sharp knife, cut into the flesh, encircling the pit from top to bottom. Then twist the two halves and pull them apart. Pry out the pit with a sharp knife and scoop the flesh out of the fruit with a spoon. Use avocado pulp right away or refrigerate it.

BANANAS
To peel bananas, cut off both ends and pull the skin off in sections. Bananas darken when exposed to the air; to keep them from discoloring, peel and add to fruit combinations just before serving. If necessary to hold, sprinkle with lemon juice. Banana skins turn brown if refrigerated; however, the fruit will be fine.

BLACKBERRIES
See directions for raspberries.

BLUEBERRIES
Spread on paper toweling and pick out any twigs, leaves, and under- or overripe fruit. Rinse in a colander under cold running water, drain, and dry well.

CACTUS PEARS
See directions for prickly pears.

CARAMBOLA
This is also called starfruit. The flavor is citruslike and makes an interesting and flavorful accompaniment to macédoines or fruit cups. The whole fruit is edible. Slice across to display the stars.

CHERRIES
Raw cherries are, of course, delicious. To use in fruit desserts, always pit the cherries. There are several different makes of cherry pitters sold in gourmet shops. They are worth the investment.

CHESTNUTS
Chestnuts can be bought dried, prepared in brine, or in syrup. For desserts, the most convenient to use are those packed in syrup. They are expensive, however, so you may choose to prepare the chestnuts yourself.

To Peel
With a sharp knife, cut a cross on one side of each chestnut. Put the chestnuts into boiling water and simmer for 20 minutes, then drain and let stand until cool. Peel the shell from each chestnut and rub off the brown skin.

To Rehydrate Dried Chestnuts
Put the chestnuts into water to cover and let stand for 12 hours. Drain, re-cover with cold water, and simmer until tender.

COCONUTS
With a screwdriver, pierce the "eyes" — the dark spots on the top of the coconut. Drain out the milky liquid and discard. Turn the coconut onto its side and, while turning it, rap around the center of the coconut with a hammer or with the back of a heavy cleaver until the nut splits

apart (this does not require great force). When split, break the halves into sections, and pry the meat from the shell. With a vegetable peeler, pare the barklike skin from the meat. Grate the coconut on a four-sided grater using the largest holes, or shred it in a food processor using the shredding blade.

DATES
Sold pitted or unpitted. If unpitted, cut a slit along one side of the date and open the flesh to remove the pit. The opening can be stuffed with marzipan, peanut butter, nuts, etc.

FIGS
Fresh figs can be peeled if desired. To peel, cut off the blossom end and peel off the skin in sections toward the stem end. Dried figs can be used without further preparation if the stem end is soft. If hard, cut off with a knife and discard.

GRAPES
Grapes can be peeled, though this tedious job is not usually necessary. If peeling is desired, use the point of a small sharp knife or your fingernail to peel the skin off in sections, working from the stem end down.

To seed grapes, cut in half and pry out the seeds. Or, if you wish to leave the grapes whole, open up a paper clip, leaving the smaller bend in place; then insert this bend into the stem end of the grape and worry out the seeds.

GRAPEFRUITS
See directions for lemons and oranges.

KIWIFRUIT
Cut off either end and peel with a vegetable peeler or small sharp knife. Cut into thin slices.

LEMONS
Lemons are used in a variety of ways in cookery.

Julienne
To remove the zest (the outermost layer of the rind), wash *well*, then use a vegetable peeler to peel off fine strips. Stack a bundle of strips and cut into the finest possible shreds with a large knife. Or use a special tool called a *zester*, which has four or five small holes and is pulled down over the fruit, removing the outer skin in long, thin strips (julienne).

Lemon Strips
Larger strips of lemon can be removed from the lemon by using another tool, called a *stripper*. This tool has a single large hole and removes strips about $1/4$-inch wide. It is used in the same fashion as a zester.

Of course, the whole rind can also be removed from the lemon and then cut into strips of any thickness. To remove the rind in one section, first cut off both ends of the lemon. Cut a slit down one side of the lemon, cutting into the pith (the white innermost portion of the rind) but not into the flesh. Then, easing a teaspoon between the flesh and the rind, pry the rind away from the lemon. Cut the rind into strips as needed.

To Grate Lemon Rind
Using the finest side of a four-sided grater, gently grate the lemon in a rotary motion, removing just the color (zest) of the lemon and none of the white pith. If you use a relaxed rolling motion, you can remove the rind without grating your knuckles.

If you need larger quantities (a half cup or more) of grated lemon rind, use a vegetable peeler or zester to remove the yellow zest, then put the zest into a processor or a blender and mince finely.

Making lemon cups

a

b

Grapefruit knife

Other styles

ward the center of the fruit. It is usually necessary then to cut the slices away from the pit.

MELONS

Melons can be served as containers for other foods, cut into wedges, scooped into balls, or decorated as a centerpiece. With the exception of watermelon, melons are cut in half, and the seeds are discarded. The melons are then cut as desired and served. Small melons can be served in individual halves.

Melon Wedges

Cut the melon in half lengthwise and then into wedges. Cut under the fruit to separate it from the rind. Then cut into crosswise slices about half an inch wide. To arrange attractively, poke alternating sections a half inch toward the center (see sketch).

Lemon Cups

Cut a slice from the top or side of the lemon about one-third the height of the lemon. With a grapefruit knife, cut out the flesh. Use a teaspoon to scoop out any flesh clinging to the inside of the shell. You can make a more elaborate shell by cutting the lemon to leave a handle at the top, or by making crenulations (notches) in the edge (see sketch).

You can use the shell to hold fresh fruits or to garnish a platter, or you can fill it with lemon mousse or sherbet. If necessary, cut a thin slice from the bottom of the lemon cup so that it will stand upright. For extra flair, you can carve designs in the shell with a zester or stripper.

LIMES

See directions for lemons.

MANGOES

Peel with a sharp knife or a vegetable peeler. To cut slices, cut lengthwise to-

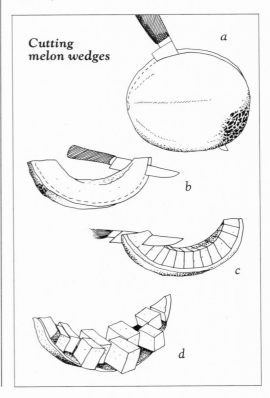

Cutting melon wedges

a

b

c

d

A more elaborate presentation is to cut into the sides of the wedge with a melon baller, pulling the flesh away from the side to give it a sculptural quality. You can also cut out melon balls from the side or down the center of each wedge and fill the spaces with melon balls of a contrasting-colored melon.

Melon Balls

Press a melon baller directly into the melon and twist to remove the ball. (Be careful, as the juices will spurt from the small hole in the center of the baller.) Snap your wrist over a bowl, and the melon ball should fall out.

Melon Flowers

Cut very thin slices from the sides of a peeled melon wedge. Wrap one or more slices around a melon ball, preferably one of a contrasting color, and secure the slices with a wooden toothpick. Anchor them in such a way that the slices are tight around the bottom, more open at the top. Use individual melon flowers to garnish a dessert or a nosegay of them to decorate a platter (see sketch).

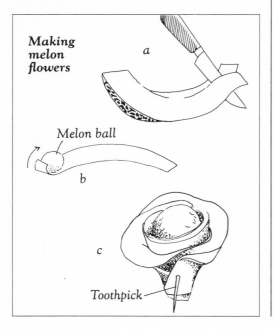

Making melon flowers

a

Melon ball

b

c

Toothpick

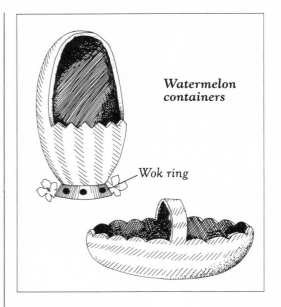

Watermelon containers

Wok ring

Melon Containers

See photograph on page 72.

Halves of small melons can be used to hold portions of other fruits for individual servings. For a larger melon, cut off the top or one side and scoop out the flesh with a melon baller, or cut it out with a knife and dice it, using the knife or scoop to make the inside as neat as possible. If desired, the edge can be scalloped, serrated, or crenulated. You can also use a lemon stripper to cut a design in the melon skin. The container may be further decorated with other fruits skewered to the edge. For example, skewer strawberries onto orange slices and arrange around the edge of a watermelon.

The melon can be carved to form a handle, or to look like a viking ship or a swan. Let your imagination run rampant! The melon can also be carved vertically or horizontally. It may be necessary to cut a thin slice off the bottom or side to ensure that the melon stays firmly in place. If you wish to serve a large watermelon vertically, it may be positioned in a wok ring to stabilize it. Decorate and camouflage the ring with fruits and flowers (see sketch).

NECTARINES

To Peel

Bring a pot of water to a full rolling boil, add the nectarines, and let blanch about 20 seconds. Transfer to a bowl of cold water to stop the cooking. Then, with a sharp knife and your thumb, pull away the skin. Rub the fruit with lemon juice to prevent it from darkening.

To Pit

With a knife, cut into the nectarine as far as the pit and then circle around the fruit. Twist the two halves of fruit to separate and pull or cut out the pit. Cut the fruit into slices. If they are to stand for more than a few minutes, toss the slices with lemon juice to prevent darkening.

ORANGES

See directions for lemons.

Orange Slices

Slice off both ends of the orange and set it on a board. With a sharp knife, cut down the orange on all sides following its contours, removing all of the rind and pith. Turn the orange onto its side and cut it into slices.

Orange Wedges

Remove the rind and pith as above. With a sharp knife, cut into the orange on one side of the section membrane, then on the other. Remove the wedge. Keep cutting around the orange until all of the wedges have been removed.

PAPAYAS

Peel the papaya with a vegetable peeler or a sharp knife. Cut in half and scoop the seeds out with a spoon. Cut the papaya into slices either lengthwise or crosswise.

PEACHES

See directions for nectarines.

PEARS

Using a vegetable peeler or a sharp knife, peel the skin. To maintain the pear shape, peel around the globular base, then, starting at the center of the pear, peel toward the stem.

Cut the pear in half, remove the core with a melon baller, and cut out the stem. Or use a special tool, a roughly pear-shaped strip of metal on a wooden handle, designed to core pears. The larger opening is used to remove the core, and the pointed end scoops out the fibrous stem.

Hollowing Pears

Several recipes in this book call for pears to be left whole with the centers hollowed from the bottom. To do this, use an apple corer to remove the core from the bottom of the pear. You can core all the way through, cutting off the stem and then reinserting it in the hole, or you can push the corer almost to the stem end and then twist it to pull out the core and much of the fibrous stem. Use a melon baller to enlarge the opening if necessary.

PINEAPPLES

Pineapple Wedges

Cut the pineapple in half from top to bottom, cutting through the frond (see sketch on next page), and cut each half into halves or thirds, still cutting in the same direction. Leave the frond on if desired. Cut out the hard core and cut under the meat of the pineapple, leaving it in its shell. Cut the wedges into $1/2$-inch slices. Push alternating slices of the pineapple about half an inch toward the center of each wedge.

To Peel

Cut off the frond and base of the pineapple. Stand it on end and cut down the sides with a heavy knife, cutting deeply enough to remove the eyes.

To Peel in a Spiral

The frond may be left on or not, depending on how you plan to serve it. Cut the base off evenly. With the tip of a knife inserted diagonally underneath a spiral of eyes, cut from top to bottom. Turn the pineapple and cut again under the same strip of eyes from the opposite side, removing a diagonal strip of eyes. Repeat the process around the pineapple (see sketch).

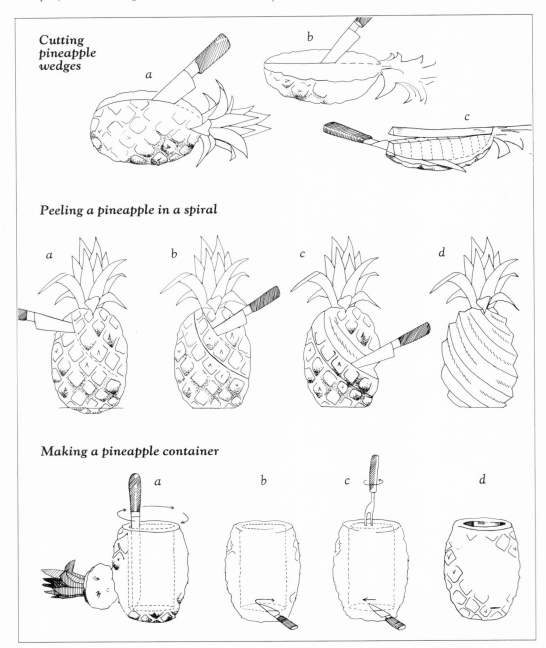

Cutting pineapple wedges

Peeling a pineapple in a spiral

Making a pineapple container

Pineapple Slices

Slice a peeled pineapple thinly. Use an apple corer or a pastry tip to cut out the center (core) of each slice.

The peeled pineapple can also be cut into halves or quarters and cut into thin slices to make half slices or wedges. Cut out the core before slicing.

Pineapple Containers

Some of the desserts given here use a whole pineapple as a serving container. To make one, you need to cut the pineapple so that the center can be removed as one solid plug, with no cuts showing from the outside. First, cut off the frond about half an inch down from the green. Then, with a sharp, long, thin knife cut straight down into the pineapple about half an inch inside the outside edge, cutting all the way around. Remove the knife. Next, to free the base of the center plug, insert the knife about an inch from the base and cut toward one side, but not all the way through the shell. Remove the knife and reinsert it in the same opening with the blade turned in the opposite direction. Cut toward the opposite side, again, not all the way through. With a kitchen fork, pull out the center, which should come out as one solid plug (see sketch). It may be necessary to go over the original vertical cuts to make sure that you have cut all the way through. Use a tiny pat of butter to seal the hole made by the knife at the base; the butter will prevent the juices from escaping.

PLUMS

Do not peel; see directions for nectarines for pitting.

PRICKLY PEARS

Also called cactus pears. Cut off both ends of the fruit, then cut a slit in the skin from end to end. Put a fork into the slit and, with the back of a knife wedged between the flesh and the skin, pull the skin away from the fruit. Slice the fruit.

PRUNES

Prunes are dried plums. They are usually steeped in a liquid such as tea, fortified wine, or a liqueur.

QUINCES

See directions for apples.

RAISINS

Raisins are often plumped before using by soaking them in a liquid for at least 15 minutes.

RASPBERRIES

Pick over carefully, discarding any leaves, twigs, or moldy berries. Wash quickly just before using; dry on paper toweling.

RHUBARB

The leaves of rhubarb are poisonous. Remove any leaves before preparing the fruit for recipes.

STARFRUIT

See directions for carambola.

STRAWBERRIES

Wash the strawberries just before using. Do not let sit in water or the fruit will become soggy.

To Hull

With a small, sharp knife, cut a circle under the hull and pull off the green top; the white core will pull out as well. Discard the core and leaves.

TANGERINES

Peel the skin from the tangerines with your fingers, then pull off the network of bitter membranes from the fruit. Separate into wedges.

SPECIAL FRUIT PRESENTATIONS

Although many of the recipes in the following chapters give rather elaborate serving directions, there are also some basic presentations that are visually outstanding. Here are a few suggestions.

FROSTED FRUITS

This simple technique makes an attractive garnish for main courses as well as for desserts. It is most often done with grapes, but also works with strawberries and can be used as a way to enhance citrus fruits.

Cut the grapes into small clusters; wash and dry well. Beat 1 or 2 egg whites until they are frothy but not stiff. Dip the grapes into the egg whites and then into a dish of granulated sugar, rolling them to coat completely. Place on a cake rack and let dry for several hours. These can be made a day ahead, but should be stored in a cool room, not in the refrigerator. (The moisture in the refrigerator can cause the sugar to "weep," so the coating falls off as a syrup.)

FRUIT CORNUCOPIA

See photograph on page 72.

One of the most impressive presentations is a cornucopia of fruits. Baskets woven to look like cornucopias are certainly effective; however, a more spectacular and personal version is one made from dough. I prefer bread dough to give the finished cornucopia a more puffy, effulgent look, although others prefer pie pastry. It does take a little time to make an attractive cornucopia, but once you get the knack of it, you will find it relatively easy to prepare. And of course, it can be reused. Once made, the cornucopia will keep weeks or even months. To preserve it even longer, you can coat it with clear polyurethane. The cornucopia is not to be eaten.

Bread Dough for a Fruit Cornucopia

> 1 package yeast
> 2 cups lukewarm water
> 1 tablespoon sugar
> 2 tablespoons salt
> 7 to 8 cups flour

In a bowl, dissolve the yeast in the water with the sugar and salt. Cover with a towel wrung out in warm water and let proof. Stir in 3 cups of flour and beat well. Add additional flour, 1 cup at a time, until the dough looks shaggy.

Turn onto a lightly floured board and knead until smooth and elastic, adding enough additional flour to make a medium-firm dough. Place the dough in a bowl, dust generously with the flour, cover the bowl with a towel wrung out in warm water, and let rise until doubled in bulk, about 1 hour. Punch down.

Proceed with directions for shaping the cornucopia (see below).

The Foil Form

Unroll several yards of aluminum foil from the roll, and crush and shape it roughly into the beginning of a cone. Keep wrapping lengths of foil around the cone until it is the size you want. Concentrate on keeping the cone shape. When the cone is the desired size, curl the point toward one side like a cornucopia. To make it easier to remove the form after it is baked, wrap one or more layers of foil lengthwise over the foil cone, and press as smooth as possible. The object is to make a casing over the crumpled foil so you will be able to remove the foil easily from the interior of the finished dough cornucopia. The

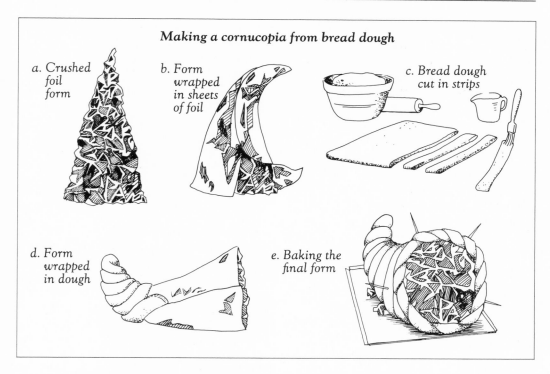

Making a cornucopia from bread dough

a. Crushed foil form

b. Form wrapped in sheets of foil

c. Bread dough cut in strips

d. Form wrapped in dough

e. Baking the final form

crumpled form must be solid enough to support the dough and to stand up under its own weight.

Wrapping the Form with Dough

When the bread dough has doubled in bulk, punch it down and roll it out on a lightly floured board into a long rectangle, about ¼ inch thick. Cut the dough into long strips, about 2 inches wide. Brush one side of each strip with cold water. With the wet side out, start at the tip and wrap the dough around the form, overlapping each piece generously. Press the end of each new strip onto the end of the preceding strip and continue wrapping until you have reached the opening. Do not allow the pastry to drape over the opening or you will have trouble removing the foil. If the dough is soft and tends to sag, use wooden toothpicks to hold the dough to the form. (Remove them after the dough is baked by twisting them in place before pulling them out; pulling them out without twisting them first could pull the cornucopia apart.) If the dough is *too* soft, you may need to work in more flour. If so, do not be concerned that the dough might be tough, since the cornucopia is not intended to be eaten.

Baking the Cornucopia

Preheat the oven to 400°F.

Lightly oil a baking sheet and set the form on it with the opening down. If the cornucopia is very large, to fit it in the oven it may be necessary to set it on its side, supporting it with crumpled balls of foil.

Prepare a glaze of 1 egg, beaten with ¼ teaspoon salt. Brush glaze over the cornucopia and bake for 35 to 50 minutes, or until it is golden brown and the pastry appears set. Check the dough, and if the interior of the cornucopia is not fully cooked, put it back into the oven and bake until the interior is done. It does not have to brown, but it should not be soggy. When fully baked, remove the cornucopia from the oven and let it cool. Then gently pull the foil from the inside. If you have trouble removing the foil near the tip, cut it off and push it firmly into the tip. No one will see it.

Note: Although the pastry will wrap more easily when circling the form, if you like you can drape strips of dough from the point toward the opening and weave in other strips to create a basket-like effect.

THE FLOWER TECHNIQUE

A lovely presentation can be made by circling the centerpiece of many cream desserts with concentric rings of sauce and then forming the cream and sauce into a flower design. This is achieved by

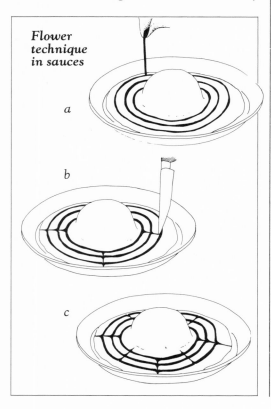

Flower technique in sauces

drawing the point of a knife from the centerpiece to the edge of the plate at 12, 3, 6, and 9 o'clock. Then, between these points, draw the knife from the edge of the plate into the center again to create the flower effect in the cream (see sketch).

An excellent example of this is found in the Figs with Raspberry Cream recipe on page 36, but it works for many other desserts as well.

FRUIT AND CHEESE PLATTERS

Fruit and cheese are natural partners; they complement each other beautifully. In addition, they can be served as an accompaniment to cocktails or wines, or served as a dessert. There are certain classic fruit and cheese associations such as apples and Cheddar, pears and Roquefort, and grapes and Brie. Pears are excellent with almost any cheese, although they do seem to have a particular affinity with blue cheese. Grapes complement most cheeses and have the added advantage of being easy and neat to eat. There are no limitations; enjoy the combinations that please you.

All manner of platters and trays are sold to serve cheese: pottery, porcelain, baskets, and slabs of marble. My preference is for a flat wicker tray lined with leaves to accent the cheese. The fruit can be served on the tray, if it is large enough, or passed separately. For formal occasions, a silver tray provides an elegant setting for fruits and cheese. Again, lining the tray with large leaves accents the colors of the cheeses and makes them stand out. Stilton cheese, by the way, is traditionally wrapped in a white linen napkin, although of course you may serve it without the wrap, or even presliced.

Crackers and breads should accompany the fruits and cheese.

SIMPLE FRUIT DESSERTS

ALTHOUGH an apple or banana eaten out of hand is obviously the simplest of desserts, there are many different preparations of single fruits that make superb desserts. Baked apples or a baked pear, perhaps embellished with a liqueur and a dash of cream, are palate pleasers that take little or no time and are satisfying without being overpowering. Very often such desserts are perfect to serve family, but they can also make a delightful surprise visit to the party table.

These are the desserts for the hectic days when you've been just too busy to cook, but dinner time is at hand and the hordes are waiting for your latest production. Many of these can be prepared, put into a serving dish, and allowed to cook while you and your guests enjoy the rest of the meal. It is part of all of us to wish to seem brilliant — capable of doing a hundred things at once and all of them perfectly. Choose your desserts from this group and you will find yourself well on the way.

Gingered Apples

Note that the first step for these tasty slices takes 3 days. After that, it's a breeze.

> 1 tablespoon minced gingerroot
> ½ cup cognac
> 3 pounds cooking apples, peeled, cored, and sliced
> 4 cups sugar
> ¾ cup lemon juice, strained
> Candied Orange Peel (see page 284)
> ¼ cup heavy cream, whipped

Crush the gingerroot with a mallet and put it into a jar with the cognac. Cover and set aside for 3 days. Strain, discarding the gingerroot. Simmer the apples

in the strained cognac, sugar, and lemon juice for about 10 minutes or until translucent. Chill. Serve cold, garnished with the orange peel and whipped cream.   YIELDS 6 SERVINGS.

Purée de Pommes au Citron

APPLESAUCE WITH LEMON AND ORANGE

> 2 pounds McIntosh apples
> Juice of ½ lemon
> ½ cup water
> Sugar to taste
> 1 unpeeled orange, thinly sliced

Peel, quarter, and core the apples. Put the apples and the lemon juice in a pot with ½ cup water. Cover and cook over low heat until the apples are soft, stirring frequently. Add sugar to taste. Serve chilled, garnished with the orange slices. Can be made 2 or 3 days ahead.   YIELDS 4 SERVINGS.

Apples and Praline-Flavored Cream

Whip the cream until it holds a soft shape so that it will fold in more easily. Then be sure to fold in as soon as the mixture reaches room temperature, before it gets too stiff.

> 8 large McIntosh apples, peeled and sliced
> 1 lemon
> 2 tablespoons butter
> ½ cup honey
> 1 teaspoon vanilla
> 1 cup Praline Powder made with walnuts (see page 284)
> ¼ to ½ cup minced crystallized ginger

¼ cup water
1 tablespoon gelatin
¼ cup light rum
1 ½ cups heavy cream
⅓ cup sugar

Place the apples in a large bowl. Grate 1 teaspoon lemon rind and set aside. Squeeze the juice from the lemon over the apples and toss gently. In a large skillet, melt the butter and add the apples, grated lemon rind, honey, and vanilla. Sauté until the apples are soft and the liquids have evaporated, about 15 to 20 minutes. Turn into a large bowl. Stir in ½ cup Praline Powder and the ginger. In a small saucepan, combine the water and gelatin and let stand until the gelatin softens. Dissolve over low heat. Stir into the apples, then blend in the rum. Set aside to cool for about 30 minutes.

Whip the cream until soft peaks form. Add the sugar and beat until almost stiff. Fold into the apple mixture. Turn into a serving bowl and chill until set, about 4 hours. Sprinkle with the remaining praline.

YIELDS 6 TO 8 SERVINGS.

Note: This cream can be made a day ahead.

■▪■

Caramelized Apple Slices

For apples with more texture, cook uncovered over moderately high heat for ten minutes rather than as given below.

6 Cortland apples, peeled, sliced,
    and cored
3 tablespoons butter
Pinch of salt
3 tablespoons firmly packed brown
    sugar
½ teaspoon cinnamon
Whipped cream to taste (optional)

In a skillet with a tight-fitting cover, cook the apples in the butter, covered, over low heat for about 10 minutes or until they begin to soften. Sprinkle with salt, sugar, and cinnamon. Cook uncovered for 15 to 20 minutes longer or until softened and glazed. Serve warm, with whipped cream if desired.

■▪■   YIELDS 6 SERVINGS.

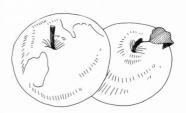

Brouillade aux Pommes

SCRAMBLED BAKED APPLES

This dessert is especially delicious accompanied by cold heavy cream.

1 pound apples, peeled, sliced,
    and cored
¼ cup plus 2 tablespoons sugar
3 eggs
Pinch of salt
4 tablespoons butter

In a bowl, toss the apples with ¼ cup sugar and leave covered overnight.

When ready, preheat oven to 350°F. Beat the eggs and salt together and fold into the apples. In a heavy skillet, heat the butter until bubbling. Stir in the apple mixture and let stand for 30 seconds. Put into the oven and bake for about 45 minutes. Every 10 minutes, stir the mixture, chopping the apples with the side of a spoon and then smoothing the surface. Sprinkle with the remaining 2 tablespoons sugar and turn oven to 450°. Bake until surface is just caramelized.   YIELDS 4 SERVINGS.

■▪■

Brandied Apples

This can be served plain, with whipped cream, or as a topping to ice cream or even griddle cakes.

½ cup butter
¾ cup firmly packed dark brown sugar
2 tablespoons lemon juice
2 tablespoons orange juice
3 Golden Delicious apples, peeled, thinly sliced, and cored
1 teaspoon dark rum
2 teaspoons cognac

In a skillet over medium heat, melt the butter; add the sugar and cook, stirring until sugar is dissolved. Stir in the lemon and orange juices. Add the apples, rum, and cognac. Mix well and simmer until the apples are tender, about 5 minutes. Remove from the heat and serve warm.   YIELDS 4 TO 6 SERVINGS.

Cold Baked Apples

6 medium apples, peeled and cored
1 tablespoon sugar
⅔ cup apple cider
1 cup currant jelly, melted
½ cup heavy cream, whipped

Preheat oven to 300°F. Arrange the apples in a 9- by 11-inch baking dish. Sprinkle the apples with the sugar and add the cider. Bake for 35 minutes, basting often until the apples are tender but still retain their shape. Stir the jelly into the juices in the bottom of the baking dish and pour over the apples to glaze them. Chill the apples and serve with whipped cream.   YIELDS 6 SERVINGS.

Minted Baked Apples

6 Cortland apples
Mint leaves to cover bottom of pan, plus 6 for garnish
12 tablespoons honey
4 tablespoons water
2 tablespoons butter, melted

Preheat oven to 375°F. Core the apples without peeling. Then peel the upper quarter of each apple. Keeping aside 6 leaves, place a layer of mint leaves in the bottom of a baking dish just large enough to hold the apples upright. Fill the cavity of each apple with 2 tablespoons honey, 2 teaspoons water, ½ teaspoon butter, and 1 mint leaf. Cover the baking pan and bake until almost tender, about 30 minutes. Remove the cover and bake, basting often until tender, about 5 minutes longer.   YIELDS 6 SERVINGS.

Apples Baked in White Wine

6 firm baking apples
3 tablespoons currants
2 tablespoons sugar
4 tablespoons chopped pecans
2 pinches cinnamon
4 tablespoons butter
¾ cup dry white wine
Whipped cream or plain heavy cream (optional)

Preheat oven to 350°F. Core the apples, leaving a small section at the base of each to act as a stopper. In a bowl, combine the currants, 1 tablespoon sugar, pecans, and half of the cinnamon; mix well. Butter a baking pan large enough to hold apples comfortably and arrange the apples in the pan; fill with the currant-pecan mixture. Dot apples with remaining butter and pour on the wine. Sprinkle the remaining tablespoon of sugar mixed with remaining cinnamon over the apples. Bake until tender, about 30 minutes. Serve hot or cold with pan juices. Accompany with whipped cream or plain heavy cream if desired. If serving cold, these can be made a day ahead. Let come to room temperature before serving.

◆◆◆ YIELDS 6 SERVINGS.

Baked Apples with Red Wine

The apples should be tender and the wine reduced to a glaze when this dessert is cooked. For a flavor variation, add a generous pinch of cinnamon.

6 thin slices French bread
5 tablespoons butter
6 apples, cored
1 cup red wine
6 tablespoons sugar

Preheat oven to 350°F. Butter both sides of the bread and arrange in a baking pan. Peel a strip of skin from around the middle of each apple and place the apples on the bread slices. Fill centers with

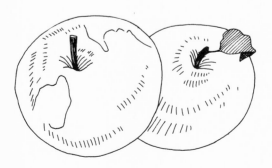

remaining butter. Pour wine over the apples and sprinkle with the sugar. Bake for about 35 minutes or until tender, basting often. Serve warm.

◆◆◆ YIELDS 6 SERVINGS.

Fransk Äppelkaka

FRENCH BAKED APPLE HALVES
WITH ALMOND TOPPING

This is a Swedish version of a favorite French dessert.

2 cups cold water
¼ lemon plus 2 teaspoons lemon juice
4 large tart apples
½ cup plus ⅔ cup sugar
2 teaspoons unsalted butter
½ pound butter, softened
3 eggs, separated
½ cup ground blanched almonds
Pinch of salt

In a saucepan, combine the water, juice of the quarter lemon, and the lemon quarter itself. Peel, halve, and core each apple and drop into lemon water. Stir in ½ cup sugar and bring to a boil. Simmer uncovered for 6 to 8 minutes, or until the apples are tender. Drain apples on a cake rack.

Preheat oven to 350°F. With the 2 teaspoons unsalted butter, butter a baking dish just large enough to hold the apples in a single layer. Place the apples, cut side down, in the dish.

In a processor, cream the ½ pound softened butter with remaining ⅔ cup sugar; add the egg yolks, almonds, and the remaining 2 teaspoons lemon juice. Process until mixed. Beat the egg whites with the pinch of salt until stiff, but not dry. Fold into the egg yolk mixture. Spread over the apples and bake for 20 minutes or until golden. Serve warm.

◆◆◆ YIELDS 6 TO 8 SERVINGS.

Cantonese Baked Apples

A non-Cantonese finish is to serve this with heavy cream.

6 baking apples
1 cup chopped Brazil nuts
½ cup chopped, pitted dates
⅓ cup chopped candied ginger
1 cup light corn syrup
1 teaspoon ground ginger
Red food coloring (optional)
Sugar

Preheat oven to 350°F. Core the apples, almost but not completely through. Peel the skin about a third of the way from the top of each apple. In a bowl, combine the nuts, dates, and candied ginger and fill apple centers with the mixture. In a small saucepan, combine the corn syrup, ground ginger, and a drop or two of red food coloring if desired. Simmer 5 minutes and brush on the apples. Place the apples in a baking dish and add just enough boiling water to cover the bottom of the dish. Bake until tender, about 40 minutes, basting often with the syrup.

Remove from the oven and sprinkle the apples with the sugar. Turn on the broiler and glaze the apples, basting often with the remaining syrup. Sprinkle with additional sugar to taste. Serve warm or at room temperature.

▼▼▼   YIELDS 6 SERVINGS.

Apple Hedgehog

For a more elaborate presentation, pipe the meringue through a pastry bag fitted with a no. 4 open-star tip.

12 Cortland apples, peeled and cored
1 cup plus 2 tablespoons
   granulated sugar
1¼ cups water

Grated rind of 1 lemon
3 egg whites
Confectioners' sugar
½ cup sliced almonds

Leave 6 apples whole; chop the remaining apples. In a medium-sized saucepan, combine the 1 cup granulated sugar, water, and lemon rind. Bring to a boil and poach the whole apples until tender, but not broken. Drain. Cook the chopped apples in the syrup until they are reduced to a thick pulp.

Preheat oven to 375°F. Pile the whole apples into a pyramid on a heatproof serving dish. Smooth the apple purée over the whole apples. Beat the egg whites with the remaining 2 tablespoons of granulated sugar until stiff, but not dry. Spread over the apple mound and sprinkle with the confectioners' sugar. Stick the almonds into the mound, leaving the tips exposed. Brown in the oven and serve warm. Can be prepared for baking several hours ahead, but do not make or spread on the meringue until just before baking.

▼▼▼   YIELDS 6 SERVINGS.

Apple Crisp

This is a wonderfully adaptable dessert. See the suggestions below.

6 tart apples
1 cup sugar
¼ teaspoon ground cloves
½ teaspoon cinnamon
2 teaspoons lemon juice
¾ cup sifted flour
Pinch of salt
6 tablespoons butter
¼ cup chopped walnuts
Whipped cream or ice cream
   (optional)

Preheat oven to 350°F. Peel, core, and slice the apples. In a bowl, combine the apples, ½ cup of the sugar, cloves, cinnamon, and lemon juice. Mix gently and turn into a buttered 1½-quart casserole. In another bowl, combine the remaining ½ cup sugar, flour, salt, and butter, working in the butter to make a mixture the consistency of cornmeal. Add the nuts and sprinkle over the apple mixture. Bake for 45 minutes or until the apples are tender and the crust is browned. Serve with whipped cream or ice cream as desired. YIELDS 6 SERVINGS.

Note: This recipe can be varied in many ways. Substitute pecans for the walnuts, or stir ¼ cup sliced almonds into the apple mixture and omit the walnuts in the topping. Flavor the apples with a generous grating of orange peel or add 1 tablespoon minced crystallized ginger.

Pommes Bourgeoises I

APPLES BOURGEOIS I

**6 tart apples, peeled, halved, and
  cored
2 cups vanilla syrup (see
  page 286)
¾ cup mixed glacéed fruits
2 cups Pastry Cream (see page 282)
½ cup toasted slivered almonds or
  macaroon crumbs
Granulated sugar**

Poach the apples in the vanilla syrup until they are soft, but retain their shape. Cool in the syrup.

Preheat oven to 450°F. Transfer the apples, cut side up, to a heatproof serving dish. Fill the apple cavities with the glacéed fruits and coat with the Pastry Cream. Sprinkle the almonds or macaroons over the cream and sprinkle generously with the sugar. Bake for 5 to 7 minutes, or until glazed. Serve hot or at room temperature. Can be prepared for baking the day before, but let come to room temperature before glazing.
YIELDS 6 SERVINGS.

Pommes Bourgeoises II

APPLES BOURGEOIS II

**1 cup rice, washed and drained
2½ cups milk, scalded
6 tablespoons sugar, plus additional
  for sprinkling
½ teaspoon salt
1 (1-inch) piece vanilla bean
1 tablespoon butter
3 egg yolks
2 tablespoons cream
6 vanilla-poached apples, halved (see
  page 286)
2 cups Pastry Cream (see page 282)
Chopped almonds**

Cover well-washed rice with cold water. Bring to boil, turn off the heat, and let stand for 5 minutes. Drain the rice, rinse well, and return the rice to the pan. Add the milk, sugar, salt, and vanilla bean. Bring the milk to a boil and add the butter. Cover and simmer gently for 30 minutes or until the rice is very tender. Toss the rice with a fork to separate the grains. Discard vanilla bean.

Preheat broiler. Mix the egg yolks with the cream, toss gently with the rice, and spread on a heatproof serving dish. Arrange the apple halves on the rice and cover them generously with the Pastry Cream. Sprinkle the top with almonds and additional sugar. Brown under the broiler. Can be prepared for browning several hours ahead. YIELDS 6 SERVINGS.

Abricots Fines Bouches

APRICOTS WITH
KIRSCH BUTTER SAUCE

1 can (1 pound 12 ounces) apricots,
  drained
2 egg yolks
2 tablespoons kirsch
1 tablespoon sugar
6 tablespoons butter
½ cup sliced almonds, toasted

Arrange the apricots on a serving platter, cut side up, and chill. In a saucepan,
beat the egg yolks, kirsch, and sugar
over low heat until mixture starts to
thicken slightly. Beat in the butter a tablespoon at a time until the mixture is
thick and creamy. Pour the sauce over
the chilled apricots. Sprinkle with the
almonds and serve. Can be prepared
several hours ahead and refrigerated until ready to serve, with the almonds added just before serving.

■▼■   YIELDS 6 SERVINGS.

Abricots au Cognac

APRICOTS WITH COGNAC

*These apricots can be served alone, or
topped with heavy cream, whipped cream,
or ice cream.*

1 pound dried apricots
⅔ cup sugar
Cognac to cover

In a bowl, combine the apricots, sugar,
and cognac. Let stand for 24 hours, or
up to two weeks. Serve chilled.

■▼■   YIELDS 6 SERVINGS.

Abricots Hélène

APRICOTS HELEN

*This is even better with fresh apricots, but
they are available for such a short season.
Canned fruit, in this instance, also works
very well.*

¼ pound stale ladyfingers
1½ cups milk, heated
4 tablespoons sugar
4 eggs
1 can (1 pound 12 ounces) apricots
Cherries
Apricot Sauce (see page 274)

Preheat oven to 350°F. Soak the ladyfingers in the milk for 10 minutes; force
through a sieve, add sugar, and beat in
the eggs. Butter and sugar a 3-quart
mold. Pour in the ladyfinger mixture
and bake for 40 minutes or until set.
Unmold and surround with apricot
halves, rounded sides down. Place a
cherry in the center of each apricot and
serve with Apricot Sauce. The pudding
can be served warm or cold.

■▼■   YIELDS 6 SERVINGS.

Avocado Chartreuse Dessert

*This dessert may well strike some readers
as strange. However, it is truly delicious
and should be tried before you reject it.*

3 large ripe avocados
1 cup sugar
4 tablespoons lime juice
2 tablespoons green Chartreuse
½ cup heavy cream
6 thin lemon slices

Cut the avocados in half and scoop out
the flesh with a spoon without damag-
ing the skins. In a processor, purée the
pulp with the sugar, lime juice, and

Chartreuse. Fill the reserved avocado shells with the avocado purée. Whip the cream and pipe onto the avocados with a pastry bag fitted with a no. 4 open-star tip. Garnish each with a lemon slice and serve cold. Can be prepared about 4 hours ahead. Do not try to prepare too far in advance, or the avocado mixture may turn brown.   YIELDS 6 SERVINGS.
❖❖❖

Bananes aux Abricots

BANANAS WITH APRICOTS

 6 medium bananas
 ⅓ cup apricot jam
 4½ tablespoons kirsch
 1½ cups heavy cream, whipped
 ¼ cup sugar

Peel off one third of each banana skin lengthwise and remove the flesh. In a bowl or a processor, crush the flesh and mix in the jam and kirsch. Refill the banana shells and cover with the cream sweetened with the sugar. The cream can be piped on with a pastry bag fitted with a no. 4 open-star tip. Chill and serve cold. Can be made about 4 hours before serving.   YIELDS 6 SERVINGS.
❖❖❖

Barquettes de Bananes

BANANA BOATS

 4 medium bananas
 1 tablespoon plus 2 teaspoons sugar
 2 to 3 tablespoons maraschino liqueur
 ⅔ cup heavy cream, whipped
 Glacéed cherries (optional)

Carefully cut each banana in half lengthwise and remove the flesh from the peels, leaving the peels intact. Cut the bananas into ½-inch slices and toss gently with the 1 tablespoon sugar and

the maraschino liqueur. Sweeten the whipped cream with the remaining sugar and fill the banana shells. Arrange the banana slices alternately with the cherries on top of the whipped cream. Serve immediately.
❖❖❖   YIELDS 4 TO 8 SERVINGS.

Bananes Meringuées

MERINGUE-TOPPED BANANAS

You can prepare the bananas early in the day, but do not coat with the meringue until shortly before serving, so that the dish will be warm.

 3 to 6 ripe bananas
 2 tablespoons orange liqueur
 2 tablespoons Clarified Butter (see page 286)
 2 egg whites
 6 tablespoons sugar
 1 egg yolk, lightly beaten
 1 tablespoon flour

Preheat oven to 300°F. Peel the bananas, and cut them in half lengthwise and again crosswise if long. Sprinkle with orange liqueur and let stand for 1 hour; drain, reserving the juices. In a skillet, sauté the bananas in butter until golden. Beat the egg whites until almost stiff; beat in sugar, 1 tablespoon at a time, and continue to beat until stiff. Fold in the egg yolk and flour. Arrange the bananas on a heatproof serving dish. Heat the reserved liqueur in the skillet, ignite it, and pour over the bananas. When the flames die out, spread the meringue over the bananas and bake until crisp and golden, about 30 to 40 minutes. Serve warm.   YIELDS 6 SERVINGS.

Note: For a prettier presentation, pipe the meringue on top of the bananas through a no. 5 star tip.
❖❖❖

Bananes Flambées

KIRSCH-FLAMED BANANAS

You can substitute almost any fruit in this dish. Select any complementary liqueur for the fruit. Apples with rum or bourbon are wonderful, but not with crème de menthe, for instance.

    6 bananas, peeled
    2 tablespoons sugar
    1 cup flour
    1 egg, lightly beaten
    3 tablespoons Clarified Butter (see
        page 286)
    ¼ cup kirsch, warmed

Cut the bananas in half lengthwise and sprinkle with half of the sugar. Dip the bananas in the flour, roll in the beaten egg, and then again in the flour. Sauté the bananas in the butter until golden on both sides. Arrange on a warm serving platter, sprinkle with remaining tablespoon sugar, and pour the kirsch over all. Ignite and serve flaming.

▪▪▪   YIELDS 6 SERVINGS.

Bananes Sautées

SAUTÉED BANANAS

    6 bananas
    2 tablespoons Clarified Butter (see
        page 286)
    2 tablespoons sugar
    ¼ cup rum

Peel the bananas and cut in half lengthwise. Sauté in the butter until they start to turn golden. Add the sugar and cook for 1 minute or until the sugar melts. Add the rum and ignite. Serve flaming.

▪▪▪   YIELDS 6 SERVINGS.

Bananas Foster

Created at Brennan's Restaurant in New Orleans almost 40 years ago for a special customer.

    4 bananas, peeled
    Lemon juice
    ¼ cup butter
    1 cup firmly packed brown sugar
    ¼ teaspoon cinnamon
    ¼ cup banana liqueur
    ¼ cup dark rum
    Vanilla ice cream

Cut the bananas in half crosswise and again lengthwise. Dip in lemon juice. In a skillet, melt the butter; add the sugar and cook until it melts. Add the bananas and sauté for 3 minutes. Sprinkle with cinnamon and banana liqueur. Add the rum, ignite it, and spoon the juices over the bananas until the flame dies down. Serve warm with ice cream.

YIELDS 6 SERVINGS.

Note: For a spectacular effect, prepare this dish in a chafing dish at the table, with the lights lowered.

▪▪▪

Bananas in Caramel Cream

    4 tablespoons unsalted butter
    3 tablespoons firmly packed
        brown sugar
    1 tablespoon grated orange rind
    ½ cup orange juice
    3 tablespoons lemon juice
    Pinch of nutmeg
    6 bananas, peeled
    2 tablespoons banana liqueur
    2 tablespoons orange liqueur
    2 tablespoons cognac
    ¼ cup golden raisins, chopped
    1 cup heavy cream

In a skillet, heat the butter and sugar until melted. Stir in the orange rind, orange juice, lemon juice, and nutmeg. Add the bananas to the skillet and cook, turning once, until heated, about 2 or 3 minutes. Remove bananas to a platter. Cook juices until syrupy. Stir in the banana liqueur, orange liqueur, and cognac. Add raisins and reduce by half. Pour in the cream and reduce by one-third. Serve sauce warm over bananas. YIELDS 6 SERVINGS.

Bananes Maltaise

BANANAS MALTESE-STYLE

  6 bananas, peeled
  2 tablespoons butter
  6 tablespoons sugar
  2 oranges
  2 to 4 tablespoons orange liqueur

Cut bananas in half lengthwise. In a skillet, sauté the bananas in the butter for 2 minutes on each side. Sprinkle with sugar and cook until the sugar is caramelized. Grate the peel from the oranges over the bananas; squeeze the orange juice over the top. Cook a few minutes longer or until the juices are syrupy. Remove from the heat, swirl in the liqueur, and ignite. Serve immediately. YIELDS 6 SERVINGS.

VARIATIONS

Bananes au Rhum: Substitute brown sugar for sugar, omit the oranges and orange liqueur, and add ½ cup dark rum.

Bananes Caribe: Preheat oven to 300°F. Bake the bananas topped with 3 oranges, peeled and sliced, dotted with butter, and sprinkled with sugar, for 30 minutes. Add ½ cup rum, ignite, and serve.

Bananas a Brasiliera

BANANAS BRAZILIAN-STYLE I

Fresh bread crumbs are best for this. To prepare your own, cut the crusts from bread that is a day or two old, but not stale or hard. Then pulverize the crumbs in a blender or a processor. The dried and toasted bread crumbs sold in markets give a heavy coating as opposed to one that is light and crisp.

  4 ripe bananas, peeled
  2 eggs, lightly beaten
  1 ½ cups bread crumbs, crusts
    discarded
  Peanut or vegetable oil
  Apricot Sauce (see page 274)

Cut the bananas into 4 sections crosswise. Roll the sections in the egg and then in the bread crumbs. Let dry on a cake rack for 10 minutes. In a skillet, heat ½ inch of oil and cook the bananas until golden. Serve immediately with Apricot Sauce. YIELDS 6 SERVINGS.

Bananas Brazilian-Style II

  6 bananas, peeled
  ¼ cup orange juice
  1 tablespoon lemon juice
  ¼ cup firmly packed brown sugar
  Pinch of salt
  2 tablespoons butter
  1 cup grated coconut

Preheat oven to 400°F. Cut the bananas in half lengthwise. Arrange in a buttered baking dish. In a bowl, combine the orange juice, lemon juice, sugar, and salt. Pour over the bananas and dot with the butter. Bake for 10 to 15 minutes or until tender. Remove from the oven and sprinkle with the coconut. Serve hot, warm, or at room temperature. YIELDS 6 SERVINGS.

Orange-Glazed Bananas

6 bananas, peeled
¾ cup orange juice
¼ cup Grand Marnier
3 tablespoons butter
⅓ cup chopped walnuts
⅓ cup firmly packed brown sugar
Vanilla ice cream, sour cream, or
    whipped cream (optional)

Preheat oven to 450°F. Cut the bananas in half lengthwise and arrange in a single layer in a baking dish. Sprinkle with the orange juice and liqueur and dot with the butter. Bake for 10 minutes, basting occasionally. Sprinkle with the nuts and sugar and bake until the sugar is melted and the nuts are glazed and toasted, about 5 minutes. Serve alone, or with ice cream, sour cream, or whipped cream. Serve hot or warm.

▾▾▾   YIELDS 6 SERVINGS.

Neruppu Vazhai

BANANAS WITH COCONUT
AND CARDAMOM

A superb dessert to serve after curries.

6 bananas, peeled
¼ cup orange juice
½ cup firmly packed light brown sugar
1 cup grated coconut
½ cup slivered blanched almonds
1 teaspoon ground cardamom
¼ cup butter, melted

Preheat oven to 400°F. Arrange the bananas in one layer in a buttered baking dish. Pour on the orange juice; sprinkle with the sugar, coconut, almonds, cardamom, and butter. Bake for 25 minutes or until the bananas are tender. Serve warm.   YIELDS 6 SERVINGS.
▾▾▾

Blueberry Crumble

An old New England favorite. Maine housewives use the same technique with whatever fruits are in season, such as rhubarb, apples, raspberries, and peaches.

1 pint blueberries
1 tablespoon lemon juice
¼ teaspoon cinnamon
¼ teaspoon allspice
½ cup butter
1 cup flour
1 cup sugar
Heavy cream or sour cream (optional)

Preheat oven to 375°F. Place the blueberries in a baking dish. Sprinkle with the lemon juice, cinnamon, and allspice. In a bowl, cut the butter into the flour until the mixture resembles coarse meal. Stir in the sugar and spread the "crumble" over the blueberries. Bake for 40 minutes or until the topping is crisp and brown. Serve hot or cold with cream or sour cream if desired.

▾▾▾   YIELDS 6 SERVINGS.

Gingered Blueberry Compote

½ pint blueberries
1 cup orange juice
1 tablespoon lemon juice
¼ cup confectioners' sugar
2 tablespoons minced preserved ginger
Mint leaves (optional)

Drain the blueberries and place in a bowl. In another small bowl, combine the orange juice, lemon juice, sugar, and ginger. Mix well, then pour over the berries. Let macerate for at least 1 hour. Serve cold, garnished with the mint leaves if desired.

▾▾▾   YIELDS 4 TO 6 SERVINGS.

Cerises au Cognac

CHERRIES IN BRANDY

These cherries are good served over ice cream or can be used in baking. The cherries may be pitted either before or after they are prepared for bottling.

3 pounds cherries
Cognac
¼ pound sugar
3 tablespoons water

Pack the fruit in wide-mouth canning jars and cover with the cognac. Be sure the fruit is firmly packed. Cover and store, sealed, for 6 weeks. Then, in a saucepan over low heat, dissolve the sugar in the water; add the juices from the cherries and mix well. Strain and pour over the packed cherries. Reseal and store until ready to use.

YIELDS 3 PINTS.

Cherry Compote

1½ pounds cherries, pitted
1 tablespoon sugar
Pinch of cinnamon
½ cup red wine
3 tablespoons currant jelly
Grated rind and juice of 1 orange
1 tablespoon arrowroot
2 tablespoons water
Vanilla ice cream (optional)

In a saucepan, combine the cherries, sugar, and cinnamon. Cover, and heat over medium heat for 5 to 10 minutes or until the juice runs from the cherries. Turn into a bowl. Reduce the wine in the same pan by half. Stir in the currant jelly, and the orange rind and juice; heat until the jelly is melted. Strain the juices from the cherries and add to the wine mixture. In a small bowl, dissolve the arrowroot in the water and then stir into the wine-cherry mixture. Bring to a boil, stirring. Pour the boiled mixture over the cherries and allow to cool. Serve cold, alone or over ice cream.

YIELDS 6 SERVINGS.

Cerises Montmorency

CHERRIES WITH ORANGE, MACAROONS, AND CREAM

1 recipe Cherry Compote (see preceding recipe)
4 sugar cubes
1 orange
1½ cups heavy cream
12 Almond Macaroons (see page 261)
2 tablespoons kirsch

Prepare the Cherry Compote and set aside. Rub the sugar cubes over the rind of the orange until well soaked with the oil. Crush the sugar cubes in a bowl with the juice from the orange. Whip the cream until it holds a soft shape. Fold in the orange syrup, and continue beating until the cream holds its shape. Arrange the cherries and macaroons in a serving bowl. Sprinkle with the kirsch and spread the orange cream over the top. Chill for several hours before serving. Can be prepared the day before serving. YIELDS 6 SERVINGS.

Cherries with Liqueurs

2½ quarts cherries, pitted
⅔ cup cassis syrup
⅓ cup framboise
Crème Fraîche (see page 286)

Place the cherries in a bowl and sprinkle with cassis and framboise. Let macerate for at least 4 hours. Serve with Crème Fraîche if desired. Can be prepared up to 2 days before serving.

YIELDS 8 SERVINGS.

Cherries in Cream

2 pounds cherries, pitted
3 tablespoons kirsch
1 cup sour cream
2 tablespoons sugar
1 teaspoon cinnamon
Grated semisweet chocolate (optional)

Place the cherries in a serving bowl, toss with the kirsch, and chill. In a separate bowl, mix the sour cream, sugar, and cinnamon together and chill. When ready to serve, pour the cream mixture over the fruit and sprinkle with grated chocolate if desired. Can be prepared 2 days ahead.   YIELDS 6 TO 8 SERVINGS.

Cherries Jubilee

For a spectacular effect, prepare in a chafing dish in the dining room with the lights lowered.

1 ½ pounds cherries, pitted
1 cup sugar
2 cups plus 2 tablespoons water
Pinch of salt
1 tablespoon cornstarch
½ cup cognac
6 scoops vanilla ice cream

In a saucepan, simmer the cherries, sugar, 2 cups water, and salt for 5 minutes. Remove from heat and cool. Drain the cherries, reserving 1 cup of juice. Combine the remaining 2 tablespoons water and the cornstarch and stir into the reserved juice. Simmer 3 minutes, stirring constantly. Add the cherries. In a small saucepan, warm the cognac, ignite, and pour over the cherries. Serve with vanilla ice cream.   YIELDS 6 SERVINGS.

Fichi alla Gritti

FIGS ALLA GRITTI PALACE

This favorite from the Gritti Palace Hotel in Venice is truly delicious and simple.

18 ripe figs, peeled
2 tablespoons kirsch
½ cup heavy cream

Place the figs in a glass dish. Combine the kirsch and cream and pour over the figs. Let stand for 1 to 2 hours at room temperature before serving. Can be made up to 24 hours ahead.   YIELDS 6 SERVINGS.

Figs with Raspberry Cream

This dessert can be presented on a large platter with the raspberries surrounding it. However, for a stunning individual presentation, spread a layer of the raspberry cream on a dessert plate, arrange a fig "flower" on top, and surround it with the fresh raspberries. Then pour the drained syrup from the raspberries in three concentric rings around the fruit and draw the point of a knife from the fruit to the edge of the plate at 12, 3, 6, and 9 o'clock. Between these points, draw the knife from the edge of the plate into the fruit to create a flower effect in the cream (see sketch on page 22).

1 cup heavy cream
4 tablespoons sugar
10 ounces frozen raspberries, thawed and drained
12 ripe figs, peeled
1 cup fresh raspberries

Beat the cream to the soft-peak stage and sweeten with the sugar. Do not beat until stiff. Press the drained frozen raspberries through a sieve, discarding the seeds but reserving the juice. Fold the raspberry purée into the cream. Cut about three-quarters of the way through each fig from top to bottom to create quarters or sixths. Open each fig like a flower and arrange on a platter or on individual serving plates. Spoon the raspberry cream around each fig and garnish with the fresh raspberries. Can be prepared up to 2 hours before serving. YIELDS 6 SERVINGS.

Figs in Crème de Cacao

1 cup sour cream
2 tablespoons crème de cacao
12 fresh figs, peeled
½ teaspoon cocoa

In a bowl, combine the sour cream and crème de cacao. Dip the figs into the mixture, coating completely. Set on a serving platter. Sprinkle with cocoa and chill. Can be prepared up to 4 hours ahead. YIELDS 6 SERVINGS.

Figs in Curaçao

12 fresh figs, peeled
1 tablespoon cognac
1 cup sweet cream
⅓ cup curaçao

Cut the figs into quarters and put into a bowl. Toss gently with the cognac and let macerate for 30 minutes. In another bowl, combine the cream and curaçao with any unabsorbed cognac from the figs, and mix well. Spoon over the figs to serve. Can be prepared up to 4 hours ahead. YIELDS 6 SERVINGS.

Figs with Port and Honey Sabayon Sauce

19 figs, peeled
¾ cup port wine (approximately)
6 egg yolks
3 tablespoons honey
1 ½ teaspoons vanilla
¾ teaspoon lemon juice

Make a slit in each fig and toss the fruit with ½ cup of the port. Let macerate for at least 4 hours or up to 24 hours. When ready, drain the port into a measuring cup and add enough additional port to make ½ cup. Place the figs on a serving platter. In a saucepan, combine the ½ cup port, egg yolks, honey, vanilla, and lemon juice. Place over medium heat and cook, beating constantly, until the mixture thickens to the consistency of mayonnaise and is tripled in bulk. Spoon the sauce over the figs. Serve immediately or let cool to room temperature. YIELDS 6 SERVINGS.

Figues au Thym
FIGS WITH THYME

1 pound dried figs
2 cups red wine
½ teaspoon dried thyme
3 tablespoons honey

In a saucepan, combine the figs, wine, thyme, and honey. Simmer about 30 minutes or until the figs are tender. Remove the figs to a bowl. Strain the liquid through a fine sieve into a saucepan; discard the thyme. Reduce the strained syrup by a third, to the consistency of light syrup. Pour over the figs. Can be prepared 2 days before serving.
YIELDS 4 TO 6 SERVINGS.

Gingered Figs

1 pound dried figs
2 lemons
1 tablespoon minced gingerroot
Sugar
Cream

Cut the stems off the figs. In a medium-sized saucepan, combine the figs, water to cover, 2 tablespoons lemon juice, 1 tablespoon thinly sliced lemon rind, and the gingerroot. Simmer until the figs are tender, about 30 minutes. Drain the figs, reserving the liquid but discarding the gingerroot and lemon rind. Place the figs in a serving dish. Measure the reserved liquid and add half as much sugar. Simmer until syrupy, about 10 minutes. Add 1 tablespoon lemon juice and 4 slices of lemon. Pour over the figs. Serve with cream. Can be prepared 2 days before serving.

▪▼▪ YIELDS ABOUT 6 SERVINGS.

Poached Figs with Chartreuse-Flavored Cheese

The cheese can, in fact, be made several days ahead. The longer it drains the firmer and drier it will become. The cheese also can be served on its own and flavored with other liqueurs, or with herbs. The figs can be done up to two days ahead.

1 pound cream cheese
1 pound farmer cheese
1 cup sour cream
1¾ cups sugar
4 tablespoons green Chartreuse
⅛ teaspoon plus a pinch ground
  cardamom
3 cups water
2 strips lemon peel
24 dried figs

In a large bowl, combine the cream cheese, farmer cheese, sour cream, ¼ cup of the sugar, 3 tablespoons of the Chartreuse, and the pinch of cardamom. Beat until smooth. Line a colander or cheese mold with cheesecloth wrung out in cold water and place the cheese on top. Fold another cheesecloth over the top of the cheese, set the colander over a bowl, and put a saucer or plate on top of the cheese. Weight the cheese with a 2-pound weight. Let drain in the refrigerator overnight.

When ready, dissolve the remaining 1½ cups sugar in the 3 cups water in a saucepan over low heat. Add the lemon peel and ⅛ teaspoon cardamom and simmer the figs in this mixture until tender. Chill until ready to serve. Drain the figs, reserving the syrup. Unmold the cheese onto a platter and surround with the drained figs. Add the remaining tablespoon of Chartreuse to the syrup and spoon over the cheese.

▪▼▪ YIELDS 6 TO 12 SERVINGS.

Fichi alla Cioccolata

FIGS WITH CHOCOLATE

1 pound large dried figs
1 cup toasted almonds
¾ cup diced candied peel
Ground cloves to taste
¾ cup cocoa
¾ cup confectioners' sugar

Preheat oven to 350°F. Trim the tough stalk from the tips of the figs and cut a slit in the side of each. Stuff each fig with an almond, a few pieces of candied peel, and a pinch of cloves. Press the opening closed. Arrange figs on a baking sheet and bake for 15 minutes or until they darken slightly. In a shallow dish, sift the cocoa and sugar together. Roll the hot figs in the cocoa mixture and set on a plate to cool. Serve at room temperature. The figs will keep a week in an airtight container.

❖❖❖ YIELDS ABOUT 20 PIECES.

White Grapes and Sour Cream

This treatment also works well with other fruits, especially berries and cherries. If you prefer, use Crème Fraîche (see page 286) instead of the sour cream.

6 cups stemmed seedless grapes
1½ cups sour cream
¾ cup firmly packed light brown sugar

Wash the grapes, dry on paper toweling, and chill. In a bowl, combine the sour cream with ½ cup of the sugar and fold into the grapes. Sprinkle with remaining sugar. Can be prepared up to 6 hours ahead. YIELDS 6 SERVINGS.

❖❖❖

Grapes in Brandy

This is also delicious with strawberries or blueberries.

¾ cup honey
6 tablespoons cognac
1 tablespoon lemon juice
1 pound seedless grapes
1 cup sour cream

In a bowl, mix the honey, cognac, and lemon juice. Fold in the grapes and stir to coat. Chill. Serve with sour cream on the side. Can be prepared up to 24 hours before serving. YIELDS 4 SERVINGS.

❖❖❖

Lemon Posset

Posset dates back to the 16th century.

2½ cups heavy cream
1½ teaspoons grated lemon peel
½ cup dry white wine
¼ cup lemon juice
½ cup plus 2 tablespoons sugar
3 egg whites
Candied violets (optional)
Mint sprigs (optional)

In a bowl, whip the cream and lemon peel until stiff. Beat in the wine until stiff. Gradually beat in the lemon juice and ½ cup of sugar. Beat the egg whites until they form soft peaks, add the remaining 2 tablespoons sugar, and beat until stiff and glossy. Fold beaten egg whites into the cream mixture. Pour into a serving dish and garnish with violets and mint, if desired. Can be prepared up to 2 hours before serving.

❖❖❖ YIELDS 8 SERVINGS.

Mango Slices with Champagne

This method of treating fruits works very well with pears, bananas, blueberries, cherries, oranges, pineapple, raspberries, and strawberries.

3 mangoes, peeled and sliced
½ cup confectioners' sugar
¼ cup framboise liqueur
1 bottle extra-dry champagne

In a bowl, combine the mangoes, sugar, and framboise. Toss gently and chill for up to 6 hours. Put the slices into individual glasses and cover with champagne. Can be prepared up to 6 hours ahead but add champagne just before serving. YIELDS 6 SERVINGS.

❖❖❖

Melon Balls with Raspberry Sauce

2 quarts melon balls
¼ cup lemon juice
2 tablespoons sugar
10 ounces frozen raspberries in syrup, thawed
¼ cup crème de cassis
4 small cantaloupes, halved and seeded
½ pint raspberries
Mint leaves

In a bowl, combine the melon balls, lemon juice, and sugar. Toss gently. Purée the berries in a processor, strain, and discard the seeds. Stir in the cassis. Fold the raspberry mixture into the melon balls. Cover and refrigerate for 3 to 4 hours. Spoon the melon balls into the cantaloupe halves and garnish with the fresh raspberries and mint leaves. Can be prepared a day ahead.

          YIELDS 8 SERVINGS.

Nectarines and Brandy

Serve peaches, apples, pears, or other fruits in this manner.

6 nectarines, peeled and quartered
¾ cup granulated sugar
1 cup water
5 tablespoons cognac
1½ teaspoons vanilla
1 cup sour cream
1 tablespoon confectioners' sugar

In a saucepan, combine the nectarines, granulated sugar, and water; simmer 1 minute. Remove from the heat and stir in 3 tablespoons cognac and the vanilla. Let cool and chill. Just before serving, drain and arrange fruit in serving dishes. In a small bowl, combine the sour cream, confectioners' sugar, and

the remaining 2 tablespoons cognac. Spoon over the nectarines and serve. The fruit can be prepared the day before.   YIELDS 6 SERVINGS.

Nectarines Flambé

1 cup sugar
1½ cups water
6 nectarines, peeled, halved, and pitted
¼ cup Cointreau
Vanilla ice cream (optional)

In a saucepan, combine the sugar and water. Bring to a boil and simmer 10 minutes. Add the nectarines and simmer until tender, about 5 minutes. Remove the nectarines and put into the blazer of a chafing dish with about ½ cup syrup. Bring to a boil and add the Cointreau. Ignite. Serve with ice cream if desired. The fruit can be poached a day ahead.   YIELDS 6 SERVINGS.

Oranges with Ginger and White Wine

10 navel oranges
1⅓ cups dry white wine
1 jar (10 ounces) preserved ginger in syrup
1 cup orange juice
2 tablespoons lemon juice
1½ tablespoons sugar
¼ cup diced crystallized ginger

With a zester, remove the zest from 2 oranges, wrap it in plastic, and refrigerate. Peel all the oranges and slice thinly. Arrange in a serving bowl. In a processor, combine the wine, preserved ginger, ginger syrup, orange juice, lemon juice, and sugar. Process with on/off turns until the ginger is minced. Pour over the oranges, toss gently, and cover. Chill for an hour or up to 36 hours. Serve sprinkled with reserved orange zest and diced crystallized ginger. Yields 10 servings.

Oranges in Red Wine

1 cup dry red wine
1 cup water
¾ cup sugar
1 cinnamon stick
2 whole cloves
2 to 3 slices tangerine (optional)
2 slices lemon
5 large oranges

In a saucepan, simmer the wine, water, sugar, cinnamon stick, cloves, tangerine, and lemon slices for 3 minutes. With a zester, remove the rind from 3 oranges and set aside. Peel the oranges, removing all of the pith. Cut the oranges into segments. Put the segments into the hot wine syrup, sprinkle with the orange julienne, and chill. Can be prepared 2 days ahead.
Yields 4 to 6 servings.

Oranges in Caramel

See photograph on page 65.

The caramel for this dish reaches 320°F. When it splatters on you, it sticks. If you should get splattered, immediately place that portion of you under cold running water, keeping it there for several minutes, at least. Do not try to peel the caramel off; instead, let the water wash it off. To protect your hand from the splattering caramel, wrap it in a towel as suggested or wear an oven mitt.

6 large navel oranges
8 toothpicks
1 cup sugar

½ cup water
½ cup *warm* water

Pare the zest from 1 orange and cut into julienne strips. Blanch strips in boiling water for 4 minutes and drain. Peel the oranges and cut into slices, keeping the slices in order. Reassemble the oranges, using the toothpicks to keep the oranges in shape. Place in a serving dish. In a saucepan, combine the sugar and ½ cup water and heat over medium heat until sugar dissolves. Turn up heat and boil until syrup is golden brown. Remove the pan from the heat. Wrap your hand in a towel; then, with the towel-wrapped hand, gently pour in the ½ cup warm water. Return to the heat and cook, stirring until the caramel has dissolved. Pour the sauce over the oranges and sprinkle with the blanched orange julienne strips. Can be prepared a day ahead. Yields 8 servings.

Arance Caramellate

6 navel oranges
1 cup sugar
4 tablespoons water
Pinch of cream of tartar
Candied Orange Peel (see page 284)
3 tablespoons cognac
½ cup glacéed fruit

Peel the oranges, and slice. Arrange oranges in a shallow serving dish. In a skillet, combine the sugar, water, and cream of tartar. Bring to a boil and cook until mixture is a deep golden caramel. Stir in ½ cup of the syrup from the Candied Orange Peel, bring to a boil, and stir in the cognac. Pour over the oranges. Sprinkle with the candied fruit and Candied Orange Peel. Chill. Can be prepared a day or two ahead; the longer the fruit stands, the thinner the sauce will become. Yields 6 servings.

Oranges Glacées au Grand Marnier

GLAZED ORANGES WITH
GRAND MARNIER

6 navel oranges
2 tablespoons honey
¼ cup orange juice
¼ cup Grand Marnier

Candy the orange rind (see recipe on page 284) and cut into julienne strips, then add the honey. Remove all of the white pith from the oranges and cut the flesh into slices. Place the slices in a shallow serving dish. Add the orange juice and Grand Marnier to the juice from the candied peel and stir gently. Pour over the oranges. Chill. Can be prepared 2 to 3 days ahead.

❖❖❖   YIELDS 6 SERVINGS.

Orange Slices with Rosemary Syrup

See photograph on page 65.

The old-fashioned idea of flavoring foods with fresh herbs is returning. If you do not have rosemary, try another favorite herb such as thyme, marjoram, or savory.

½ cup sugar
2 tablespoons minced rosemary
1 cup water
4 navel oranges, peeled and sliced
Rosemary sprigs

In a saucepan, combine the sugar, minced rosemary, and water. Simmer 5 minutes; remove from heat and allow to cool. Arrange orange slices in a shallow serving dish and pour the syrup over them. Let stand for 2 to 3 hours. Serve garnished with rosemary sprigs. Can be made a day ahead.   YIELDS 4 SERVINGS.
❖❖❖

Buttered Oranges

10 oranges
¼ cup sugar
5 egg yolks
4 tablespoons butter, softened
¼ cup heavy cream, whipped to soft peaks
2 teaspoons rose water (optional)
4 tablespoons Candied Orange Peel (see page 284)

Grate the zest from 2 oranges and squeeze the juice into a saucepan. Cut the top half inch from each remaining orange, set aside, and remove the pulp from the rest of the orange, forming a hollow shell. Squeeze the juice into the saucepan. Add the grated zest, sugar, and egg yolks. Over medium heat, cook, stirring constantly until thickened. Remove from the heat and cool to just below room temperature. Beat in the butter, bit by bit, and fold in the cream. Fold in the rose water, if desired, and the Candied Orange Peel. Fill the hollowed orange shells with the mixture and cover with the reserved tops. Refrigerate for at least 4 hours. Can be prepared 24 hours ahead.

❖❖❖   YIELDS 8 SERVINGS.

Baked Oranges with Sabayon Sauce

4 large navel oranges
5 tablespoons plus 1 teaspoon sugar
3 egg yolks

Peel 1 orange into julienne strips. Peel remaining oranges, removing all the pith. Cut oranges into segments and squeeze juices from the membranes into a bowl. Add the orange segments to the bowl with the orange zest. Let macerate for at least 30 minutes with 2 tablespoons of the sugar. Drain, reserving juice. Place the sections and the zest strips in a 2-cup gratin or in 4 individual ramekins.

Preheat the broiler. In a saucepan, beat the egg yolks, 3 tablespoons sugar, and the reserved juices. Place over medium heat and cook, beating constantly, until the mixture is the consistency of a foamy mayonnaise and about tripled in bulk. Spoon over the oranges and sprinkle with the remaining teaspoon of sugar. Brown under the broiler, watching carefully, as it can burn quickly. Serve immediately. YIELDS 4 SERVINGS.

Note: The oranges for this recipe can be prepared ahead and the ramekins filled. But make the sauce at the last moment.
▪▪▪

Baked Papayas

3 ripe papayas, peeled and seeded
2 tablespoons butter
2 teaspoons vanilla
4 tablespoons firmly packed brown
  sugar
Cream (optional)

Preheat oven to 350°F. Arrange the papayas, cut side up, in a baking dish and add ½ inch of water. Dot the center of each with butter, and sprinkle with vanilla and sugar. Bake until tender, about 45 minutes. Serve hot or cold. Accompany with cream if desired.
▪▪▪
YIELDS 6 SERVINGS.

Peaches in White or Red Wine

6 large peaches, peeled, stoned,
  and sliced
Red or white wine to cover
Sugar to taste

Arrange the peaches in a bowl, pour on enough wine to cover, and sprinkle with sugar. Let macerate for at least 1 hour or up to 12. YIELDS 6 SERVINGS.
▪▪▪

Peaches with Honey-Lime Sauce

6 peaches, peeled, stoned, and sliced
2 tablespoons honey
2 tablespoons lime juice
1 teaspoon grated lime zest
Dash of mace

Place the peaches in a large bowl. In another smaller bowl, whisk the honey, lime juice, zest, and mace together. Spoon over the fruit, mixing lightly. Can be prepared up to 6 hours ahead.
▪▪▪ YIELDS 6 SERVINGS.

Pêches à la Fermière

PEACHES FARMER-STYLE

6 peaches, peeled, stoned, and sliced
2 tablespoons granulated sugar
⅓ cup peach brandy
8 ounces cream cheese
½ cup confectioners' sugar
1 cup heavy cream
2 cups blueberries

Place the peaches in a bowl, sprinkle with granulated sugar and brandy, cover, and chill for 3 hours. Beat the cream cheese and confectioners' sugar until smooth. Beat the cream to the soft-peak stage and fold into the cream cheese mixture. Shortly before serving, drain the peaches and arrange in a bowl. Fold the blueberries and cream cheese mixture together, thinning with some of the macerating liquid if necessary. Spoon over the peaches and serve. Can be prepared up to 6 hours before serving.
▪▪▪ YIELDS 6 SERVINGS.

Pêches au Sabayon Mousseline

PEACHES WITH FLUFFY
SABAYON SAUCE

Although this recipe suggests Sabayon flavored with sauterne, you can prepare it with any liqueur. You might want to use peach brandy, bourbon, or one of the almond-flavored liqueurs.

> 6 peaches, peeled and stoned
> Juice of 1 lemon
> ½ cup peach brandy
> 2 tablespoons sugar
> 2 cups Sabayon Sauce flavored with
>   sauterne (see page 272)
> Pinch of cinnamon
> Pinch of nutmeg
> ½ cup heavy cream
> Toasted almond slices (optional)

Place peaches in a bowl and toss with the lemon juice. Add the brandy and sugar and mix until the sugar is dissolved. Chill for 4 hours. Prepare the Sabayon Sauce and season with cinnamon and nutmeg. Chill. Beat the cream to the soft-peak stage and fold into the sauce. Pour over the peaches and garnish with the toasted almonds. Can be prepared up to 6 hours before serving.
▰▰▰   YIELDS 6 SERVINGS.

Pesche Ripiene I

STUFFED PEACHES I

Try this with nectarines, pears, apples, or plums. See Note.

> 6 ripe peaches, peeled, halved,
>   and stoned
> 2 tablespoons lemon juice
> 2 cups dry white wine
> ¾ cup sugar
> ½ teaspoon vanilla

> 1 cup heavy cream, whipped
> 12 amaretti, crushed
> 1 egg yolk, lightly beaten

Scoop part of the pulp out of each peach half and reserve. Brush peach halves with lemon juice. In a saucepan, bring the wine, sugar, and vanilla to a boil. Add peach halves and poach for 2 minutes. Remove from heat and cool. Drain peaches, reserving the syrup. Simmer the syrup until thickened. Purée the reserved pulp and mix with the whipped cream, 10 crushed amaretti, and the egg yolk. Fill peach halves with this mixture. Place on a serving dish and chill. This portion of the recipe can be prepared up to 6 hours before serving. When ready to serve, coat with reserved syrup and sprinkle with remaining 2 amaretti.   YIELDS 6 SERVINGS.

Note: Nectarines and other fruits can be treated in the same fashion. Amaretti are cookies made from apricot kernels. They can be found in specialty stores.
▰▰▰

Pesche Ripiene II

STUFFED PEACHES II

> 6 peaches, peeled, halved, and stoned
> 5 stale macaroons, crushed
> 2 egg yolks
> 2 tablespoons sugar
> 4 tablespoons butter

Preheat oven to 375°F. Scoop out enough pulp from the center of each peach to make a deep hollow. Mince the pulp and add it to the macaroons, egg yolks, sugar, and butter. Fill the peaches with the mixture. Arrange in a buttered baking dish in a single layer. Bake about 25 minutes or until the peaches are tender, basting often. Serve warm or at room temperature. Can be baked the day before and reheated.
▰▰▰   YIELDS 6 SERVINGS.

Glazed Baked Peaches

6 peaches, peeled, stoned, and sliced
2 tablespoons butter
1 to 2 tablespoons sugar
½ cup cognac

Preheat oven to 350°F. Butter a baking dish and arrange peach slices in the bottom. Sprinkle with the sugar and bake 30 minutes. In a small saucepan, warm the brandy; pour over the peaches and ignite. Can be baked several hours before serving and reheated, but do not flame with cognac until ready to serve.
❖ YIELDS 6 SERVINGS.

Peaches in Orange Liqueur

6 peaches, peeled, halved, and stoned
¼ cup butter
1 cup sugar
½ cup orange liqueur
¼ cup lemon juice
¼ cup almonds, slivered

Preheat oven to 375°F. Arrange peaches, cut side down, in a single layer in a shallow baking pan. Cream the butter and sugar in a processor or by hand, and beat in the orange liqueur and lemon juice. Spoon over the peaches. Sprinkle with the almonds and bake for 35 to 45 minutes or until the peaches are soft. Baste with juices once or twice. Serve warm. Can be made the day before and reheated. YIELDS 6 SERVINGS.
❖

Nut-Stuffed Peaches, Pears, or Nectarines

Poaching fruits in vanilla syrup enhances their flavor, especially if they are not fully ripe. The syrup can be kept in the refrigerator and used over again. If it becomes too thick, thin with some water.

½ cup raspberry jam
¾ cup finely chopped pecans
6 vanilla-poached peaches, pears, or nectarines (see page 286)
12 (3-inch) circles Génoise (see page 279)
1 cup heavy cream, whipped and sweetened to taste

In a bowl, combine the jam and pecans to make a stiff mixture. Cut the poached fruit in half and remove each pit or core. Fill with the jam mixture; it will resemble the stone of the peaches or nectarines. Arrange the fruit halves on the cake slices and garnish with the cream, piped through a no. 4 open-star tip. Can be prepared up to 4 hours before serving. YIELDS 6 TO 12 SERVINGS.
❖

Poires en Cointreau

PEARS IN COINTREAU

6 pears, peeled, sliced, and cored
1 tablespoon sugar
1 cup orange juice
¼ cup Cointreau
1 teaspoon lemon juice
Julienned rind of 1 orange (optional)

In a bowl, combine the pears and sugar. Pour on the orange juice, Cointreau, and lemon juice. Macerate in the refrigerator for 1 hour. Garnish with orange rind, if desired. Can be prepared up to 6 hours before serving.
❖ YIELDS 6 SERVINGS.

Poires Belle Angevine

PEARS IN RED WINE

6 pears, peeled and cored
3 cups red wine
3 to 4 tablespoons sugar
1 cinnamon stick
1 tablespoon pear brandy

In a saucepan, combine the pears, wine, sugar, and cinnamon stick. Simmer gently until the pears are tender. Drain pears, reserving the liquid. Arrange pears in a serving dish. Continue cooking the poaching liquid until it is a light syrup. Cool, then flavor with the pear brandy. Discard cinnamon stick. Pour syrup over the fruit and chill. Serve cold or at room temperature. Can be prepared the day before serving.
YIELDS 6 SERVINGS.

VARIATIONS

Pears in Port: Substitute 1 cup port and 2 cups water for the wine, and add the rind of ½ an orange and 1 strip of lemon peel. Omit the pear brandy.

Poires à la Bordelaise (Pears Bordeaux-Style): Omit the pear brandy and substitute 2 tablespoons rum or cognac.

Pere al Vino (Pears with Wine): Replace wine with 4 cups Chianti and 1 cup tawny port. Omit the cinnamon and pear brandy; add juice of ½ lemon and a strip of lemon peel.

Poires Bourguignon (Pears Burgundy-Style): Omit pear brandy and add 2 tablespoons kirsch or Cointreau. Omit the cinnamon stick.

Poached Pears with Wine and Basil: Omit the cinnamon; add the julienned peel of ⅓ lemon. When pears are tender, reduce liquid to a syrup and swirl in ½ tablespoon of butter. Add 20 basil leaves, chopped, and let stand, stirring occasionally, for 1 hour. Strain syrup, discarding the leaves and lemon. Spoon sauce over pears.
▚▚▚

Pears in Cider

6 pears
1 lemon, halved
2½ cups apple cider
½ cup sugar
Strip of lemon peel
1 vanilla bean, split
1 cinnamon stick
1½ cups heavy cream
1½ tablespoons cognac

Leave stems intact and rub pears with lemon half. Trim bases of pears to allow them to stand straight. In a saucepan, simmer cider, sugar, lemon peel, vanilla bean, and cinnamon stick for 2 minutes. Add pears and poach until tender. Let cool in liquid. Discard the cinnamon stick. Whip the cream in a bowl and blend in the cognac. Transfer pears to a serving dish. Reduce cooking liquid to a syrup and pour over the pears. Pass the cream separately. Can be prepared a day ahead.   YIELDS 6 SERVINGS.
▚▚▚

Pere alla Gelatina di Frutta

PEARS WITH CURRANT JELLY

6 pears, peeled, with stems left intact
⅓ cup currant jelly
2 cups water
2 tablespoons sugar as needed
1 tablespoon maraschino or
   amaretto liqueur

Stand the pears upright in a saucepan. Add the jelly and 2 cups water. Add more water, if needed, so that only the stems of the pears are above the liquid. Cover and simmer until tender, about 25 minutes. Cool the pears in the liquid, then remove the fruit and arrange on a serving platter. Boil the juice until it is thick enough to coat the back of a spoon, adding the sugar if needed. Add the maraschino or amaretto and pour the syrup over the pears. Let cool, preferably without refrigerating. Can be prepared up to 24 hours ahead.

◆◆◆ YIELDS 6 SERVINGS.

Poires au Sirop

PEARS IN PEPPER AND HONEY SYRUP

Pepper and fruit may sound like a strange combination, but it is truly delicious. The little fire of the pepper brings out the flavors of the fruit.

> 4⅓ cups water
> 1¾ cups sugar
> ⅔ cup honey
> 3 whole bay leaves
> 2 whole cloves
> ¾ teaspoon black peppercorns
> 6 pears, peeled

In a saucepan, simmer the water, sugar, honey, bay leaves, cloves, and peppercorns for 2 minutes. Add the pears and simmer 15 minutes. Let cool in syrup overnight. Strain syrup before serving. Can be prepared 2 days before serving.

◆◆◆ YIELDS 6 SERVINGS.

Poires Glacées

CHILLED GLAZED PEARS

> 6 pears, peeled
> 4 cups dry white wine

> 1 cup sugar
> 1 teaspoon vanilla
> 1 pint strawberries
> 1 pint raspberries
> 2 cups heavy cream
> ½ cup red port

In a large saucepan, poach the pears with the wine, ⅔ cup sugar, and vanilla. Let cool in the syrup. Force the berries through a sieve, discarding the seeds. Chill. Beat the cream with the remaining ⅓ cup sugar to the soft-peak stage. Beat in the port and continue to beat until stiff. Chill. Fill a serving dish with the chilled whipped cream. Drain the pears and arrange on the whipped cream, then top each pear with the fruit purée. Assemble no more than 1 hour before serving. YIELDS 6 SERVINGS.

◆◆◆

Pears in Zabaglione

Zabaglione is an Italian egg sauce made with Marsala wine. The French version is Sabayon Sauce.

> 6 pears, peeled
> 1 lemon, sliced
> ¼ to 1 cup sugar
> 1 recipe Zabaglione Sauce (see
>   page 272)
> Candied mint leaves (optional)

Cut a slice off the bottom of each pear so that it will stand up. In water to cover, poach the pears until tender with the lemon and sugar. Drain and chill the pears. When ready to serve, place pears in serving dishes and spoon on the Zabaglione Sauce. Garnish with mint leaves. Can be prepared 24 hours ahead.

YIELDS 6 SERVINGS.

Note: Candied mint leaves are available in gourmet shops.

◆◆◆

Gingered Pears

2 cups water
2 cups sugar
1 cinnamon stick
2 strips lemon peel
1 teaspoon whole cloves
2 tablespoons chopped fresh
   gingerroot
6 pears, peeled, sliced, and cored

In a saucepan, simmer the water, sugar, cinnamon stick, lemon peel, cloves, and gingerroot for 2 minutes. Add the pears and poach until tender. Let cool in the syrup. Chill. Strain sauce and discard cinnamon stick, lemon peel, cloves, and gingerroot. Can be prepared the day before serving.   YIELDS 6 SERVINGS.
▼▪▼

Pears with Ginger

6 pears, peeled, halved, and cored
2 cups water
¾ cup sugar
⅛ teaspoon ginger
1 slice lemon

Poach the pears in 2 cups water for 10 minutes. Add the sugar, ginger, and lemon and poach until tender, about 15 to 20 minutes longer. Chill. Can be made 2 days before serving.
▼▪▼   YIELDS 6 SERVINGS.

Pears in Caramel Syrup

8 pears, peeled
3 cups water, plus enough
   to cover pears
Juice of 1 lemon
2 cups sugar
⅓ cup coffee liqueur
Whipped cream (optional)

Leave the pears whole. Cover pears in water acidulated with the lemon juice. In a saucepan, simmer 3 cups water and 1 cup sugar for 2 minutes; add the pears and poach until tender. Remove pears and set aside. Pour 1 cup of the syrup into a saucepan, add remaining 1 cup sugar, and boil until it starts to caramelize. Remove from the heat and add the remaining syrup. Bring to a boil again and add the coffee liqueur. Pour the sauce over the pears. Chill. Serve with whipped cream if desired. Can be prepared 2 days ahead.
▼▪▼   YIELDS 8 SERVINGS.

Sautéed Pears with Raspberry Sauce

If you like, substitute other fruits for the pears. If the fruit is already tender, do not cover and cook until tender, but instead cook quickly over high heat.

6 pears, peeled, sliced, and cored
Juice of ½ lemon
4 tablespoons butter
¼ cup Grand Marnier
½ cup raspberry preserves, strained
¼ cup sliced almonds, toasted
½ cup heavy cream, whipped

Toss the pear slices in the lemon juice. In a large skillet, sauté the pears over high heat for 5 minutes, tossing to coat with the butter. If needed, cover and steam another minute or two until tender. Transfer the pear slices to a serving platter or to individual plates. Add the liqueur and raspberry preserves to the skillet. Cook, stirring over high heat until slightly thickened. Pour over the pear slices and sprinkle with the nuts. Serve the whipped cream on the side.
▼▪▼   YIELDS 6 SERVINGS.

Pears in Orange Sabayon Sauce

6 pears, peeled, halved, and cored
3 cups vanilla syrup (see page 286)
½ cup diced candied fruit, soaked in
   ¼ cup orange liqueur
Sabayon Sauce flavored with orange
   liqueur (see page 272)

Poach the pears in the syrup until tender. Drain pears; arrange on a platter and fill with candied fruit. Serve with the Sabayon Sauce. The pears can be poached 2 days before serving.

▪▪▪   YIELDS 6 SERVINGS.

Poires à la Cardinale

PEARS WITH RASPBERRY SAUCE
See photograph on page 66.

A pretty, delicious, not-too-rich dessert that is a perfect finish for an elaborate meal.

½ cup plus 2 tablespoons sugar
1¾ cups water
Dash of salt
6 pears, peeled, halved, and cored
4 teaspoons lemon juice
1 cup raspberries
Chopped blanched almonds

In a saucepan, simmer ½ cup sugar, water, salt, pears, and 2 teaspoons lemon juice until pears are tender, about 10 to 20 minutes. Chill in the syrup. Transfer the pears to a serving dish. Sieve the raspberries, discarding the seeds. Add the remaining 2 teaspoons lemon juice and 2 tablespoons sugar. Stir until the sugar is dissolved. Chill. Just before serving, coat the pears with the raspberry sauce and sprinkle with the almonds. The pears can be poached up to 2 days before serving.   YIELDS 6 SERVINGS.

▪▪▪

Poires à la Vigneronne

PEARS WINE GROWERS-STYLE

6 pears, peeled, sliced, and cored
2 cups dry white wine
½ cup sugar
Zest of 1 lemon
1 cinnamon stick or ¼ teaspoon
   ground cinnamon
1 (1-inch) piece vanilla bean
   or 1 teaspoon extract
¼ cup orange marmalade
¼ cup apricot preserves

Place the pears in a saucepan with the wine and sugar. Cut the lemon zest into julienne strips and add to the pan. Simmer the pears gently until tender, about 7 to 10 minutes. Remove the pears and zest to a serving dish. Add the cinnamon stick, vanilla bean, marmalade, and apricot preserves to the poaching liquid and boil for about 10 minutes or until syrupy. Pour over the pears, discarding the cinnamon stick and vanilla bean. Chill. Serve cold or at room temperature.   YIELDS 6 SERVINGS.

Note: If you use the ground cinnamon and vanilla extract, add them to the liquid after it has been reduced.

▪▪▪

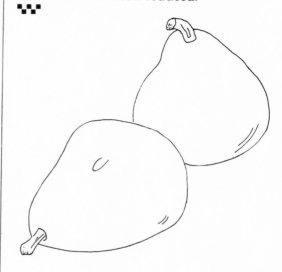

Poached Pears with Chestnuts

The chestnuts in syrup for this recipe are available in many gourmet shops and supermarkets.

> 2 cups water
> 2 tablespoons lemon juice
> ¾ cup sugar
> 1 (1-inch) piece cinnamon stick
> 6 pears, peeled, halved, and cored
> 12 whole chestnuts in syrup
> 2 cups Custard Sauce (see page 273)
> ½ cup chopped chestnuts in syrup
> ¼ cup syrup from chestnuts

In a saucepan, simmer the water, lemon juice, sugar, and cinnamon stick 3 minutes. Add the pears and simmer until tender. Let pears cool in the syrup; then drain and chill the pears. Discard sugar syrup. Arrange the pears, cut side up, on a serving plate and fill each cavity with a whole chestnut. Combine the Custard Sauce, chopped chestnuts, and ¼ cup of syrup. Mix well and pour over the pears. Can be prepared for assembly the day before.   YIELDS 6 SERVINGS.

Poached Pears Mary Garden

Mary Garden, an opera singer at the turn of the century, was often honored by chefs naming dishes for her. One way of knowing you were a star was to have a dish given your name.

> 4 vanilla-poached pears (see page 286)
> ½ cup raspberry jam
> 1 teaspoon cornstarch
> 1 tablespoon water, plus warm water as needed
> 1 tablespoon kirsch

> ¼ cup candied cherries
> 1 cup heavy cream, whipped

Cool the pears in the poaching syrup as directed, and drain well. In a small saucepan, melt the jam and then strain. In a small bowl, combine the cornstarch with 1 tablespoon water and stir into the jam. Bring to a boil and cook until thickened. Cool and add the kirsch. Pour warm water over the candied cherries and let stand until softened. Drain and dry on paper toweling. Add the cherries to the jam mixture. Arrange the raspberry-cherry sauce in the bottom of a serving dish. Arrange pears on top and coat with whipped cream. The pears can be prepared the day before serving, but do not coat with cream until just before serving.

     YIELDS 4 SERVINGS.

Poires Susanne

PEARS SUSANNA

In the tradition of naming desserts for people, I created this dessert for Susanna Gourley because it combined so many of her favorite flavors.

> 6 vanilla-poached pears (see page 286)
> 4 ounces cream cheese
> ¼ cup ground walnuts
> 1 tablespoon kirsch
> Sugar to taste
> Grated semisweet chocolate

Chill the pears and core by cutting through the bottom of each, leaving the stem intact. In a bowl, cream the cheese with the walnuts, kirsch, and sugar until mixture is light and fluffy. Stuff the pears with the cheese mixture and arrange upright on a platter. Pour the poaching syrup around the pears and sprinkle the chocolate over the pears. Can be prepared the day before serving. ◆◆◆ YIELDS 6 SERVINGS.

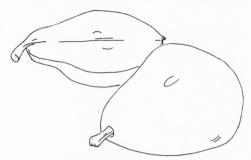

Poires Vefour

POACHED PEARS GRAND VEFOUR

Named for the Restaurant Grand Vefour in Paris. The violets may seem a conceit, but they are required to give the dessert color. If you wish, use raspberries, strawberries, or blueberries on top to give the dessert color. This is a delicious dessert, but without a touch of color, it seems undistinguished. The violets are available in gourmet shops and, although they are somewhat costly, one can pull a dessert together visually.

6 pears, poached in vanilla syrup (see page 286)
2 cups Pastry Cream (see page 282), cooled
Vanilla to taste
Grand Marnier to taste
12 Almond Macaroons (see page 261)
1 cup heavy cream
Sugar to taste
Crystallized violets

Cool pears in syrup. In a bowl, combine the Pastry Cream with the vanilla and Grand Marnier to taste. Make a thin layer of the Pastry Cream on a serving dish. Dip each macaroon in the Grand Marnier and place on top of the Pastry Cream. Cover with the remaining Pastry Cream. Arrange the pears on top. Beat the heavy cream to the soft-peak stage and beat in sugar and more Grand Marnier to taste. Beat until stiff. With a pastry bag fitted with a no. 4 open-star tip, garnish the pears. Top with crystallized violets. YIELDS 6 SERVINGS.
◆◆◆

Poires Pralinées au Porto Blanc

PEARS POACHED IN PORT WITH PRALINE

Praline powder is used in many desserts. Prepare it ahead and keep in an airtight container for months. If your kitchen is warm, keep it in the freezer lest the nut oil turn rancid.

6 pears, peeled, halved, and cored
3 cups white port
¼ cup sugar
¼ teaspoon vanilla
6 egg yolks
¾ cup heavy cream, whipped
⅓ cup Praline Powder (see page 284)

Poach the pears in the port until tender. Let pears cool in liquid. Drain pears, reserving the wine. In a saucepan, beat the sugar, vanilla, and egg yolks together until they form a ribbon. Add 1 cup of reserved wine and cook over medium heat, stirring constantly, until the mixture is thick and frothy. It is best to use a hand-held electric mixer. Remove from the heat and cool. Fold in the cream. Place the pears in a heatproof baking dish, cut side down. Spread the sauce over them and sprinkle with the Praline Powder.

Preheat the broiler. Brown under the broiler. Watch carefully; it can burn quickly. Cool and chill. Can be prepared the day before serving.
◆◆◆ YIELDS 6 SERVINGS.

Poached Pears Flambé

6 vanilla-poached pears (see
   page 286)
1 cup apricot preserves
2 tablespoons cornstarch
2 tablespoons cold water
½ cup rum

Drain pears, reduce poaching syrup to 1
cup, then add the apricot preserves and
bring to a boil. In a bowl, combine the
cornstarch with the cold water. Stir into
the syrup and cook until thickened and
clear. Pour over the pears and keep hot
in a chafing dish or oven. When ready
to serve, warm the rum; then pour it
over the pears and ignite. The pears can
be prepared the day before serving and
reheated.   YIELDS 6 SERVINGS.

Pere Ripiene alla Gorgonzola I

PEARS STUFFED WITH GORGONZOLA I

*If the pears are not perfect for eating, they
can be poached in vanilla syrup (see page
286) before using in this recipe.*

6 pears, peeled
1½ tablespoons lemon juice
3 ounces Gorgonzola cheese
3 tablespoons butter, softened
3 tablespoons ground walnuts,
   pistachios, or pine nuts

Cut the pears in half lengthwise, leaving
the stem attached to one half. Core and
scoop out a scant tablespoon of pulp.
Brush the pear inside and out with lemon juice. In a bowl, cream the Gorgonzola and butter until soft and fluffy. Fill
the cavities of the pears with the cheese
mixture and press the halves back together. Roll the pears in the nuts and
chill for 2 hours before serving. Can be
prepared about 6 hours before serving.
          YIELDS 6 SERVINGS.

Pere Ripiene alla Gorgonzola II

PEARS STUFFED WITH GORGONZOLA II

6 pears, peeled
12 very thin slices gingerroot
1 cup dry white wine
½ cup water
3 tablespoons sugar
Juice of ½ lemon
½ pound Gorgonzola, at room
   temperature
⅔ cup pistachio nuts, chopped

Cut the pears in two pieces horizontally
about a third down from the stem. With
a melon baller, hollow out the larger
section of each pear and set in a casserole, then place the top back on. Scatter
the gingerroot around the pears; add
the wine, water, sugar, and lemon juice.
Cover and simmer 10 minutes or until
tender but firm. Mash the Gorgonzola
until softened. Remove the pears from
casserole, remove tops, and stuff with
the cheese. Replace tops and set aside.
Reduce cooking liquid to ¼ cup. Dip
bottom of each pear first in syrup, then
in the nuts. Return pears to the casserole and spoon any remaining sauce
over all. Sprinkle with remaining pistachios. Serve warm. Can be reheated in a
slow oven if made earlier in the day.
          YIELDS 6 SERVINGS.

Pere Ripiene alla Gorgonzola III

PEARS STUFFED WITH GORGONZOLA
III

*The pears for this dessert should be at the
point of eating perfection, as should the
cheese. Do not use pears that have been
poached in vanilla syrup.*

3 pears, peeled, halved, and cored
Lemon juice
5 ounces Gorgonzola, softened

Brush the pears with the lemon juice. Fill the cavities with the cheese and refrigerate until 15 minutes before serving. Should be prepared no more than 2 hours before serving.

YIELDS 6 SERVINGS.

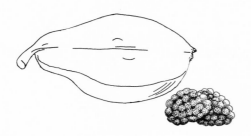

Almond-Filled Pears with Raspberry Sauce

1 cup blanched almonds, toasted
¼ cup sugar
2 tablespoons rose water
¼ teaspoon almond extract
6 vanilla-poached pears, cored from the bottom, stems left intact (see page 286)
20 ounces frozen raspberries, thawed and drained
Framboise or kirsch to taste

In a processor, combine the almonds, sugar, rose water, and almond extract. Process until mixture forms a paste. Stuff pears with almond mixture. Place pears in a serving dish. Combine the raspberries with ¾ cup poaching liquid and purée in processor. Press through a sieve, discarding the seeds. Add more poaching syrup to taste and flavor with framboise or kirsch. Chill until serving time. Serve pears coated with sauce. Pears can be prepared the day before serving. YIELDS 6 SERVINGS.

Poires Fioretta

PEARS LITTLE FLOWER

The several steps to this dessert can be done ahead. It is a lovely presentation.

¼ cup semolina flour
½ cup sugar
½ teaspoon salt
2 cups milk
1 (2-inch) piece vanilla bean
1 tablespoon gelatin
¼ cup cold water
1 cup heavy cream, whipped
6 wine-poached pears (see page 286)
¼ cup red currant jelly
10 small circles Candied Orange Peel (see page 284)
¼ cup grated pistachio nuts

In a saucepan, combine the semolina, sugar, salt, milk, and vanilla bean. Bring to a boil, stirring constantly; then reduce heat to a simmer. Cook 5 to 10 minutes or until the mixture thickens, stirring often. Soften the gelatin in the cold water and blend into hot semolina mixture. Remove vanilla bean from mixture. Turn the mixture into a bowl and place in a pan of ice water. Let cool, stirring often. When cool to the touch, fold in the whipped cream and turn into a lightly oiled 8-inch ring mold. Chill until set, about 2 hours.

When the pears have been poached, boil the syrup until it reaches 230°F. and spins a short thread. Add the jelly and mix well. Stir and cook slowly until the sauce coats a spoon. Unmold the semolina mixture onto a serving plate. Drain the pears, then dip 4 of them into the jelly and place in the center of the mold. Cut remaining 2 pears in half lengthwise; core them and arrange around the outside of the mold. Top mold with circles of Candied Orange Peel and sprinkle with the pistachios.

YIELDS 6 SERVINGS.

Baked Pears

6 pears, peeled, halved, and cored
¾ cup dry white wine, or more if
   needed
6 tablespoons sugar
1 teaspoon cinnamon
8 tablespoons butter
¼ pound shredded Cheddar cheese

Preheat oven to 375°F. Place the pears in a shallow baking dish and set aside. Simmer wine, sugar, cinnamon, and butter for 5 minutes. Pour syrup over the pears and bake for 25 minutes or until tender, basting often; add more wine if needed. When cooked, remove pears and cool. Sprinkle pears with cheese. Simmer baking syrup, if needed, to thicken slightly; pour over the pears. The pears can be baked the day before and reheated before serving.   YIELDS 6 SERVINGS.
▼▼▼

Almond-Baked Pears

6 pears, peeled
3 egg yolks
½ cup plus 2 tablespoons
   confectioners' sugar
¼ teaspoon almond extract
2 cups slivered almonds, toasted
   and chopped
1½ cups dry white wine
6 tablespoons amaretto liqueur
½ cup heavy cream

Preheat oven to 375°F. Scoop out the bottoms of the pears. In a bowl, combine the egg yolks and ½ cup sugar, and beat until light and fluffy. Stir in ⅛ teaspoon almond extract and all but 2 tablespoons almonds. Stuff pears and stand upright in an ovenproof baking dish. Pour in the wine and amaretto liqueur. Cover and bake the pears for about 30 minutes or until tender, basting often.

Transfer pears to a serving dish. Reduce cooking liquid to 6 tablespoons and spoon over the pears. Whip the cream and fold in the remaining 2 tablespoons sugar and ⅛ teaspoon almond extract. Spoon over the pears and sprinkle with the reserved almonds. Can be prepared the day before. Rewarm pears and add cream just before serving.
▼▼▼   YIELDS 6 SERVINGS.

Pere Ripiene alla Milanese
STUFFED PEARS MILAN-STYLE

6 pears, halved and cored
¾ cup confectioners' sugar
4 maraschino cherries, minced
½ cup toasted almonds, ground
¼ teaspoon almond extract
½ cup dry sherry

Preheat oven to 375°F. Arrange the pears in a single layer in a baking dish, cut side up. In a bowl, combine the sugar, cherries, almonds, and almond extract and mix well. Fill the pears with the mixture. Pour on the sherry. Bake for 15 minutes or until the pears are tender. Serve hot or cold. Can be prepared 2 days before serving.
▼▼▼   YIELDS 6 SERVINGS.

Pears Stuffed with Amaretti
See photograph on page 66.

6 pears
12 amaretti cookies
3 egg yolks
1½ tablespoons butter
6 tablespoons sugar
1½ cups white wine
Custard Sauce (optional; see page 273)

Preheat oven to 375°F. Core each pear from the bottom, making a hollow in the middle. In a processor, grind the cookies to a powder, then add the flesh from inside the pears, plus egg yolks, butter, and half the sugar; blend together. Stuff mixture into each pear. Bake for 40 to 50 minutes or until the pears are soft. Pour the wine and remaining 3 tablespoons sugar into the baking pan and scrape up the juices. Simmer until liquid is reduced to a thin syrup. Glaze the pears with the sauce. Serve warm or cold, with warm or cold Custard Sauce if desired. Can be prepared 2 days before serving. YIELDS 6 SERVINGS.

Note: Amaretti biscuits are available in specialty shops and some supermarkets.

Baked Pears with Brandy

This recipe is equally delicious with apples.

¼ cup brandy
2 tablespoons dried currants
4 tablespoons butter
¼ cup firmly packed light brown sugar
1 teaspoon minced lemon rind
4 pears, peeled and cored from the bottom

Pour the brandy over the currants and let macerate for 15 minutes.

Preheat oven to 375°F. Drain currants, reserving brandy. In a bowl, cream the butter and sugar until light and fluffy. Fold in the currants and lemon rind. Fill the pears with the butter mixture and arrange them in a baking dish just large enough to hold them. Pour on the brandy and bake until tender, about 25 minutes, basting often. Let cool to room temperature. Serve with juices. Can be prepared the day before serving, but let pears come to room temperature before serving.

YIELDS 4 SERVINGS.

Cardamom-Flavored Pears

6 pears, peeled, cored, and sliced
¼ cup sugar
½ cup orange liqueur
1 teaspoon ground cardamom
1 cup heavy cream, whipped and flavored with 2 tablespoons orange liqueur

Preheat oven to 375°F. Arrange the pears in a shallow baking dish. Sprinkle with the sugar, liqueur, and cardamom. Bake for 20 to 30 minutes or until tender. Cool and chill. Serve topped with cream. Can be prepared the day before serving. YIELDS 6 SERVINGS.

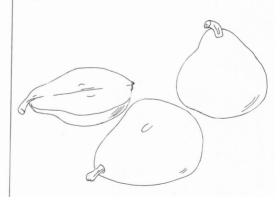

Honey-Baked Pears

6 pears, peeled, halved, and cored
3 tablespoons lemon juice
½ cup honey
¾ teaspoon cinnamon
2 tablespoons butter

Preheat oven to 350°F. Place pears in a baking dish and sprinkle with lemon juice, honey, and cinnamon; dot with butter. Bake until tender; test with a hot knife after 20 minutes. Serve hot or cold. Can be prepared 2 days before serving. YIELDS 6 SERVINGS.

Pears with Meringue and Chocolate Sauce

See photograph on page 66.

1 jar (12 ounces) apricot jam
1 cup sugar
½ cup water
6 pears, peeled and cored
½ cup mixed candied fruit
1 tablespoon rum
2 egg whites
6 ounces semisweet chocolate, grated

Preheat oven to 425°F. In a saucepan, simmer jam, ½ cup sugar, and water until syrupy. Poach the pears in the syrup until tender, about 20 minutes, basting often. Mix the candied fruit with the rum. Remove pears from the baking dish and fill centers with candied fruit. Arrange on a serving dish. Beat the egg whites until stiff, then carefully fold in 7 tablespoons sugar. With a pastry bag fitted with a no. 4 star tip, pipe a rosette on each pear. Sprinkle with remaining 1 tablespoon sugar, and brown in the oven. Stir the grated chocolate into the syrup and continue stirring over low heat until melted. Pour the sauce around the pears just before serving. Can be prepared about 6 hours before serving.   YIELDS 6 SERVINGS.

Baked Pears with Maple Nut Sauce

You can also use walnuts or Brazil nuts instead of pecans.

6 pears, peeled, halved, and cored
½ cup water
½ cup maple syrup
½ cup firmly packed dark brown sugar
2 tablespoons butter, melted
¼ cup chopped pecans

Preheat oven to 350°F. Place pear halves, cut side up, in a small deep casserole. Add the water, syrup, sugar, and butter. Cover and bake until the pears are tender, about 30 minutes. Sprinkle with nuts and serve. Can be made a day before and reheated before serving.   YIELDS 6 SERVINGS.

Poires Cuites à la Savoyarde

BAKED PEARS SAVOYARD

This simply prepared dessert is one of my favorites. It can bake while dinner is being eaten.

6 pears, peeled, cored, and quartered
¾ cup sugar
6 tablespoons butter
2 tablespoons water
½ cup cream

Preheat oven to 400°F. Place pears in a buttered baking dish. Sprinkle with sugar, dot with butter, and sprinkle with water. Bake for 40 minutes. When the sugar is caramelized, pour in the cream. Serve hot. Can be prepared for baking about 2 hours before needed.   YIELDS 6 SERVINGS.

Vermouth-Glazed Pears

6 pears, peeled, with stems attached
Juice and grated peel of 1 lemon
⅔ cup apricot preserves
⅓ cup vermouth
½ cup crushed amaretti crumbs
¼ cup chopped toasted almonds
3 tablespoons dark rum
1 pint vanilla ice cream, softened

Preheat oven to 350°F. Core the pears from the bottom. Arrange in a baking dish no more than 1 inch apart. Pour the lemon juice over the pears. In a saucepan, bring the apricot preserves, vermouth, and lemon peel to a boil. Pour over the pears. Sprinkle with the crumbs and nuts. Bake, basting often, until the pears are tender, about 30 minutes. In a bowl, beat the rum into the softened ice cream. Transfer the pears to a plate and serve with rum cream. Serve warm. Can be prepared for baking about 2 hours before serving.

YIELDS 6 SERVINGS.

Pineapple with Gingered Yogurt Sauce

2 cups yogurt
1 tablespoon sugar or to taste
1 teaspoon minced crystallized ginger
12 pineapple rings

In a bowl, combine the yogurt, sugar, and ginger. Arrange the pineapple on plates and coat with the sauce, or serve separately. Can be prepared the day before serving.　　YIELDS 6 SERVINGS.

Ananas Romanoff

PINEAPPLE WITH RUM CREAM

1 large pineapple, cut into wedges
½ cup confectioners' sugar
3 tablespoons rum
3 tablespoons Cointreau
1½ cups heavy cream
3 tablespoons kirsch
Grated rind of 1 orange

In a bowl, toss the pineapple wedges with ¼ cup sugar. Place in a serving bowl. Pour on the rum and Cointreau and refrigerate for up to 24 hours. One hour before serving, whip the cream with the remaining ¼ cup sugar and kirsch. Spoon onto the pineapple and toss until each piece is coated with the mixture. Rearrange in the bowl and sprinkle with the grated orange rind. Can be started up to 24 hours before serving.　　YIELDS 6 SERVINGS.

Pineapple in Pernod

2 pineapples, cut into wedges
Pernod to taste

In a bowl, combine the pineapple with Pernod to taste; use about 3 tablespoons for a subtle flavor. Do not be tempted to use too much Pernod. Can be prepared the day before serving.

YIELDS 6 SERVINGS.

Note: Generally pineapples are sweet enough, but if needed, sprinkle with sugar to taste.

Pineapple in Rum Custard

2 pineapples
2 cups Custard Sauce flavored with rum (see page 273)

Cut the pineapples in half through the fronds, then into quarters through the fronds. With a sharp knife, cut the flesh from each section, then cut off the core and return the flesh section to the pineapple shell. Cut into ½-inch slices and poke alternating sections toward the center of the pineapple. Arrange on a platter or on individual serving plates. Serve with sauce on the side.

YIELDS 8 SERVINGS.

Ananas à l'Orange

PINEAPPLE IN ORANGE SYRUP

> 1 large orange
> 2 cups sugar
> 2 cups water
> 1 large pineapple, peeled, cored, and
>   cut into ½-inch slices
> ¼ cup Grand Marnier

Julienne the orange peel. Slice the orange. In a 1½-quart casserole, combine the sugar and water, and simmer 1 minute. Add the orange peel, orange slices, and pineapple slices. Poach for 5 to 10 minutes, depending on the ripeness of the fruit. Remove the fruit with a slotted spoon, letting the juices drain back into the casserole. Cook the syrup until slightly thickened. Stir in the Grand Marnier and pour the sauce over the pineapple. Can be prepared a day ahead.
▄▀▄   YIELDS 6 SERVINGS.

Ananas au Rhum

PINEAPPLE WITH RUM

This dessert can be prepared in a chafing dish at the table.

> 6 tablespoons Clarified Butter (see
>   page 286)
> 1 pineapple, peeled, cored, and cut
>   into ½-inch slices
> Sugar to taste
> 2 tablespoons fresh butter
> ¼ cup rum

In a large skillet, heat the Clarified Butter. Sauté the pineapple slices until golden on both sides. Sprinkle with sugar to taste and add fresh butter. Cook, shaking the pan gently until the sugar starts to caramelize. Pour on the rum and ignite. Serve immediately.
                          YIELDS 6 SERVINGS.

Note: Virtually any fruit can be treated like this.
▄▀▄

Pineapple Flambé

> ¼ cup sugar
> ½ cup sherry
> ½ cup water
> 1 pineapple, peeled, cored, and thinly
>   sliced
> 1½ cups currant jelly
> ½ cup cognac
> Vanilla ice cream
> Macaroon crumbs

In a saucepan, combine the sugar, sherry, and water. Simmer the pineapple slices in the liquid for 5 minutes; drain. In a skillet, melt the jelly and add pineapple slices. Heat, spooning the jelly over the pineapple slices, for about 5 minutes. Add the cognac to the pan and ignite. Spoon over the fruit while flaming. Serve the fruit over ice cream and sprinkle with macaroon crumbs. Can be prepared ahead and reheated just before serving.   YIELDS 6 SERVINGS.
▄▀▄

Ananas Brûlés

BROILED PINEAPPLE

> 4 tablespoons butter
> 1¼ cups firmly packed dark
>   brown sugar
> ½ cup dark rum
> ½ teaspoon lemon juice
> ¼ teaspoon almond extract
> 2 pineapples, quartered lengthwise,
>   with fronds left on

In a saucepan, cook the butter, 1 cup of the sugar, rum, lemon juice, and almond extract, stirring, for 10 minutes. Leaving the pineapple in the shell, cut the flesh free from the skin, cut out the core, and slice into 1-inch-thick wedges.

Preheat the broiler. Wrap the fronds with foil. Spoon the sauce over each pineapple section and sprinkle with remaining ¼ cup sugar. Broil until sugar begins to bubble. Remove foil from fronds and serve.   YIELDS 8 SERVINGS.
■.■.■

Piñas Natillas
BAKED PINEAPPLE

Prepare the pineapple for baking several hours ahead. For a party, place the unwrapped, baked pineapple on a platter decorated with fresh leaves and exotic flowers.

    1 egg, plus 2 yolks
    1 teaspoon cornstarch
    1 teaspoon vanilla
    2 cups light cream, scalded
    1 large pineapple
    ¼ cup sugar
    2 to 3 tablespoons rum
    4 tablespoons butter

In a saucepan, combine the egg, egg yolks, cornstarch, and vanilla. Beat in the cream and cook over medium heat, stirring, until smooth and slightly thickened. Strain into a bowl, cover with plastic wrap, and chill for at least 1 hour.

Preheat oven to 350°F. Cut the pineapple to use as a container (see page 19), and cut the flesh into bite-sized pieces. In a bowl, toss the fruit with the sugar and rum and return to the pineapple shell. Dot with the butter, cover with the pineapple frond, and wrap in foil. Bake for 20 minutes. Serve immediately with the cold sauce on the side.
■.■.■   YIELDS 4 TO 6 SERVINGS.

Plums and Port

    2 pounds fresh plums, pitted
    2 cups tawny port
    ⅔ cup sugar
    2 tablespoons julienned orange peel
    1 cinnamon stick
    6 whole cloves
    1 cup heavy cream, whipped

In a saucepan, simmer the plums, port, sugar, orange peel, cinnamon stick, and cloves for about 10 minutes or until plums are tender. Discard the cloves and cinnamon. Chill overnight. Serve with whipped cream. Can be prepared up to 2 days before serving.
■.■.■   YIELDS 6 SERVINGS.

Prunes Suédoise
PLUMS SWEDISH-STYLE

    1½ pounds plums, pitted
    ½ cup sugar
    1½ cups water
    1 tablespoon gelatin
    Blanched almonds as needed
    Cream or Vanilla Custard Sauce (see
      page 273)

Poach the plums in the sugar and water for 15 minutes or until tender. Drain, reserving the syrup. Separate out a few of the best-looking plum halves; purée the remaining halves. Measure out 1 cup of poaching syrup and add 1½ cups of the fruit purée. Sprinkle the gelatin over ½ cup of remaining syrup and let soften. Dissolve over low heat. Stir into the plum purée. Put a blanched almond in the center of each reserved plum half and arrange plums, cut side down, in a 1-quart soufflé dish. Pour in the purée and chill until set. Serve with cream or Vanilla Custard Sauce.
■.■.■   YIELDS 4 TO 6 SERVINGS.

Croûtes aux Prunes

PLUM TOAST
See photograph on page 68.

A slice of bread, some fruit, butter, and sugar create a dessert fine enough to be served in the best restaurants, yet also perfect for the simple family meal. See Note.

    6 (½-inch-thick) slices bread
    ¾ cup butter
    12 to 18 plums, stoned
    6 tablespoons firmly packed
        brown sugar

Preheat oven to 350°F. Butter the bread slices on both sides and arrange in a baking dish. Place 4 to 5 plum halves on each slice and dot with the remaining butter. Sprinkle with the sugar and press down gently. Cover lightly with foil and bake for about 30 minutes. The bread slices should be golden and crispy and the plums coated with a sugary syrup. If necessary, bake 10 minutes longer without the foil. Serve warm.
                    YIELDS 6 SERVINGS.

Note: Can also be prepared with peaches, apricots, nectarines, or pears.
❖❖❖

Baked Quince

    6 quinces, peeled
    Lemon juice
    1 cup sugar, plus extra for sprinkling
        and serving
    ½ cup butter
    ¼ cup heavy cream, plus extra
        as accompaniment

Preheat oven to 375°F. Hollow out the cores of the quinces from the top about three-quarters of the way through. Sprinkle with lemon juice and stand in a buttered baking dish. In a bowl, com-

bine ⅔ cup sugar, butter, and 3 tablespoons cream. Pour into the hollowed quinces. Add the remaining ingredients halfway through the cooking. Bake 1 hour or until tender. To serve, sprinkle with sugar and pass heavy cream and additional sugar.   YIELDS 6 SERVINGS.
❖❖❖

Quince Compote

This dish can be served with cream or as part of a compote of other fruits.

    6 large quinces, peeled, quartered,
        and cored
    3 cups water
    2 cups sugar
    1 stick cinnamon
    2 whole cloves
    1 tablespoon lemon juice

Slice each quince quarter into thirds. In a saucepan, simmer the slices with the water, sugar, cinnamon stick, cloves, and lemon juice for about an hour or until the fruit is tender. Cool. Can be prepared up to 2 days before serving.
❖❖❖   YIELDS 6 SERVINGS.

Raspberries in Sherry Cream

Strawberries or blueberries may be substituted for the raspberries here.

    2 large eggs, separated
    2 tablespoons sugar
    1 cup heavy cream, scalded
    2 tablespoons dry sherry
    ½ teaspoon almond extract
    Pinch of salt
    1 quart raspberries, chilled

In a saucepan, beat the egg yolks and sugar until they form a ribbon. Pour in the hot cream, beating constantly, and heat until the mixture is smooth and thickened. Stir in the sherry, almond extract, and salt. Beat the egg whites until stiff but not dry, and fold into the sauce. Serve the warm sauce over the chilled berries. YIELDS 4 TO 6 SERVINGS.

Raspberries Hamilton

My good friend William Hamilton created this marvelous dessert on a camping trip in the backwoods of Maine after he found a wild raspberry patch.

   1½ quarts raspberries
   ¼ cup honey
   1 tablespoon lemon juice
   Heavy cream, sour cream, or whipped
     cream to taste

In a saucepan, combine 2 cups raspberries, honey, and lemon juice and bring to a boil, stirring constantly. Place the remaining raspberries in individual dessert glasses. Spoon the hot sauce over them and serve with heavy, sour, or whipped cream. YIELDS 6 SERVINGS.

Note: This is the ultimate raspberry dessert. It can be made with strawberries or blueberries, but if possible prepare it with fresh raspberries.

Country Cheese with Berries

A wonderful accompaniment for all sorts of berries, either alone or in combination.

Of course, you can use any fruit, but for me at least, the summer fruits have the greatest appeal.

   4 cups sour cream
   6 egg yolks
   8 ounces cream cheese
   1 cup sugar
   3 to 4 strips lemon peel
   1 pint strawberries, blueberries,
     or raspberries

In a saucepan, heat the cream until hot but not boiling. In a bowl, combine the egg yolks and 1 cup of the hot cream. Beat in the cream cheese and sugar. Stir in the remaining 3 cups hot cream and the lemon peel. Turn into the saucepan and cook, stirring, over low heat until thickened. Remove from the heat and let stand in hot water for 15 minutes. Discard the lemon peel. Line a strainer with fine cheesecloth and place over a deep bowl. Pour in the cheese mixture and drain for 2 hours. Cover the cheese with the ends of the cloth and drain in the refrigerator for 24 hours more. Unwrap the cheese and turn out onto a plate. Serve garnished with the berries. Can be prepared 2 days before serving. YIELDS 6 TO 8 SERVINGS.

Fragole al Limone

STRAWBERRIES WITH LEMON

   1½ quarts strawberries
   ½ to 1 cup confectioners' sugar
   Juice of 2 lemons

Crush ½ cup strawberries and stir in sugar to taste. Stir in lemon juice and toss with whole berries. Chill at least 1 hour before serving. YIELDS 4 TO 6 SERVINGS.

Strawberries in Liqueur

This dessert can also be made with blueberries, peaches, nectarines, or cactus pears.

> 1 quart strawberries, sliced
> ½ cup confectioners' sugar
> 1 tablespoon Cointreau
> 1 tablespoon kirsch
> 2 tablespoons cognac
> 6 slices Sponge Cake, 3 inches in
>   diameter (see page 278)
> Whipped cream (optional)

Place the strawberries in a bowl and sprinkle with the sugar. Pour on the Cointreau, kirsch, and cognac and mix carefully. Macerate in refrigerator for 3 to 4 hours. Serve over slices of Sponge Cake. Garnish with whipped cream if desired.   YIELDS 6 SERVINGS.

Fraises au Rhum

STRAWBERRIES IN RUM CUSTARD

> 1 pint strawberries
> 1 pint vanilla ice cream
> 2 cups Custard Sauce (see page 273)
>   flavored with dark rum

Prepare the sauce using ¼ cup packed light brown sugar and 2 tablespoons dark rum. Arrange the strawberries in a bowl and cover with scoops of softened vanilla ice cream. Pour the sauce over all.   YIELDS 6 SERVINGS.

Fraises Cordon Bleu I

STRAWBERRIES CORDON BLEU I

> 6 sugar cubes
> 1 large orange
> ¼ cup cognac
> 1 pint strawberries

Rub sugar cubes over the orange rind until they are soaked with oil. In a bowl, crush the sugar cubes and add the juice from the orange and the cognac. Stir until the sugar is dissolved. Pour over the berries. Chill 2 to 3 hours before serving.   YIELDS 4 TO 6 SERVINGS.

Fraises Cordon Bleu II

STRAWBERRIES CORDON BLEU II

Be sure to use almond macaroons, not coconut.

> 1 pint strawberries
> ½ cup macaroon crumbs
> Grated rind and juice of 1 orange
> 1 tablespoon sugar
> ¾ cup heavy cream

In a serving bowl, layer the berries and macaroon crumbs. Moisten with half of the orange juice. In another bowl, combine the remaining juice, orange rind, and sugar. Stir until the sugar is dissolved. Whip the cream until stiff and fold in the orange syrup. Pile onto the berries. Chill 1 hour before serving.   YIELDS 4 TO 6 SERVINGS.

Fraises à la Cardinale

STRAWBERRIES WITH
RASPBERRY SAUCE

> 1 pint strawberries
> 1 cup raspberries, sieved
> 4 tablespoons sugar

2 teaspoons lemon juice
Chopped blanched almonds

Arrange the strawberries in a bowl. Combine the raspberry purée, sugar, and lemon juice, and stir until the sugar is dissolved. Pour over the raspberries. Sprinkle with the almonds.

YIELDS 4 TO 6 SERVINGS.

Strawberries and Pistachios

2 pints strawberries
Sugar to taste
⅓ cup Cointreau
¼ cup chopped pistachios

In a serving bowl, combine the berries, sugar, and Cointreau. Toss together gently. Sprinkle with the pistachios just before serving. Can be prepared a day before serving. YIELDS 6 TO 8 SERVINGS.

Strawberries in Raspberry Cream

1 pint strawberries
Granulated sugar to taste
Juice of ½ orange
1 tablespoon kirsch
1 cup raspberries
¼ cup confectioners' sugar
1½ cups heavy cream

In a bowl, combine the strawberries, granulated sugar to taste, orange juice, and kirsch. Cover and chill. Force the raspberries through a sieve, discarding the seeds. Beat in the confectioners' sugar. Whip the cream until it holds soft peaks, then fold in the raspberry purée. Spoon over the strawberries. The strawberries and raspberry purée can be prepared the day before serving; however, do not make the raspberry cream until just before serving.

YIELDS 4 TO 6 SERVINGS.

Fragole al Aceto

STRAWBERRIES WITH VINEGAR

The touch of vinegar gives this dessert a sweet-sour complexity that proves impossible for guests to identify.

1 pint strawberries
1 cup red or white wine
2 tablespoons white vinegar
Confectioners' sugar

Macerate the berries in the wine for 5 minutes, then pour off the wine. (The wine is only for washing the berries.) Fill a bowl with the berries and add the vinegar and sugar to taste. Toss together gently. Can be prepared the day before serving.   YIELDS 4 TO 6 SERVINGS.

Pickled Strawberries

2 pints strawberries, sliced
2 tablespoons sugar
Pinch of cinnamon
2 teaspoons Balsam vinegar
1 bottle dry sparkling wine

In a bowl, combine the strawberries, sugar, and cinnamon and toss gently. Let macerate at room temperature for 30 minutes, stirring 2 or 3 times. Sprinkle with the vinegar and mix. Refrigerate until ready to serve. Distribute among goblets, pouring the wine over the berries. Except for adding wine, can be prepared up to 8 hours before serving.

YIELDS 6 SERVINGS.

Strawberries Jubilee

½ cup water
⅓ cup sugar
2 teaspoons cornstarch
1 pint strawberries
4 tablespoons kirsch
1 quart vanilla ice cream

In a small saucepan, combine the water, sugar, and cornstarch. Heat, stirring, until mixture reaches a boil. Add the strawberries and bring again to a boil, stirring only to mix. To serve, reheat the strawberry mixture, add the kirsch, and ignite. Serve over scoops of ice cream.

 YIELDS 6 SERVINGS.

Tangerines in Kirsch

6 tangerines
Confectioners' sugar to taste
2 tablespoons kirsch

Peel the tangerines, separate into segments, and put into serving dishes. Sprinkle with sugar and the kirsch. Let macerate for at least 2 hours before serving. Can be prepared up to 2 days before serving.　　YIELDS 6 SERVINGS.

Sherried Watermelon

Other melons also work well for this dessert, and other wines such as port or Madeira can be substituted for the sherry.

4 cups cubed watermelon, seeded
¼ cup sugar
1 cup dry sherry
Mint leaves

Sprinkle the watermelon with the sugar and sherry. Let macerate for 2 hours. Serve garnished with mint leaves. Can be prepared 24 hours before serving.
YIELDS 6 SERVINGS.

Wined Watermelon

Fourth of July and Labor Day parties are perfect times to serve this. Let guests carve up slices to suit their appetites.

1 whole watermelon
1 bottle red wine

Cut a plug from one end of the watermelon. Stand it on end and slowly pour in the bottle of wine. Return the plug and let chill for 24 hours. To serve, cut as usual for watermelon slices.
YIELDS 10 TO 30 SERVINGS.

Note: You can use a wok ring to help stabilize the melon while you pour in the wine.

Oranges for Every Occasion Clockwise from the candle: Orange Slices with Rosemary Syrup *(recipe on page 42)*, Oranges in Caramel *(page 41)*, and Orange Tart I *(page 224)*.

Perfect Pear Desserts Clockwise from the flowers at top: Almond Pear Pie *(recipe on page 228)*, Pears Stuffed with Amaretti *(page 54)*, Poires à la Cardinale *(page 49)*, and Pears with Meringue and Chocolate Sauce *(page 56)*.

Simple Elegance Clockwise from the flowers at top: Lemon Mousse II *(recipe on page 138)*, Viennese Food for the Gods *(page 98)*, and, on the cookie tray, Madeleines *(page 265)*, Palmiers *(page 265)*, and Nut Butter Cookies *(page 262)*.

Winter Desserts Above: Plum Toast *(recipe on page 60)*, Braised Pears Bresse-Style *(page 83)*.

Afternoon Tea At right, clockwise from the center: Zuccotto alla Michelangelo *(recipe on page 239)*, Mandarin Slices *(page 250)*, Strawberry Cheesecake *(page 258)*, and Purple Plum Torte *(page 254)*.

Apples Abound Clockwise from the flowers and candle: Apple Charlotte (*recipe on page 129*), Apples in Phyllo Dough (*page 219*), and Tarte Tatin (*page 218*).

Something Formal Clockwise: Chocolate-Coated Fruits *(recipe on page 267)*, Pamelas *(page 266)*, Chocolate-Coated Orange Peel *(page 267)*, and Meringue Mushrooms *(page 268)*.

A Harvest of Fruits A Fruit Cornucopia *(instructions on page 20)* and a Melon Container *(instructions on page 16)*.

MACÉDOINES, MÉLANGES, CUPS & COMPOTES

MIXTURES of fruits, whether called macédoines, fruit cups, compotes, or mélanges, are a step beyond fruits served by themselves.

The combinations can be as simple as strawberries and blueberries topped with a dollop of sour cream, or a cantaloupe half-filled with raspberries sprinkled with kirsch. A more elaborate combination may be a large watermelon hollowed and filled with a glorious mélange of fresh seasonal fruits, perhaps enhanced by a judicious measure of wine or a liqueur, or accompanied by a Sabayon sauce lightened with whipped cream. As with single fruit desserts, combination dishes can be topped with many sauces — from fresh fruit purées to whipped cream, from pastry cream to caramel, and more.

There does not seem to be any clear definition of the differences between macédoines, mélanges, cups, and compotes of fruit. However, when I think of macédoines, mélanges, and cups, I think of cool, refreshing fresh fruit dishes composed of two or more fruits. When I think of compotes, I think of cooked fruits, with the fruits poached gently in sugar syrup flavored with lemon, vanilla, or cinnamon.

Many years ago a well-known chef and food writer wrote that fruit cups, macédoines, and the like had to include citrus fruit. Although citrus fruits are delicious, attractive to look at, and refreshing to the palate, such didacticism is invalid. However, citrus fruits do mix beautifully with other fruits and they have the added advantage of keeping certain fruits, such as bananas, apples, pears, and peaches, from turning brown. One of the joys of fruit compotes is that they do allow for substitutions. When preparing them, you should consider what is best in flavor as well as what is freshest and in season. These may not always be the fruits specified in the recipe. If the peaches are green and hard, leave them out and perhaps use nectarines or pears instead. And when raspberries are not available, other berries can be used.

Generally, the fruit mixtures can be kept in the refrigerator for 6 to 12 hours; after that some of the more delicate fruits become mushy and possibly lose their color. If you are using fruits that tend to turn brown when exposed to the air, plan to prepare and add them to the mixture shortly before serving. Bananas have a strong aroma that can overpower more subtle fruits. Wait until just before serving before adding to the macédoine.

Should you have any questions when preparing the assorted fruits for the recipes in this section, be sure to refer back to the specific preparation suggestions given for each fruit in the opening chapter on preparation and presentation.

Fruits with Zabaglione

**6 vanilla-poached pears, apples, or
   peaches (see page 286)
1 recipe Zabaglione (see page 272)**

The fruit can be warm or cold. Arrange in individual serving dishes or on a platter. Coat with the sauce. The sauce may also be warm or cold, depending on the season of the year. If serving cold, both fruit and sauce can be prepared a day before.   YIELDS 6 SERVINGS.

Macedonia di Frutta

MACÉDOINE OF FRUIT I

Never feel confined to the fruits listed. Use what is fresh, bountiful, and in season. Except for the peaches, the fruits can macerate in the kirsch for 24 hours before serving; the peaches should be prepared on the day they are to be served.

1 pound cherries, pitted
2 quarts strawberries, halved
1 pound seedless grapes, halved
2 bananas, peeled and sliced
½ cup kirsch, or to taste
2 tablespoons confectioners' sugar, or to taste
4 peaches, peeled, stoned, and sliced
6 tablespoons lemon juice

In a bowl, combine the cherries, strawberries, grapes, and bananas. Stir in the kirsch and sugar, and toss gently. Refrigerate until ready to serve, stirring occasionally. In a bowl, combine the peach slices and lemon juice. Chill. Shortly before serving, drain the peaches and stir into the other fruits. Add more sugar or kirsch if desired.   YIELDS 6 SERVINGS.

Variation: Add 1½ cups orange juice and grated rind of 1 lemon.

Macédoine de Fruits I

MACÉDOINE OF FRUIT II

1½ cups seedless grapes
1½ cups seedless orange sections
3 cups peaches or plums, sliced
1½ cups fresh berries
5 tablespoons confectioners' sugar
3 tablespoons cognac
3 tablespoons kirsch
3 tablespoons Grand Marnier

In a bowl, combine the grapes, orange sections, peaches, and berries. Mix gently and sprinkle with sugar. Mix again and chill for at least 2 hours before serving. Just before serving, add the cognac, kirsch, and Grand Marnier. Stir gently to blend. This much of the macédoine can be prepared up to 24 hours before serving. However, the peaches should be added only a couple of hours before and tossed well with the orange mixture. (To prevent them from darkening, toss the peaches in lemon juice before adding to the other fruits.)
YIELDS 6 SERVINGS.

Macédoine de Fruits II

MACÉDOINE OF FRUIT III

1 pineapple, peeled and diced
½ pound peaches, peeled and diced
1 pint strawberries, halved
1 teaspoon minced gingerroot
1 teaspoon grated lemon rind
¼ cup port
Sugar to taste (optional)

In a bowl, combine the pineapple, peaches, strawberries, gingerroot, and lemon rind. Toss together gently and add the port. Mix again. If desired, add sugar to taste. Can be made up to 24 hours before serving. Before adding the peaches to the other fruits, toss them with lemon juice to prevent their darkening.   YIELDS 6 SERVINGS.

Macédoine de Fruits III
MACÉDOINE OF FRUIT IV

2 grapefruits, cut into sections
3 oranges, cut into sections
1 small melon, cut into balls
2 pears, peeled and sliced
½ pound plums, halved
2 bananas, sliced
¼ pound cherries, pitted
3 peaches, sliced
¼ pound seeded grapes
Juice of 1 lemon
Kirsch or Cointreau to taste
Candied Orange, Lemon, and Lime
    Rinds in Syrup (see page 285)

In a glass serving bowl, place the fruits in layers and sprinkle with the lemon juice and kirsch or Cointreau. Chill until serving time. Just before serving, pour some of the rind syrup over the fruits and garnish with the candied rinds. The fruits for this can be prepared up to 6 hours before serving. However, do not add the syrup until ready to serve, or it will thin out with the juices from the fruits.

YIELDS 6 TO 8 SERVINGS.

Mélange de Fruits
MIXTURE OF FRUITS

2 cups strawberries, halved, or pears
    or apples, sliced
1 orange, cut into sections
2 tablespoons orange juice
3 tablespoons confectioners' sugar
2 tablespoons Grand Marnier
1 tablespoon kirsch
1 tablespoon cognac
1 tablespoon framboise

In a bowl, combine the strawberries, pears, or apples, and the orange sections. Add the orange juice and sugar and toss gently. Refrigerate for 1 hour. When ready to serve, add the Grand Marnier, kirsch, cognac, and framboise. Can be prepared up to 3 hours before serving.   YIELDS 4 SERVINGS.

Miveh Makhlout
PERSIAN FRUIT MÉLANGE

Although rose water lends more aroma than taste, it gives this recipe an exotic quality. It is available in pharmacies and gourmet shops.

1 honeydew melon, cut into balls
1 cantaloupe, cut into balls
1 pint strawberries
2 tablespoons slivered almonds
¼ cup chopped pistachios
1 cup seedless grapes
2 tablespoons rose water
1½ cups orange juice
½ cup kirsch

In a bowl, combine the melon balls, strawberries, almonds, pistachios, grapes, rose water, orange juice, and kirsch. Mix together gently. Let macerate for up to 6 hours before serving.   YIELDS 6 TO 8 SERVINGS.

Fruits au Vin Rouge
FRUITS IN RED WINE

1¼ cups red wine, preferably a
    Bordeaux
½ cup water
3 tablespoons sugar
1 vanilla bean, split lengthwise
6 cups assorted fresh fruits in season
    (pears, peaches, grapes, oranges,
    cherries, strawberries, raspberries,
    etc.)
8 small mint leaves

In a saucepan, simmer the wine until it is reduced by half. Add the water, sugar, and vanilla bean. Simmer 2 minutes. Cool and chill. Over a bowl, peel and core or pit the fruits according to type and cut into slices. Add fruit to bowl. Add the wine and chill at least 1 hour. Discard the vanilla bean and garnish with the mint leaves. Can be prepared the day before serving.

❖❖❖   YIELDS 6 SERVINGS.

Fruit Loaf with Raspberry Sauce

Easy to prepare ahead, this is a great dessert for a large crowd. Use whatever fruits are in season.

    5 teaspoons gelatin
    1½ cups milk
    1 vanilla bean, split lengthwise
    1 cup plus 2 tablespoons sugar
    4 egg yolks
    1 cup heavy cream
    2 cups peeled and cubed peaches
    ½ pint raspberries
    ¾ cup strawberries, halved if large
    ¾ cup blackberries
    2 cups Raspberry Sauce (see page 276)

Line a 9- by 5- by 3-inch loaf pan with plastic wrap, and oil lightly. In a small saucepan, sprinkle gelatin over ½ cup milk and let soften. In a heavy saucepan, combine remaining 1 cup milk, vanilla bean, and 1 cup sugar. Heat, stirring, until the sugar is dissolved. In a bowl, beat the egg yolks with the remaining 2 tablespoons sugar until they are thick and lemon-colored. Whisk in ¼ cup of the hot milk and mix well. Return yolks to the saucepan of hot milk and cook, stirring, until thickened enough to coat the back of a spoon, about 180°F. *Do not boil.* Immediately remove from the heat

and strain into a clean bowl. Stir in the softened gelatin and let cool until thick enough to mound but not set. Beat the heavy cream until it is just beyond the soft-peak stage. The cream and custard should be of the same temperature and consistency when combined.

Fold the cream and custard together and then gently fold in the fruits. Pour into the loaf pan and bang once or twice on the counter to settle. Chill until set, at least 4 hours.

Turn out onto a chilled platter, peel off the plastic wrap, and cut into ¾-inch slices. Serve each slice on a bed of Raspberry Sauce. Can be prepared 24 hours before serving.

❖❖❖   YIELDS 10 TO 12 SERVINGS.

Fruits Rafraîchis au Kirsch

FRESH FRUITS WITH KIRSCH

    ½ cup sugar
    1 cup water
    2 teaspoons lemon juice
    Dash of salt
    2 apricots, peeled and quartered
    ½ cup pitted cherries
    ½ cup strawberries
    2 nectarines, peeled and quartered
    ½ cup pineapple wedges
    2 to 3 tablespoons Cointreau, kirsch,
      or framboise

In a saucepan, combine the sugar, water, lemon juice, and salt. Bring to a boil and simmer 5 minutes. Let cool. In a bowl, combine the apricots, cherries, strawberries, nectarines, and pineapple. Just before serving, pour on the sugar syrup and sprinkle with the liqueur of your choice. The fruits can be prepared up to 6 hours before serving.

❖❖❖   YIELDS 4 TO 6 SERVINGS.

Fruits Frais à la Gelée d'Amande

FRESH FRUITS WITH ALMOND JELLY

This dessert is Chinese in origin and is one of the most popular Chinese desserts for westerners. This recipe is a French version. To create the Chinese version, try to obtain some of the more exotic fruits such as arbutus, lychee, and loquats.

> 1½ teaspoons gelatin
> 1 tablespoon cold water
> ½ cup milk
> ½ teaspoon almond extract
> Assortment of 8 to 9 fruits (berries, cherries, grapes, oranges, pears, apples, etc.)

In a bowl, soak the gelatin in cold water until soft. Bring the milk to a boil and stir into the gelatin mixture. When no granules of gelatin show on the back of a spoon, stir in the almond extract and pour into a 7-inch cake pan. Chill until set. Prepare fruits according to types and arrange attractively on a serving platter or on individual plates. Use 2 to 3 pieces of each fruit for each serving. Cut the almond mixture into diagonals, squares, rectangles, or other fancy shapes. Place the almond jelly shapes on the serving platter or plates. The almond jelly can be made the day before, but the fruits should be prepared within 2 to 3 hours of serving.

❖❖❖   YIELDS 6 TO 8 SERVINGS.

Rote Grütze I

MOLDED FRUIT PUDDING I

> 20 ounces frozen strawberries, thawed
> 20 ounces frozen raspberries, thawed
> ¼ teaspoon salt

> ⅓ cup cornstarch
> ½ cup water
> 1 cup Custard Sauce (see page 273)

In a 2-quart saucepan, bring the strawberries and raspberries to a boil, stirring occasionally. Strain through a fine sieve, discarding the seeds. Return the pulp and juice to the saucepan and add the salt. In a bowl, combine the cornstarch and water and then stir into the berries. Stirring constantly, bring to a boil over medium heat. Boil 1 minute. Pour into a 1-quart mold. Chill for 4 hours or until set. Serve with Custard Sauce. Can be prepared the day before serving.

❖❖❖   YIELDS 6 SERVINGS.

Rote Grütze II

MOLDED FRUIT PUDDING II

Black currant juice is available in German and Scandinavian delicatessens and gourmet shops.

> 3 cups black currant juice
> 2 cups fresh raspberries
> 2 cups blackberries
> 2 cups canned cherries, undrained
> 1 (2-inch) piece vanilla bean, split
> Grated rind and juice of 1 lemon
> ½ to 1 cup sugar to taste
> ½ cup cornstarch
> ½ cup water
> Heavy cream

In a saucepan, combine the black currant juice, raspberries, blackberries, and undrained cherries. Add the vanilla bean, lemon rind and juice, and sugar to taste. Bring to a boil, stirring until the sugar is dissolved. In a bowl, combine the cornstarch and water and add to the saucepan of fruit, stirring constantly. Remove the vanilla bean. Pour into a bowl and chill completely, about 4 hours. Serve with the cream, whipped or not as desired. Can be prepared the day before serving.

■▪■   YIELDS 12 SERVINGS.

Broiled Fruit with Pastry Cream Brûlé

Interestingly, this dessert has great appeal for men; women like it but men rave.

4 cups assorted fruits (blueberries, strawberries, pears, cherries, grapes, oranges, etc.)
2 tablespoons superfine sugar
2 tablespoons framboise, kirsch, or Grand Marnier
1 cup Pastry Cream (see page 282)
¼ cup firmly packed dark brown sugar

Preheat the broiler. Prepare the fruits according to their type and combine in a bowl with the sugar and liqueur. Toss to blend. Spoon into individual ramekins or a 1-quart shallow baking dish. Coat with the Pastry Cream and smooth over. Put the brown sugar into a sieve and sprinkle evenly over the fruit. Brown under the broiler until the sugar is melted. Can be prepared for broiling up to 2 hours before serving.

■▪■   YIELDS 4 TO 6 SERVINGS.

Gratin de Fruits

BROILED FRUITS WITH
SABAYON SAUCE

3 peaches or pears, peeled and sliced
2 tablespoons lemon juice
2 oranges, sectioned
1 pint strawberries
5 egg yolks
½ cup plus 2 tablespoons dry fruit white wine
¾ cup sugar

Preheat the broiler. Put the peaches or pears in a bowl; toss with lemon juice and drain. Put into a bowl with the oranges and strawberries and refrigerate. In a saucepan, combine the egg yolks and wine until blended. Place over low heat and beat in the sugar, 2 tablespoons at a time. Beat constantly until tripled in volume, about 10 minutes. Remove from the heat and beat until cooled slightly. Arrange the fruit in a 1-quart shallow baking dish, coat with the sauce, and broil until golden. Serve immediately. The fruits can be prepared several hours ahead. The sauce can be prepared several hours ahead and beaten until cooled. Assemble and brown just before serving.

■▪■   YIELDS 4 TO 6 SERVINGS.

Warm Fruit Compote

This once-fashionable dessert can be made with any variety of dried fruits. The results are far better than you'll get by trying to use woody strawberries, underripe pears, or other out-of-season fruits.

2 apples, peeled and sliced
6 ounces pitted prunes
6 dried figs, quartered
3 ounces dried apricots
⅓ cup water
⅓ cup apple juice
Juice of 1 lemon
2 to 3 cinnamon sticks
½ teaspoon ground cloves
2 pears, peeled and sliced
2 oranges, peeled and sectioned
1 cup seedless grapes
Yogurt

In a saucepan, simmer the apples, prunes, figs, apricots, water, apple juice, lemon juice, cinnamon sticks, and cloves for 4 minutes. Add the pears and cook until the fruit is tender. Just before serving, add the orange sections and grapes. Remove the cinnamon sticks. Serve with yogurt on the side. Can be prepared up to adding the oranges and grapes the day before, then reheated and finished just before serving.

■▪■   YIELDS 6 TO 8 SERVINGS.

Apricot Compote

Who doesn't love apricots? This is a lovely way to present them.

> ½ **pound dried apricots**
> ½ **cup sugar**
> 2 **cups water**
> ¼ **cup currants**
> ¼ **cup golden raisins**
> 2 **cups sauterne**
> 3 **whole cloves**
> ⅓ **cup crystallized ginger, chopped**
> 2 **tablespoons pine nuts**

In a saucepan, simmer the apricots, sugar, and water for about 30 minutes, or until the apricots are soft. Drain off the cooking liquid and set the fruit aside. Boil the liquid until reduced to 1 cup. In a bowl, combine the apricots, syrup, currants, raisins, sauterne, and cloves for 12 to 34 hours. Remove cloves and add the ginger and pine nuts before serving. Can be prepared 2 days before serving.   YIELDS 6 SERVINGS.

Note: This dessert can be served alone, but it is enhanced with a custard sauce, heavy cream, whipped cream, yogurt, vanilla ice cream, or sour cream.

■▪■

Bananas and Grapes in Caramel Syrup

> 6 **tablespoons water**
> ¾ **cup sugar**
> ¼ **teaspoon ginger**
> **Grated rind and juice of 1 lime**
> 3 **tablespoons rum**
> 4 **bananas, peeled and sliced**
> 1½ **cups seedless grapes**

In a small saucepan, combine 2 tablespoons water with sugar and heat over low heat until the sugar is dissolved. Cook over high heat until the mixture starts to turn golden. Add the remaining 4 tablespoons water and stir until the mixture is smooth. Remove from the heat and stir in the ginger, lime juice, and rum. Chill. Place the bananas and grapes in a serving dish. Just before serving, pour the chilled syrup over the fruit and sprinkle with the grated lime rind. The syrup can be made 2 or 3 days before serving, but the fruits should be cut up just before serving.

■▪■   YIELDS 6 SERVINGS.

Spiced Cherries with Pineapple

These cherries are particularly good with ice cream and make a delicious accompaniment to ham.

> 2 **pounds dark sour cherries**
> 2 **pounds sweet bing cherries**
> 3 **slices pineapple, cut into chunks**
> 2 **cinnamon sticks**
> 2 **tablespoons ground cloves**
> 1 **cup sugar**
> ½ **cup cognac**

Remove stems from cherries and pit. Combine cherries with pineapple. Sterilize two 1-quart preserving jars and fill each with fruit to within 1 inch of the top. Insert 1 cinnamon stick and 1 tablespoon cloves into each jar. Add ½ cup sugar to each jar. Pour ¼ cup cognac over the top of each and seal the lids tightly. Let stand for about an hour, then turn the jars over. Keep turning the jars over every hour or so until the sugar is dissolved. Store in a cool place for 90 days before serving. The fruit will keep for at least a year.

YIELDS 6 TO 8 SERVINGS.

Figs, Dates, and Walnuts in Sherried Whipped Cream

1 ½ cups figs, stemmed and halved lengthwise
4 ounces pitted dates
4 tablespoons cream sherry
1 cup chopped walnuts
2 cups heavy cream
½ cup confectioners' sugar

In a bowl, macerate the figs, dates, and 2 tablespoons sherry for about 30 minutes at room temperature. Add the walnuts to the figs and mix well. Whip the cream with the sugar until stiff and fold in the remaining 2 tablespoons sherry. Spoon the fig mixture into individual bowls or 1 large serving dish and top with the whipped cream. Can be prepared 24 hours before serving.

YIELDS 6 SERVINGS.

Melon de Scheherazade

FRUIT-STUFFED MELON

This dessert is not only beautiful, it is also wonderful to eat. If you cannot get all of the fruits listed, use more of others or substitute. For a large party, prepare a large closed melon and surround it with hollowed-out melon or pineapple halves to be used as serving dishes.

1 large Persian melon
Salt
2 pineapple slices, cored and diced
2 peaches, sliced
1 banana, sliced
18 raspberries
18 strawberries
3 ½ tablespoons sugar
2 cups champagne
½ cup crème de menthe
¼ cup maraschino liqueur
¼ cup kirsch
1 tablespoon butter, softened

Cut off the top third of the melon. With a melon baller, scoop balls out of the top and bottom sections. With a knife, cut the interior of the melon as smoothly as possible without breaking through the shell. The idea is to remove the remaining fruit, leaving just the shell. Lightly salt the inside of the bottom melon section, then turn it upside down and let drain for at least 20 minutes. Do the same with the top.

In a bowl, macerate the pineapple, peaches, banana, raspberries, strawberries, melon balls, and sugar. Let stand for about 1 hour.

Add the champagne, crème de menthe, maraschino, and kirsch. Fill the melon with the fruit, then pour the juices into the shell. Butter the rim of the top section of the melon and press firmly into place. Let stand in the refrigerator for 2 hours before serving. Can be kept on ice for up to 6 hours.

YIELDS 6 TO 8 SERVINGS.

Note: If you do not wish to seal the melon with butter, you can wrap the entire melon securely in plastic wrap.

Melon, Orange, and Blueberry Mélange

3 quarts honeydew melon balls
¾ cup orange juice
¼ cup Cointreau
2 tablespoons sugar
2 teaspoons grated orange peel
1 pint blueberries
Mint sprigs

In a serving bowl, combine the melon balls, orange juice, Cointreau, sugar, and orange peel. Mix gently and refrigerate, covered, for up to 6 hours. When ready to serve, pour the blueberries over the melon balls and garnish with the mint. Serve at room temperature.

          YIELDS 8 SERVINGS.

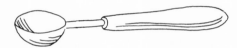

Minted Cantaloupe and Blueberries

Other melons can be substituted for the cantaloupe. The delicate green of honeydew is particularly attractive with the blueberries.

½ cup sugar
1 cup water
1 tablespoon minced mint
1 cup blueberries
2 cups cantaloupe balls
Mint sprigs

In a small saucepan, boil the sugar, water, and minced mint for 3 minutes. Strain the liquid and chill. Add the blueberries and melon balls to the syrup just before serving. Garnish with the mint sprigs. The syrup can be prepared several days before using.

          YIELDS 4 TO 6 SERVINGS.

Orange-Apricot Chantilly

1 pound dried apricots
1 orange, finely shredded (both rind and pulp)
½ cup sugar
2 to 3 tablespoons Cointreau
⅔ cup heavy cream, whipped
2 to 3 tablespoons blanched slivered almonds

In a saucepan, combine the apricots and shredded orange pulp and rind with enough water to cover. Simmer gently, uncovered, for 15 minutes. Stir in the sugar and cook until most of the liquid is absorbed and the apricots are tender. Add more water if needed. Stir in the Cointreau. Fold in the whipped cream and almonds. Place in individual soufflé dishes and chill. Can be prepared 1 day before serving or frozen.

          YIELDS 6 SERVINGS.

Chestnut and Orange Compote

This dessert is especially good when accompanied by a pitcher of heavy cream or sour cream passed separately.

2 cups water
¾ cup sugar
1 (1-inch) piece vanilla bean
1 pound chestnuts, peeled and skinned (see page 13)
3 large oranges, peeled and thinly sliced

In a 1-quart saucepan, boil the water, sugar, and vanilla for 5 minutes. Add the chestnuts and simmer 30 minutes, or until soft. Cool. Discard the vanilla bean. Add the orange slices and mix gently. The chestnuts can be prepared several days ahead. Add the oranges only shortly before serving.

          YIELDS 4 TO 6 SERVINGS.

Poires Braisée à la Bressane

BRAISED PEARS BRESSE–STYLE
See photograph on page 68.

6 pears, peeled, cored, and halved
¼ cup sugar
3 tablespoons butter, cut into bits
2 cups heavy cream
3 to 4 tablespoons cognac
2 to 3 tablespoons honey
½ teaspoon vanilla

Preheat oven to 400°F. Arrange the pears, cut side down, in one layer in a 9-by 13-inch baking dish. Sprinkle with sugar and dot with the butter. Bake 35 to 40 minutes or until tender. Reduce the heat to 350° and pour 1 cup of heavy cream over the pears. Bake until the sauce is thick and caramel-colored, about 10 minutes, basting several times. Whip the remaining 1 cup cream and flavor with the cognac, honey, and vanilla. Serve the pears at room temperature with the whipped cream. The pears can be baked the day before and reheated. YIELDS 6 SERVINGS.

Note: If preferred, the pears can be served without the whipped cream immediately after baking.

Pear and Apple Compote

Red Delicious apples make an eye-appealing contrast to the pears for this compote.

4 cups sauterne
1½ cups sugar
1 large piece lemon rind
1 cinnamon stick
1 (3-inch) piece vanilla bean
3 whole cloves
3 pears, peeled, cored, and quartered
2 Red Delicious apples, peeled and sliced
½ cup apricot preserves

In a saucepan, simmer the wine, sugar, lemon rind, cinnamon stick, vanilla bean, and cloves for about 20 minutes. Add the pears and apples and poach until just tender. With a slotted spoon, transfer the fruit to a serving bowl. Add the apricot jam to the syrup and simmer 3 minutes. Strain through a sieve over the fruit. Chill. Can be prepared 2 days before serving. YIELDS 4 TO 6 SERVINGS.

Pommes et Poires Flambées

APPLES AND PEARS FLAMBÉ

For a little drama when serving this fine dessert, add the rum to the warm syrup and ignite at the table before pouring the syrup over the fruits.

2 pounds apples, peeled, cored, and chopped
1½ cups sugar
½ cup chopped walnuts
6 pears, peeled and cored from the bottom
3 cups red wine
¼ teaspoon cinnamon
¼ cup rum

In a saucepan, cook the apples with ½ cup sugar, covered, until very soft. Force the apple mixture through a sieve. Stir in the walnuts and spread on a heat-proof serving platter. In a saucepan, simmer the pears, wine, remaining cup of sugar, and cinnamon until the pears are tender. Arrange the pears on the apple purée. Reduce the poaching liquid to a syrup. Stir in the rum and ignite. Pour over the pears. Serve hot or cold. Can be prepared a day before and allowed to come to room temperature before serving. YIELDS 6 SERVINGS.

Pears and Plums in Wine

2 oranges
¼ cup orange liqueur
8 pears, peeled
2 tablespoons lemon juice
3 cups dry red wine
1½ cups sugar
1 cinnamon stick
1 (2-inch) strip of lemon peel
3 whole cloves
16 plums
½ cup currant jelly

With a zester or sharp knife, remove peel from oranges and cut into julienne strips. Blanch the strips in boiling water for 10 minutes; then drain, place in a bowl, and pour on the orange liqueur. Drop the pears into water acidulated with 1 tablespoon of the lemon juice.

In a 2-quart saucepan, boil the wine, sugar, cinnamon, lemon peel, and cloves for 2 minutes, being sure the sugar is dissolved. Lower the heat, add 2 or 3 pears, cover, and poach until tender, about 20 minutes. Remove pears to a bowl and repeat with remaining pears. When all the pears have been cooked, add the plums to the poaching liquid and simmer, covered, over low heat for 10 minutes. Remove to the bowl with the pears.

Reduce poaching liquid until it becomes syrupy and lightly coats the back of a spoon. Add the jelly, remaining lemon juice, and 1 tablespoon orange peel–liqueur mixture. Strain over the fruit and chill thoroughly. Can be prepared 24 hours before serving.

❖❖❖   YIELDS 8 SERVINGS.

Poires Rosemond

PEARS ROSAMOND

I do not know who Rosamond was, but we do owe her a debt for this luscious dessert.

3 cups water
1½ cups sugar
4 pears, peeled and cored from
    the bottom
¼ cup pineapple, cut in ¼-inch cubes
⅓ cup plus 1 tablespoon rum
3 egg yolks
Grated peel of 1 lime
⅓ cup Chablis

In a saucepan, bring water and 1 cup sugar to a boil. Add the pears and poach until tender. Drain pears and cool. Macerate the pineapple and rum in a bowl. In a saucepan, beat the egg yolks until light and fluffy, then beat in the remaining ½ cup sugar and grated lime peel and blend well. Over low heat, add the wine and cook, whisking constantly, until light and fluffy. Stuff the insides of the pears with the macerated pineapple and arrange on a platter. Top pears with the sauce. Except for the sauce, the dessert can be prepared a day ahead. The sauce should be prepared within an hour of serving.   YIELDS 4 SERVINGS.
❖❖❖

Ananas Frais Crème Chantilly

FRESH PINEAPPLE CREAM

1 pineapple, peeled, cored, and cut
    into slices (reserve juice)
1 cup heavy cream
1 vanilla bean, split
1 teaspoon kirsch
Sugar to taste
Candied violets

Place the pineapple slices on a platter. Gather the juices from the cut pineapple and put into a bowl with the cream. Scrape the vanilla seeds into the bowl and add the kirsch. Beat until stiff, adding sugar to taste. Mound on top of the pineapple and decorate with the violets. The pineapple and cream can be prepared the day before serving, as long as they are kept in covered bowls. Do not assemble until ready to serve.

▼▼▼ YIELDS 6 SERVINGS.

Ananas Surprise

PINEAPPLE SURPRISE

Like many pineapple desserts, this is a striking presentation. A small effort on your part will bring raves from your guests.

- 1 grapefruit, cut into sections
- 2 oranges, cut into sections
- 2 apples, peeled and diced
- 1 pineapple, cut into a container (see page 19)
- 6 ounces candied cherries
- ½ cup maraschino liqueur or kirsch
- ½ cup sugar

In a bowl, combine the grapefruit, oranges, apples, the fruit from the pineapple cut into ¾-inch cubes, cherries, maraschino liqueur, and sugar. Mix gently and let stand for 10 minutes. Fill the pineapple shell with the fruit mixture, replace the top, and chill. Can be prepared the day before serving.

YIELDS 6 SERVINGS.

Variation: Use 2 apricots, pitted and diced; 4 cherries, pitted and halved; 1 peach, peeled and diced; and 4 strawberries.

▼▼▼

Apple, Pineapple, and Papaya Mélange

- 3 pineapples, halved
- 1 papaya, peeled and diced
- 1 apple, thinly sliced

With a sharp knife, hollow out the inside of each pineapple half, leaving a shell ½-inch thick. Cut the fruit from the shells into dice-sized pieces and mix gently with the papaya and apple in a bowl. Fill the pineapple shells with the fruit. Chill for up to 6 hours before serving.

YIELDS 6 SERVINGS.

▼▼▼

Ananas et Fraises Créoles

PINEAPPLE AND STRAWBERRIES CREOLE-STYLE

- 1 large pineapple
- 3 to 4 tablespoons kirsch
- 2 tablespoons sugar
- 2 cups strawberry purée (see Note)
- ½ cup heavy cream, beaten until stiff, sweetened to taste and flavored with kirsch

Cut the pineapple into quarters or sixths, lengthwise, through the frond. Remove the pulp and cut into thin slices. Reserve the shells. Put the slices into a bowl and sprinkle with the kirsch and sugar. Mix gently. Cover and chill until serving time. At serving time, arrange a pineapple shell on each plate and set the slices back into the shells. Coat with the strawberry purée. With a pastry bag fitted with a no. 5A tip, pipe rosettes of whipped cream down the center of each serving. Fruit mixture can be prepared the day before serving. Depending on size of the pineapple,

YIELDS 4 TO 6 SERVINGS.

Note: To make the strawberry purée, purée 1 pint strawberries in a food processor, sweeten to taste with sugar, and strain through a fine sieve, discarding the seeds.

▼▼▼

Chistera aux Fruits

PINEAPPLE BASKETS

2 to 3 pineapples, halved
3 bananas, quartered and halved
½ cup maraschino liqueur
½ cup apricot brandy
½ cup white rum
10 tablespoons sugar
1 quart vanilla ice cream
¼ cup rum, warmed

Remove the pulp from the pineapples, leaving ¼-inch-thick shells. Cut the pulp into wedges. In a skillet, warm the pineapple pulp, bananas, maraschino, apricot brandy, white rum, and sugar. When heated, spoon into the shells and top with the ice cream. Pour the warmed rum over all and ignite. The fruits can be set into the skillet for heating 5 or 6 hours before serving. However, serve as soon as ignited.

▚▚▚   YIELDS 4 TO 6 SERVINGS.

Compote de Pruneaux et Pommes

PRUNE AND APPLE COMPOTE

24 prunes
2 cups tawny port
2 cups red wine
10 tablespoons sugar
2 tablespoons vanilla
6 apples, peeled
1 tablespoon butter
½ cup heavy cream

Soak the prunes in the port for 24 hours. Then simmer the prunes and port in a saucepan with the wine, 9 tablespoons sugar, and vanilla until reduced by two-thirds, about 2 hours, over very low heat. Remove and chill the prunes. Save the liquid. Cut the top and bottom off each apple and hollow out the center. Sauté the apples in the butter until they are tender, then add 1 tablespoon sugar and cook until the sugar is caramelized. When ready to serve, arrange the apples in a serving dish, fill the hollows with the heavy cream, and surround with the prunes and prune liquid. The prunes and liquid can be prepared 24 hours before serving. The apples can be sautéed early in the day and reheated just before serving.

▚▚▚   YIELDS 6 SERVINGS.

Fraises à la Nino

28 strawberries
3 ounces tawny port
4 canned figs
3 ounces kirsch
2 cups sweetened whipped cream
4 scoops vanilla ice cream, softened
4 macaroons, crushed
2 teaspoons Grand Marnier

In a bowl, combine the strawberries and port, piercing the fruit with a fork so it will absorb the wine. Chill 1 hour. Add the figs to the strawberries; mix together and partially crush. Add kirsch and mix. Add the whipped cream and fold together. Fold in the ice cream just enough to blend with the other ingredients. Transfer to individual serving dishes and sprinkle with the macaroons and the Grand Marnier. Serve immediately. The strawberries can be set to macerate several hours before serving. However, the final assembly must be done just before serving.

▚▚▚   YIELDS 4 SERVINGS.

FOOLS, WHIPS, SNOWS & CREAMS

FOOLS, whips, snows, and creams are old-fashioned desserts that are unknown to many people and long-since forgotten by many others. They are similar in that each uses a purée of fruit lightened with whipped cream or egg whites, sometimes firmed with gelatin. They are very easy to prepare, taking only moments, and are delicious. The creative cook's imagination will allow him or her to create unending varieties and presentations. Do not hesitate to exchange one fruit for another, or to alter, or add to, the suggested liqueurs. The one drawback to some of these desserts, if it can be called that since the desserts are so easily assembled, is that most of them should be made close to serving time. Those that are made with gelatin or are to be frozen can be made a day or two ahead. The others, however, will lose their airy lightness if they aren't served within a few hours.

FOOLS

Fools are among the simplest of these desserts to make. To prepare them, simmer any fruit in a little water until tender. Then strain, sweeten to taste with sugar, and chill completely. This can be done several days before serving. For each cup of fruit, add 2 cups of whipped cream and fold together so that the fruit streaks through the cream, creating a marbled effect. Serve in parfait glasses, large wine glasses, glass bowls, or — for a party — a single large bowl. Some of the recipes suggest cooking the fruit with cornstarch to make a thicker mixture.

WHIPS

The difference between whips and fools is that, while with fools the fruit purée is folded into whipped cream, with whips it is folded into egg whites beaten until stiff. Again, whips are piled into parfait glasses or other such containers and served chilled. They should be served within a few hours of preparing, or the egg whites will lose their fluffiness. The exception is prune whip, which is baked after assembling and is then chilled before serving. You can, if desired, use the same method on other whips to make them more stable.

SNOWS

Snows are the same as whips except that they have dissolved gelatin folded into the mixture. The snow is then allowed to set and is usually left in a mold. Snows are often made with fruit juices, especially citrus juices.

CREAMS

Creams are made to be served as accompaniments to fruit desserts; the fruit is not folded into the cream mixture. The cream can have a base of whipped cream and cheese, or of egg whites. Sometimes it is stiffened with gelatin. Very often, especially if gelatin has been added, or if it is allowed to drain in a basket, the cream is molded in a standard mold. Metal molds make unmolding easier. Pottery pudding molds, though attractive, require too much heat to release cold desserts and often end up melting much of the dessert.

To Prepare a Basket to Drain Creams

Cut 2 sheets of cheesecloth large enough to line the bottom and sides of the basket. Wring the cheesecloth out under cold running water and line the basket. Set the basket in a bowl or baking pan (see sketch). Add the cream and

Preparing a basket to drain creams

In a saucepan, heat the cream, milk, sugar, and salt over low heat until the sugar is dissolved. Soften the gelatin in the cold water and stir into the cream mixture. When the gelatin is dissolved, beat in the sour cream with a wire whisk until thoroughly blended and smooth. Then blend in the flavorings. Pour into individual bowls and chill until set, about 4 hours. Serve garnished with the fruit of your choice. YIELDS 6 SERVINGS. ▼▼▼

let drain for at least 6 hours and up to 36 hours. The longer it drains, the drier and firmer the cream will become. When ready to serve, unmold the cream onto a serving platter, remove the cheesecloth, and garnish with your choice of seasonal fruit. Some chefs recommend pouring on a coating of heavy cream. It is your choice whether or not you wish to add this enrichment.

Crème Louisa

A tasty cream to serve with whatever fresh fruit you might have at hand.

> 1 cup heavy cream
> ½ cup milk
> ½ cup sugar
> Pinch of salt
> 1 tablespoon gelatin
> 2 tablespoons cold water
> 1 cup sour cream
> ½ teaspoon almond extract
> 2 tablespoons cognac or Cointreau
> 3 cups crushed and sweetened berries,
>   peaches, apricots, nectarines,
>   or oranges

Coeur à la Crème

CREAM HEART

The cheese for this recipe can be changed to suit personal tastes. Try using Chèvre or even some Roquefort for part or all of the cottage cheese. If desired, add sugar to taste. For added richness, coat the unmolded dessert with heavy cream. If you do not have the special molds or a suitable basket, the cheese can be drained in a sieve lined with very fine cheesecloth. The traditional fruit for this dessert is strawberries, served whole and rolled in sugar, or crushed and sprinkled with sugar. However, any fresh fruit in season will serve to accompany this dessert.

> 1 pound cottage cheese
> 1 pound cream cheese, softened
> Pinch of salt
> 2 cups heavy cream
> 3 or 4 cups fruits of choice

Line a mold or molds with cheesecloth (see above). Sieve the cottage cheese and combine with the cream cheese and salt. Beat well, then gradually beat in the heavy cream. Continue beating until the mixture is smooth. Turn the mixture into the mold and allow to drain in refrigerator overnight. Unmold onto a serving platter, remove the cheesecloth, and surround with the fruits of your choice. Can be prepared up to 36 hours before serving. YIELDS 6 TO 8 SERVINGS.

Note: Any leftover cheese can be left to drain several days longer. If desired, beat in a suitable herb (that is, if you have not added sugar) and perhaps some garlic; let flavor develop for several hours and use as a spread for hors d'oeuvres.

Angela Pia

ANGEL CREAM

A truly delicious old-fashioned dessert.

   3 eggs, separated
   ½ cup sugar
   2 tablespoons cognac
   2 tablespoons rum
   1 tablespoon gelatin
   ¼ cup cold water
   1 cup heavy cream, whipped
   1 teaspoon vanilla
   Seasonal fruits or fruit sauces of choice

In a medium-sized bowl, beat the egg yolks and sugar until lemon-colored. Beat in the cognac and rum. In a small saucepan, soak the gelatin in the cold water until softened. Heat over low heat, stirring, until the gelatin is dissolved. Stir into the egg yolk mixture. Beat the egg whites until stiff and fold into the egg yolk mixture with the heavy cream and vanilla. Pour into sherbet glasses and chill until set, about 2 hours. Serve with a mixture of fruits or a fruit sauce of your choice. Can be prepared 24 hours before serving.

YIELDS 6 SERVINGS.

Cremets d'Angers

MOLDED CREAM

   1½ cups heavy cream
   3 egg whites
   3 or 4 cups strawberries, raspberries, or apricots

In a bowl, beat 1 cup heavy cream until almost stiff. In another bowl, beat the egg whites until almost stiff, then fold the two ingredients together. Line a sieve or heart-shaped mold with cheesecloth (see pages 88–89). Place the mold over a bowl to collect the liquid and transfer the cream–egg white mixture to the mold. Refrigerate overnight. Unmold onto a serving platter and pour the remaining ½ cup cream over all. Serve garnished with the fruits. Can be prepared 2 days before serving. The longer it is allowed to drain, the drier it will become.   YIELDS 6 SERVINGS.

Pommes à la Neige

APPLE SNOW

   4 apples (Cortlands or Rome Beauties)
   1½ teaspoons gelatin
   1 tablespoon water
   1 lemon
   3 tablespoons sugar
   2 egg whites

Preheat oven to 350°F. Make an incision a third of the way down each apple around the circumference to prevent the skin from bursting. Pour a film of water over the bottom of a baking dish and add the apples. Bake for 30 minutes. Remove and cool.

In a small saucepan, soften the gelatin in the tablespoon of water. Dissolve over low heat. Pare the rind from the lemon and dice finely. Squeeze the juice and strain. Blanch the rind in boiling water for 3 minutes, drain, and refresh under cold water.

When the apples are cool enough to handle, slice off the caps; scoop out the pulp, keeping the shells intact, and discard the cores. Purée the apple pulp in a processor with 1½ tablespoons sugar, the lemon juice, and the dissolved gelatin. Turn into a bowl and fold in the lemon rind. Beat the egg whites until stiff with the remaining 1½ tablespoons sugar and fold into the apple mixture. Spoon the snow back into the apple shells and replace the caps. Chill for 1 hour. Can be made up to 24 hours before serving.   YIELDS 4 SERVINGS.

Note: If you do not wish to use the apple skins or if they get broken, the mixture can be placed in sherbet glasses to chill. Serve garnished with a dollop of whipped cream and a bit of grated apple, if desired.

Apple Whip

¾ cup Apple Purée (see page 283)
1 tablespoon sugar, or to taste
3 egg whites
1 cup Custard Sauce (see page 273)

In a bowl, combine the Apple Purée and sugar. Beat the egg whites until stiff and fold into the purée. Pour into a serving dish and chill. Serve with Custard Sauce. Do not prepare more than 6 hours before serving.

                 YIELDS 4 SERVINGS.

Crème aux Abricots

APRICOT CREAM

12 ounces dried apricots
1 tablespoon gelatin
¼ cup cold water
½ cup almonds
1 tablespoon milk
1 cup heavy cream, whipped, sweetened to taste, and flavored with vanilla to taste
Fresh or stewed apricots (optional)

Lightly oil a 3-cup mold and refrigerate. In a saucepan, simmer the apricots in water to cover until tender, about 30 minutes. Purée in a food processor. Soak the gelatin in the ¼ cup cold water until softened and stir into the hot apricot purée. Cool until the mixture is just about to set. Grind the almonds in a processor with the milk to form a paste. Stir into the apricot mixture. When the apricot mixture is almost ready to set, fold in the cream and pour the mixture into the mold. Refrigerate for at least 3 hours. Unmold onto a platter and serve. Garnish with fresh or stewed apricots, if desired. Can be prepared 24 hours before serving.   YIELDS 6 SERVINGS.

Note: If desired, the cream can be accompanied by a raspberry or chocolate sauce.

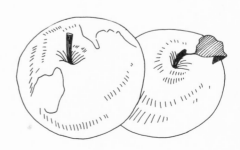

Banana Whip with Orange Sabayon Sauce

4 bananas
¼ cup plus 3 tablespoons sugar
1½ cups orange juice
¼ cup light rum
3 eggs, separated, plus 1 yolk
Pinch of salt

In a processor, purée the bananas with ¼ cup sugar, ½ cup orange juice, and the rum, adding more sugar if desired. In a bowl, beat the 3 egg whites and salt until almost stiff. Fold the whites into the banana mixture and chill for several hours. In a saucepan, beat the 4 egg yolks with the remaining 3 tablespoons sugar until they are thick and lemon-colored. Over low heat, beat the egg mixture, slowly adding the remaining cup of orange juice. Continue beating until the mixture gets light and foamy and is tripled in bulk. *Do not let it boil.* Remove from the heat and beat for 3 minutes, then pour into a bowl and chill. Serve with the banana whip. Can be prepared 24 hours before serving.
▪▪▪　　　　　YIELDS 6 SERVINGS.

Blueberry Fool

6 cups blueberries
3 large strips lemon rind
1 cup sugar
2 tablespoons crème de cassis or ¼ cup
　Grand Marnier
3 cups heavy cream

In a 2-quart saucepan, simmer the blueberries, lemon rind, and sugar, covered, for 4 minutes. Uncover and boil gently until the mixture is thick and sticky, about 15 minutes, stirring occasionally. Remove the lemon rind and purée the blueberries through a food mill or in a processor. The mixture should be quite thick; if necessary, cook a little longer. Chill, then stir in the cassis or Grand Marnier. In a large kettle, boil the heavy cream until it is reduced to 1½ cups. Chill. Whip the cream to the soft-peak stage. Partly fold the cream into the chilled blueberry mixture, leaving a striated appearance. Turn into a serving dish. Chill for up to 12 hours before serving.　　　YIELDS 6 TO 8 SERVINGS.
▪▪▪

Chestnut Fool

Although it is possible to prepare your own chestnut purée, it is much easier, and just as good, to buy it in cans. Be sure to get the sweetened purée.

2 cups sweetened chestnut purée
Maraschino liqueur
1 cup heavy cream
Vanilla to taste

In a bowl, beat the chestnut purée until smooth and stir in the maraschino liqueur. Whip the cream until stiff, flavoring with the vanilla. Fold into the chestnut mixture, leaving a striated appearance. Pour into serving glasses and chill for 1 hour before serving. Can be prepared up to 12 hours before serving.
　　　　　YIELDS 6 SERVINGS.

Note: This mixture can be used to fill meringue nests or individual tart shells.
▪▪▪

Gooseberry Fool

This fool can be made equally well with blackberries, raspberries, tamarinds, or plums in place of the gooseberries.

1 pint gooseberries, hulled
Sugar to taste
2 teaspoons orange flower water

3 egg yolks
1 teaspoon cornstarch
1 cup milk, scalded
1¼ cups heavy cream
Ladyfingers or butter cookies
    (optional)

In a saucepan, combine the gooseberries with water to cover and simmer 15 minutes. Drain, reserving the juice, and purée the fruit. Strain to remove the seeds. Measure the purée and add enough reserved juice to make 2½ cups. Add sugar to taste and orange flower water. Chill.

In a saucepan, beat the egg yolks with the cornstarch until stiff, then stir in the milk. Cook, stirring, until thickened. Simmer 2 minutes and stir in the gooseberry purée. Chill.

Whip the cream until it holds soft peaks and fold into the gooseberry mixture, leaving a striated appearance. Pour into a glass bowl or individual dessert glasses. Serve with the cookies, if desired. Can be prepared up to 24 hours before serving.   YIELDS 6 SERVINGS.

Note: Orange flower water is available at gourmet shops, Middle Eastern markets, drugstores, and supermarkets.

Kiwi Fool

14 kiwifruit, peeled
⅓ cup sugar
2 tablespoons water
4 teaspoons cornstarch
2 cups heavy cream

In a bowl, beat 12 kiwifruit with a whisk to form a coarse purée. In a small saucepan, combine 1 cup of purée with the sugar. In a bowl, stir the water and cornstarch until smooth. Add to the sugared kiwifruit purée. Simmer over medium heat, stirring, until the mixture is clear and very thick. Scrape it into a bowl and let it cool slightly. Beat in the remaining unsugared kiwifruit purée and mix well. Chill.

In a 1½-quart saucepan, boil the cream until it is reduced to 1 cup. Chill.

Beat the chilled cream to the soft-peak stage, and fold into the fruit purée, leaving a striated appearance. Turn the fool into a serving dish and garnish with slices of the remaining 2 kiwifruit. Serve. Can be prepared 24 hours before serving.   YIELDS 6 SERVINGS.

Lemon Snow

2 tablespoons gelatin, softened in
    ½ cup water
1⅓ cups sugar
2½ cups boiling water
⅔ cup lemon juice
½ teaspoon grated lemon rind
6 egg whites
1 cup heavy cream, whipped and
    sweetened to taste
Candied violets (optional)

In a large bowl, combine the gelatin and sugar. Stir in the boiling water and continue stirring until the gelatin is dissolved. Stir in the lemon juice and rind and chill until the mixture is syrupy, about 1 hour in the refrigerator.

Beat the egg whites until stiff and fold them into the lemon mixture. Pour into a serving dish and chill until set, about 2 hours.

Garnish with whipped cream and candied violets if desired. Can be prepared up to 12 hours before serving.
                      YIELDS 6 SERVINGS.

Note: If desired, the whipped cream can be folded into the lemon mixture for a more subtle flavor.

Lemon Cream

This cream is also delicious used to fill meringue or tart shells.

4 egg yolks
½ cup sugar
3 tablespoons lemon juice
2 tablespoons grated lemon rind
1 cup heavy cream, whipped
Strawberries, blueberries,
  or raspberries

In a medium-sized saucepan, beat the egg yolks and sugar until thick and lemon-colored. Beat in the lemon juice and rind and cook over low heat about 10 minutes or until thickened (about 180°F. on a thermometer). Let cool. Fold in the whipped cream and pour into a glass bowl. Garnish with the fruit of your choice. Can be prepared up to 12 hours before serving, but garnish with fruit just before serving.
▀▄▀ YIELDS 6 SERVINGS.

Orange Chantilly

6 oranges
1 cup heavy cream
6 tablespoons sugar
2 tablespoons maraschino liqueur
5 tablespoons chopped walnuts

Cut off the top third of each orange and scoop out the flesh, saving both the juices and the pulp. Cut the pulp free of seeds and filaments, and dice. Whip the cream until stiff; fold in the sugar, maraschino liqueur, walnuts, and reserved orange pulp and juices. Fill the orange shells with the mixture. Chill.
YIELDS 6 SERVINGS.

Note: If you prefer, this dessert can be frozen.
▀▄▀

Crème aux Pêches

PEACH CREAM

1 tablespoon gelatin
¼ cup cold water
1 cup chopped fresh peaches
½ cup confectioners' sugar
1 tablespoon dark rum
1 cup heavy cream
2 egg whites
Peach slices

Oil a 1½-quart mold. Soften the gelatin in the cold water and heat until dissolved. Combine the chopped peaches with the sugar and rum and marinate for at least 10 minutes. Add the dissolved gelatin to the peaches. Beat the cream to the soft-peak stage. Beat the egg whites to the soft-peak stage. Fold the cream and egg whites into the fruit. Pour into the mold and chill at least 2 hours. Unmold and garnish with peach slices. Can be prepared 1 day before serving. YIELDS 6 SERVINGS.
▀▄▀

Pear Snow

1 cup heavy cream
4 cups Pear Purée (see following
  recipe)
4 egg whites
Pinch of salt
¼ cup granulated sugar
½ teaspoon almond extract
Brown sugar to taste

In a bowl, beat the cream until stiff. Fold in the Pear Purée. Beat the egg whites and salt to the soft-peak stage, then beat in the granulated sugar and almond extract. Continue beating until almost stiff. Fold into the pear mixture. Refrigerate, covered, for 2 hours. Serve in individual bowls sprinkled with brown sugar to taste. Can be prepared up to 6 hours before serving.

❖❖❖   YIELDS 8 SERVINGS.

Pear Purée

This purée can be used in many ways. Try it as a filling for a tart or meringue shell. Serve it as a base for fresh raspberries or serve it over chocolate ice cream or fresh gingerbread.

  4 pounds pears, peeled, cored, and sliced
  3 tablespoons water
  2 ounces toasted almonds, ground
  ⅓ cup sugar
  2 tablespoons pear brandy
  1 tablespoon lemon juice

In a saucepan, place the pears in the water and cook, stirring occasionally, until soft, about 25 minutes. Drain the pears and purée in a processor. Stir in the almonds, sugar, pear brandy, and lemon juice. Can be prepared 2 to 3 days before using.   YIELDS 4 SERVINGS.

❖❖❖

Pineapple Fool

  2 cups fresh pineapple, minced
  1 cup heavy cream
  2 tablespoons confectioners' sugar
  1 teaspoon vanilla

Place the pineapple in a colander for 20 minutes to drain. Whip the cream until it begins to thicken. Gradually add the sugar and vanilla, beating until stiff. Cover with plastic wrap and chill. Just before serving, fold the pineapple into the mixture, leaving a striated appearance. Then pour into large bowl or individual glasses. Can be made up to 6 hours before serving.

❖❖❖   YIELDS 4 SERVINGS.

Prune Whip

The pastry cook at the Quisset Harbor House in Falmouth, Massachusetts, used to prepare this once a week. When I tried it again recently I found it as good as my childhood memory.

  ⅓ pound prunes
  ½ cup sugar
  5 egg whites
  ½ teaspoon lemon juice
  Custard Sauce (optional; see page 273)

Preheat oven to 350°F. Butter an 8- by 11-inch baking dish. Simmer the prunes in water to cover until soft. Stone, if necessary, and purée in a processor. Add the sugar and simmer over low heat for 5 minutes or until the mixture is thick. Cool to room temperature. Beat the egg whites until stiff but not dry, and fold into the prune mixture with the lemon juice. Pour into the prepared baking dish and bake for 20 minutes. Cool. Serve cold with the Custard Sauce. Can be prepared the day before serving.

❖❖❖   YIELDS 6 SERVINGS.

Raspberry Whip

  1¼ cups raspberries
  1 cup confectioners' sugar
  3 egg whites
  Custard Sauce (optional; see page 273)

In a processor, purée the raspberries with the sugar. Strain through a sieve, rubbing diligently on the seeds to remove all of the fruit. Discard the seeds. Beat the egg whites until stiff and fold into the purée. Pour into a serving bowl and chill. Serve with Custard Sauce, if desired. Can be prepared up to 6 hours before serving.   YIELDS 6 SERVINGS.

❖❖❖

Prune Fool with Port Wine

½ pound dried prunes
⅔ cup granulated sugar, plus more as needed
Rind of 1 lemon, in julienne strips
1 cup port wine, or more as needed
1 cup heavy cream
3 tablespoons confectioners' sugar
Slivered blanched almonds

In a saucepan, simmer prunes, granulated sugar, and lemon rind in water to cover until tender. Drain, leaving the prunes and lemon peel in the pan. Add the port and simmer 20 minutes longer. Discard the rind and stone the prunes, if necessary. Purée fruit in a processor. If necessary, add more port to make the prunes moist. Sweeten to taste with more granulated sugar. Whip the cream and mix half of it with the prunes. Spoon the mixture into a serving bowl. Sweeten the remaining whipped cream with the confectioners' sugar and garnish the dessert with the whipped cream and almonds. Can be prepared up to 12 hours before serving.
▼▼▼   YIELDS 6 SERVINGS.

Raspberry Coeur à la Crème

20 ounces frozen raspberries, thawed
4 tablespoons raspberry liqueur
8 ounces cream cheese
½ cup confectioners' sugar
1½ cups heavy cream

Line eight ½-cup *Coeur à la Crème* molds or one 2-cup *Coeur à la Crème* basket with 2 layers of dampened cheesecloth (see pages 88–89); set aside.

Drain 10 ounces raspberries, reserving the juice. In a processor, purée the remaining 10 ounces of raspberries and the reserved juices from all the berries. Strain, discarding the seeds, and stir in 2 tablespoons raspberry liqueur. Chill.

In a processor, cream the cream cheese and sugar until light and fluffy. Whip the heavy cream until stiff and fold into the cheese mixture with the reserved raspberries and remaining 2 tablespoons raspberry liqueur. Fill the molds or basket with the mixture, tap to settle, and place ends of cheesecloth over the top. Place in a shallow pan and let drain overnight, refrigerated. Unmold, remove the cheesecloth, and serve with the raspberry sauce. Can be prepared up to 36 hours before serving.
▼▼▼   YIELDS 8 SERVINGS.

Raspberry Parfait

This delicious dessert is a mix of a fool, a whip, and a frozen dessert. You can substitute two cups of any puréed fruit for the raspberries. Try tamarind, blueberries, pineapple, or apple.

1 pint fresh raspberries or 10 ounces unsweetened frozen raspberries
2 egg whites
½ cup sugar
1½ cups heavy cream

Strain raspberries, discarding the seeds. Put the purée into an ice cube tray, cover with foil, and freeze overnight. About 1 hour before serving, beat egg whites until they hold soft peaks. Gradually beat in the sugar and continue beating until stiff. Whip the heavy cream in a separate bowl to the soft-peak stage. Remove the frozen purée from the refrigerator and place in a bowl. Beat with a whisk to break down the ice crystals.

Fold the cream and egg whites together and quickly fold in the semifrozen raspberry purée. Pile into parfait glasses and keep in coldest part of the refrigerator. Do not attempt to assemble more than 2 hours before serving.

YIELDS 6 SERVINGS.

Rhubarb Fool

1½ pounds rhubarb stalks, cut into 1-inch pieces
½ to ¾ cup sugar
2 cups heavy cream

Preheat oven to 350°F. Place the rhubarb in a baking dish; cover tightly. Bake for 45 minutes or until the rhubarb is so tender it becomes a purée when stirred. Stir in sugar to taste. Chill. In a 1½-quart saucepan, boil the cream until reduced to 1 cup. Chill. Whip the cream until soft peaks form. Fold in the rhubarb, leaving a striated appearance, and pour into a serving dish. Can be prepared up to 6 hours before serving.   YIELDS 6 SERVINGS.

Fraises Eugénie

STRAWBERRY CREAM

1 pint strawberries
2 tablespoons kirsch or framboise
5 tablespoons sugar
1½ cups heavy cream
1 tablespoon gelatin
¼ cup cold water
Raspberry Sauce (see page 276)

Oil an 8-cup soufflé dish and chill. Cut the berries into eighths, reserving a few whole berries for garnish, and place in a bowl with 1 tablespoon kirsch and 2 tablespoons sugar. In a bowl, beat the cream until it reaches the soft-peak stage, then add the remaining 3 tablespoons sugar and beat until stiff. In a saucepan, soften the gelatin in the water and heat, stirring, until dissolved. Turn into a bowl and fold in the remaining tablespoon kirsch and 1 cup of the whipped cream. Fold in the cut-up strawberries and the remaining whipped cream. Pour into the mold and chill until set, about 4 hours. When ready to serve, unmold onto a serving dish and garnish with the whole strawberries. Serve the Raspberry Sauce on the side. Can be prepared 24 hours before serving.   YIELDS 6 SERVINGS.

Strawberry Whip

1½ cups strawberries
1 cup confectioners' sugar
3 egg whites
Custard Sauce (optional; see page 273)

In a processor, purée the strawberries with the sugar and strain through a fine sieve. Beat the egg whites until stiff, but not dry, and fold into the purée. Chill. Serve with Custard Sauce, if desired. Can be prepared up to 6 hours before serving.   YIELDS 6 SERVINGS.

Strawberries Romanoff I

Named for the last ruling czars of Russia. And it is a dessert worthy of a czar.

  1 quart strawberries
  6 tablespoons Cointreau
  2 tablespoons sugar
  ½ cup heavy cream
  1 cup vanilla ice cream
  1 teaspoon lemon juice

In a bowl, toss the berries gently with 3 tablespoons Cointreau and sprinkle with sugar. Macerate in the refrigerator for 1 hour. Whip the heavy cream until stiff; whip the ice cream until softened. Add lemon juice to the ice cream. Fold the strawberries into the ice cream, then fold in the whipped cream and remaining Cointreau. Serve immediately.
❖   YIELDS 6 TO 8 SERVINGS.

Strawberries Romanoff II

  1 orange
  2 tablespoons sugar
  1 cup heavy cream
  1 pint strawberries

Grate the orange rind and squeeze juice from half the orange. In a bowl, combine the sugar with the juice and rind. Stir until the sugar dissolves. Whip the heavy cream until it holds soft peaks, then stir in the syrup. Halve or lightly crush the strawberries and fold into the orange cream mixture. Pile into a bowl and cover. Chill for 30 minutes. Can be prepared up to 2 hours before serving.
❖   YIELDS 6 SERVINGS.

Wiener Götterspeise

VIENNESE FOOD FOR THE GODS
See photograph on page 67.

One of the best desserts ever, truly a food for the gods.

  1 cup crushed almond macaroon
    crumbs
  2 tablespoons rum, plus more for
    dipping
  1 egg yolk
  2 tablespoons granulated sugar
  1 cup heavy cream, whipped
  1 quart strawberries
  Confectioners' sugar

Rinse a 3-cup mold in cold water and set aside. In a bowl, mix the macaroon crumbs with the 2 tablespoons rum, the egg yolk, and the granulated sugar. Fold the mixture into the whipped cream and pour into the mold. Freeze for 2 hours. Dip the strawberries into the additional rum and roll in the confectioners' sugar. Unmold the cream and surround with the berries. The whipped cream mixture can be frozen for several weeks. If frozen more than 2 hours, let temper in the refrigerator for 2 to 3 hours before serving.   YIELDS 6 SERVINGS.
❖

CUSTARDS

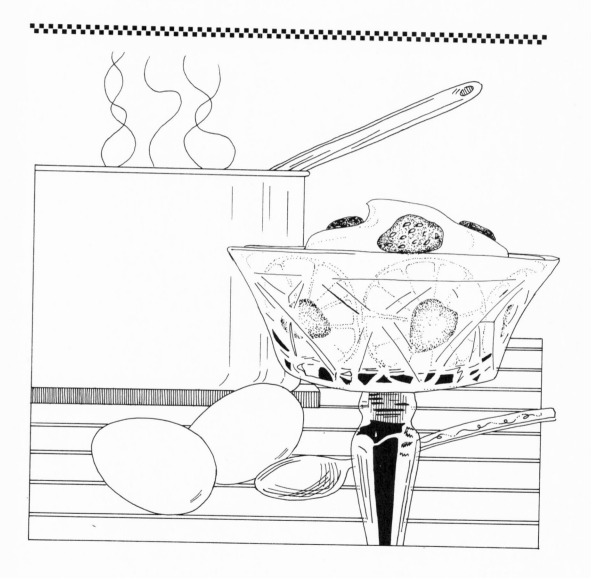

PREPARATIONS called custards range from sauces to puddings to flans and even to *crèmes brûlées.* They are all based on egg yolks, cream, sugar, and flavorings. The final consistency depends on how the ingredients are cooked and the number of egg yolks used in relation to the amount of liquid.

WATER BATHS

A custard is mixed together and then strained into a heatproof baking dish. It is baked in a water bath (*bain-marie*) or in a moderately low oven until just set. The water protects the custard from overcooking and from browning on the sides and bottom. To prepare a water bath, put the custard into its mold and place that in another pan. Fill that pan with enough hot water to come halfway up the sides of the mold. The water in the water bath must be very hot when the custard is put into it, but it *must not boil* or else the custard will have holes, and possibly become watery and split apart when unmolded. The worst that can happen is that the dessert will curdle completely, in which case it is ruined. The degree of damage depends on how long the water boils. If you find the water boiling when you check the custard, immediately drop some ice cubes into the water to stop the boiling, then lower the temperature and continue baking until done. If the liquid has boiled only briefly, the custard may still come out perfect. If it has boiled too long, however, any of the above problems may occur.

TO TEST FOR DONENESS

To test a baked custard for doneness, insert a thin-bladed knife halfway between the edge of the custard and the center. It should come out clean. The center of the custard will still be slightly undercooked at this point, but it will finish cooking as the custard cools. If you cook the custard until the center is firm, it can become overcooked as it cools. Cool the custard out of the water bath.

TO COOK ON TOP OF THE STOVE

Some versions of *crème brûlée* and *pots de crème* require a less firm custard mixture. They are made by cooking the egg-cream mixture on top of the stove until it is thick enough to coat the back of a spoon. Some insist that these custards be cooked in a double boiler. My experience is that there is no difference in the result whether cooked in a double boiler or over direct heat. What *is* necessary is that the heat be no more than moderate (the water in the double boiler should barely simmer), and that the custard be stirred constantly until it has thickened. Cook the custard until it is thick enough to coat the back of a spoon: To test for doneness, dip a spoon into the custard, turn it over, and run your fingertip down the center. There should be a distinct line in the custard, and it should register 180°F. on a candy thermometer. Once it has reached this point, the custard should be strained immediately through a fine sieve into another container, as the retained heat in the original pot can overheat the custard and cause it to curdle. There is no remedy for a curdled custard except to discard it and start again. Do not be intimidated, though; with care and a little practice you will find that custards are really simple to prepare.

Occasionally, custards have softened gelatin dissolved in them so that they will be firmer when set. If these mixtures are then lightened with whipped cream, they become the Bavarian creams you will find in the next chapter.

To Coat a Mold with Caramel

Crèmes renversées au caramel (caramel custards) and flans are customarily baked in molds that have been lined with sugar cooked to the caramel stage. The sugar is boiled until it turns golden brown and is about 356°F. If it is overcooked, it will have a distinctly burned taste. Because of the extremely high temperature and the fact that sugar syrup is sticky, molten caramel can create some of the most painful and disfiguring burns. The instructions below teach you to handle this material safely. Follow them!

1. Keep everyone out of the way, especially children. Little children should be sent completely out of the room for their safety, or confined in a playpen.

2. Heat the sugar, lemon juice, and water to a full rolling boil, stirring gently. When it boils, cover the pan and boil, covered, for five minutes (the steam will wash any sugar crystals from the sides of the pan). Remove the cover and boil until the syrup starts to turn golden. If it turns in only one spot, gently swirl the pan to caramelize the entire mixture.

3. Immediately pour the caramel into a heatproof mold and, using potholders, twist and tilt the mold to cover the bottom and about three-quarters of the way up the sides of the mold with the caramel. It is best not to let the caramel coat higher than the custard mixture, as it will not soften after baking and can cause a problem when trying to unmold the dessert. When the mold is well covered and the caramel is running as slowly as molasses, you can turn it upside down on a rack and let it drain until ready to fill. You can also leave it right side up until ready to use if you prefer.

4. If you should spill any of the molten caramel on you, plunge the affected area under cold running water and keep it there. *Do not try to peel off the caramel.* Let the cold water stop the cooking and burning and dissolve the caramel. If you try to peel off the caramel, you may well peel off some of your skin.

5. If the caramel should burn, do not pour it down the sink until it has cooled. The viscous molten caramel can turn the drain into a form of cannon with the explosion blowing up into your kitchen and onto you. Let the caramel cool to room temperature. Do not worry about the pan. Let it sit in water until the caramel has dissolved. It may take a day or two, but it *will* dissolve and the pan will be fine. If you try to scrape and scour it out, you will probably ruin the pan's finish.

These rules are not intended to frighten you, but to give you the information you need to work with caramel safely. Do not be afraid; just use common sense to create wonderful desserts.

To Unmold a Caramel-Lined Dessert

It is necessary to chill the dessert completely after baking. The chilling helps to firm the custard and, at the same time, the period involved helps dissolve the caramel so that it will turn into a sauce. When the custard is completely chilled and ready to serve, dip the mold in hot water, run a knife around the edge, and invert the mold onto a platter. The dessert should fall out easily. If it does not, give it a firm shake while on the platter. If it still does not unmold, re-dip it in the hot water.

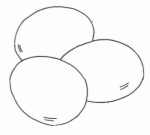

Crème à la Vanille Caramelisée

1 cup sugar
1 ½ tablespoons water
3 drops lemon juice
4 ½ cups milk
1 vanilla bean
4 whole eggs, plus 8 yolks
1 ⅓ cups Custard Sauce (optional; see
    page 273)

Preheat oven to 325°F. In a small saucepan, bring ¼ cup sugar, water, and lemon juice to a boil, stirring constantly. Cover and boil 5 minutes. Remove the cover and continue boiling until the mixture is a rich golden brown. Pour into 6 individual molds or one 1½-quart mold. Turn and tilt the mold to coat it evenly. Set aside.

In a 2-quart saucepan, scald the milk and vanilla bean. In a bowl, beat the eggs, egg yolks, and remaining ¾ cup sugar together until light and lemon-colored. Stirring constantly, add the milk to the egg mixture and cook, stirring, until the mixture coats the back of a spoon. Then strain into the mold or molds. Bake in a *bain-marie* until set, about 30 minutes. The water in the water bath *must not boil*. The individual molds may be done sooner than 30 minutes; the larger mold, depending on its depth, may take longer. Test for doneness by inserting a knife before removing the custard from the oven. It should come out clean. When done, remove custard from the water bath and let cool. Chill completely, about 4 hours, before unmolding.

To unmold, dip the mold into hot water, then invert it onto a platter. Serve the sauce on the side if desired. Can be prepared 2 days before serving.

         YIELDS 6 TO 8 SERVINGS.

Variations: The flavor of the custard can be changed as you desire. Instead of the vanilla bean, add your favorite liqueur to taste to the custard mixture before putting it into the mold. Or, if desired, you can season it with cinnamon, nutmeg, or allspice.

Crème Renversée au Citron
LEMON-FLAVORED CARAMEL CUSTARD

1 quart milk
Grated rind of 2 lemons
6 eggs
1 ¼ cups sugar
2 teaspoons water

Preheat oven to 325°F. In a saucepan, simmer the milk and grated lemon rinds for 5 minutes. Strain; discard the grated rinds. In a bowl, beat the eggs with ¾ cup sugar until lemon-colored. Pour in the strained milk, stirring constantly. Skim off any froth that forms on the top. Cook, stirring, until mixture coats spoon. In a saucepan, bring the remaining ½ cup sugar and the water to a boil; cover and simmer 5 minutes. Remove the cover and boil until a rich caramel color. Pour into a 1½-quart mold and tilt the mold to coat. Strain the egg mixture into the mold and bake in a water bath until it tests done. Chill completely, at least 3 hours. Can be prepared 2 days before serving.

         YIELDS 6 SERVINGS.

Ginger and Orange Flan

When preparing this flan, remember that the water in the water bath must not boil, or else the flan will have holes, or worse, turn into sweet scrambled eggs.

1 cup sugar
1 tablespoon lemon juice
½ cup plus 2 tablespoons water
¾ cup minced, peeled gingerroot

1 cup heavy cream
1 cup milk
1 teaspoon grated orange rind
2 whole eggs, plus 4 yolks
Pinch of salt

Preheat oven to 325°F. In a skillet, bring ½ cup sugar, lemon juice, and 2 tablespoons water to a boil, stirring constantly. Cover and boil for 5 minutes. Remove the cover and continue to boil until golden. Pour into a 9-inch pie plate or cake pan and tilt the pan to coat evenly. In a saucepan, simmer the remaining ½ cup sugar, gingerroot, and ½ cup water until reduced by half, stirring occasionally. Stir in the cream, milk, and orange rind and heat until hot. In a bowl, beat the eggs, egg yolks, and salt until well mixed. Gradually stir in the hot milk mixture.

Strain into the caramel-lined mold, pressing firmly on the gingerroot to extract all the flavor. Bake in a water bath for 45 minutes or until it tests done. Cool, then chill until cold. Unmold onto a serving platter. Can be prepared 2 days before serving.   YIELDS 4 SERVINGS.
▟▖

Flan de Naranja

ORANGE CARAMEL CUSTARD

2½ cups sugar
¼ cup water
3 navel oranges
1 quart milk
2 cinnamon sticks
1 teaspoon vanilla
6 whole eggs, plus 2 yolks

Preheat oven to 325°F. In a saucepan, bring 1 cup sugar and the water to a boil, stirring constantly. Cover and boil 5 minutes. Remove the cover and boil until mixture is a rich golden brown. Pour into a 1½-quart mold and tilt to coat evenly. Peel the orange rind, without removing

any of the white pith, and set aside. Peel the oranges completely and cut into segments. Set aside.

In a 2-quart saucepan, scald the milk, orange peel, and cinnamon sticks. Stir in the vanilla. In a large bowl, beat the eggs and egg yolks with the remaining 1½ cups sugar until thick and lemon-colored. Stirring constantly, add the hot milk. Press the orange segments into the caramel and chill for 10 minutes in the freezer.

Strain the egg-milk mixture into the caramel-lined mold and bake in a water bath until it tests done, about 45 minutes. Chill completely, about 4 hours. Unmold onto a serving platter. Can be prepared 2 days before serving.
▟▖   YIELDS 6 SERVINGS.

Puerto Rican Pineapple Flan

3 cups pineapple juice
3 cups sugar
¼ cup water
7 eggs

In a saucepan, boil the pineapple juice and 2 cups sugar until mixture reaches 222°F. on a candy thermometer. Remove from heat and cool completely.

Preheat oven to 325°. In a saucepan, bring the remaining cup sugar and the water to a boil. Cover and boil for 5 minutes. Remove the cover and continue to boil until a rich golden brown. Pour into a 9-inch cake tin and swirl to coat the bottom and sides. In a bowl, break the eggs and mix until blended but not frothy. Strain the eggs into the pineapple mixture and mix gently. Pour into the caramel-lined pan. Bake in a *bain-marie* for about 55 minutes or until set. Chill completely, about 4 hours. Can be prepared 2 days before serving.
▟▖
     YIELDS 4 TO 6 SERVINGS.

Pumpkin Flan

This custard can be baked in a pie shell for pumpkin pie, and if you like, you can add to the flavor with cloves, nutmeg, cinnamon, ginger, and allspice.

> ¼ cup plus 4 tablespoons sugar
> 2 tablespoons water
> 1 cup pumpkin purée
> 1 cup milk
> ½ cup cream
> 4 eggs
> ¼ teaspoon vanilla

Preheat oven to 350°F. In a small saucepan bring ¼ cup sugar and the water to a boil, stirring constantly. Cover and boil 5 minutes. Remove the cover and continue to boil until a rich golden brown. Pour into a 1-quart baking dish and tilt to coat evenly. In a bowl, combine the pumpkin purée, milk, cream, eggs, remaining 4 tablespoons sugar, and vanilla. Stir well. Strain into the baking dish. Bake in a water bath for about 45 minutes or until flan is set. Chill completely, about 4 hours. Can be prepared 2 days before serving.
▼▪▪   YIELDS 4 SERVINGS.

Flan de Potiron

RUM-FLAVORED PUMPKIN FLAN

> 1 ½ cups milk
> Grated zest of 1 lemon
> ½ cup heavy cream
> ½ cup plus 2 tablespoons sugar
> 2 tablespoons water
> ¾ cup cooked or canned pumpkin
>   purée
> ⅓ cup honey
> ¼ cup dark rum
> ¼ teaspoon salt
> 3 whole eggs, plus 2 yolks

Preheat oven to 325°F. In a saucepan, scald the milk, lemon zest, and cream; re-move from heat, cover, and let stand for 10 minutes. In a saucepan, bring the ½ cup sugar and the water to a boil, stirring constantly. Cover and boil for 5 minutes. Remove cover and continue to boil until a rich golden brown. Pour into a 5-cup mold and tilt to coat the bottom and sides. Force the pumpkin purée through a sieve into a bowl; beat in the honey, rum, salt, and remaining 2 tablespoons of sugar. Blend in the eggs and egg yolks. Strain into the mold and bake in a water bath for about 1 hour, or until flan tests done. Chill completely, about 4 hours. Unmold onto a serving platter. Can be prepared 2 days before serving.
▪▪▪   YIELDS 4 TO 6 SERVINGS.

Crème Brûlée

> 6 egg yolks
> 6 tablespoons granulated sugar
> 1 teaspoon cornstarch
> 2 ½ cups heavy cream, scalded
> 1 teaspoon vanilla
> 1 cup sieved light brown sugar

In a saucepan, beat the egg yolks until thick and lemon-colored. Beat in the granulated sugar and cornstarch, then whisk in the cream, stirring constantly. Put over low heat and cook, stirring constantly, until the custard is thick enough to coat the back of a spoon (180°F.). Remove from the heat and stir in the vanilla. Strain into a 1-quart heatproof serving dish or 6 individual dishes. Wrap tightly in plastic wrap to prevent a skin from forming; chill completely.

Preheat the broiler. Shortly before serving, sprinkle the brown sugar in an even layer over the cream. Broil until the sugar is bubbly and has melted. Take care not to let it burn. Remove from the broiler and chill for about an hour or until ready to serve. Can be prepared for broiling 2 days before serving.

YIELDS 6 SERVINGS.

Note: You can flavor the cream with almond extract, rum, cognac, framboise, kirsch, or any other flavor you like.

Crème Brûlée au Potiron et Bourbon

PUMPKIN AND BOURBON-FLAVORED CRÈME BRÛLÉE

2 cups heavy cream
¾ cup granulated sugar
4 eggs
1 ⅔ cups cooked or canned pumpkin purée
1 ½ teaspoons cinnamon
1 teaspoon ginger
½ teaspoon nutmeg
¼ teaspoon ground cloves
3 tablespoons bourbon
½ cup dark brown sugar

Preheat oven to 325°F. In a saucepan, combine the cream and granulated sugar and heat, stirring until the sugar is dissolved. In a bowl, beat the eggs until pale yellow. Beat in the pumpkin, cinnamon, ginger, nutmeg, cloves, and bourbon. Stir in the hot cream mixture and strain into a 5-cup baking dish. Bake in a water bath for about 1 hour, or until set. Remove from the water bath and chill completely, about 4 hours.

Preheat the broiler. Sieve the dark brown sugar and sprinkle evenly over the surface. Broil until the sugar melts and is shiny. Take care not to let it burn. Chill completely and serve. Can be prepared 2 days before serving, but the sugar should be added no more than an hour or two before serving.   YIELDS 6 SERVINGS.

Orange Custard

1 cup heavy cream
3 eggs, lightly beaten
1 cup orange juice
1 ½ teaspoons grated orange rind
¼ cup sugar
Pinch of salt

Preheat oven to 325°F. In a bowl, combine the cream, eggs, orange juice, orange rind, sugar, and salt. Beat well. Strain into 6 custard cups or one 3-cup mold. Bake in a water bath until set, about 45 minutes. Insert a knife into the custard to test for doneness. It should come out clean. Chill before serving. Can be made 1 day before serving.   YIELDS 6 SERVINGS.

Orange Pots de Crème

There are sets of covered pots and a tray for just this dessert. You might try checking local antiques shops.

4 egg yolks
5 tablespoons sugar
Pinch of salt
2 cups heavy cream, scalded
1 tablespoon grated orange rind
2 tablespoons Grand Marnier
Candied violets (optional)

Beat the egg yolks, sugar, and salt until they form a ribbon. Gradually stir in the cream. Place over low heat and cook, stirring, until the custard is thick enough to coat the back of a spoon (180°F.). Set the pan in cold water to stop the cooking. Stir in the orange rind and Grand Marnier. Pour into individual custard cups or crème pots. Chill. Garnish each dish with a violet if desired. Can be prepared a day before serving.   YIELDS 6 SERVINGS.

Papaya Custard

1 ½ cups light cream
3 large whole eggs, plus 1 yolk
1 ½ cups puréed papaya
½ teaspoon salt
¼ cup sugar
Juice and rind of 1 orange
½ cup toasted coconut
1 papaya, peeled and sliced

Preheat oven to 325°F. Beat the cream, eggs, egg yolk, papaya purée, salt, sugar, orange juice, and orange rind together until well blended. Pour into 6 individual custard cups or one 1-quart baking dish. Bake in a water bath for 40 to 45 minutes for the individual servings or up to an hour for the single mold. Cool. Unmold onto individual serving plates or a serving platter and garnish with the coconut and papaya slices. Serve warm. Can be prepared for baking an hour or two before.   YIELDS 6 SERVINGS.

Poires à la Joinville

POACHED PEARS WITH CUSTARD

This custard is very delicate. You may prefer to arrange the pears around the outside rather than in the center.

1 cup sugar
3 tablespoons water
1 ½ cups milk
1 cup light cream
1 (2-inch) piece vanilla bean
4 whole eggs, plus 2 yolks
¼ teaspoon salt
6 pear halves, vanilla-poached (see page 286)
1 cup heavy cream, whipped
Candied cherries (optional)
Pistachio nuts (optional)

Preheat oven to 350°F. In a saucepan, bring ¾ cup sugar and the water to a boil, stirring constantly. Cover and continue to boil for 5 minutes. Remove cover and cook to a rich golden brown. Pour into a 9-inch ring mold and tilt to coat evenly. In a saucepan, scald the milk and light cream with the vanilla bean. In a bowl, beat the eggs, egg yolks, and remaining ¼ cup sugar until thick and lemon-colored. Stir in the salt. Stirring constantly, add the milk-cream mixture, then strain into the ring mold. Bake in a water bath for 1 hour or until it tests done. Chill completely, about 4 hours.

Unmold onto a serving platter, fill the center with pear halves, and garnish with whipped cream, cherries, and pistachios. The pears and custard can be prepared the day before serving, but assemble no more than 2 hours before serving.   YIELDS 6 SERVINGS.

Pistachio Cream Custard with Custard and Strawberry Sauce

2 cups heavy cream
¼ cup peeled pistachios, minced
1 cup plus 2 tablespoons sugar
4 eggs
2 cups Custard Sauce (see page 273)
1 cup strawberries
Juice of 1 lemon
Whole pistachios

Preheat oven to 350°F. Butter eight 5-ounce custard cups. In a saucepan, combine the cream and minced pistachios and bring to a boil, stirring, then remove from heat. Let steep 10 minutes. Beat ¾ cup sugar and eggs until they form a ribbon and are thick and lemon-colored. Whisk in the pistachio cream and strain into custard cups. Rinse pistachios caught in strainer and spread to dry on paper toweling. Bake custards in a water bath for 20 minutes or until set. Chill completely, about 4 hours.

When ready to serve, spread some of the Custard Sauce on each plate. In a processor, purée the strawberries, remaining sugar, and lemon juice. Strain through a fine sieve; discard the seeds. Spoon a ribbon of strawberry purée around the edge of the Custard Sauce. With a knife point, draw thin lines alternately toward and away from the center (see sketch on page 22). Unmold the custard in the center of the plate and sprinkle with the reserved pistachios. Can be prepared a day ahead.

■❖■ YIELDS 8 SERVINGS.

Coppa Primavera
SPRING CUP

A dessert that is as good to look at as it is to eat.

1 tablespoon gelatin
2 tablespoons cold water
2 eggs, separated, plus 1 white
7 tablespoons sugar
Juice of 2 oranges
3 tablespoons Cointreau or
    Grand Marnier
1 pint strawberries
½ cup dry white wine
1 cup heavy cream
2 oranges, peeled and sliced
1 pint strawberries, sliced

In a 1-quart saucepan, soften the gelatin in the cold water. In a bowl, beat the 2 egg yolks with 3½ tablespoons sugar until thickened. Dissolve the gelatin over low heat, then stir in the orange juice and 2 tablespoons Cointreau. Stir gelatin mixture into the egg-yolk mixture and heat until thickened, stirring constantly. Remove from the heat and let cool until almost set.

Beat 2 egg whites until stiff but not dry

and fold into the custard. In a 1-quart saucepan, simmer the 1 pint strawberries, remaining 3½ tablespoons sugar, and wine for 5 minutes. Purée and chill.

Beat the extra egg white until stiff, and fold into the chilled purée. Beat ½ cup cream until stiff and fold into the purée. Marinate the orange slices in the remaining Cointreau for 15 minutes.

Place a strawberry slice in the center of each orange slice and arrange in wine glasses with the strawberries facing out. Make a thin layer of strawberry slices in the glass; add a layer of orange custard, a layer of strawberry cream, and more orange custard. Whip the remaining ½ cup cream. Garnish with the whipped cream, and the remaining sliced strawberries. Can be prepared several hours before serving. YIELDS 6 SERVINGS.
■❖■

Pots de Crème aux Fraises
CUSTARD WITH STRAWBERRIES

¾ cup milk
½ cup heavy cream
2 large whole eggs, plus 2 yolks
⅓ cup sugar
1 teaspoon vanilla
1 pint strawberries
1 cup currant jelly
2 tablespoons orange liqueur

Preheat oven to 350°F. In a saucepan, scald the milk and heavy cream. In a bowl, beat the eggs, egg yolks, sugar, and vanilla until well mixed. Pour in the scalded milk-cream mixture and strain into six 6-ounce custard cups or *pots de crème* pots. Bake in a water bath for 15 minutes or until just set. Chill. Garnish with strawberries. In a saucepan, melt the currant jelly, stir in the orange liqueur, and glaze the strawberries. Chill again. Can be prepared 1 day before serving.
■❖■ YIELDS 6 SERVINGS.

Crème Josephine Baker

An adaptation of a recipe created by Alice B. Toklas to honor the great jazz singer.

> 2¼ cups milk
> 2 tablespoons flour
> 3 eggs
> 3 tablespoons sugar
> 2 teaspoons kirsch
> 3 tablespoons Pernod
> 3 bananas, thinly sliced
> Grated rind of 1 lemon

Preheat oven to 400°F. In a bowl, gently stir a small amount of milk into the flour to make a paste. Stir in the remaining milk gradually until the mixture is smooth. Beat in the eggs and sugar. Strain. Stir in the kirsch, Pernod, bananas, and lemon rind. Pour into a 1-quart baking dish and bake for 20 minutes, or until set. Cool. Serve cold or at room temperature. Can be prepared the day before serving. YIELDS 6 SERVINGS.

Norwegian Cream

> 2 tablespoons apricot jam
> 3 eggs
> 1 tablespoon sugar
> ½ teaspoon vanilla
> 2 cups milk, scalded
> ½ cup heavy cream
> Chocolate Caraque (see following recipe)

Preheat oven to 350°F. Spread the jam over the bottom of a 3-cup soufflé dish and set aside. Beat 2 whole eggs and the yolk of 1 egg with the sugar and vanilla until creamy. Stir the milk into the egg mixture and strain into the soufflé dish. Bake in a water bath covered with foil for 45 to 50 minutes, or until it tests done. Chill. Whip the remaining egg white until it holds firm peaks. Beat the heavy cream until it holds peaks, then fold together with the egg white. Sprinkle the Chocolate Caraque over the custard and pile the cream-egg white mixture on top. Decorate with more Caraque. Can be prepared 1 day before serving.

YIELDS 6 SERVINGS.

Chocolate Caraque

SHAVED CHOCOLATE

> 3 ounces semisweet chocolate, melted

Spread the melted chocolate on a marble slab, or the back of a baking sheet. Leave until nearly set. Hold a sharp long, thin knife almost at a right angle and shave off long chocolate scrolls or flakes, using a slight sideways sawing motion. Can be prepared a week or two before using, if stored in an airtight tin in a cold place (not the refrigerator).

Lemon Sponge Custard

> ¾ cup sugar
> 2 tablespoons butter
> 2 teaspoons grated lemon peel
> 3 eggs, separated
> 3 tablespoons flour
> ¼ cup lemon juice
> 1 cup light cream
> Pinch of salt
> Whipped cream

Preheat oven to 350°F. Butter a 1-quart soufflé dish. In a processor, cream the sugar, butter, and lemon peel until light and fluffy. Beat in the egg yolks one at a time. Stir in the flour, lemon juice, and cream. Beat the egg whites with the salt until stiff but not dry and fold into the egg yolk mixture. Pour into the prepared mold and bake in a water bath for 1 hour or until it tests done. Serve hot or cold, garnished with whipped cream. Can be prepared 1 day before serving.

YIELDS 6 SERVINGS.

BAVARIAN CREAMS

BAVARIAN CREAMS, *Charlotte Russe*, and frozen soufflés are desserts of ethereal lightness and subtlety. However, ▪▪▪▪▪they are sometimes, perhaps a little derogatorily, referred to as "nursery" desserts. Years ago good mothers knew that spicy, highly flavored foods excited children. Therefore, to keep their tempers quiet, the children were fed bland foods. Often desserts such as these were made with pallid flavors. However, properly made, these often-neglected desserts are delicious. In their more adult versions, the flavorings frequently include liqueurs — they certainly should not be relegated only to small children.

These desserts are a perfect example of how a few ingredients can be used with skill and thought to create many different tastes and textures. The desserts that follow consist of eggs, sugar, cream, and extract, plus a purée of fruit or a liqueur. Some may need gelatin, others a ring of ladyfingers, but the essence of each is the eggs and cream. Although the desserts are rich, their essential lightness makes them a delicious offering after a full dinner.

Bavarians provide an opportunity to garnish desserts beautifully. A pastry bag fitted with a star tip can ruffle and flourish the dessert. Sauces can enhance the cream with more of the same fruit flavor used, or with a contrasting flavor, and can add welcome color.

Bavarian creams have been mentioned in literature for at least two centuries. No one seems to know where the name comes from. The most reasonable explanation is that the dessert was a favorite in Bavaria. *Larousse Gastronomique* with typical chauvinism indicates that the dessert was created by a French chef in Bavaria. Whoever created the dessert is to be thanked.

Bavarian creams are composed of four basic ingredients: English custard (*crème à l'Anglaise*), gelatin, cream, and a flavoring. The gelatin is softened in cold water, dissolved in the hot custard, then allowed to cool until near the setting point. Lightly whipped cream is then folded into the mixture with the flavoring. Sometimes the flavoring is added to the custard mixture. Once assembled, the mixture is usually put into a mold and allowed to chill until set. It is then unmolded onto a platter and garnished.

ENGLISH CUSTARD, CRÈME À L'ANGLAISE, OR CUSTARD SAUCE

This is a wonderfully light egg-cream sauce that has caused terror for many cooks over the years — unnecessarily. The eggs must not be overheated or the sauce will curdle and turn into sweet scrambled eggs. With a little care, however, it is possible to produce exquisite, velvety smooth sauces. In the Sauces chapter of this book you will find a basic recipe for custard sauce for easy reference throughout. The recipes in this section have the quantities and instructions incorporated in them. The principal point to remember is not to overheat the egg mixture. Cook over low heat, in a double boiler, if desired, stirring constantly. The eggs will be done at 180°F. If you use an instant-read thermometer, you can check the temperature as the eggs cook. When they reach 180°F., remove the pan from the heat and strain the sauce immediately to prevent it from overcooking. If you do not have a thermometer, cook the sauce, stirring constantly, until it thickens enough to coat the back of a spoon.

GELATIN

All the recipes in this book that call for gelatin refer to plain, or unflavored, gelatin; flavored gelatin mixtures will not work. The amount of gelatin is not the same because the packaged mixture also has sweetening and flavoring in the package. To use plain gelatin (available in packages containing envelopes of one tablespoon each), sprinkle the gelatin over cold water or other liquid and let stand for a few minutes until the gelatin becomes translucent and is softened. At that point, stir it into a hot liquid, or dissolve over low heat. Be careful not to get it too hot because it is protein and burns easily. Do not sprinkle the dry gelatin over a hot liquid; it will not dissolve properly and the result will be lumpy.

WHIPPED CREAM

When preparing whipped cream for Bavarians, it must be whipped until stiff enough to hold soft, firm peaks, but not until it is stiff. At the soft-firm stage the cream can be folded into the other ingredients smoothly. If it is very stiff, you will have a difficult time folding the cream into the mixture and you will have a greater chance of deflating the air from the cream. Properly speaking, the cream is beaten to the Chantilly stage.

PREPARING THE MOLD

Any lightly flavored or flavorless vegetable oil is suitable for oiling the mold. Use just enough to coat the mold, but not so much that it puddles. It is wise to turn the oiled mold upside down over paper toweling to let the excess oil drain off. Butter is not suitable because the chilling sets the butter too firmly; when unmolding, it is often necessary to use so much heat to melt the butter that you end up melting the Bavarian.

UNMOLDING

Once the Bavarian has set, dip the mold into a bowl of hot water and let it stand for 10 to 20 seconds. Run a small knife around the edge. Hold the mold at a slight angle and let it pull away from one side and let some air into the mold. Place a serving plate over the top of the mold and turn the mold over in one quick movement. If you stop halfway through, you could end up with a disaster. Once the mold has been turned over completely, give the mold and platter a firm shake and lift off the mold. If the Bavarian does not unmold, repeat the procedure.

PREPARING AHEAD

Bavarians are best when served within 12 to 36 hours of assembling. After that the cream loses its velvety smoothness and lightness. Bavarians can be frozen, but should then be served before completely thawing. They are not as velvety when frozen.

Vanilla Bavarian Cream

1 cup milk
1 (1-inch) piece vanilla bean or
  1 teaspoon vanilla extract
4 egg yolks
½ cup sugar
1 tablespoon gelatin
2 tablespoons cold water
1 cup heavy cream

Oil a 3-cup mold; set aside. In a saucepan, scald the milk with the vanilla bean and let stand for 10 minutes to absorb the flavor. In a heavy saucepan, beat the egg yolks with the sugar until they are light and form a ribbon. Pour the scalded milk into the egg yolk mixture, stirring constantly. Heat over low heat and cook, stirring, until the mixture is smooth and thick, about 180°F. on a thermometer. Strain the cream into a bowl and discard the vanilla bean. (If you are using vanilla extract, stir it into the cream.)

In a small bowl, soften the gelatin in the cold water and stir it into the hot cream until it is dissolved. Cool the cream in the refrigerator, stirring often, until it is about the consistency of egg whites. Beat the heavy cream until it holds soft peaks. Fold into the cream and pour into the mold. Can be prepared the day before serving.

YIELDS 6 SERVINGS.

Note: The Bavarian can be flavored with any favorite flavoring, such as fruit liqueurs, in place of the vanilla.
▼▪■

Blackberry Bavarian Cream

You can substitute raspberries, cherries, blueberries, or strawberries for the black-berries in this Bavarian if you like.

1 pint blackberries, plus extra whole berries for garnish

1 cup water

3 tablespoons sugar, plus more to taste

3 egg yolks

1½ cups milk, scalded

2 tablespoons gelatin

2 cups heavy cream

Oil a 1-quart ring mold. In a saucepan, simmer 1 pint blackberries and ½ cup water for 5 minutes. Purée in a processor and strain to remove the seeds. Sweeten with sugar to taste. In a saucepan, beat the egg yolks and 3 tablespoons sugar until thick and light in color. Beat in the milk and cook, stirring, until the custard coats the back of a spoon (180°F.). Cool.

In a small saucepan, soften the gelatin in the remaining ½ cup water and dissolve over low heat. Stir into the berry purée. Stir in the custard and chill, stirring, until it is almost ready to set.

Beat 1 cup of cream to the soft-firm stage and fold into the blackberry custard mixture. Pour into the mold. Chill until set, about 4 hours. Unmold the Bavarian onto a platter and garnish with remaining cup of cream, whipped, and whole blackberries. Can be prepared 1 day before serving. YIELDS 6 SERVINGS.
▼▪■

Bavarois de Cassis
BLACK CURRANT BAVARIAN CREAM

¾ cup granulated sugar

½ cup plus 1 tablespoon milk

3 tablespoons gelatin, softened in ½ cup cold water

2 cups strained black currant purée

3 cups heavy cream

½ cup plus 2 tablespoons confectioners' sugar

Oil a 2-quart mold. In a saucepan, scald the granulated sugar and all the milk. Stir in the softened gelatin until dissolved. Stir in the black currant purée and cool until almost ready to set. Beat 2¼ cups cream and ½ cup confectioners' sugar until the mixture holds soft peaks. Fold into the currant mixture. Pour into the mold and chill until set. Unmold onto a platter. Whip remaining ¾ cup cream with 2 tablespoons of confectioners' sugar until stiff. Pipe designs around the dessert. Can be prepared the day before serving.
▼▪■ YIELDS 6 SERVINGS.

Ginger Bavarian Cream

2 tablespoons gelatin

½ cup cold water

1 cup Custard Sauce, heated (see page 273)

3 tablespoons minced preserved ginger
¼ cup syrup from preserved ginger
1 teaspoon vanilla
2 cups heavy cream, whipped
Whipped cream, sweetened and
    flavored with ginger syrup
Crystallized ginger, coarsely chopped

Oil a 5-cup mold. Soften the gelatin in the cold water and stir into the hot custard until dissolved. Stir in the minced ginger, syrup, and vanilla. Cool until almost set. Fold in the 2 cups heavy cream, whipped, and pour into the mold. Chill until set, about 4 hours. Unmold the Bavarian and garnish with the sweetened whipped cream and crystallized ginger. Can be prepared 1 day before serving; however, garnish no more than 2 hours before serving.
▼▼▼   YIELDS 6 SERVINGS.

Bavarois à l'Orange

ORANGE BAVARIAN CREAM

1 tablespoon gelatin
½ cup orange juice
1½ cups milk
1 (2-inch) piece vanilla bean
½ cup sugar
4 large egg yolks
Pinch of salt
1 tablespoon grated orange rind or
    1 teaspoon grated lemon rind
1½ cups heavy cream, whipped
Orange sections
Glacéed cherries

Oil a 6-cup mold. In a small bowl, soften the gelatin in the orange juice and set aside. Scald the milk and vanilla bean over low heat; remove from heat, cover, and let steep for 10 minutes.

In a saucepan, beat the sugar, egg yolks, and salt until thickened and light in color. Stir in the milk and cook over low heat until thickened and custard

coats the back of a spoon (180°F.). Stir in the gelatin, mix well, and strain into a bowl. Stir in the grated orange or lemon rind. Chill, stirring often, until mixture begins to thicken.

Fold 2 cups of whipped cream into the custard and pour into the mold. Chill until set, about 4 hours.

Unmold the Bavarian onto a platter, garnish with remaining whipped cream piped through a pastry bag, and decorate with the orange sections and cherries.
▼▼▼   YIELDS 6 SERVINGS.

Bavarois à l'Ananas

PINEAPPLE BAVARIAN CREAM

For an added flair, garnish this dessert with sweetened whipped cream and pineapple rings macerated in rum.

4 eggs, separated
¾ cup sugar
2 cups milk, scalded
2 envelopes gelatin, softened in ¼ cup
    cold water
1 cup heavy cream, whipped
2 cups crushed pineapple
1 cup rum

Oil an 8-cup mold. In a saucepan, beat the egg yolks and sugar until thick and light in color. Stir in the hot milk and place over low heat. Cook, stirring, until thickened enough to coat the back of a spoon (180°F.). Stir in the softened gelatin until it dissolves. Strain custard into a bowl and chill until almost syrupy.

Beat the egg whites until stiff and fold into the custard. Fold in the whipped cream. In a saucepan, bring the pineapple and rum to a boil and allow to cool. Fold the pineapple and rum into the almost-set custard and pour into the mold. Chill until set, about 4 hours.

Unmold to serve. Can be prepared 24 hours before serving.
▼▼▼   YIELDS 6 SERVINGS.

Ananas Georgette

PINEAPPLE BAVARIAN CREAM
GEORGETTE

1 large pineapple, cut into a container
    (see page 19)
½ cup rum
2 tablespoons gelatin
¼ cup cold water
4 eggs, separated
¾ cup sugar
2 cups milk, scalded
1 cup heavy cream, whipped

Cut the core from the center of the pineapple and crush the fruit. In a saucepan, bring the pineapple and rum to a boil and chill. In a small bowl, soften the gelatin in the cold water. In a 1½-quart saucepan, beat the egg yolks and sugar until thickened and light in color. Stir in the hot milk and cook over low heat, stirring constantly, until thick enough to coat the back of a spoon (180°F.). Stir in the gelatin until it is dissolved, strain into a bowl, and cool until almost set.

Beat the egg whites until stiff but not dry and fold into the egg yolks. Gently fold in the pineapple mixture and then the whipped cream. Pour as much as possible into the pineapple container and chill until set.

Pour remaining cream into 1 large mold or a number of individual molds and chill until set.

When ready to serve, arrange the pineapple on a platter with the frond on top. Arrange the large mold (cut into portions) or the individual molds around the pineapple. Serve the molds first and finally scoop the filling from the shell. Can be prepared 24 hours before serving.   YIELDS 6 TO 8 SERVINGS.

Mirabelle-Flavored Bavarian Cream

5 egg yolks
⅔ cup plus 1 tablespoon sugar
2 cups milk, scalded
Pinch of salt
1 tablespoon gelatin
¼ cup mirabelle or kirsch
1 cup heavy cream
Candied violets (optional)

In a saucepan, beat the egg yolks and ⅔ cup sugar until thickened and light in color. Stir in the milk and salt and cook over low heat until thick enough to coat the back of a spoon (180°F.). Soften the gelatin in the liqueur and stir into the custard until dissolved. Strain into a bowl and chill until almost ready to set. Beat the cream until soft-firm with the remaining tablespoon sugar and fold into the custard. Spoon into 6 to 8 dessert or wine glasses and let set. Garnish with the candied violets if desired. Can be prepared 1 day before serving.
         YIELDS 6 TO 8 SERVINGS.

Bavarois Praliné

PRALINE BAVARIAN CREAM

Serve this with a favorite fruit sauce such as raspberry or apricot, or a chocolate sauce flavored with kirsch or orange liqueur.

1½ cups Custard Sauce, heated (see
    page 273)
1 tablespoon gelatin, softened in
    2 tablespoons cold water
3 tablespoons kirsch
½ cup Praline Powder (see page 284)
1 cup heavy cream, whipped

Oil a 3-cup mold. Stir the gelatin into the heated Custard Sauce and strain into a bowl. Add the kirsch and Praline Powder. Chill until almost set. Fold in the whipped cream and pour into the mold. Chill until set, about 4 hours. Unmold and serve. Can be prepared 24 hours before serving.

✦✦ YIELDS 6 SERVINGS.

Bavarois Rubané aux Framboises

STRIPED BAVARIAN CREAM WITH RASPBERRIES

1¼ cups granulated sugar
2 tablespoons gelatin
4½ cups milk
9 egg yolks
1 teaspoon vanilla
20 ounces frozen raspberries, thawed, puréed, and strained
2 cups heavy cream, whipped
½ vanilla bean, split
1¼ cups confectioners' sugar
Whole fresh raspberries (optional)

In a saucepan, combine ¾ cup granulated sugar, gelatin, and 2½ cups milk and let stand 5 minutes. Over medium heat, stirring constantly, heat until the gelatin is dissolved. In a 2-quart saucepan, beat 5 of the egg yolks until light in color. Stir in the hot milk and cook, stirring, until thick enough to coat the back of a spoon (180°F.).

Divide the custard between 2 bowls. Stir the vanilla into one bowl and half of the raspberry purée into the second bowl. Cool until thick and syrupy. Fold half the whipped cream into one bowl and the rest into the other.

Pour a third of the raspberry custard into a 3-quart glass bowl and chill 10 minutes. Pour on one third of the vanilla cream and chill 10 more minutes. Add another third of raspberry custard and chill 10 minutes, then add another third of the vanilla cream and chill 10 minutes. Then add the final third of the raspberry custard and chill 10 minutes. Pour on the remaining vanilla cream and chill completely, at least 4 hours.

In a saucepan, combine the remaining 2 cups milk, ½ cup granulated sugar, and the vanilla bean and scald. In a 1-quart saucepan, beat the remaining 4 egg yolks until light and stir in the hot milk. Cook, stirring, until thick enough to coat the back of a spoon. Strain; discard vanilla bean. Chill, covered. Meanwhile, combine the remaining raspberry purée with the confectioners' sugar, then set aside.

Unmold custard onto a serving platter and garnish unmolded custard with the whole raspberries. Serve the raspberry and custard sauces separately. Can be prepared 24 hours before serving.

✦✦ YIELDS 8 TO 10 SERVINGS.

Crème Margot

STRAWBERRY BAVARIAN CREAM I

For the strawberry purée, process 1¼ cups of hulled berries in a processor or blender until smooth.

3 egg yolks
3 tablespoons sugar
1¼ cups milk, scalded
1 tablespoon gelatin
¼ cup cold water
¾ cup strawberry purée
1 cup heavy cream
1 egg white
Whole strawberries
Pistachio nuts

In a saucepan, beat the egg yolks and sugar until thickened and light in color. Stir in the scalded milk and cook, stirring, until the custard coats the back of a spoon (180°F.). Sprinkle the gelatin over the cold water and let soften. Stir into the hot custard until dissolved. Stir in the strawberry purée. Chill until almost set.

Whip ½ cup heavy cream until soft-firm and fold into the custard. Whip the egg white until it holds soft-firm peaks and fold into the strawberry mixture. Pour into a 4-cup glass bowl to set. Whip the remaining ½ cup heavy cream. Decorate the dessert with rosettes of cream and garnish with whole strawberries and pistachios. Can be prepared the day before.

▀▄▀   YIELDS 4 TO 6 SERVINGS.

Bavarois aux Fraises
STRAWBERRY BAVARIAN CREAM II

1 quart plus 1 cup strawberries
¾ cup confectioners' sugar
Juice of 1 lemon
1 to 2 drops red food coloring
   (optional)
1½ tablespoons gelatin
½ cup cold water
1 cup heavy cream, whipped
1 cup heavy cream, whipped (optional)

Oil a 6-cup mold. In a processor, purée 1 quart strawberries with the sugar and lemon juice. When the sugar has dissolved, stir in the red food coloring, if desired, to obtain a subtle deep pink. Soften the gelatin in the cold water in a small saucepan. Heat, stirring until dissolved. Stir into the strawberry purée. Chill until mixture becomes syrupy.

Fold in the whipped 1 cup heavy cream, pour into the mold, and chill until set, about 4 hours.

Unmold onto a serving dish and garnish with 1 cup whole strawberries. Decorate with additional whipped cream, if desired. Can be prepared a day ahead.   YIELDS 6 SERVINGS.
▀▄▀

Bavarois au Kirsch et Fraises
BAVARIAN CREAM WITH KIRSCH AND STRAWBERRIES

3 whole eggs, separated, plus 2 yolks
4 tablespoons sugar
1 tablespoon gelatin
¼ cup cold water
1½ cups milk, scalded
½ cup heavy cream
9 tablespoons kirsch
1 pint whole strawberries

Oil a 1-quart mold. In a 1-quart saucepan, beat the 5 egg yolks and sugar until they are thickened and light in color. Soften the gelatin in the cold water and add to the egg yolk mixture. Stir in the milk. Cook, stirring, until the mixture is thick enough to coat the back of a spoon (180°F.). Strain into a bowl and chill until almost set.

Beat the 3 egg whites until stiff and fold into the custard. Beat the heavy cream until soft-firm and fold into the custard. Fold in the kirsch. Pour into the mold and chill until set, about 4 hours.

Unmold onto a platter and garnish with the strawberries. Can be prepared 1 day before serving.
▀▄▀   YIELDS 4 TO 6 SERVINGS.

CHARLOTTES

CHARLOTTE is the name of two rather different desserts. The first, commonly known as *Charlotte Russe*, was probably originated by the great chef Antonin Carême (Carême was chef to Czar Alexander; the Prince Regent of England, later George IV; and Talleyrand). Carême, according to *Larousse Gastronomique*, originally called the dessert *Charlotte Parisienne*, and he prepared it as a take-out dessert for the great houses of Paris.

Charlotte Russe is usually made in a straight-sided mold, although, as the recipes indicate, not in every case. The mold is lined with ladyfingers, sponge cake slices, or slices of jellyroll, and filled with a Bavarian cream filling. The original filling was Vanilla Bavarian Cream; however, many versions have been created over the years, from the butter, cream, and almond filling of *Charlotte Malakoff* to the vanilla ice cream in *Charlotte Glacée à la Vanille*. When the filling has set, the charlotte is unmolded and often decorated with whipped cream and served with a suitable sauce.

The second type of charlotte is a fruit-filled dessert that was probably created long before the *Charlotte Russe*. It is a home-cooked dessert of the first order. A few basic ingredients, found in most kitchens and certainly in the kitchens of long ago, are combined to make a delicious, nourishing, and visually interesting dessert. Bread slices are dipped into melted butter and used to line a straight-sided mold. A thick fruit purée — apple is the most common — is piled into the center and covered with more sliced buttered bread. The charlotte is baked to a deep golden brown. After baking, the charlotte is allowed to rest not only to settle the fruit filling, but also to cool it. It is best served warm. If it were served directly from the oven, the fruit purée would be not only too hot to eat but also, because of the high internal temperature of the dish, potentially dangerous. This charlotte can be accompanied by a fruit sauce, ice cream, or whipped cream.

TO LINE A MOLD WITH LADYFINGERS

On page 280 I have provided a recipe for ladyfingers. They are easy and quick to prepare and are far superior to any you can buy. Ladyfingers can be frozen for several months or left out for a week before using in these desserts. They should be dry and crispy when used. If you do not wish, or do not have the time, to make your own ladyfingers, then go to a good bakery and buy good crisp ladyfingers. Avoid the spongy ladyfingers that are usually found in supermarkets.

Once the ladyfingers are in hand, you are ready to proceed. Lightly oil a charlotte mold, spring-form pan, or soufflé dish. Line the bottom with waxed paper, and then cut some of the ladyfingers into long, triangular sections to arrange neatly in the bottom of the mold. If desired, cut a 1-inch circle from a ladyfinger to place in the center. The ladyfingers should be placed rounded side out. Cut one end off the remaining ladyfingers. Then stand them around the edges of the pan, rounded side out and flat end down (see sketch). Once the filling has been put into the mold, you can trim the tops of the ladyfingers evenly.

Often ladyfingers are dipped into a liqueur or a flavored syrup. The moisture helps to hold the ladyfingers in place until you add the filling. However, do not let the ladyfingers sit in the liqueur, or they may disintegrate. An alternative and perhaps safer method is to

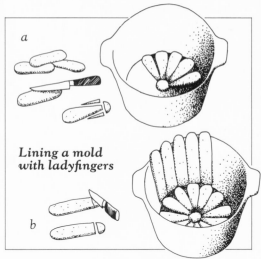

Lining a mold with ladyfingers

brush the ladyfingers with the liqueur while they are in place.

In some of the desserts given here, only the sides of the mold are lined with ladyfingers, not the bottom. Of course, when the charlotte is unmolded, the bottom becomes the top of the dessert, so do spend some time arranging the bottom attractively.

TO LINE A MOLD WITH SPONGE ROLLS

Lightly oil a charlotte mold, soufflé dish, or spring-form pan. Line the bot-

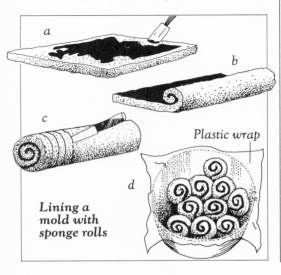

Plastic wrap

Lining a mold with sponge rolls

tom with a circle of waxed paper. Slice the sponge roll (see sketch) ¼- to ½-inch thick and arrange the slices, cut side down, around the bottom and sides of the mold. Sometimes the dessert is molded in a round bowl. For ease in unmolding, line the bowl with plastic wrap.

TO LINE A MOLD WITH BREAD SLICES

Lightly butter a charlotte mold or soufflé dish. Do not use a spring-form pan — the butter and juices from the filling will drain out during the baking. Cut the bread into ½-inch-thick, 2-inch-wide fingers. To establish how much bread is needed and the correct shapes, arrange the slices, overlapping them in the bottom of the mold in a fan shape. Arrange remaining slices around the sides of the mold, overlapping (see sketch). Remove all of the bread slices and dip in melted butter, then rearrange in mold. Be sure that the fruit purée is thick before putting it into the mold, or it may be too soft to unmold. After the

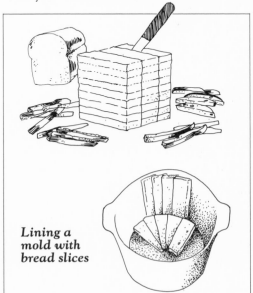

Lining a mold with bread slices

charlotte has baked, let it stand at least 30 minutes to allow it to settle and cool before unmolding.

Charlotte Nesselrode

CANDIED FRUIT CHARLOTTE

Nesselrode was a Russian statesman and foreign minister in the last century. A dessert with this name means candied fruits and chestnuts that have been macerated in rum or brandy.

> 1 teaspoon oil
> 32 to 36 ladyfingers (see page 280)
> 2 tablespoons gelatin
> ¼ cup cognac, kirsch, or rum
> 8 egg yolks
> 1 cup sugar
> 2 cups milk, scalded
> 2 cups Nesselrode (see following recipe)
> 1 cup heavy cream, whipped, plus additional for garnish

Lightly oil a 12-cup mold and line with ladyfingers (see page 118). Soften the gelatin in the liqueur. In a saucepan, beat the egg yolks and sugar until lemon-colored. Beat in the hot milk, stirring constantly. Cook, stirring, over low heat until the custard is thick enough to coat the back of a spoon (180°F.). Stir in the gelatin until dissolved. Strain into a bowl and chill until mixture is almost syrupy.

Fold in most of the Nesselrode and the 1 cup heavy cream. Pour into the mold lined with ladyfingers and chill until set. When ready to serve, dip the mold into hot water and unmold onto a serving platter. Garnish with additional whipped cream and Nesselrode mixture, if desired. Can be prepared 24 hours before serving.

YIELDS 10 TO 12 SERVINGS.

Nesselrode

This liqueur-flavored candied fruit and chestnut mix is used in certain pies and puddings as well as in the charlotte here.

> 1½ cups diced candied fruits
> 12 chestnuts in syrup, chopped
> ¼ cup dark rum or cognac

Combine the candied fruits, chestnuts, and rum in a bowl or glass jar. Let macerate at least 1 hour. Can be prepared ahead and stored in a sealed jar for up to 6 months.   YIELDS ABOUT 2 CUPS.
▼▼▼

Charlotte aux Abricots

APRICOT CHARLOTTE

> 4 cups pitted fresh apricots
> 2 cups sugar
> 1 cup water
> 3 tablespoons light Karo syrup
> Juice of 1 lemon
> 2 tablespoons gelatin, softened in ¼ cup cold water
> 2 tablespoons kirsch
> 1 cup heavy cream, whipped, plus extra for garnish
> 1 (9-inch) kirsch-flavored layer Génoise (see page 279)
> Apricot sections

Simmer the 4 cups apricots in the sugar, water, and Karo syrup for 15 minutes or until very soft. Purée the fruit in a blender; set juice aside. Stir the lemon juice and softened gelatin into the apricot purée and cool. Stir in the kirsch. When the purée is almost ready to set, fold in the whipped cream.

Cut the Génoise into 2 thin layers and line an oiled 9-inch spring-form pan with 1 layer. Add the apricot mixture, cover with the remaining Génoise, and chill for 6 hours. Serve garnished with whipped cream and apricot sections.
▼▼▼   YIELDS 8 SERVINGS.

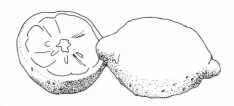

Lemon-Blueberry Charlotte

½ cup plus 1 tablespoon water
1¼ cups plus 1½ tablespoons sugar
¾ cup plus 2 tablespoons lemon juice
32 to 36 ladyfingers (see page 280)
1 tablespoon gelatin
4 eggs, separated
1 teaspoon grated lemon rind
Pinch of cream of tartar
1 cup heavy cream, whipped
4 cups blueberries
1 tablespoon cornstarch
1 tablespoon mirabelle liqueur

Lightly oil a 9-inch charlotte mold or spring-form pan. Heat 3 tablespoons of water and the 1½ tablespoons sugar until dissolved. Stir in the 2 tablespoons lemon juice. Line bottom and sides of a mold with ladyfingers. Brush with lemon mixture and set aside.

In a small pan, soften the gelatin in 2 tablespoons water. Beat the egg yolks into the gelatin with the remaining ¾ cup lemon juice and ½ cup sugar. Cook, stirring, over low heat until thickened. Strain into a bowl; stir in ½ teaspoon lemon rind. Chill until almost set.

Beat the egg whites and cream of tartar until soft peaks form, then beat in ¼ cup sugar and beat until stiff and glossy. Fold into the lemon mixture. Fold in the whipped cream and 2 cups blueberries. Fill the lined mold with the mixture and refrigerate until set, about 4 hours.

In a skillet, combine the remaining ½ cup sugar, cornstarch, ¼ cup water, and 2 cups more blueberries. Cook, stirring, over medium heat, until the mixture begins to boil and becomes clear. Stir in remaining ½ teaspoon lemon rind. Cool and stir in the mirabelle. Unmold the charlotte and serve, with the blueberry sauce passed separately. Can be prepared 1 day before serving.

YIELDS 10 TO 12 SERVINGS.

Lemon Charlotte

32 to 36 ladyfingers (see page 280)
¾ cup plus 1 tablespoon sugar
3 tablespoons kirsch
¼ cup plus 2 tablespoons cold water
1 tablespoon gelatin
1½ tablespoons grated lemon rind
⅔ cup strained lemon juice
4 egg whites
Pinch of salt
1 cup heavy cream, whipped

Lightly oil a 6-cup charlotte mold and line with waxed paper. Line the mold with ladyfingers. In a bowl, stir 1 tablespoon sugar, kirsch, and 2 tablespoons water together. Brush over the ladyfingers, reserving 1 to 2 tablespoons of syrup. In a small saucepan, soften the gelatin in ¼ cup cold water for 5 minutes, then heat over low heat until dissolved. Stir in remaining ¾ cup sugar and heat until the sugar is dissolved. Remove from the heat and stir in the grated lemon rind and strained juice. Pour into a bowl and chill until almost set. Beat the egg whites and salt until soft peaks form. Fold into the gelatin mixture. Fold in the whipped cream. Pour half into the mold, top with a layer of ladyfingers, and sprinkle with reserved syrup. Add remaining custard mixture and chill until set, about 4 hours. Unmold onto a platter and remove waxed paper. Can be prepared 1 day before serving.

YIELDS 6 TO 8 SERVINGS.

Peach Charlotte

1 pound peach halves poached in
   vanilla syrup (see page 286)
3 tablespoons sugar
1 tablespoon gelatin
6 tablespoons water
2 cups heavy cream, whipped
20 cats' tongues or ladyfingers,
   approximately (see pages 264
   and 280)

Lightly oil a 1¼-quart charlotte mold.
Reserve 1 peach half for garnishing. Purée the remainder and measure. Add
enough poaching syrup to make 2 cups.
Stir in the sugar. In a small saucepan,
soften the gelatin in the water, then dissolve over low heat. Stir into the peach
purée. Chill until almost ready to set.
Fold 1 cup cream, whipped, into the
mixture and pour into the mold. Chill
until set, about 4 hours.

When ready to serve, unmold the
charlotte. Beat the remaining 1 cup
cream until stiff. Spread over the cats'
tongues or ladyfingers to serve as "glue"
and arrange around the sides. Garnish
the top with rosettes of remaining
whipped cream and the peach half cut
into slices. Can be prepared 1 day before
serving.   YIELDS 6 SERVINGS.
▀▖▀

Charlotte à la Chambourienne

PEAR CHARLOTTE
WITH RASPBERRY SAUCE I

*A perfect summer dessert — light, refresh-
ing, and attractive.*

   30 ladyfingers, approximately (see
      page 280)
   2 vanilla-poached pears, sliced (see
      page 286)

2 tablespoons pear brandy
1½ teaspoons gelatin
¼ cup water
1 cup milk
1 vanilla bean
5 egg yolks
¾ cup sugar, plus more to taste
1½ cups heavy cream
5 ladyfingers, diced
1 pound fresh raspberries
Juice of ½ lemon

Oil a charlotte mold and line with
waxed paper. Cover bottom and sides of
charlotte mold with ladyfingers. Soak
poached pears in brandy. In a saucepan,
soften the gelatin in the water; dissolve
over low heat. In a saucepan, scald the
milk and vanilla bean; steep 10 minutes.
In a bowl, beat the egg yolks and ½ cup
sugar until thick and light in color. Add
the hot milk, stirring. Stir in the gelatin
and cook the mixture until thick
enough to coat the back of a spoon
(180°F.). Strain and cool until almost
ready to set.

Fold in the brandied pears. Whip the
cream with ¼ cup sugar and fold into
the custard. Fold diced ladyfingers into
the mixture. Pour into the lined mold
and chill until set, about 4 hours.

In a processor, purée the raspberries,
adding sugar to taste and lemon juice.
Chill. Unmold the charlotte and serve
with the raspberry sauce. Can be prepared 1 day before serving.
▀▖▀   YIELDS 6 TO 8 SERVINGS.

Charlotte aux Poires avec Coulis de Framboise

PEAR CHARLOTTE
WITH RASPBERRY SAUCE II

*The Poire William called for in this recipe
is a pear brandy. It is clear and potent.
Although expensive, it is worth the cost.*

Confectioners' sugar
1 (10-inch) Nutted Génoise layer (see page 279)
5 vanilla-poached pears (see page 286 and Note below)
¼ cup plus 2 tablespoons Poire William liqueur
4 egg yolks
⅔ cup granulated sugar
1 cup milk, scalded
1½ teaspoons gelatin
2 egg whites
1 cup heavy cream
Raspberry Sauce (see page 276)

Butter a 10-inch spring-form pan and sprinkle the bottom with confectioners' sugar. Place the cake layer in the pan and brush with 2 tablespoons of poaching liquid mixed with 2 tablespoons of Poire William. Set aside. In a saucepan, beat the egg yolks and granulated sugar until thick and light-colored. Stir in the milk and cook over low heat until thick enough to coat the back of a spoon (180°F.). In a bowl, sprinkle the gelatin over ½ cup cool poaching liquid to soften. Stir into the hot custard. Let cool until almost set.

Drain the pears and reserve the liquid. Cook the liquid until reduced to 2 cups. In an electric mixer, beat the egg whites to the soft-peak stage. Slowly pour in ⅔ cup of poaching liquid in a steady stream, beating constantly until the egg whites form stiff peaks. Fold into the custard. Whip the heavy cream, flavor with the remaining ¼ cup Poire William, and beat to the soft-peak stage. Fold into the custard. Spread half of the cream over the cake. Cut the pears into small dice and sprinkle over the custard. Cover with remaining custard and chill until set, about 4 hours. Remove the sides of the pan and put the dessert on a platter. Serve with the Raspberry Sauce passed separately. Can be prepared 1 day before serving.   YIELDS 12 SERVINGS.

Note: Use 3 cups of water and 1¼ cups of sugar for the poaching liquid. This will produce the proper density of sugary syrup to beat into the egg whites.
▾▾▾

Charlotte de Potiron
PUMPKIN CHARLOTTE

For nontraditionalists, this could replace pumpkin pie for the holidays.

18 to 24 ladyfingers (see page 280)
⅔ cup plus 1 tablespoon granulated sugar
¼ cup plus 2 tablespoons water
3 tablespoons plus 4½ teaspoons dark rum
½ cup gingersnap crumbs
½ cup firmly packed brown sugar
4 eggs, separated
2 tablespoons gelatin
1 cup milk, scalded
1 can (1 pound) pumpkin purée
2 teaspoons grated orange peel
¼ teaspoon plus a pinch of cinnamon
¼ teaspoon plus a pinch of allspice
¼ teaspoon plus a pinch of nutmeg
1½ cups heavy cream
¼ cup blanched slivered almonds
1 tablespoon confectioners' sugar

Lightly oil a 9-inch spring-form pan and line with ladyfingers. In a saucepan, simmer ⅓ cup granulated sugar and the water until the sugar is dissolved; remove from heat and stir in 3 tablespoons rum. Brush the ladyfingers with the rum syrup, and sprinkle generously with the gingersnap crumbs. In a 1-quart saucepan, beat the brown sugar and egg yolks until thick enough to form a ribbon. Stir in the gelatin and let stand 5 minutes. Stir in the scalded milk and cook, stirring, over low heat until thick enough to coat the back of a spoon

(180°F.). Remove from heat and stir in the pumpkin, orange peel, ¼ teaspoon cinnamon, ¼ teaspoon allspice, and ¼ teaspoon of nutmeg. Mix well. Cool until almost ready to set.

Whip 1 cup cream with ⅓ cup granulated sugar to the soft-firm stage. Fold into the custard. Whip the egg whites until stiff and fold into the pumpkin mixture. Pour into the prepared mold and chill until set, about 4 hours.

In a skillet, mix the almonds and remaining 1 tablespoon granulated sugar with pinches of allspice, nutmeg, and cinnamon. Cook until the sugar melts and coats the almonds, turning occasionally. Turn onto a buttered pie plate and let cool. When ready to serve, unmold the charlotte. Beat the remaining ½ cup cream until stiff with 4½ teaspoons rum and the confectioners' sugar. Pipe onto the charlotte and garnish with the sugar-coated almonds. Can be prepared 1 day before serving.

▚▚▚ YIELDS 10 TO 12 SERVINGS.

Charlotte Malakoff aux Framboises

RASPBERRY MALAKOFF

Named for a French victory in the Crimean War. Use the filling in cream puffs, or serve large dollops with fresh fruit or berries.

12 to 14 ladyfingers (see page 280)
3 tablespoons framboise
½ cup unsalted butter
⅔ cup plus 2 teaspoons sugar
1 cup blanched almonds, powdered
1 cup heavy cream
1 pint raspberries, plus extra berries
   for garnish
½ teaspoon vanilla
Melba Sauce (see page 276)

Lightly butter a 5-cup charlotte mold and line the bottom with waxed paper. Line the sides of the mold with ladyfingers, trimming them to fit tightly. Sprinkle with 1 tablespoon framboise. In a processor, cream the butter and ⅔ cup sugar until very soft and light. Add the almonds and 1 tablespoon framboise and process until well mixed. Beat ½ cup cream to the soft-peak stage and fold it into the almond mixture. *Do not do this in the processor.* Gently fold the raspberries into the mixture. Pour into the mold and top with ladyfingers, then sprinkle with remaining tablespoon framboise. Cut ends of ladyfingers even with the top of the filling. Cover with plastic wrap, and set a saucer and a 1-pound weight on top. Chill at least 12 hours.

When ready to serve, beat the remaining ½ cup cream with the remaining 2 teaspoons sugar and the vanilla. Unmold the dessert and pipe the cream around the base and the top of the charlotte; garnish with whole raspberries. Serve the Melba Sauce separately. Can be prepared 2 days before serving.

▚▚▚ YIELDS 6 TO 8 SERVINGS.

Charlotte Russe

RASPBERRY AND PINEAPPLE CHARLOTTE

Although this charlotte version calls for the cake to be rolled, it can also be spread with the jam, stacked into sandwiches, and cut into long strips, with the strips then placed cut side down in a 1½-quart bowl. The dessert will appear striped when unmolded.

2 (10- by 15-inch) Sponge Cake layers,
   rolled (see page 278)
1 pound seedless raspberry jam
½ cup cognac or kirsch
8 egg yolks

¾ cup sugar
2 cups milk, scalded
2 tablespoons gelatin
1½ cups heavy cream
Pinch of salt
2 teaspoons vanilla
1½ cups pineapple, poached for 1
  minute (see Note)
Apricot Glaze (see page 283)
Raspberry Sauce (see page 276)

Unroll the sponge rolls and set aside. Beat the jam and ¼ cup cognac or kirsch together until well mixed; brush over the sponge roll. Roll tightly (if the jam is not smooth, heat it with the liqueur so that it can be spread easily). Line a 1½-quart round bowl with plastic wrap. Cut the jellyroll into ¼-inch-thick slices and line the bowl with the cut side down (see sketch on page 119). Press the slices as close together as possible. Set aside.

In a saucepan, beat the egg yolks and sugar until thick and light in color. Stir in the scalded milk and cook, stirring, over low heat until thick enough to coat the back of a spoon. Strain. Soften the gelatin in ½ cup heavy cream and stir into the egg yolk cream with a pinch of salt. Stir in the vanilla and cool until almost set. Whip the remaining 1 cup cream until thickened, beat in the remaining ¼ cup liqueur, and beat to the soft-peak stage and fold into the custard mixture. Pour the cream into the cake-lined bowl and set aside. Cool the poached pineapple, drain well, and pour over the cream, pressing gently into the cream. Chill until set, about 4 hours.

Turn out onto a serving platter and remove the plastic wrap. Melt the Apricot Glaze and brush over the charlotte. Serve garnished with any additional pineapple and pass the Raspberry Sauce separately. Can be prepared 1 day before serving. YIELDS 12 SERVINGS.

Note: It is necessary to poach the pineapple; otherwise, it will prevent the gelatin in the cream from setting.

❖❖❖

Rhubarb Charlotte

The langues de chat, or cats' tongues, called for in this recipe are crisp cookies shaped like a cat's tongue. They would become soggy if used to line the mold; therefore, put them on shortly before serving. If preferred, you can line the mold with ladyfingers or sponge slices.

¼ cup currant jelly
1 pound rhubarb, cut in 1-inch pieces
1 tablespoon gelatin
¼ cup water
2 egg whites
¼ cup sugar
1¼ cups heavy cream
12 to 16 Cats' Tongues (see page 264)

Preheat oven to 350°F. Lightly oil a 5- or 6-cup charlotte mold and line the bottom with waxed paper. In a casserole, spread 2 tablespoons of jelly over the bottom and sides. Add the rhubarb and cover with the remaining jelly, cover dish, and bake for 30 minutes or until tender. Purée in a processor and cool. In a small pan, soften the gelatin in the water and dissolve over low heat. Stir into the rhubarb. Cool until almost set. Beat the egg whites until frothy and beat in the sugar until the mixture holds stiff peaks. Fold into the rhubarb mixture. Beat 1 cup cream to the soft-peak stage and fold into the rhubarb. Pour into the mold and chill until set, about 4 hours.

Unmold onto a platter. Whip the remaining ¼ cup cream and spread around the sides of the charlotte. "Glue" the cats' tongues to the sides of the dessert with the cream. Garnish the dessert with any remaining whipped cream. Can be prepared 1 day before serving. YIELDS 6 SERVINGS.

❖❖❖

Individual Strawberry Charlottes

1 (10- by 15-inch) Sponge Cake sheet
    (see page 278)
⅔ cup milk
2 teaspoons grated orange peel
1 whole egg, separated, plus 1 white
2 tablespoons sugar
1 teaspoon gelatin, softened in 2
    tablespoons water
1 pint strawberries, mashed
1 cup heavy cream, whipped, plus
    extra for garnish
2 tablespoons Cointreau
Red food coloring (optional)
Raspberry Cream (see following
    recipe)
12 whole strawberries

Butter twelve ½-inch dariole molds or custard cups (see Note). Cut the Sponge Cake into 2-inch strips. Cut each strip in half horizontally. Cut 12 circles from the strips and fit into the bottom of the molds. Cut 6-inch-long strips to fit around the insides of the molds.

In a small saucepan, scald the milk and orange peel, stirring occasionally. Beat the egg yolk with 1 tablespoon sugar and stir in the hot milk and orange peel. Stir in the softened gelatin and mix well. Chill until almost set.

Fold into the mashed strawberries in a bowl, then fold in the whipped cream flavored with the Cointreau. If desired, add enough red food coloring to make it a rich pink color. Beat the egg whites until stiff with the remaining tablespoon sugar and fold into the strawberry mixture. Fill each mold with about ⅓ cup of the strawberry mixture and chill until firm, about 4 hours.

Unmold onto a platter or individual plates. Spread with the Raspberry Cream and top with a rosette of whipped cream and a strawberry. Can be prepared 1 day before serving.
YIELDS 12 SERVINGS.

Note: Dariole molds, also called timbales or baba molds, are round, flat-bottomed cups. The cake must be no more than ¼-inch thick. Slice each piece horizontally if needed.

Raspberry Cream

1¼ cups heavy cream
¼ teaspoon vanilla
10 ounces frozen raspberries, thawed,
    drained, puréed, and strained
2 tablespoons confectioners' sugar
1 tablespoon framboise

In a bowl, beat the cream and vanilla until stiff. Fold in the raspberry purée, confectioners' sugar, and framboise. Refrigerate until needed, up to 6 hours before using. YIELDS ABOUT 2½ CUPS.
❖❖❖

Charlotte Malakoff aux Fraises

STRAWBERRY CHARLOTTE MALAKOFF

24 ladyfingers (see page 280)
⅓ cup plus ½ cup orange liqueur
⅔ cup water
½ pound unsalted butter, softened
1 cup sugar
¼ teaspoon almond extract
1⅓ cups finely ground almonds
3 cups heavy cream, whipped
1 quart strawberries

Line the bottom of a charlotte mold with waxed paper. Line the bottom and sides of the mold with ladyfingers, reserving extras. In a bowl, mix ⅓ cup orange liqueur and the water together and brush over the ladyfingers. In a processor, cream the butter and sugar until pale and fluffy. Beat in the remaining ½ cup orange liqueur and the almond extract. Beat until the sugar is dissolved. Beat in the almonds until well mixed, and remove to a bowl. Fold in the 2 cups of heavy cream, whipped. Turn a third of the mixture into the mold and cover with a layer of ladyfingers, dipped in the orange liqueur. Add another layer of the almond-egg cream, then another layer of ladyfingers, and cover with remaining almond-egg cream. Cover top with any remaining ladyfingers and cut off the ends of any ladyfingers that stick up above the filling. Cover with plastic wrap and set a saucer on top. Place a weight on the saucer and chill for at least 6 hours.

To serve, remove the waxed paper, run a knife around the edges, and unmold onto a platter. Peel the waxed paper from the top. Decorate with remaining whipped cream and strawberries. Can be prepared 2 days before serving.

❖❖❖ YIELDS 6 TO 8 SERVINGS.

Charlotte aux Fraises
STRAWBERRY CHARLOTTE

- 3 pints strawberries, halved
- ¾ cup sugar, plus more for sweetening cream
- 2½ tablespoons kirsch
- 24 ladyfingers, approximately (see page 280)
- ½ cup maraschino liqueur
- ½ cup water
- 1½ cups heavy cream, whipped, plus more for garnish
- Vanilla to taste

In a bowl, macerate the strawberries with 6 tablespoons sugar and the kirsch. Line the bottom and sides of a 2-quart charlotte mold with ladyfingers. Brush the ladyfingers with a mixture of the maraschino liqueur and the water. Place a layer of strawberries over the bottom of the mold, cover with a layer of whipped cream sweetened with remaining sugar and flavored with vanilla to taste, then cover with a layer of moistened ladyfingers. Continue filling the

mold, finishing up with the ladyfingers. Chill at least 6 hours.

Unmold and serve with additional sweetened whipped cream. Can be prepared 24 hours before serving.

❖❖❖ YIELDS 6 SERVINGS.

Chippolata
TANGERINE AND GINGER CHARLOTTE

A South African dessert based on the traditional charlotte, Chippolata is made with a tangerine liqueur called Van der Hum.

- 1 tablespoon vegetable oil
- 24 ladyfingers (see page 280)
- ½ cup tangerine liqueur
- 1 tablespoon gelatin
- ¼ cup cold water
- 2 cups milk
- 1 tablespoon grated tangerine peel
- 2 whole eggs, separated, plus 2 yolks
- ⅓ cup granulated sugar
- 8 tablespoons minced preserved ginger
- 2 tablespoons confectioners' sugar
- 1 cup heavy cream

Lightly oil a 1½-quart charlotte mold with 2 teaspoons vegetable oil. Line the bottom with waxed paper and spread with 1 teaspoon oil. Line the mold with the ladyfingers and brush with the liqueur. Soften the gelatin in the cold water and set aside. Scald the milk and tangerine peel in a saucepan. In another saucepan, beat the 4 egg yolks and granulated sugar until thick and light in color. Stir in the milk with the softened gelatin. Cook over low heat until thick enough to coat the back of a spoon (180°F.). Strain into a bowl and cool until almost set. Beat the 2 egg whites until stiff and fold into the custard mixture with 4 tablespoons minced preserved ginger. Pour into the lined mold and chill until set, about 4 hours.

Unmold onto a platter and sprinkle

with the confectioners' sugar. Beat the cream until stiff and pipe around the dessert, then garnish with the remaining 4 tablespoons preserved ginger. Can be prepared 1 day before serving.

❖❖❖   YIELDS 6 SERVINGS.

Charlotte Makrauer

MANDARIN ORANGE AND GINGER CHARLOTTE

I created this dessert for Suzie Makrauer, using her favorite flavors.

- 1 (11- by 16-inch) Sponge Cake sheet (see page 278)
- 1½ cups Apricot Glaze (see page 283), thinned with Cointreau
- ¼ cup Cointreau
- ½ cup water
- 1 recipe Vanilla Bavarian Cream (see page 111)
- ½ cup chopped mandarin orange segments
- ½ cup finely diced preserved ginger
- 1½ cups heavy cream, whipped, sweetened, and flavored to taste with Cointreau
- 1 cup mandarin orange segments
- Slices of preserved ginger
- 2 cups chocolate sauce

Place a circle of waxed paper in the bottom of a 2-quart charlotte mold, soufflé dish, or other straight-sided mold. Spread the sponge sheet with the thinned Apricot Glaze and roll tightly into a long jellyroll. Slice into ¼-inch-thick slices. Arrange the slices in the bottom and against the sides of the mold (see sketch on page 119). Brush with ¼ cup Cointreau mixed with the water. Make the Bavarian. When just about to set, fold in the chopped mandarin segments and the diced ginger. Pour into the mold and chill until set, about 4 hours.

Unmold onto a serving plate. With a pastry bag fitted with a no. 5A star tip, pipe the whipped cream around the charlotte. Garnish with the whole mandarin orange segments and the preserved ginger slices. Serve with chocolate sauce passed separately. Can be prepared 1 day before serving.

❖❖❖   YIELDS 6 TO 8 SERVINGS.

Charlotte with Tangerines

- 36 ladyfingers (see page 280)
- ¼ cup plus 3 tablespoons tangerine liqueur
- 6 ounces semisweet chocolate, melted
- 1½ tablespoons gelatin
- ¾ cup orange juice
- 5 egg yolks
- ¾ cup granulated sugar
- 3¼ cups heavy cream
- 1 teaspoon vanilla
- 1 teaspoon butter
- 6 tangerines, peeled, sectioned, and seeded
- 2 tablespoons confectioners' sugar

Brush the ladyfingers with 2 tablespoons of the liqueur. Then arrange most in a spring-form pan and brush with melted chocolate. Spread remaining ladyfingers with chocolate and arrange on a baking sheet; chill until set. In a small bowl, soften the gelatin in the orange juice. In a saucepan, beat the egg yolks and granulated sugar until thick and light in color. Scald ¾ cup heavy cream and whisk into the egg mixture with the gelatin. Cook, stirring, until thick enough to coat the back of a spoon (180°F.). Strain; stir in ¼ cup tangerine liqueur, vanilla, and butter. Chill until almost set.

Beat 1½ cups heavy cream until it reaches the soft-peak stage, then fold into the custard. Spoon a ½-inch-thick layer of the tangerine-egg cream into the lined mold and cover with a layer of chocolate-coated ladyfingers, then spoon in a third of the remaining cream mixture and top with half the tangerine sections. Repeat once, and top with remaining filling. Refrigerate until set.

Beat remaining 1 cup heavy cream with confectioners' sugar and the remaining 1 tablespoon liqueur until stiff. Unmold the charlotte and spread three-quarters of the cream on top. Pipe remainder around the base. Can be prepared 1 day before serving.

YIELDS 6 SERVINGS.

Charlotte Comtoise

APPLE CHARLOTTE COMTOISE

It is necessary to cool this dessert at least 30 minutes so the apple mixture sets. If you unmold it and it collapses, serve it on individual plates. It will still taste as good.

- ½ cup plus 1 tablespoon sugar, plus additional for sprinkling
- 1 pound loaf bread, crusts removed, thickly sliced
- ¼ pound butter, melted
- 6 apples, peeled and cored (preferably Cortlands or Golden Delicious)
- ½ teaspoon cinnamon
- 6 tablespoons dry white wine
- 2 tablespoons sherry
- 1 cup heavy cream, whipped, sweetened, and flavored

Preheat oven to 375°F. Butter a 1-quart charlotte mold or soufflé dish. Sprinkle with 1 tablespoon sugar. Cut the trimmed bread into fingers about 2 inches wide. Dip the bread into the melted butter and roll in the remaining sugar. Use to line the bottom and sides of the mold (see sketch on page 119). Thinly slice the apples and arrange in layers in the soufflé dish, sprinkling each layer with a little sugar and cinna-mon. The apples should mound on the top. Sprinkle with the white wine and sherry. Bake until the apples are translucent and completely softened, about 1 hour. They should look rather dry.

Let rest out of the oven for 30 minutes, then unmold and serve warm or at room temperature. Serve garnished with the whipped cream. Can be baked 2 days before serving. Let warm to at least room temperature before serving or reheat in a 350° oven.

YIELDS 6 SERVINGS.

Note: The apples must cook up dry. If they are too juicy, you will have trouble unmolding.

Charlotte aux Pommes

APPLE CHARLOTTE
See photograph on page 70.

Be sure to use a dry cooking apple, such as a Cortland or Golden Delicious, for this dessert.

- 6 pounds apples, peeled, quartered, and cored
- ½ cup apricot preserves
- 1 cup plus 2 tablespoons sugar
- 2 teaspoons vanilla
- ¼ cup plus 3 tablespoons dark rum
- 3 tablespoons butter
- 1 cup butter, melted
- 1 loaf (1 pound) bread, crusts removed, thickly sliced
- ½ cup sieved apricot preserves
- 1 cup heavy cream, whipped, sweetened, and flavored with rum to taste

Preheat oven to 425°F. Slice apples roughly and put into a heavy saucepan. Cover and cook over low heat, stirring occasionally, for 20 minutes. Uncover and beat in the ½ cup apricot preserves,

1 cup sugar, vanilla, ¼ cup rum, and 3 tablespoons butter. Raise heat and boil, stirring often, for 10 minutes or until the mixture holds a solid mass in a spoon. Line a charlotte mold with the bread slices dipped into the melted butter (see sketch on page 119). Pack the apples into the mold and let dome in the center. Top with remaining bread slices dipped in butter. Set the mold on a baking sheet and bake for 30 minutes or until the bread is golden and apples are tender. Remove and allow to rest for 30 minutes before unmolding.

Serve hot, warm, or cool, but preferably not refrigerated. Make a glaze by combining the ½ cup sieved apricot preserves, 3 tablespoons rum, and 2 tablespoons sugar in a saucepan and heating until thickened slightly. Spread over the top of the charlotte. Serve the whipped cream separately. Can be baked 2 days before serving.   YIELDS 6 SERVINGS.

Note: The dessert can also be served with a sauce composed of ½ cup raspberry jam, ¼ cup rum, and 2 tablespoons sugar. Heat to the boiling point and serve warm.

▀▀▀

Charlotte à l'Indienne

BANANA CHARLOTTE

> **1 loaf (1 pound) bread, crusts**
>   **removed, thickly sliced**
> **1 cup butter, melted**
> **6 bananas, sliced**
> **2 tablespoons butter**
> **1 tablespoon sugar**
> **1 tablespoon raisins**
> **½ cup Apricot Sauce (see page 274)**
> **1 tablespoon kirsch**

Preheat oven to 400°F. Trim the bread crusts and cut bread to fit the mold (see sketch on page 119). Dip the bread into the melted butter and line a charlotte mold. In a saucepan, cook the bananas with the 2 tablespoons butter until thoroughly warmed. Stir in the sugar and raisins. Fill the charlotte mold with the banana mixture. Bake for 1 hour.

In a saucepan, combine the Apricot Sauce with the kirsch. Unmold the dessert onto a platter and pour on the Apricot Sauce. Serve hot, warm, or cool. Can be prepared 1 day before serving. Reheat in 350° oven before serving.

▀▀▀   YIELDS 6 SERVINGS.

Charlotte aux Poires

HOT PEAR CHARLOTTE

> **1 loaf (1 pound) bread, crusts**
>   **removed, thickly sliced**
> **1 cup butter, melted**
> **12 to 14 pears, quartered and cored**
> **1 ½ cups boiling water**
> **Sugar to taste**
> **1 teaspoon vanilla**
> **Whipped cream (optional)**

Preheat oven to 400°F. Dip the bread slices into the melted butter and line a charlotte mold with the slices overlapping (see sketch on page 119). In a saucepan, cook the pears in the boiling water until soft, then put through a food mill. Add an equal amount of sugar and the vanilla. Return the mixture to the saucepan and simmer, stirring often, until very thick. Pour into the lined mold and bake 30 to 35 minutes or until the mixture is solid enough to hold its shape and bread is golden.

Cool for 30 minutes, then unmold carefully, and serve warm or cold with whipped cream if desired. Can be prepared 1 day before serving.

▀▀▀   YIELDS 6 SERVINGS.

MOUSSES

MOUSSES are served hot or cold as first courses, main courses, or desserts. Obviously, dessert mousses are of immediate interest to us. They consist of a purée, in this instance, of fruit, that is lightened with heavy cream and possibly egg whites. Mousses are served in large bowls, individual serving bowls, large wine glasses, or in a soufflé dish. When served in a soufflé dish, the dish is customarily wrapped with a collar and the mixture is made with gelatin to give it firmness. After the dessert sets, the collar is removed.

The basic preparation of mousses is similar to that of Bavarian creams. Often they can be interchanged. If the recipe has gelatin, it will probably work as a Bavarian cream, charlotte, mousse, or cold soufflé. The title depends on the presentation. Mousses made without gelatin are more delicate and must be served in individual bowls, or in one large bowl, but will not hold their shape for soufflés, charlottes, or Bavarians. Garnish mousses with a dollop of whipped cream or, in a large bowl, decorate the whole surface with whipped cream and garnish further with fruits or chocolate cutouts.

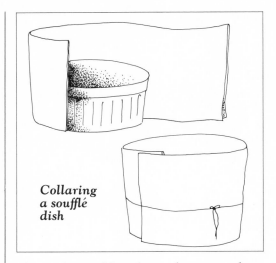

Collaring a soufflé dish

TO COLLAR A SOUFFLÉ DISH
Lightly oil the inside of a soufflé dish or other straight-sided mold; cut a strip of aluminum foil long enough to encircle the mold and overlap by two inches. Fold the foil in half lengthwise and lightly oil one side. Wrap the foil around the outside of the dish, oiled side in, and extending above the rim of the mold. Secure by crimping, using a paper clip, or tying a string around the dish (see sketch).

Add the soufflé mixture to the dish. The mixture should be at least one inch above the mold and may be as much as twice the height of the dish. Chill until set. Then carefully peel the foil from around the soufflé. If desired, you can press cake crumbs or finely minced nuts into the side of the soufflé to make it look baked. Garnish the top with fruit or whipped cream.

PASTRY SOUFFLÉ DISH
Line a soufflé dish or other straight-sided mold with foil, leaving a two-inch overhang. Press the foil securely into all the corners of the dish to make it as smooth as possible. Oil the foil lightly, and preheat the oven to 400°F. Roll the sweet pastry dough (see page 213) between sheets of waxed paper to ½-inch thickness. Peel off the waxed paper and line the dish with the pastry. If the pastry should split, simply press a piece of dough into the split, dampening the dough scrap with cold water to make it adhere, if necessary. If you are lining a large dish, roll the dough in two sections: line half of the dish with one section and the other half with the remaining pastry, overlapping slightly and pressing to seal. Use scraps to fill any holes. Trim the top edges evenly. Try to keep the sides at least ¼-inch thick. Line

the inside of the pastry with foil and fill the shell with dried beans or rice.

Bake for 20 minutes. Check to see if the pastry has set and is starting to brown by pulling the inner foil gently away from the side. If the side stands, remove the beans and inside foil, but if it starts to give, pat it gently back into place and bake another five minutes. Remove the foil and beans and bake until golden.

Using the overlapping edges of the outer foil liner, carefully remove the pastry from the soufflé dish and peel off the foil. Re-line the mold with the foil and replace the pastry shell. Wrap a collar around the outside of the mold and fill the shell with the soufflé mixture. Chill until set. When ready to serve, carefully remove the foil collar and, with the help of the foil liner, carefully lift the soufflé onto a platter. Gently peel the foil from the sides and slide out from under the pastry shell. Serve some of the shell with each serving of soufflé. This is the ultimate chiffon pie.

The shell can be baked a day or two before using and put in an airtight container until ready to fill. It can be frozen for up to two months. Do not fill the shell more than six hours before serving lest it soften from the moisture of the filling.

CHOCOLATE SOUFFLÉ SHELL

Line a soufflé dish or other straight-sided mold with foil, pressing it firmly into all corners and leaving a two-inch overhang. Press as smoothly as possible against the sides of the dish. Put mold into the freezer. In a double boiler over low heat, melt one pound of semisweet chocolate. When smooth and liquid, remove the chocolate from the heat. With a pastry brush, brush a layer of chocolate onto the chilled dish, concentrating especially on the sides. Chill the dish until the chocolate starts to set. Continue painting layers of chocolate onto the dish until it is ¼-inch thick. Chill until completely set. Carefully remove the chocolate shell from the mold and peel off the foil. Line the mold with foil and return the chocolate shell. Put a collar around the outside of the mold and fill with the mousse mixture. Chill until set. With the help of the foil, remove to a serving platter and carefully peel the foil from the chocolate. The mold can be prepared two or three days before using.

OTHER MOUSSE PRESENTATIONS

Mousse mixtures can also be served in hollowed fruits, such as hollowed orange or lemon shells, or atop hollowed poached peaches or pears.

Apple Mousse

1 tablespoon vegetable oil
3 pounds McIntosh apples, peeled, halved, and cored
½ cup sugar
2 tablespoons gelatin
4 tablespoons cold water
1½ tablespoons Calvados
3 large whole eggs, plus 1 white
Pinch of cream of tartar
Pinch of salt
¾ cup heavy cream, whipped
2 cups apricot preserves
1 apple, cored
1 tablespoon Calvados or rum

Brush inside of a 6-cup loaf pan with 1 teaspoon vegetable oil. Brush remaining 2 teaspoons oil on an 8- by 15-inch length of waxed paper and place, oiled side up, in loaf pan. Reserving 1 for garnish, place the apples in a 6-quart saucepan with the sugar and cook, covered, over low heat, stirring occasionally until tender, about 35 to 40 minutes. Remove the cover and simmer over moderate heat until the liquid evaporates, stirring occasionally. Purée and strain through a fine sieve. Measure 3½ cups of hot purée. In a small bowl, soften the gelatin in the cold water; add to the hot purée, stirring to dissolve. Stir in the 1½ tablespoons Calvados and cool to room temperature.

Stir in the 3 egg yolks; set aside. Beat the 4 egg whites with cream of tartar and salt until stiff but not dry. Fold into the apple purée. Fold in the whipped cream, then pour the mixture into the prepared pan. Chill until set, about 4 hours.

Unmold onto a serving platter and remove the waxed paper. Heat the apricot preserves in a saucepan, then strain. Cool slightly and brush the top of the mousse with 3 tablespoons preserves. Slice the remaining apple and arrange the slices on top. Stir the tablespoon Calvados or rum into the remaining preserves and pour over the apple slices, letting the preserves drizzle down the sides. Chill for 2 hours. Can be prepared 1 day before serving.

▼▼▼   YIELDS 10 TO 12 SERVINGS.

Mousse aux Pommes Calvados

APPLE MOUSSE WITH CALVADOS

   2 pounds apples, peeled, cored, and
      sliced
   Grated rind of 1 lemon
   2 tablespoons firmly packed brown
      sugar
   5 tablespoons apricot jam
   2 tablespoons butter
   3 whole eggs, plus 2 yolks
   3 tablespoons granulated sugar
   1 tablespoon gelatin
   Juice of 1 lemon
   4 tablespoons hot water

   2 tablespoons whipped cream
   ¼ cup Calvados
   2 oranges, peeled and cut into
      segments
   1 apple, peeled, cored, and thinly
      sliced

In a deep, heavy pan, cook the apples, lemon rind, brown sugar, and 2 tablespoons jam until mixture is a thick purée. Stir in the butter and rub through a sieve. Cool.

In a mixer, beat the eggs and egg yolks with the granulated sugar until thick and light in color. In a small saucepan, soften the gelatin in the lemon juice and dissolve in 1 tablespoon hot water, heating gently if required. Mix into the egg mixture, then fold in the apple purée, whipped cream, and Calvados. Pour into individual cups or a large bowl and chill until set, about 4 hours.

Place the orange slices on the mousse and top with the remaining apple slices. Simmer the remaining 3 tablespoons jam with 3 tablespoons water until melted and slightly thickened, about 2 minutes. Brush over the fruits. Can be prepared the day before serving.

▼▼▼   YIELDS 6 SERVINGS.

Apple Mousse Brittany-Style

   5 apples, peeled, cored, and sliced
   ¼ cup apricot preserves
   ½ teaspoon cinnamon
   ¼ teaspoon grated lemon rind
   Pinch of nutmeg
   4 egg yolks
   ¾ cup sugar
   1 teaspoon cornstarch
   1½ cups milk, scalded
   1 tablespoon gelatin
   1 tablespoon water
   1 teaspoon vanilla

1 cup heavy cream
Apricot Sauce (see page 274)

In a large saucepan, cook the apples, apricot preserves, cinnamon, lemon peel, and nutmeg over low heat until very soft, stirring often. In a saucepan, beat the egg yolks, sugar, and cornstarch until thick and light in color. Stir in the milk and cook, stirring, until thick enough to coat the back of a spoon (180°F.). Soften the gelatin in the water and stir into the hot custard with the vanilla until the gelatin dissolves. Chill until the mixture just begins to set.

Whip the cream and fold into the custard with the apple purée. Add more nutmeg and cinnamon if desired. Pour into a 6-cup mold and chill until set, about 4 hours.

Just before serving, unmold and surround with some of the Apricot Sauce. Serve remaining sauce separately. Can be prepared 1 day before serving.
◆◆◆   YIELDS 6 TO 8 SERVINGS.

Mousse de Pommes à la Bénédictine

APPLE MOUSSE WITH BÉNÉDICTINE

Of course you can use any favorite liqueur in place of the Bénédictine. For some unusual but delicious suggestions, try Pernod, kümmel, or Chartreuse.

½ cup granulated sugar
1 tablespoon water
2 pounds apples, peeled, cored, and
    sliced
1 cup confectioners' sugar
5 egg whites
3 tablespoons Bénédictine
2 cups heavy cream, whipped,
    sweetened, and flavored to taste

Preheat oven to 400°F. In a small saucepan, dissolve the granulated sugar in the water and bring to a boil, stirring. Cover and simmer 5 minutes. Remove the cover and boil until a rich golden brown. Pour into the bottom of a charlotte mold and coat evenly with the caramel (see page 101 for details). Simmer the apples in ⅓ cup confectioners' sugar in a covered saucepan, stirring often, until tender. Purée. If apples are very wet, cook over high heat, stirring often, until the mixture becomes a dry purée. Let cool while preparing the egg whites. Beat the egg whites with the remaining ⅔ cup confectioners' sugar until they hold stiff peaks. Fold into the apple purée with the Bénédictine and pour into the mold. Bake, covered with foil, in a water bath (see page 100) for 40 minutes. Cool in the mold and chill until set, about 4 hours.

Unmold and serve with the whipped cream on the side. Can be prepared 1 day before serving.
◆◆◆   YIELDS 4 TO 6 SERVINGS.

Banana Mousse I

1 tablespoon gelatin
1 cup orange juice
¼ cup boiling water
2 tablespoons lemon juice
4 medium bananas
¼ teaspoon salt
1 cup heavy cream
¾ cup confectioners' sugar

In a blender or a processor, soften the gelatin in the orange juice. With the machine running, add the boiling water, lemon juice, bananas, and salt; blend until smooth. Chill until mixture starts to set. Whip the heavy cream with the sugar and fold into the banana mixture. Pour into a serving bowl and chill until set, about 3 hours. Can be prepared 24 hours before serving.
◆◆◆   YIELDS 6 SERVINGS.

Mousse de Bananes

BANANA MOUSSE II

⅓ cup golden raisins
¼ cup dark rum
½ pound white chocolate, chopped
4 bananas, cut into ½-inch slices
2 tablespoons lemon juice
1 tablespoon gelatin
2 tablespoons water
¾ cup sweetened condensed milk
½ cup heavy cream

Macerate the raisins in the rum for 2 hours. Melt the chocolate in a double boiler over hot, not boiling, water. In a processor, purée the bananas and lemon juice. Turn into a bowl. In a small saucepan, soften the gelatin in the water and heat over low heat until dissolved. Stir into the banana mixture and add the milk, melted chocolate, macerated raisins, and rum. Beat the heavy cream until stiff and fold into the mousse. Turn into 8 to 10 ramekins or dessert dishes. Chill until set, about 2 hours. Can be prepared the day before serving.
■▪■   YIELDS 8 TO 10 SERVINGS.

Fresh Fig Mousse

¾ cup Pastry Cream (see page 282)
½ cup plus 2 tablespoons sugar
⅓ cup water
1 (1½-inch) piece vanilla bean, split
3 (2-inch) strips lemon peel
5 large, ripe, fresh figs, stemmed
1 tablespoon gelatin
2 tablespoons lemon juice
½ cup heavy cream, whipped
½ teaspoon vanilla extract
2 egg whites
Pinch of salt

Prepare the Pastry Cream and chill. In a saucepan, boil the sugar, water, vanilla bean, and lemon peel until the sugar is dissolved. Poach the figs in this mixture for 3 minutes and set aside. Soften the gelatin in the lemon juice. Remove 1 fig from the poaching liquid and reserve. Add the softened gelatin to the remaining figs and stir to dissolve. Purée in a processor and cool. Fold the Pastry Cream into the fig purée and refrigerate, covered, until almost set. Fold in the whipped cream and vanilla extract. Beat the egg whites with the salt until soft peaks form. Fold into the fig mixture. Pour into a glass bowl. Swirl the top of the mousse and chill until set, about 2 hours. Garnish with the reserved fig. Can be prepared 1 day before serving.   YIELDS 6 SERVINGS.
■▪■

Ginger Mousse

1 tablespoon gelatin
¼ cup cold water
2 cups evaporated milk, scalded
4 eggs, separated
½ cup sugar
Pinch of salt
½ cup rum
1 cup minced crystallized ginger

In a small bowl, soften the gelatin in the water. Stir into the hot milk. In a saucepan, beat the egg yolks and sugar until thick and light in color. Stir in the milk and cook over low heat until thick enough to coat the back of a spoon (180°F.). Cool until almost ready to set. Beat the egg whites with a pinch of salt to the soft-peak stage and fold into the custard mixture. Fold in the rum and ginger. Pour into dessert dishes. Can be prepared 1 day before serving.
■▪■   YIELDS 6 SERVINGS.

Coppette alle Nocciole

HAZELNUT MOUSSE

3 eggs, separated
1/3 cup sugar
1 tablespoon gelatin
2 tablespoons water
4 ounces hazelnuts, toasted and
    ground
3 tablespoons cognac
1 cup heavy cream

In a bowl, beat the egg yolks with the sugar until thickened and light in color. In a small saucepan, soften the gelatin in the water and dissolve over low heat. Fold into the egg yolks with the hazelnuts and cognac. Beat the egg whites to the soft-peak stage and fold into the nut mixture. Beat the cream to the soft-peak stage and fold into the nut mixture. Pour into individual cups or 1 large bowl and chill until set, about 1 hour for cups or 4 hours for bowl. Can be prepared 1 day ahead.   YIELDS 6 SERVINGS.

Note: This is particularly good if served with a raspberry or strawberry sauce. (See the Sauces chapter.)

Mousse de Kiwi

KIWI MOUSSE

3 eggs
3/4 cup sugar
6 tablespoons Cointreau
2 cups heavy cream
3 drops vanilla
3 kiwifruit, peeled and minced
1 kiwifruit, peeled and sliced

In a double boiler, beat the eggs, 1/2 cup sugar, and 4 tablespoons Cointreau over hot, not boiling, water until thickened to the consistency of mayonnaise. Remove from the heat and whisk until cooled. Beat the cream to a soft-peak stage. Beat in the remaining 1/4 cup sugar and the vanilla, and continue beating until stiff. Fold in the minced kiwifruit and remaining 2 tablespoons Cointreau. Fold into the egg mixture and pour into sherbet glasses. Chill until ready to serve, at least 30 minutes.

Garnish with the kiwi slices. Can be prepared up to 12 hours before serving.
        YIELDS 8 TO 10 SERVINGS.

Lemon Mousse I

If desired, fold in minced Candied Lemon Peel (follow recipe for Candied Orange Peel on page 284).

1 cup plus 3 tablespoons sugar
4 lemons
2 tablespoons dry white wine
2 tablespoons gelatin
2/3 cup cold water
8 egg yolks
1/4 teaspoon salt
2 cups heavy cream, whipped

Put 3 tablespoons sugar in a saucepan. Grate the lemon rind and add to the sugar. Squeeze the juice from the lemons into the saucepan and add the wine. Cook over medium heat until the sugar is dissolved. Soften the gelatin in 1/3 cup cold water and add to the lemon mixture. In another saucepan, combine 1 cup sugar with the remaining 1/3 cup water and cook mixture over low heat until it forms a soft ball (238°F. on a candy thermometer).

Using an electric mixer, beat the egg yolks and salt until thickened and add the hot sugar syrup in a thin steady stream, beating constantly. Beat until the mixture is only warm, then fold into the lemon mixture. Cool until almost set, then fold in the whipped cream. Pour into a mold and chill until set, about 2 hours. Can be prepared 1 day before serving.   YIELDS 6 SERVINGS.

Lemon Mousse II

See photograph on page 67.

2 lemons
4 eggs, separated
¼ cup sugar
1 tablespoon gelatin
¾ cup heavy cream
Sweetened whipped cream
Candied violets

Grate the rind of the lemons and reserve. Squeeze the juice and reserve. In a bowl, combine the egg yolks, lemon rind, and sugar and beat until thickened and light in color. In a small saucepan, soften the gelatin in the lemon juice and dissolve over low heat. Stir into the egg yolk mixture. Beat the ¾ cup cream to the soft-peak stage and fold into the lemon mixture. Beat the egg whites to the soft-peak stage and fold in. Pour into a 2-quart bowl or a 1-quart soufflé dish fitted with a collar. Chill until set, about 4 hours. Garnish with the sweetened whipped cream and candied violets. Can be prepared 1 day before serving.   YIELDS 6 TO 8 SERVINGS.

Citronfromage

LEMON "CHEESE"

1 tablespoon gelatin
¼ cup cold water
3 eggs, separated
⅔ cup plus 2 tablespoons sugar
Grated rind and juice of 2 lemons
1 cup white wine
Pinch of salt
2 cups heavy cream

In a small saucepan, soften the gelatin in the cold water and dissolve over low heat. Beat the egg yolks with ⅔ cup sugar until thick and light in color. Stir in the lemon rind, lemon juice, and dis-solved gelatin. Stir in the white wine. Chill until almost set. Beat the egg whites with the remaining 2 tablespoons sugar and the salt until stiff but not dry. Fold into the lemon mixture. Whip 1 cup cream to the soft-peak stage and fold into the lemon mixture. Pour into a glass bowl and chill until firm, about 4 hours. Whip remaining cup cream and use to garnish the dessert. Can be prepared 1 day before serving.   YIELDS 6 SERVINGS.

Cold Lemon Soufflé

4 whole eggs, plus 3 yolks
¼ cup sugar
2 tablespoons gelatin
¼ cup lemon juice
Grated rind of 1 large lemon
1 cup heavy cream, whipped
1 cup heavy cream, whipped, sweetened, and flavored with vanilla

Put a collar on a ¾-quart soufflé dish. In a bowl, beat the eggs, egg yolks, and sugar until the mixture is very thick. In a small saucepan, soften the gelatin in the lemon juice and dissolve over low heat. Beat into the egg mixture and strain. Fold in the lemon rind and the 1 cup whipped cream. Pour into the serving dish and chill until set, about 4 hours. Carefully remove the paper collar and garnish the dessert with rosettes of sweetened whipped cream. Can be prepared a day before serving.   YIELDS 6 TO 8 SERVINGS.

Lime Soufflé

1 tablespoon gelatin
1 cup strained lime juice
1 tablespoon cornstarch
¼ cup water

1 cup evaporated milk
4 eggs, separated
1 ½ cups sugar
3-4 tablespoons grated lime rind
Pinch of salt
½ cup grated coconut

In a small bowl, soften the gelatin in the lime juice and set aside. In a saucepan, combine the cornstarch and water. Stir in the milk and cook over low heat, stirring, until thick and smooth. In a bowl, beat the egg yolks and sugar until they form a ribbon. Stir in the milk, then return the mixture to the saucepan and cook until thickened and smooth. Stir in the gelatin until dissolved. Stir in 3 tablespoons of the grated rind. Cool until almost set. Beat the egg whites with salt until stiff. Fold into the almost-set custard; pour into individual serving dishes. Chill until set, about 2 hours.

In a 325°F. oven, toast the coconut until golden. Sprinkle the coconut on the soufflé and sprinkle with remaining lime rind. Can be made the day before serving.   YIELDS 6 TO 8 SERVINGS.
▾.▾.

Cold Lime Soufflé I

This pretty soufflé can be made as much as a month before serving and frozen until wanted.

1 cup sugar
¼ cup water
7 egg yolks
½ cup lime juice
2 cups heavy cream, whipped
Green food coloring (optional)

In a saucepan, cook the sugar and water until mixture registers 240°F., the softball stage, on a candy thermometer. In a mixer, beat the egg yolks until combined. With the machine still running, add the sugar syrup in a slow, steady stream until blended. Continue beating until cool and tripled in volume. Add the lime juice. Fold in the whipped cream and the food coloring if desired. Pour into 8 to 10 individual soufflé dishes and freeze, covered with plastic wrap.   YIELDS 8 TO 10 SERVINGS.

Note: When ready to serve, garnish with whipped cream rosettes, candied lime rind, or grated lime rind.
▾.▾.

Cold Lime Soufflé II

1 tablespoon gelatin
¼ cup cold water
¾ cup milk
4 eggs, separated, plus 3 whites
½ cup sugar
½ cup fresh lime juice
2 cups heavy cream, whipped
Green food coloring (optional)

Oil a 1-quart soufflé dish and tie a collar around it. Oil the collar. In a small bowl, soften the gelatin in the cold water. In a saucepan, scald the milk. In a bowl, beat the 4 egg yolks and sugar until light in color and thickened. Pour in the hot milk, stirring constantly. Return to the saucepan and stir in the gelatin. Cook over moderate heat until thick and creamy (180°F. on a thermometer). *Do not let it boil.* Remove from the heat and cool. Stir in the lime juice and chill until it is almost ready to set. Whip 1 cup cream to the soft-firm stage and fold into the custard with the food coloring if desired. Beat the 7 egg whites until stiff but not dry and fold into the mixture. Pour into the prepared mold and chill until set, about 4 hours. Garnish with remaining whipped cream. Can be prepared the day before serving.
▾.▾.   YIELDS 6 TO 8 SERVINGS.

Melon Mousse

½ cup sugar
¾ cup water
2 cups diced cantaloupe or honeydew
   or Persian melon
1 tablespoon gelatin
Green or orange food coloring
   (optional)
2 cups heavy cream, whipped

Dissolve the sugar in ½ cup water and simmer 5 minutes. Add the melon and cook over low heat for 5 minutes. Strain the syrup into a bowl. In a saucepan, soften the gelatin in the remaining ¼ cup water and dissolve over low heat. Add gelatin to syrup. Chill until the syrup just begins to set, then beat until foamy and add the poached melon and a few drops of green or orange food coloring if desired. Fold in the whipped cream and turn into a mold. Chill until set, about 4 hours. Can be prepared 1 day before serving. YIELDS 6 SERVINGS.
•.•

Mousse à l'Orange

ORANGE MOUSSE

3 whole eggs, plus 2 yolks
½ cup sugar
Grated rind and juice of 1 large orange
2 tablespoons gelatin
½ cup heavy cream, whipped
2 oranges, peeled and cut into sections
3 tablespoons currant jelly
2 tablespoons water

Beat the eggs and egg yolks with the sugar until thickened and light in color. Stir in the grated orange rind. In a small saucepan, soften the gelatin in the orange juice and dissolve over low heat. Pour into the egg mixture and fold in the whipped cream. Pour into cups and chill until set, about 4 hours.

Arrange the orange sections on the mousse. In a small saucepan, melt the jelly with the water and cook until slightly thickened. Glaze the oranges with the syrup. Can be prepared 1 day before serving. YIELDS 6 SERVINGS.
•.•

Mousse au Cointreau

ORANGE MOUSSE WITH COINTREAU

If desired, blueberries or orange segments can be used in place of the raspberries in this dessert.

5 eggs, separated
¾ cup plus 2 tablespoons sugar
1 cup milk, scalded
⅓ cup Cointreau
3 tablespoons cognac
1 tablespoon gelatin
¼ cup orange juice
1 tablespoon grated orange rind
1 teaspoon vanilla
1 cup heavy cream, whipped
2 cups raspberries

In a heavy saucepan, beat the egg yolks with all but 4 tablespoons of the sugar until thick and light in color. Stir in the milk, Cointreau, and cognac. Cook over low heat until the mixture is thick enough to coat the back of a spoon (180°F.). Remove from the heat. Soften the gelatin in the orange juice and stir into the hot custard. Stir in the orange rind and vanilla. Chill, stirring occasionally, until almost set. Beat the egg whites with 2 tablespoons sugar until they hold firm peaks. Fold into the custard. Fold in the whipped cream. Pour into a serving dish and chill at least 2 hours or until ready to serve. Toss the raspberries with the remaining 2 tablespoons sugar and pour over the mousse. Can be prepared 1 day before serving.
•.•   YIELDS 6 SERVINGS.

Peach and Blueberry Mousse

The perfect dessert for Labor Day. If you wish to take it on a picnic, serve it from a bowl rather than trying to unmold it.

3 pounds peaches, peeled and diced
Juice of 1 lemon
½ cup sugar, plus extra to taste
5 egg yolks
1½ cups milk, scalded
1 teaspoon vanilla
3 tablespoons gelatin softened in ½
    cup cold water
2 tablespoons peach brandy (optional)
1 pint blueberries
1 cup heavy cream, whipped

Purée all but 1 cup of diced peaches and sprinkle with half the lemon juice. Sprinkle remaining lemon juice over the dice. Set aside. Sweeten purée to taste with sugar. Beat the egg yolks and ½ cup sugar until thick, then stir in the hot milk and vanilla. Cook, stirring, over low heat until thick enough to coat the back of a spoon (180°F.). Stir in the softened gelatin and strain. In a bowl, combine the peach purée with the custard and stir in the brandy if desired. Fold in the diced peaches and the blueberries, then fold in the whipped cream. Pour into a large mold and chill until set, about 4 hours. Unmold. Can be prepared 1 day before serving.

YIELDS 8 TO 10 SERVINGS.

Note: The mousse can be accompanied by a raspberry or blueberry sauce. (See Sauces chapter.)

Pear and Currant Mousses

The Poire William called for by this recipe is a pear brandy. It is clear and potent, and although expensive, it is well worth the cost.

2¼ cups water
1 cup sugar
4 to 5 pears, peeled, cored, and halved
1 tablespoon gelatin softened in 2
    tablespoons water
4 to 5 tablespoons Poire William
¾ cup heavy cream, whipped
4 jars (12 ounces) black currants in
    syrup
6 pears, peeled, cored, and left whole
Mint leaves (optional)

In a saucepan, simmer the water and sugar until the sugar is dissolved. Cook the halved pears, turning until tender. Drain well and reserve the liquid. Finely dice ½ cup cooked pears and set aside. In a processor, purée the remaining cooked pears. Stir the softened gelatin into 1 tablespoon of hot pear poaching liquid until dissolved. Cool to room temperature. Fold in the pear purée and the diced pear. Stir in the Poire William and fold in the whipped cream. Pour into 6 dariole molds or custard cups and chill until set, about 4 hours.

Meanwhile, purée all but 1 tablespoon of the currants in their syrup. In a saucepan, poach the whole pears in the currant syrup until tender. Remove pears; drain and cool. When ready to serve, spoon the currant purée onto serving plates and place a poached pear on one side of each. Unmold a mousse next to each pear and garnish with the mint leaves if desired. Garnish the mousses with the reserved currants. Can be prepared 1 day before serving.

YIELDS 6 SERVINGS.

Rum Pumpkin Mousse

2 tablespoons gelatin
½ cup dark rum
4 eggs, separated
1 cup sugar
Pinch of salt
¾ cup milk
1 teaspoon cinnamon
½ teaspoon ginger
¼ teaspoon nutmeg
1⅔ cups puréed pumpkin
Pinch of cream of tartar
1½ cups heavy cream
Toasted chopped walnuts

Soften the gelatin in the rum and set aside. In a heavy saucepan, beat the egg yolks, ½ cup sugar, and salt until thick and light in color. Add the milk and softened gelatin and cook, stirring, until the mixture is thick enough to coat the back of a spoon (180°F.). Beat in the cinnamon, ginger, nutmeg, and pumpkin. Cool until almost ready to set.

Beat the egg whites and cream of tartar to the soft-peak stage. Beat in remaining ½ cup sugar, 1 tablespoon at a time, until egg whites form stiff peaks. Fold into the pumpkin mixture. Beat 1 cup cream and fold in. Turn into a 2-quart soufflé dish, or collar a 1-quart soufflé dish. Chill until set, about 4 hours.

Beat the remaining ½ cup cream and pipe around the dessert; garnish with the walnuts. Can be prepared 1 day before serving. YIELDS 8 TO 10 SERVINGS.

▸▸▸

Cold Rum Soufflé

This basic recipe can be varied by using other liqueurs such as framboise, Grand Marnier, etc. Create your own favorite.

1 tablespoon cornstarch
¼ cup plus 2 tablespoons cold water
1 cup light cream
4 eggs, separated
½ cup sugar
1 tablespoon gelatin
½ teaspoon vanilla
½ cup dark rum
Pinch of salt
1 cup heavy cream, whipped, sweetened, and flavored with rum
8 Chocolate Wedges (see recipe following)

Collar a ¾-quart soufflé dish. In a saucepan, mix the cornstarch and 2 tablespoons water until smooth; stir in the cream and cook over low heat until thickened. In a bowl, beat the egg yolks and sugar until they form a ribbon. Soften the gelatin in ¼ cup cold water. Stir the egg yolk mixture and gelatin into the cream and cook, stirring, over low heat for 5 minutes. Remove from the heat and stir in the vanilla and rum. Beat the egg whites with the salt until they are stiff. Fold into the egg yolk mixture and pour into the soufflé dish. Chill until set, about 4 hours.

Shortly before serving, pipe on the sweetened and flavored whipped cream through a pastry bag fitted with a no. 5 open-star tip. Pipe 8 rows of cream from the center to the edges in spoke fashion. Place a Chocolate Wedge slanted against each row of cream. Pipe a rosette in the center of the dessert on top of the chocolate points. Can be prepared for garnishing the day before.

YIELDS 8 SERVINGS.

Chocolate Wedges

In a saucepan over hot, but not boiling, water melt 3 ounces semisweet chocolate, stirring until smooth. Line the bottom of an 8-inch cake pan with a circle of waxed paper. Pour the chocolate into the pan and tilt to coat evenly. Chill until set. Run a knife around the edge of the pan and turn out the chocolate disk. Warm a long knife under hot water and wipe dry. Cut the disk into 8 wedges. Set aside until ready to use. Can be prepared a day or two before using.

YIELDS 8 WEDGES.

Frozen Raspberry-Macaroon Mousse

This is one of the best recipes in this book. It is fabulous even without being frozen. In that case, refrigerate it for 3 to 24 hours after preparing.

1 quart raspberries (see Note)
1 cup sugar
1 cup macaroon crumbs
Pinch of salt
⅓ cup framboise
1 quart heavy cream, whipped
Whipped cream
Whole raspberries

Purée the raspberries in a processor and force through a sieve. If using frozen berries, strain off the juice.

Discard the seeds. Stir the sugar into the purée. Add the macaroon crumbs, salt, and framboise. Fold the cream into the purée and pour into a glass serving bowl. Chill for at least 4 hours before serving. This dessert can be frozen until mushy, beaten well, and then frozen until solid. Garnish the dessert with sweetened and flavored whipped cream and whole raspberries. Serve with a raspberry sauce. Can be prepared the day before, or if frozen, up to 2 weeks before serving.   YIELDS 8 TO 10 SERVINGS.

Note: If fresh raspberries are not available, substitute 40 ounces frozen raspberries, thawed and drained.

Mousse aux Framboises
RASPBERRY MOUSSE

1 cup sugar
1½ cups water
2½ cups raspberries
2 tablespoons gelatin
3 egg whites
1 cup heavy cream

In a saucepan, boil the sugar and 1 cup water to 350°F. Reserve about ½ cup whole raspberries for garnish; add remainder to the syrup and cook until soft. Force through a fine sieve, discarding the seeds. In a small bowl, soften the gelatin in ½ cup cold water and stir into the hot raspberry purée until dissolved. Chill until almost ready to set. Beat the egg whites until stiff but not dry and fold into the purée. Beat the cream until stiff and fold half of it into the mixture. Pour into individual dessert glasses or a large bowl. Chill until set, about 2 hours. Garnish with the raspberries and reserved cream. Can be prepared 1 day before serving.   YIELDS 6 SERVINGS.

Mousse aux Fraises
STRAWBERRY MOUSSE I

¾ pint strawberries
1 teaspoon lemon juice
1¼ cups heavy cream, whipped
½ cup sugar
2 egg whites, beaten until stiff

In a processor, purée the strawberries; mix in lemon juice. Fold the cream into the strawberries with the sugar. Fold in the egg whites. Pour into a serving bowl and chill until set, about 2 hours. Can be prepared 1 day before serving.

YIELDS 6 SERVINGS.

√ Strawberry Mousse II

1 pint strawberries, crushed
1 pint whole strawberries
1 cup confectioners' sugar, sifted
2 teaspoons gelatin
6 tablespoons Cointreau
3 cups heavy cream

Sprinkle the crushed berries with the sugar and mix until the sugar is dissolved. Reserve 6 to 8 of the prettiest whole strawberries for garnish. Cut the remaining berries in half. In a small saucepan, soften the gelatin in the Cointreau and dissolve over low heat. Cool to room temperature. Stir into the fruit purée. Beat 2 cups cream and fold into fruit purée. Fold in the strawberry halves and put into a 1½-quart decorative mold. Cover and chill until firm, about 4 hours.

Unmold onto a serving platter. Beat remaining 1 cup cream. Garnish with the whipped cream and reserved berries. Can be prepared 1 day before serving.
❖❖❖   YIELDS 6 SERVINGS.

only make ¼ of recipe

Strawberry Mousse III

2 pints strawberries, puréed
1 cup sugar
1 tablespoon gelatin
¼ cup lemon juice
2 egg whites
1½ cups heavy cream
Whole strawberries
2 tablespoons chopped pistachio nuts

In a bowl, mix the purée and sugar together. In a saucepan, soften the gelatin in the lemon juice and dissolve over low heat. Stir into the purée. Beat the egg whites until they are at the soft-peak stage and fold into the purée. Freeze until partially frozen, 45 to 60 minutes.

Purée in a processor until pale pink. Transfer to a bowl. Whip 1 cup of cream and fold into the purée. Place in serving dishes and chill until firm. Decorate with whipped cream rosettes from remaining ½ cup cream and top with whole strawberries and pistachio nuts. Can be prepared 1 day before serving.
❖❖❖   YIELDS 6 TO 8 SERVINGS.

FROZEN DESSERTS

T HESE frozen desserts are composed of fruits and whipped cream frozen to a semihard state. They can be as simple as lemon and cream beaten together (see page 152) or more elaborate presentations such as the Frozen Cranberry Cassis Mousse (see page 151). Of course, the most popular frozen dessert is ice cream. For many people, no dessert is more exciting or delightful. You can make your own ice cream using any of the varieties of ice cream freezers, from wooden-barreled, hand-cranked salt-and-ice machines to the new completely refrigerated electric ice cream makers from Italy.

If you choose to prepare your own ice cream, please do so. However, for reasons of space, it is not possible for us to provide the recipes for the many flavors of ice cream possible. The ice cream found in your market will serve very well — providing you select a good brand, as the quality of ice cream varies greatly. This becomes clear when you pack it into a mold. If the ice cream has had a lot of air and gum beaten into it, you will notice the difference. Test several brands, and choose a brand with a high butterfat content and with superior flavor. In many areas small firms have started preparing their own ice cream that is often better than major commercial brands.

There are two major ice cream preparations: coupes and bombes.

COUPES

Coupe is French for cup and, in this instance, English for ice cream sundae. A scoop of ice cream is placed in a serving dish and garnished. The garnishes can be fruit, sauces, whipped cream, chocolate, decorations, and/or cookies. The problem with coupes is that at the end of dinner when most of us would prefer to sit back and enjoy praise for having produced a glorious meal, we have to go into the kitchen and arrange the individual dessert glasses on the counter, then fill them with ice cream, top with a fruit, coat with a sauce, decorate with whipped cream, and possibly add a decoration to that. When you bring the desserts in to the guests, they say, "How lovely, sundaes." After all that effort, the praise is really not that wonderful.

BOMBES

Bombes are layers of ice cream packed into large molds, often with a mousse-like mixture as the center filling. The bombe is unmolded onto a platter and garnished. It can include the same ingredients as a coupe; however, instead of going through the steps of preparing the garnish a number of times, you only have to do it once. When you bring a platter topped with a large, beautifully decorated dessert the guests will *ooh!* and *aah!* The plaudits will make the rafters ring. As always, presentation is as important as the taste and quality of the cooking.

Because the desserts are frozen, there is a temptation to prepare the desserts, including the garnishes, and keep them in the freezer. The drawback to this is that the fruits then freeze, as does the whipped cream, and the resulting textures are not as pleasing. Freeze the ice cream ahead, but garnish just before serving.

Once you understand the principles of bombes and coupes, you will be able to create many exciting variations. Although the ice cream is always cold, warm sauces can be used, such as in Coupe Nectarine Sultane, Cherries Jubilee, or Bananas Foster, to provide an interesting counterpoint.

Note: With a little forethought, any coupe can be served as a bombe and in most instances vice versa. If the bombe has a mousselike filling and several flavors, instead of lining small molds, which, of course, is easily accomplished, you can place separate scoops of each flavor in the serving dish.

TO LINE A MOLD WITH ICE CREAM

If possible, use a metal mold. The next best choice is a somewhat flexible plastic container such as the half-gallon containers in which some ice cream is sold. Let the ice cream temper in the refrigerator for two hours or at room temperature for about half an hour. Pack the ice cream into the mold. If using more than one flavor, make a one-inch outer layer, freeze for about 30 minutes, then add the next flavor and freeze again until the mold is filled (see sketch). Once the mold is filled, wrap securely and freeze until solid. The mold can be prepared up to a month before using. If you know you are going to have a dinner

Lining a
bombe mold
with
ice cream

party, you can get most of the dessert prepared well ahead.

For a dramatic presentation for a large crowd, you can stack ice cream molds of different sizes, similar to the tiers of a wedding cake. For example, fill a 12-inch round cake tin with ice cream, and freeze. Continue with a 9-inch and a 6-inch tin. Finally, fill a 5-inch decorative mold and freeze it. When ready to assemble, unmold the layers and stack with the decorative mold on top. Use a dowel to keep the layers together. Garnish the whole dessert with the appropriate fruit sauce and whipped cream. When this is brought into the room, the guests will gasp with pleasure.

Fruits Beatrice

Spun Sugar gives a lovely, airy finish to this and other desserts. It is tricky to prepare and should be served immediately. The dessert will be as delicious, if not as fantastic, without it. If you wish to use Spun Sugar, see the instructions on page 285.

1 quart raspberry sherbet
3 cups fresh fruits or berries
Sauce Riche flavored with anisette (see page 274)
Spun Sugar (optional)
Crystallized violets

Pack a mold with the raspberry sherbet and freeze until firm. Unmold onto a serving platter and surround with the fruits. Coat some of the fruits with the sauce and surround the dessert with Spun Sugar, if using. Garnish with crystallized violets. Serve the remaining sauce separately. Can be prepared for garnishing several days ahead.

YIELDS 6 TO 8 SERVINGS.

Note: Crystallized violets are available in gourmet shops.

Bombe Esperanza

ORANGE AND PISTACHIO
ICE CREAM MOLD

½ cup chopped glacéed fruit
¼ cup orange liqueur
1 pint orange sherbet, softened
2 pints pistachio ice cream
1 cup Raspberry Sauce (see page 276)
1 cup heavy cream, whipped and
    sweetened to taste
Chocolate shavings

Macerate the fruit in the orange liqueur for 4 hours. Beat the fruit and liqueur into the softened sherbet. Line the bottom and sides of a 1-quart mold with three-quarters of the pistachio ice cream and freeze for 30 minutes. Fill the center with orange sherbet mixture and spread the remaining pistachio ice cream over the top. Freeze until firm. When ready to serve, pour a pool of Raspberry Sauce on a tray. Unmold the ice cream and decorate with the whipped cream. Sprinkle with chocolate shavings. Can be prepared several days ahead.
YIELDS 6 SERVINGS.

Note: For a more interesting appearance, pour plain heavy cream in 2 thin concentric circles around the dessert. With the tip of a knife blade, draw through the cream toward the bombe every 2 inches and toward the edge of the platter between those lines.

Coupe St. André

MIXED FRUIT SUNDAE

1 pear
1 slice pineapple, diced
½ banana, diced
12 maraschino cherries
1 peach, diced
½ orange, diced

1 teaspoon lemon juice
2 tablespoons sugar
6 scoops vanilla ice cream
6 peach slices

In a bowl, macerate the pear, pineapple, banana, 6 cherries, peach, and orange in the lemon juice and sugar for 5 minutes. Divide the mixture among 6 dessert glasses and top each glass with a scoop of ice cream. Garnish with peach slices and remaining 6 cherries. Must be served immediately.   YIELDS 6 SERVINGS.

Coupe Clo-Clo

1 cup candied chestnut pieces
¼ cup maraschino liqueur
1 quart vanilla ice cream, softened
6 whole candied chestnuts
1 cup heavy cream
1 cup strawberry purée

In a small bowl, macerate the chestnut pieces in the maraschino liqueur for at least 4 hours. Fold the macerated, drained chestnuts into the ice cream and pack into a 1-quart mold. Freeze until firm. Unmold the ice cream and decorate with the whole chestnuts. Beat the cream until stiff and fold in the strawberry purée. Spoon around the base of the mold. The cream will be too soft to pipe through a pastry bag. Can be prepared for garnishing several days ahead.   YIELDS 6 TO 8 SERVINGS.

Bombe Lilian

1 quart lemon sherbet
1 pineapple, diced
1 cup seedless grapes
Kirsch to taste
1 cup Apricot Sauce (see page 274)
½ cup toasted almonds

Pack the lemon sherbet into a mold and freeze until serving time. Macerate pineapple and grapes in kirsch for at least 1 hour. Unmold the sherbet, surround with the fruit, and pour on the Apricot Sauce. Sprinkle with almonds. Can be prepared for garnishing several days ahead.　　YIELDS 6 TO 8 SERVINGS.

Bombe aux Myrtilles

LEMON-BLUEBERRY BOMBE

   1 quart vanilla ice cream
   1 quart lemon sherbet
   Blueberry Cassis Sauce (see page 275)
   1 cup heavy cream, whipped, flavored
      with vanilla or Myrtilles liqueur

Pack the ice cream into a 2-quart mold, leaving the center hollow. Freeze for 30 minutes, then pack the center with the sherbet. Freeze until firm. Unmold onto a serving platter and surround with the Blueberry Cassis Sauce. Decorate the dessert with the whipped cream piped through a pastry bag. Can be prepared for garnishing several days before.　　YIELDS 8 TO 10 SERVINGS.

Sformata Dolce Fantasia

RUM AND CHOCOLATE FRUIT BOMBE

   1 pint chocolate ice cream
   ½ pound black cherries, pitted and
      halved
   1 (9-inch) Sponge Cake layer (see
      page 278)
   ½ cup rum
   1 pint vanilla ice cream
   1 banana, thinly sliced
   Whipped cream (optional)

Line the bottom of a 9-inch spring-form pan with the chocolate ice cream. Fill with the cherries. Split the cake in half horizontally. Place 1 layer over the cherries and sprinkle with ¼ cup rum. Top with the vanilla ice cream and then with banana slices. Cover with the remaining Sponge Cake layer and sprinkle with remaining ¼ cup rum. Cover with waxed paper and freeze for 6 hours. Garnish with the whipped cream if desired.　　YIELDS 8 SERVINGS.

Cherries Los Angeles

   6 scoops orange sherbet
   1 ½ cups Cherry Compote (see
      page 35)
   Sauce Parisienne (see page 273)
   Candied violets

Place orange sherbet in dessert glasses and surround with cherries. Spoon on the Sauce Parisienne and garnish with violets. Serve immediately.
　　YIELDS 6 SERVINGS.

Cerises Pompadour: Omit Sauce Parisienne and garnish with 1 cup heavy cream, whipped, sweetened, and flavored to taste with kirsch.

Cherries Monte Carlo

   1 ½ cups Cherry Compote (see
      page 35)
   1 tablespoon maraschino liqueur
   6 scoops tangerine or orange sherbet
   1 cup heavy cream, whipped

Macerate the cherries in the liqueur for up to 12 hours. Spoon the fruit into serving dishes and top with the sherbet. Pipe the whipped cream through a pastry bag to garnish. Serve immediately.
　　YIELDS 6 SERVINGS.

Cerises des Gourmets

CHERRY AND PINEAPPLE SUNDAES

>   6 scoops pineapple sherbet
>   1½ cups Cherry Compote (see
>   page 35)
>   1 tablespoon prunelle liqueur
>   Sauce à la Ritz (see page 273)

Place the sherbet in serving dishes, cover with the cherries, and sprinkle with the liqueur. Spoon on the sauce. Serve immediately.   YIELDS 6 SERVINGS.
▼▼▼

Cherries Laurette

>   6 scoops raspberry sherbet
>   1½ cups Cherry Compote (see
>   page 35)
>   Sauce Cardinale (see page 276)
>   1 cup heavy cream, whipped,
>   sweetened, and flavored to taste
>   Spun Sugar (optional; see page 285)

Place the sherbet in serving dishes. Spoon on the cherries and top with the Sauce Cardinale. Decorate with the whipped cream and surround with Spun Sugar, if desired. Serve immediately.   YIELDS 6 SERVINGS.
▼▼▼

Bombe Edna May

CHERRY BOMBE
WITH RASPBERRY SAUCE

>   1 quart vanilla ice cream
>   2 cups Cherry Compote (see page 35)
>   1 cup heavy cream, whipped
>   ¼ cup raspberry purée

Pack the ice cream into a 1-quart mold and freeze until firm. Unmold the ice cream onto a platter and surround with the cherries. Fold the whipped cream and purée together and spoon over the dessert. The cream will be too soft to pipe through a pastry bag. Can be prepared for garnishing several days ahead.
▼▼▼   YIELDS 6 TO 8 SERVINGS.

Bombe Germaine

CHERRY AND CHESTNUT BOMBE

>   1 quart vanilla ice cream
>   2 cups cherries, pitted
>   2 to 4 tablespoons kirsch
>   1 tablespoon sugar, plus additional
>   to taste
>   1 cup chestnut purée
>   1 cup heavy cream
>   1 tablespoon kirsch or rum

Pack the ice cream into a flat-bottomed 1-quart mold. Freeze. In a bowl, macerate the cherries in the 2 to 4 tablespoons kirsch and sugar to taste for 2 hours. Unmold the ice cream onto a serving platter. Force the chestnut purée through a ricer on top of the ice cream. Surround the base of the dessert with the cherries. Beat the heavy cream until stiff; sweeten and flavor with 1 tablespoon sugar and the kirsch or rum. Pipe around the base of the dessert. Can be prepared for garnishing several days ahead.   YIELDS 6 TO 8 SERVINGS.

Note: Chestnut purée is available in gourmet shops.
▼▼▼

Coupe Germaine

CHERRY AND CHESTNUT SUNDAE

>   1½ cups pitted cherries
>   1 tablespoon kirsch
>   6 scoops vanilla ice cream
>   1 cup chestnut purée
>   1 cup heavy cream, whipped and
>   sweetened to taste

Macerate the cherries in the kirsch for at least 30 minutes. Place the ice cream in individual serving dishes and arrange the cherries around each serving. Press the chestnut purée through a ricer onto the ice cream. Garnish with the whipped cream piped through a pastry bag. Serve immediately.

YIELDS 6 SERVINGS.

Note: Chestnut purée is available in gourmet shops.

Frozen Cranberry Cassis Mousse

4 eggs, separated, plus 4 yolks
1 cup bottled cranberry juice
5 cups cooked cranberries, drained
  (reserve the juice)
⅓ plus ¼ cup crème de cassis
1 cup heavy cream
½ cup sugar
¼ cup water
1 tablespoon arrowroot

In a saucepan, beat the 8 egg yolks until thickened. Add the bottled cranberry juice and beat until blended. Cook over medium heat until the mixture coats the back of a spoon. Cool. Add 4 cups cooked cranberries to the custard, blend well, and chill the mixture until it begins to thicken. Stir in ⅓ cup crème de cassis and mix well. Beat the cream until it is soft-firm and fold into the cranberry mixture. Beat the 4 egg whites until foamy, then beat in the sugar a tablespoon at a time and continue beating until stiff and glossy. Fold into the cranberry mixture and pour into a 2½-quart mold. Freeze until firm.

Bring 1 cup reserved cranberry juice to a simmer. In a bowl, combine the water and arrowroot and stir into the cranberry juice. Cook, stirring, until thickened. Remove from the heat and stir in remaining 1 cup cranberries.

Cool and stir in the remaining ¼ cup crème de cassis. Unmold the mousse and serve with the cranberry sauce. Mousse can be prepared several weeks before serving.

YIELDS 8 TO 10 SERVINGS.

Bombe Palm Springs

For an amusing finish, melt ½ cup chocolate, place in a paper pastry bag, and pipe out a palm tree onto a baking sheet lined with waxed paper. Let chill until set. Peel off the paper and stand in the center of the dessert. If desired, make a tree for each guest.

¼ ounce dates, chopped
¼ cup cognac
1 quart vanilla ice cream
1 cup heavy cream, whipped,
  sweetened, and flavored with
  additional cognac

In a bowl, macerate the dates in ¼ cup cognac for at least 3 hours, or up to 6 months. Pack the ice cream into a 1-quart mold and freeze until firm. Unmold the ice cream, surround with the macerated dates, and decorate with the whipped cream put through a pastry bag. Can be prepared for garnishing several days before.   YIELDS 6 SERVINGS.

Frozen Lemon Soufflé

6 whole eggs, separated, plus 6 yolks
1¾ cups plus 2 teaspoons sugar
¾ cup lemon juice
Grated rind of 1 lemon
½ cup heavy cream
Whipped cream
Candied violets

In a large bowl, beat the 12 egg yolks and 1½ cups sugar until light in color and thickened. Add the lemon juice. Place the bowl over a pan of boiling water. Do not let the water touch the bottom of the bowl. Beating constantly, heat the mixture until it is very thick, smooth, and creamy. The mixture should be about 180°F. Fold in the grated rind. Cool and chill.

Put a collar around a 5-cup soufflé dish. Beat the cream with the 2 teaspoons sugar until stiff, then fold into the egg-lemon mixture. Beat the 6 egg whites to the soft-peak stage and beat in the remaining ¼ cup of sugar. Continue beating until stiff. Fold into the egg-lemon mixture. Pour into the prepared dish and freeze until firm. When ready to serve, remove the collar and garnish with the whipped cream piped through a pastry bag and the violets. Can be prepared several days ahead.

YIELDS 6 SERVINGS.

Frozen Lemon Cream in Lemon Shells

For an attractive touch, arrange the lemon shells on a large green leaf.

1 cup milk
1 cup heavy cream
1 cup sugar
8 lemons

In a bowl, stir the milk, heavy cream, and sugar until sugar is dissolved. Pour into an ice tray and freeze until mushy. Grate the rind of 2 lemons and squeeze out their juice. Beat into the mushy cream mixture and beat well. Freeze for 2 hours.

Remove the tops from the remaining lemons and scoop out the pulp (see page 15). Cut a thin slice off bottom of each lemon shell so it will not roll. You can store the shells in the freezer for up to a month if desired. When the cream has frozen for the required 2 hours, fill the shells by piping cream through a pastry bag into each shell. Arrange the cut-off lids askew and freeze until solid. Can be prepared several days ahead, but wrap each frozen lemon in plastic wrap to protect it.   YIELDS 6 SERVINGS.

Coupe Nectarine Sultane

6 scoops pistachio ice cream
6 vanilla-poached nectarines, halved
  (see page 286)
Sabayon Sauce flavored with kirsch
  (see page 272)
Chopped pistachio nuts

Arrange the ice cream on dessert plates. Top with nectarines and pour the Sabayon Sauce over the fruit. Sprinkle the nuts on top. Serve immediately.

YIELDS 6 SERVINGS.

Bombe Grimaldi

TANGERINE AND PINEAPPLE BOMBE

1 quart tangerine or orange sherbet
1 pineapple, peeled, cored, and diced
2 tablespoons kirsch
Sugar
1 cup heavy cream, whipped and
  sweetened to taste
Candied violets

Pack the sherbet into a 1-quart ring mold and freeze. Macerate the pineapple in kirsch for 1 hour. Sweeten with sugar if needed. Unmold the sherbet onto a serving platter. Put the pineapple in the center or around the edges. With a pastry bag, pipe the cream around the dessert and garnish with the violets. Can be prepared for garnishing several days ahead.   YIELDS 6 TO 8 SERVINGS.

Fujiyama I

1 (8-inch) layer Orange Génoise (see page 279)
¼ cup Cointreau or other orange-flavored liqueur
1 pint vanilla ice cream
1 pint orange sherbet
1 cup heavy cream
¼ cup Cointreau
Orange slices

Place the Génoise on a serving platter. Sprinkle with liqueur and cover with scoops of ice cream and sherbet, piling them into a pyramid. Whip the heavy cream to the soft-peak stage with the ¼ cup Cointreau and drizzle over the ice cream. Decorate with orange slices. Serve immediately.

❖❖❖   YIELDS 6 TO 8 SERVINGS.

Fujiyama II

1 (9-inch) Orange Génoise layer (see page 279)
Grand Marnier
1 quart vanilla ice cream
1 quart orange sherbet
1 cup heavy cream, whipped
1 cup Grand Marnier Sauce (see page 273)
Orange slices

Place the Orange Génoise on a platter, sprinkle with Grand Marnier to taste, and let soak. Line a 2-quart peaked decorative mold with vanilla ice cream, leaving the center hollow. Freeze 1 hour or until firm. Fill the center with the sherbet; freeze until firm, at least 1 hour longer. Unmold the ice cream onto the cake. Fold the whipped cream and Grand Marnier Sauce together and pour over ice cream. Garnish with the orange slices. Can be prepared for garnishing several days ahead.

❖❖❖   YIELDS 8 TO 10 SERVINGS.

Bombe Eunice

ORANGE-WALNUT BOMBE

Eunice Ehrlich gave me the recipe for this sauce, which in turn inspired the dessert.

1 quart vanilla ice cream
1 pint orange sherbet
1 pint maple walnut ice cream
3 oranges, peeled and sliced
1 recipe Eunice's Walnut-Orange Sauce (see page 275)
1 cup heavy cream, whipped, sweetened, and flavored to taste

In a 2-quart mold pack the vanilla ice cream 1-inch thick. Freeze 30 minutes. Pack in the orange sherbet, leaving the center hollow. Freeze 30 minutes. Pack in the maple walnut ice cream and freeze until firm, about 2 hours. Unmold, surround with the orange slices, and coat with some of the sauce. Pipe whipped cream onto the dessert to garnish. Pass remaining sauce separately. Can be prepared for garnishing several days ahead.

❖❖❖   YIELDS 8 TO 10 SERVINGS.

Coupe à l'Orange au Chocolat

ORANGE SHERBET WITH ORANGES AND CHOCOLATE SAUCE

3 navel oranges, sectioned
⅓ cup orange liqueur
2 ounces unsweetened chocolate
¼ cup water
2 tablespoons cognac
½ cup sugar
3 tablespoons butter, thinly sliced
6 scoops orange sherbet
1 tablespoon grated orange rind

Macerate the orange sections in the liqueur for 1 hour. In a small saucepan over low heat, melt the chocolate in the water, stirring until smooth. Add the

cognac and sugar and stir until the sugar is dissolved. Stir in the butter until smooth. Let cool, loosely covered. Scoop sherbet into dishes, surround with the orange sections, and top with the chocolate sauce. Sprinkle with the grated orange rind. Serve immediately.
▼.▼   YIELDS 6 SERVINGS.

Frozen Orange Meringues

8 navel oranges
Orange juice as needed
4 cups water
2 cups plus 6 tablespoons sugar
¼ cup lemon juice
3 egg whites

Slice a cap off each orange and scoop out the shells, reserving the pulp and cut-off cap. Chill shells. Squeeze and strain juice from pulp, adding more juice if needed to make 2 cups. Grate rind from the cut-off caps.

Boil the water and 2 cups sugar for 4 minutes. Cool. Add the lemon and orange juices, then the grated rind. Freeze until mushy, about 1 hour, then beat until smooth in a processor; repeat twice.

Fill the chilled orange shells with the sherbet and freeze. Preheat the broiler. Beat the egg whites with the remaining 6 tablespoons sugar until stiff and pipe over the top of the sherbet with a pastry bag fitted with a no. 4 star tip. Broil until golden. Serve immediately or freeze for up to six hours.
▼.▼   YIELDS 8 SERVINGS.

Orange Shells Glacé

9 navel oranges
1 cup sugar
6 egg yolks
2 cups heavy cream, whipped

2 teaspoons vanilla
2 tablespoons lemon juice
4 teaspoons grated lemon peel

Slice off the tops of 8 oranges, scoop out the fruit, and set the shells aside. Measure ¾ cup of juice from the fruit into a saucepan (use remaining fruit for another purpose). Add the sugar and boil until it reaches 220°F. on a candy thermometer. In another saucepan, beat the egg yolks until thick and lemon-colored. Slowly beat in hot syrup and cook over medium heat, beating constantly, for 7 minutes. Remove from the heat and beat over cold water until cold. Fold in the cream, vanilla, lemon juice, and lemon peel. Grate the rind from remaining orange and beat into the mixture. Spoon into orange shells, cover with tops of oranges, and freeze until firm. Can be prepared several days ahead.
▼.▼   YIELDS 6 SERVINGS.

Mousse Glacée Grand Marnier

FROZEN GRAND MARNIER MOUSSE

2 egg whites
Pinch of salt
6 tablespoons sugar
1 cup heavy cream, whipped
¼ cup Grand Marnier
Berry sauce (see recipes in Sauces chapter)

Beat egg whites with salt until they form soft peaks. Gradually beat in sugar, 1 tablespoon at a time, until stiff and shiny. Blend the Grand Marnier into the cream and fold into the egg white mixture. Turn into a 1-quart bowl and freeze until firm, at least 2 hours. Unmold and serve with berry sauce of your choice. Can be prepared for garnishing 2 days before.   YIELDS 4 SERVINGS.
▼.▼

Peach-Raspberry Bombe

2 (9-inch) Nutted Génoise layers (see page 279)
4 tablespoons plus ½ teaspoon framboise
4 cups raspberry ice cream
2¼ cups peach ice cream
1½ cups heavy cream
¼ cup plus 1 tablespoon confectioners' sugar
¼ teaspoon almond extract
1 to 2 peaches, peeled and sliced
2 tablespoons ground toasted almonds
Fresh whole raspberries

Divide each Génoise layer in half horizontally. Sprinkle each resulting layer with 1 tablespoon framboise. Place a layer on a serving plate and spread with half the raspberry ice cream (see Note). Top with another sponge layer and spread with the peach ice cream; cover with another layer and spread with remaining 2 cups raspberry ice cream. Cover with final cake layer and press down lightly. Cover and freeze until firm, at least 2 hours.

About 1 hour before serving, beat the heavy cream to the soft-peak stage and beat in ¼ cup sugar and almond extract until stiff. Spread a thin layer evenly over the top of the cake. Put remaining cream into a pastry bag fitted with a no. 5 open-star tip and pipe a border. Sprinkle cut peaches with remaining ½ teaspoon framboise and remaining 1 tablespoon confectioners' sugar. Macerate for 10 minutes. Arrange peaches on top of cake, sprinkle sides with almonds, and garnish with whole raspberries. Can be prepared for garnishing several days ahead.   YIELDS 8 TO 10 SERVINGS.

Note: To make the sides of the dessert straighter and neater, you can stack the cake layers and ice cream into a 9-inch spring-form pan.

Pêches Melba

PEACH MELBA

½ pint vanilla ice cream
4 vanilla-poached peaches (see page 286)
1 cup Raspberry Sauce (see page 276)

Place a scoop of vanilla ice cream in each serving dish and top with 2 peach halves. Coat with Raspberry Sauce. Serve immediately. YIELDS 4 SERVINGS.

Bombe Mascotte

PEACH AND KIRSCH BOMBE

1 pint peach ice cream
½ pint vanilla ice cream
3 tablespoons kirsch
6 peaches, sliced
1 cup heavy cream, whipped, sweetened, and flavored to taste with additional kirsch

Pack the peach ice cream into a 1½-pint mold, leaving the center hollow. Freeze for 30 minutes. Soften the vanilla ice cream and beat in 2 tablespoons kirsch. Pack into the mold and freeze until firm, at least 2 hours. Macerate the peaches in 1 tablespoon kirsch for 1 hour. Unmold the ice cream onto a platter, surround with the peaches, and decorate with the whipped cream. Can be prepared for garnishing several days ahead.   YIELDS 6 SERVINGS.

Poires Belles Dijonnaises

RASPBERRY AND PEAR BOMBE

Spun Sugar is tricky. It must be made and then served immediately, not always a possibility if you are dressed for an elegant dinner party. No one will really know if you omit it.

6 vanilla-poached pears (see recipe on page 286)
1 quart raspberry sherbet
Sauce Riche (see page 274)
Candied violets
Spun Sugar (optional; see page 285)

Chill the pears. Fill a 1-quart ring mold with the raspberry sherbet and freeze. Unmold the raspberry sherbet onto a platter and place the chilled pears in the center. Pour some of the sauce over the pears. Garnish with candied violets. Serve the remaining sauce separately. Garnish with Spun Sugar if desired. Can be prepared for garnishing several days before.   YIELDS 6 SERVINGS.

Poires Geraldine Farrar

PEAR AND ORANGE SHERBET SUNDAE

6 vanilla-poached pears, halved and cored (see recipe on page 286)
6 scoops orange sherbet
Apricot Sauce (see page 274)
1 cup whipped cream
Candied violets

Chill the pears. Arrange pear halves in individual serving dishes and top each with a scoop of sherbet. Mask the pears with the Apricot Sauce and garnish each dish with whipped cream and a candied violet. Serve immediately.
                         YIELDS 6 SERVINGS.

Poires Belle Hélène

PEAR AND FUDGE SAUCE SUNDAES

6 vanilla-poached pears, halved and cored (see recipe on page 286)
6 scoops vanilla ice cream
Creamed Fudge Sauce (see page 272)
1 cup heavy cream, whipped and sweetened to taste

Arrange pear halves in dessert dishes and top each with a scoop of ice cream. Spoon on the sauce and garnish with the whipped cream. Serve immediately.
                         YIELDS 6 SERVINGS.

Ananas Glacé à la Bourbonnaise

PINEAPPLE ICE CREAM MOLD

1 pineapple, cut as a container (see page 19)
4 tablespoons rum
3 tablespoons sugar
1 quart rum ice cream

Dice the flesh from the pineapple and macerate in 3 tablespoons rum and 2 tablespoons sugar for 2 hours. Sprinkle the inside of the pineapple shell with the remaining 1 tablespoon rum and 1 tablespoon sugar 1 hour before serving. Fill the shell with alternate layers of ice cream and pineapple. Freeze at least 2 hours or until ready to serve. Serve with the frond on top. Can be prepared 1 day before serving.   YIELDS 6 SERVINGS.

Bombe Mayerling

PINEAPPLE AND VANILLA BOMBE

1½ quarts vanilla ice cream
1 (9-inch) Génoise layer (see page 279)
Grand Marnier to taste

2 cups diced pineapple
1 cup heavy cream, whipped

Pack the ice cream into a 1½-quart mold and freeze until firm, at least 2 hours. Place the cake layer on a serving dish and sprinkle generously with the Grand Marnier. Unmold the ice cream onto the cake, and garnish with the pineapple and whipped cream. Can be prepared for garnishing several days ahead.
▀▄▀ YIELDS 8 SERVINGS.

Coupe Jamaïque

COFFEE ICE CREAM WITH PINEAPPLE

1 quart coffee ice cream
2 cups cubed pineapple
2 tablespoons rum
1 cup heavy cream, whipped and sweetened with sugar to taste
Candied coffee beans (see Note)

Pack the ice cream into a 1-quart mold and freeze until firm, at least 2 hours. Macerate the pineapple in rum for at least 1 hour. Unmold the ice cream onto a platter. Surround with drained pineapple. Beat the cream with the sugar until stiff and flavor with the maceration liquid. Pipe the cream onto the pineapple and ice cream and top with candied coffee beans. Can be prepared for garnishing several days before.
YIELDS 6 SERVINGS.

Note: Candied coffee beans are available in gourmet shops.
▀▄▀

Bombe de Rêve de Bébé

BABY'S DREAM BOMBE

1 pint pineapple sherbet
1 pint raspberry sherbet
1 pint strawberries
½ cup orange juice, sweetened and flavored with Cointreau

1 cup heavy cream, whipped
Candied violets

Line a 1-quart mold with pineapple sherbet, leaving the center hollow. Fill the hollow with the raspberry sherbet and freeze until firm, at least 2 hours. Macerate the strawberries in the orange juice for 2 hours. Unmold the ice cream onto a platter and surround with the strawberries. Pipe the cream through a pastry bag and garnish with violets. Can be prepared for garnishing several days before serving. YIELDS 6 SERVINGS.
▀▄▀

Frozen Pumpkin Mousse

¾ cup sugar
¾ cup water
3 egg whites
Pinch of salt
Pinch of cream of tartar
½ cup pumpkin purée
Pinch of cinnamon
Pinch of ginger
Pinch of nutmeg
1 cup heavy cream
1 to 2 tablespoons rum

In a saucepan, boil the sugar and water until mixture reaches 238°F. on a candy thermometer, or the soft-ball stage. In an electric mixer, beat the egg whites until foamy. Add the salt and cream of tartar and beat until soft peaks form. With the machine running, add the syrup in a slow, steady stream. Continue beating until the meringue cools, about 10 minutes. Fold in the pumpkin, cinnamon, ginger, and nutmeg. Beat 1 cup cream to the soft-peak stage and fold in the rum, then fold into the pumpkin mixture. Pour into a 1½-quart mold and freeze for 4 hours. Can be prepared the day before. YIELDS 6 SERVINGS.
▀▄▀

Raspberry Bombe

3 pints raspberry sherbet
¾ cup plus 1 teaspoon sugar
¼ cup water
4 egg yolks
1 tablespoon grated orange peel
1¼ cups heavy cream
¼ cup Cointreau
3 cups raspberries
½ cup heavy cream, whipped
Mint leaves

Line the bottom and sides of a 2-quart mold with sherbet. Freeze, covered, until the sherbet is hard, at least 1 hour. In a saucepan, boil ¾ cup sugar and the water until mixture reaches the soft-ball stage (238°F. on a candy thermometer). In an electric mixer, beat the egg yolks until they are light in color. With the mixer going, add the syrup in a slow, steady stream. Beat until the mixture cools to room temperature, about 15 minutes. Refrigerate, covered, until cold.

In a small bowl, mash the orange peel and remaining 1 teaspoon sugar together. Whip the 1¼ cups cream to the soft-peak stage and fold in the Cointreau and orange peel–sugar mixture. Fold into the egg yolk. Spoon into the mold. Freeze, covered, overnight. Unmold and garnish with raspberries, whipped cream, and mint leaves. Can be prepared for garnishing several days ahead.
❖❖❖   YIELDS 10 TO 12 SERVINGS.

Frozen Raspberry Torte

24 ladyfingers (see page 280)
20 ounces frozen raspberries, thawed
1¼ cups sugar, plus more to taste
⅓ cup water
1 teaspoon light corn syrup
3 egg whites

2 tablespoons kirsch
2 cups heavy cream
Whole raspberries

Line the sides of a 9-inch spring-form pan with the ladyfingers and set aside. Purée the thawed raspberries in a processor and force through a sieve. There should be 2 cups of purée. Add sugar to taste, if needed. Combine 1¼ cups sugar, water, and corn syrup in a saucepan and boil until mixture reaches the soft-ball stage (238°F. on a candy thermometer). In an electric mixer, beat the egg whites until they reach the soft-peak stage. With the mixer running, slowly add the hot syrup in a long, steady stream. Beat until the mixture reaches room temperature. Fold in the raspberry purée and kirsch. Whip the cream until stiff and fold into the mixture. Pour into the prepared pan and freeze until firm. Remove the sides of the pan and garnish with the whole raspberries. Can be prepared several days ahead.
❖❖❖   YIELDS 12 SERVINGS.

Le Pavé aux Framboises

FROZEN RASPBERRY DESSERT

This dessert can be frozen for longer if desired; however, let it soften in the refrigerator before serving.

1¼ cups sugar
2 cups water
4 egg yolks
2⅓ cups raspberries
⅓ cup lemon juice
1 cup heavy cream, whipped
1 cup framboise
20 ladyfingers (see page 280)
1⅓ cups whipped cream, sweetened
   and flavored to taste

In a saucepan, boil ¾ cup sugar and 1 cup water to the hard-ball stage (250°F.

on a candy thermometer). In an electric mixer, beat the egg yolks until thick and light in color. With the mixer running, add the syrup in a slow, steady stream and continue beating until the mixture is cold. Force 1 cup of raspberries through a sieve, discarding the seeds. Add the lemon juice and fold in the whipped cream. Fold into the egg yolk mixture.

Boil the remaining ½ cup sugar with the remaining cup water until just dissolved. Remove from the heat and cool 5 minutes. Add the framboise. Spread a thin layer of raspberry mixture on the bottom of a 2-quart mold. Dip the ladyfingers into the framboise syrup and place on top. Keep layering the ingredients, ending with the mousse. Freeze at least 2 hours. Unmold and garnish with remaining raspberries and sweetened and flavored whipped cream. Can be prepared up to 6 hours before serving. ▚▚▚ YIELDS 6 TO 8 SERVINGS.

Fraises de Jeanne Granier

STRAWBERRY AND ORANGE
SHERBET SUNDAES

⅓ cup sugar
¼ cup water
¼ cup orange juice
3 egg yolks
5 tablespoons Grand Marnier
1 cup heavy cream, whipped
1 quart strawberries, halved
8 scoops orange sherbet

In a saucepan, cook the sugar, water, and orange juice until mixture reaches 232°F. on a candy thermometer. In an electric mixer, beat the egg yolks until light in color. With the mixer running, add the syrup in a slow, steady stream, beating constantly. Continue beating until mix-

ture is cool, thick, and opaque. Refrigerate until cold, about 30 minutes.

Fold in 3 tablespoons Grand Marnier and the whipped cream and refrigerate again. Macerate the strawberries in the remaining 2 tablespoons Grand Marnier for 15 minutes. Arrange the sherbet in 8 serving dishes, surround with strawberries, and spoon the mousse on top. Serve immediately. The mousse can be prepared the day before. However, macerate the strawberries no more than four hours. YIELDS 8 SERVINGS. ▚▚▚

Frozen Strawberry Soufflé

6 eggs, separated
3 cups sugar
2 cups strawberry purée
½ cup Grand Marnier
⅓ cup orange juice
3½ cups heavy cream
½ cup chopped walnuts or pistachios
Whole strawberries
Raspberry Sauce (see page 276)

Lightly oil and collar a 1½-quart soufflé dish (see page 132). In a saucepan, beat the egg yolks and 2 cups of sugar until thick and lemon colored. Stir in ½ cup of strawberry purée. Cook over low heat until thickened, stirring constantly. Remove from the heat, stir in the Grand Marnier, and cool. In a small saucepan, heat the remaining cup of sugar and the orange juice over medium heat, stirring until the sugar is dissolved. Raise heat and cook, without stirring, until the mixture reaches the hard-ball stage (250°F.).

While the orange juice and sugar are cooking, beat the egg whites until soft peaks form. With the machine running, slowly pour in the hot syrup, and continue beating until stiff peaks form.

Whip 3 cups of cream and fold into the mixture. Fold in the remaining 1½ cups strawberry purée. Turn into the soufflé dish and freeze until firm.

When ready to serve, remove the collar and press the chopped nuts around the edges. Whip the remaining cream and pipe rosettes with a pastry bag fitted with a no. 4 open-star tip. Garnish with whole strawberries. Serve the Raspberry Sauce on the side. Can be prepared a week or more before serving. If so, once the soufflé has frozen, wrap it in freezer paper to keep out freezer odors.

❖❖❖   YIELDS 12 SERVINGS.

Bombe Alhambra

STRAWBERRY-MANDARIN
ORANGE BOMBE

- 1 quart vanilla ice cream
- 1 pint strawberry ice cream
- 1 quart strawberries
- 2 tablespoons kirsch
- 1 cup heavy cream, whipped, sweetened, and flavored with kirsch
- 2 cups Sauce Riche flavored with mandarin liqueur (see page 274)

Pack the vanilla ice cream into a 1½-quart mold, leaving the center hollow. Freeze for 30 minutes, then fill the center with the strawberry ice cream. Freeze until firm, at least 2 hours.

Macerate the strawberries in the kirsch for 1 hour. When ready to serve, unmold the ice cream onto a platter. Decorate with whipped cream piped through a pastry bag and surround with the strawberries. Pour some of the Sauce Riche over the strawberries and pass the remainder separately. Can be prepared for garnishing several days ahead.   YIELDS 6 SERVINGS.
❖❖❖

Bombe Teixeira

COFFEE ICE CREAM, RASPBERRY
SAUCE, AND STRAWBERRIES

I created this dessert for Eugene Teixeira, who would rather eat ice cream.

- 1 quart coffee ice cream
- 1½ cups Raspberry Sauce (see page 276)
- 3 tablespoons kirsch
- 1 cup heavy cream, whipped
- 1 tablespoon sugar
- 1 pint strawberries

Pack the ice cream into a 1-quart mold and freeze at least 2 hours. Combine the Raspberry Sauce with 2 tablespoons kirsch and set aside. Unmold ice cream onto a serving platter. Pour a layer of sauce over the top. Whip the cream until stiff, adding the sugar and remaining tablespoon of liqueur. Pipe the whipped cream onto the top of the ice cream and arrange the strawberries, dipped in Raspberry Sauce, on top of the cream and around the base. Serve the remaining sauce separately. Can be prepared for garnishing several days before.
❖❖❖   YIELDS 6 SERVINGS.

PUDDINGS

PUDDING is not a pretty word, not even the French version, *pouding*. It hardly indicates anything edible, never mind delectable. Its stodgy name reminds us of school lunchrooms and undistinguished cafeterias. Fortunately, however, the results *can* be superior. They can even reach the heights of the most elegant cooking, suitable for the most *luxe* of tables. In addition, most puddings are easy to make, requiring inexpensive ingredients that are readily available in most homes.

Perhaps the greatest problem with puddings is the memories. If I tell a class that the dessert will be rice pudding, I can watch the faces sink into despair and disappointment. Rice pudding ranks in the minds of many of us as one of the more unpleasant childhood trials. The very idea conjures up thoughts of the culinary tortures of schools and camps.

In fact, a well-made rice pudding can reach heights of excellence to appease the most demanding of gourmets. Please take the time to prepare one of these desserts. You will realize that rice pudding does not have to mean hard pellets in a gluey mix with a carefully counted number of raisins, blanketed with poor-quality cinnamon. Try *Riz à la Maltaise* (Orange-Flavored Rice Pudding) or one of the other rice puddings, and you will soon realize how truly delicious these desserts can be. To ease into the situation, you might make one of the recipes in which rice pudding is the base for fruit garnishes, such as Blueberry Conde; that way the pudding-weary will have the fruit to entice them to taste the rice.

The rice for rice pudding should be a short-grained rice that will cook to a truly soft consistency. If you use converted rice or the extra-fancy, extra-long-grain rice selected to cook into separate grains, the results will not be as creamy.

There are no rules on what constitutes a pudding. Puddings can be as heavy as a dense, fruit-packed Christmas plum pudding or as ethereally light and delicate as a *Pouding aux Liqueurs*. Puddings can be served hot, warm, at room temperature, or cold, depending on the type. However, a very important point when serving rice pudding and many of the other denser puddings is to serve them not too cold. All too often the desserts are served directly from the refrigerator, whereas, for the best flavor and consistency, they should be served at just a degree or two below room temperature.

Many puddings are steamed. For steaming, the pudding is put into a buttered mold, covered securely, and placed in a kettle with hot water halfway up the sides of the mold, or baked in a water bath in a slow oven. The pudding is then steamed until done.

PUDDING MOLDS

Pudding molds are made of porcelain or metal. The metal molds often have tight-fitting lids with bail handles. They can be plain or elaborately detailed. Porcelain molds may be as simple as a bowl or far more elaborate, with interior designs such as lions couchant or floral arrangements. If you use a covered metal mold, butter the mold, including the inside of the lid, and fill it with pudding. Place a piece of buttered paper over the pudding and push the cover on securely. Set it to steam. If you wish to use a mold without a lid, crimp foil around the top and tie it securely with string.

Porcelain molds often have a lip around the outside edge to which you can secure a cheesecloth or towel han-

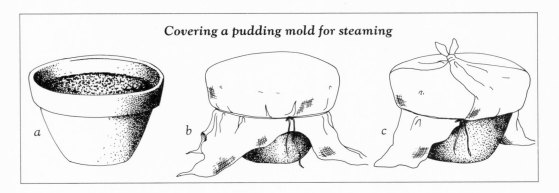

Covering a pudding mold for steaming

dle. Cover the mold with a piece of buttered waxed paper or foil. Cut a square of cheesecloth twice as wide as the opening, or use a kitchen towel. Center the cloth over the filled pudding basin. Tie a string around the mold over the towel and under the lip of the basin. Bring the opposite corners of the cloth back up over the top and tie securely (see sketch). The knot of fabric on the top of the mold can now be used as a handle to lower the pudding into or remove it from the kettle. This handle, although not entirely necessary, is wise, as the steam in the kettle is very hot and potentially dangerous. The handle allows you to reach in and get a firm grip on the pudding to remove it — or, more safely, to insert the prongs of a kitchen fork into the handle. Trying to reach into the kettle with a pair of pot holders can be extremely awkward, at best.

Steamed puddings can be made a day or two ahead, steamed, allowed to cool, and resteamed before serving. Steamed puddings can be frozen and many improve with a period of curing.

To Cure a Pudding

Plum pudding is the most common steamed pudding and is best if allowed to cure before serving. Other puddings filled with dense fruit mixtures can also benefit from a period of curing. After the pudding has been steamed, unmold it and let it cool. Saturate a piece of cheesecloth or sheeting with cognac, rum, or orange liqueur and wrap it around the pudding. Wrap the package in foil and put it into an airtight container. Keep in a cool place for a month or longer; it will keep for months. Many families prepare their Christmas puddings a year or more in advance so the flavor will have a chance to develop. Be sure to check the pudding periodically to check that the cloth is still damp, and add more liqueur if needed.

Vanilla and Chocolate Puddings

For many people, the word pudding does not conjure up rice, plum, or bread desserts, but rather the creamy vanilla and chocolate concoctions that are all too often made from packaged mixes. True, they can be ready in an instant, but they are usually loaded with additives and taste awful. Creamy puddings are, in fact, easy to prepare at home. They are no more than flavored pastry cream, or crème pâtissière. Rather than give specific recipes here, I have listed the basic recipe in the chapter on Basic Recipes along with several suggestions for flavoring.

Summer Pudding I

This pudding makes a good alternative to shortcake.

2 cups heavy cream
2 tablespoons sugar
1 (8-inch) Sponge Cake layer (see page 278)
1 cup currant jelly
4 cups peaches, peeled and thinly sliced
4 cups strawberries, thinly sliced

Whip the cream and sweeten with the sugar. Reserve some for garnish. Slice the Sponge Cake into 4 layers. Place 1 layer in the bottom of a glass bowl. In a small bowl, beat the currant jelly until thin enough to spread. Spread ¼ cup of the jelly over the cake and cover with a layer of peaches and strawberries. Coat with a layer of whipped cream. Continue, using all of the ingredients, ending with a layer of fruits. With a pastry bag fitted with a no. 8 open-star tip, garnish the dessert with the remaining whipped cream. Chill for at least 2 hours before serving. Can be prepared for garnishing the day before.   YIELDS 6 SERVINGS.
❖❖❖

Summer Pudding II

An old English favorite, which uses the bounteous fruits of summer to advantage.

1 pint blackberries, raspberries, or loganberries
½ cup water
Sugar to taste
½ pound white bread, crusts removed, thinly sliced
1 teaspoon arrowroot mixed with 1 tablespoon water
Cold heavy cream

Butter a 1½-quart soufflé dish or bowl. In a saucepan, simmer the fruit with the ½ cup water, covered, for 5 minutes. Strain, reserving the juice. Purée the fruit in a blender and strain to remove any seeds. Add the reserved juice and sweeten well. Pour a little fruit purée into the bottom of the mold. Put in 1 or 2 slices of bread on top and add more purée. Continue until the dish is very full, making sure each layer is well soaked with purée. Reserve a cup of purée for the sauce. Put a plate on top of the pudding and a 2-pound weight on top of the plate. Refrigerate overnight.

In a small saucepan, combine the arrowroot and 1 tablespoon water and stir in the remaining purée. Heat, stirring, until thickened and clear. Cool. Just before serving, turn out the pudding and spoon the sauce on top. Serve cold heavy cream separately. Can be prepared 2 or 3 days before serving.
YIELDS 6 SERVINGS.

Note: You can substitute cherries or currants, as well as blueberries, for the fruits listed above.
❖❖❖

Gâteau aux Fruits

MIXED FRUIT BREAD PUDDING

For the best flavor, toast the bread for this pudding until just barely golden.

2 cups mixed glacéed fruits
1 cup rum
6 slices bread, lightly toasted
4 eggs, separated
¾ cup sugar
2 cups milk
1 teaspoon vanilla
2 cups Caramel Sauce (see page 271)

Preheat oven to 325°F. Macerate the fruits in the rum for 2 hours and drain.

Cut the toast into small cubes. Put a layer of toast cubes in the bottom of an 8-cup baking dish. Top with a layer of fruits. Continue layering loosely until all the ingredients are used. The last layer should be toast. Put the egg yolks into a bowl and gradually stir in the sugar, milk, and vanilla. Beat the egg whites until stiff and fold into the yolk mixture. Stir carefully into the bread and fruits. Set into a water bath and bake for about an hour or until a knife inserted in the center comes out clean. Serve warm or cold, with Caramel Sauce. Can be prepared the day before.

▼▼ YIELDS 6 SERVINGS.

Swiss Pudding

An easy family dessert — excellent for a cold winter's night.

2 pounds Cortland apples, peeled and
  sliced
¼ cup granulated sugar
Grated rind of 1 lemon
½ teaspoon cinnamon
2 tablespoons water
4 cups bread crumbs
⅔ cup firmly packed light brown sugar
½ cup butter
Cold heavy cream or Custard Sauce
  (see page 273)

Preheat oven to 350°F. In a saucepan, cook the apples, sugar, lemon rind, cinnamon, and water over moderate heat until the apples are tender. Mix the bread crumbs and brown sugar together. Layer the apples and bread crumb mixture in a 1½-quart ovenproof baking dish, ending with the bread crumbs. Dot with the butter. Bake until browned and crisp, about 25 to 30 minutes. Serve hot or warm with cold cream or warm Custard Sauce passed separately. Can be reheated. YIELDS 6 SERVINGS.
▼▼▼

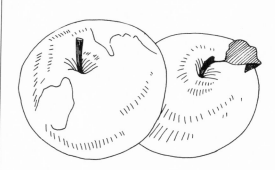

Apple Layer Pudding

1 pound tart cooking apples, cut into
  ¼-inch slices
3 tablespoons lemon juice
1 teaspoon grated lemon rind
⅓ cup raisins
½ cup firmly packed brown sugar
½ teaspoon cinnamon
1 cup plus 2 tablespoons flour
1 teaspoon baking powder
¼ teaspoon salt
⅔ cup grated suet
6 tablespoons cold water
Custard Sauce (optional; see page 273)

In a bowl, toss the apples with the lemon juice, rind, raisins, brown sugar, and cinnamon. In a bowl, mix the flour, baking powder, and salt. Stir the suet into the flour and sprinkle with the cold water. Work gently to form a soft, not sticky, dough. Turn the dough onto a lightly floured board and roll ¼-inch thick. Cut into a 3-inch circle, a 5-inch circle, and a 7-inch circle. Place the smallest circle in the bottom of a well-buttered 4-cup pudding basin. Top with half the apple mixture, place the next pastry layer on top, add apples, and cover with the largest circle. Trim to fit inside the basin. Cover the basin for steaming (see pages 162–163). Cover and steam for 2 hours. Unmold and serve with Custard Sauce if desired. Can be resteamed. YIELDS 6 SERVINGS.
▼▼▼

Gâteau des Pommes Reinettes

Aᴘᴘʟᴇ Pᴜᴅᴅɪɴɢ I

Reinettes are a variety of French apples. In their place, I recommend Cortlands or Granny Smiths.

½ cup raisins
¾ cup rum
1 cup day-old bread crumbs
2 pounds apples, peeled, cored, and
    sliced
3 tablespoons lemon juice
4 eggs, separated
¾ cup sugar
Grated rind of 1 orange
½ teaspoon vanilla
1½ teaspoons cinnamon
3½ tablespoons Clarified Butter (see
    page 286)
½ cup red currant jelly, melted

Preheat oven to 375°F. Macerate the raisins in the rum for 15 minutes, drain, and add the rum to the bread crumbs. Sprinkle the apple slices with the lemon juice. In a bowl, beat the egg yolks with ½ cup sugar until light in color. Stir in the raisins, orange rind, soaked bread crumbs, and apples. Add the vanilla and cinnamon. In a bowl, beat the egg whites until they reach the soft-peak stage. Beat in the remaining ¼ cup sugar until the whites hold stiff peaks. Stir a fourth of the egg whites into the apple mixture, to lighten the mixture; do not worry about deflating these egg whites. Gently fold in the remaining egg whites. In a 2½-quart heatproof casserole or saucepan, melt the butter over high heat. When the butter is hot, add the apple mixture. Cook over high heat for 3 minutes without stirring.

Cover and bake for 35 to 40 minutes or until the mixture has puffed and drawn away from the sides. Unmold onto a serving platter. Pour the jelly over the top and serve. Can be served hot, warm, or at room temperature. It's best if served shortly after baking.

▼▼▼   Yɪᴇʟᴅѕ 6 ѕᴇʀᴠɪɴɢѕ.

Apple Pudding II

4 tablespoons butter
3 pounds McIntosh apples, peeled and
    cored
½ cup apricot jam
Grated rind of 1 orange
½ cup dark rum
⅔ cup sugar
1 (2-inch) piece vanilla bean
2 cups water
4 Golden Delicious apples, peeled,
    cored, and thinly sliced
1½ cups macaroon crumbs

Preheat oven to 350°F. In a heavy saucepan, melt the butter and add the McIntosh apples, jam, and orange rind; simmer for 15 to 20 minutes or until very soft. Add ¼ cup dark rum and cook, stirring occasionally, until a thick purée is formed. Pour into a 9- by 13-inch baking dish and set aside.

In a saucepan, combine the sugar, vanilla bean, and water and simmer, covered, for 15 to 20 minutes. Add the Golden Delicious apple slices and poach 2 to 3 minutes or until just tender. Drain slices and set aside. Sprinkle the macaroon crumbs on the apple purée and sprinkle with the remaining ¼ cup dark rum. Arrange the poached apple slices neatly over the surface. Bake until hot and bubbly, about 20 minutes. Can be prepared for baking several hours ahead. Serve hot or warm.

▼▼▼   Yɪᴇʟᴅѕ 6 ѕᴇʀᴠɪɴɢѕ.

Pain de Pommes Râpées

GRATED APPLE LOAF

> 1 pound apples, peeled and grated
> 1/3 cup sugar (approximately)
> Pinch of cinnamon
> 5 slices day-old bread, crusts removed, crumbled
> 3/4 cup butter, softened
> Cold heavy cream (optional)

Preheat oven to 375°F. In a bowl, toss the apples, 1/4 cup sugar, and cinnamon. In another bowl, use a fork to mash the bread crumbs with the remaining 2 to 3 tablespoons sugar and 1/2 cup softened butter. Melt the remaining 1/4 cup butter in a 9-inch frying pan, and pack the bread crumb mixture against the bottom and sides with a fork to form an evenly thick shell. Fill the center with the apple mixture, packing with a fork, and cook over low heat, covered, for about 15 minutes or until the edges of the bread begin to brown. Finish uncovered in the oven for 15 minutes.

Slide out onto a serving platter. Serve the cream separately. Serve immediately or let cool to room temperature.

YIELDS 4 TO 6 SERVINGS.

Spiced Apple Pudding

> 4 cups finely diced apples
> 3/4 cup sugar
> 1/4 teaspoon salt
> 1/2 teaspoon ground cloves
> 1/4 teaspoon grated lemon rind
> 1/2 cup orange juice
> 3 tablespoons medium-dry sherry
> 1/4 cup butter, melted
> 3 cups soft, fresh bread crumbs
> Vanilla ice cream or cold heavy cream

Preheat oven to 350°F. Butter a 1-quart charlotte mold. In a large bowl, mix the apples, sugar, salt, cloves, lemon rind, orange juice, and sherry. Set aside. In another bowl, combine the melted butter and bread crumbs and mix well. Fill the mold with layers of bread crumbs and apples, beginning and ending with the crumbs. Cover and bake for 30 minutes. Uncover and bake 15 minutes longer or until the pudding is browned and the apples are tender. Serve hot or warm with ice cream or cold heavy cream. Can be prepared the day before and reheated. YIELDS 6 SERVINGS.

Bondepige med Slør I

VEILED COUNTRY LASS I

One of several versions of this Danish favorite. The browned bread crumbs are supposed to represent a tanned farm girl and the cream, of course, is the veil.

> 2 pounds plums, halved and pitted
> 1 1/4 cups sugar
> 1/4 cup butter
> 2 cups fresh bread crumbs
> 3/4 cup heavy cream
> 1 egg white

Preheat oven to 400°F. Place the plums in a buttered baking dish, sprinkle with 1/2 cup of the sugar, cover with foil, and bake for 25 minutes or until soft. Cool. In a skillet, heat the butter and sauté the crumbs, stirring constantly until golden. Sprinkle with remaining 3/4 cup sugar and mix well. Make a layer of the plums in a 1-quart soufflé dish and sprinkle with crumbs. Keep layering until all ingredients are used. Whip the cream to the soft-peak stage and whip the egg white until it holds soft peaks. Fold the beaten egg white and cream together, and spread over the plums. Chill. Can be prepared, except for the cream, the day before. Prepare cream no more than 4 hours before serving.

YIELDS 4 TO 6 SERVINGS.

Bondepige med Slør II
VEILED COUNTRY LASS II

This dessert can also be prepared with apples or strawberries.

1½ pounds rhubarb, sliced
¾ cup sugar, plus more as needed
½ cup plus 2 tablespoons water
4½ tablespoons cornstarch
Pinch of ground mace or nutmeg
4 tablespoons butter
1¼ cups zwieback crumbs
¼ teaspoon cinnamon
1 cup heavy cream

In a saucepan, poach the rhubarb, a third at a time, in ½ cup sugar and ½ cup water until tender, about 5 minutes. Remove with a slotted spoon to a sieve set over a bowl to catch the juice. Repeat with remaining fruit. Return the juices to the syrup and bring to a boil. In a small bowl, combine the cornstarch with the remaining 2 tablespoons water and stir into the syrup. Simmer until thickened and cleared. Correct seasoning with sugar as needed. Stir in the rhubarb and the mace or nutmeg.

In a skillet, sauté the butter and crumbs with the remaining ¼ cup of sugar and cinnamon, stirring constantly until the crumbs are toasted and golden. In a deep bowl, make a layer of a third of the crumbs and a third of the rhubarb. Repeat using the remaining ingredients. Just before serving, beat the cream until stiff and spread over the dessert. Can be prepared up to 2 days before serving, but bring to room temperature before serving. YIELDS 6 SERVINGS.

Bondepige med Slør III
VEILED COUNTRY LASS III

Another version of this wonderful Danish dessert.

10 tablespoons butter
3 cups dark rye pumpernickel bread crumbs
3 tablespoons sugar
2 tablespoons grated semisweet chocolate
2½ cups applesauce
1 cup heavy cream
2 to 3 tablespoons raspberry jam

Preheat oven to 375°F. Lightly butter a 1-quart mold. In a skillet, cook 8 tablespoons butter, bread crumbs, and sugar over low heat until the mixture is evenly browned and the crumbs are dry and crisp. Remove from the heat and stir in the chocolate until melted. Cover the bottom of the mold with ½ inch of crumbs and spoon on a thick layer of applesauce; continue to layer the ingredients, ending with crumbs. Dot with remaining 2 tablespoons butter and bake for 25 minutes. Let cool to room temperature. Shortly before serving, beat the cream in a bowl to soft-peak stage. Pour over the pudding and garnish with dabs of jam. Can be prepared the day before. YIELDS 6 SERVINGS.

Diplomate aux Bananes
BANANA PUDDING

4 tablespoons golden raisins
18 to 24 ladyfingers (see page 280)
3 cups milk
½ cup rum
6 bananas, sliced
6 tablespoons sugar
3 egg yolks

Macerate the raisins in warm water for 2 hours; drain well. Dip the ladyfingers into a mixture of 1 cup milk and the rum. Line the bottom and sides of a charlotte mold with the ladyfingers. Place a layer of bananas in the mold. Sprinkle with raisins and cover with a layer of moistened ladyfingers. Continue filling the mold, finishing with ladyfingers. Scald the remaining 2 cups milk with the sugar. Beat the egg yolks in a bowl and gradually add the hot milk, stirring constantly. Pour mixture into the mold and let stand for 30 minutes.

Preheat oven to 350°F. and bake pudding in a water bath for 45 minutes. Cool to lukewarm before unmolding. Can be prepared the day before and served at room temperature.

▪▪▪ YIELDS 6 SERVINGS.

Blueberry Conde

A conde is a particularly delicate form of rice pudding, elegant enough for the finest dinner party. Any fruit can be used.

3 tablespoons rice
2 cups milk
1 vanilla bean, split
3 tablespoons sugar, plus more to taste
1 pint blueberries
¾ cup orange juice
1 tablespoon gelatin
3 tablespoons cold water
6 tablespoons plus approximately
    1 cup heavy cream
1 egg white

Lightly oil a 1-quart charlotte mold or soufflé dish. Wash the rice and simmer slowly in the milk in a covered pan with the vanilla bean for 45 minutes or until very soft. Stir from time to time to prevent sticking. Remove from heat, remove vanilla bean, and stir in 3 tablespoons sugar. Cool. Sprinkle berries

with sugar to taste and ¼ cup orange juice. Chill. In a small saucepan, soften the gelatin in the water. Dissolve over low heat and stir into the rice with the remaining ½ cup orange juice. Cool until almost ready to set. Whip the 6 tablespoons heavy cream to the soft-firm stage and fold into the rice. Whip the egg white until stiff and fold into the rice. Pour into the mold and chill until set, at least 2 hours.

Unmold onto a serving platter, surround with the blueberries, and decorate with the additional 1 cup heavy cream, whipped and put through a pastry bag. Can be prepared the day before.
▪▪▪ YIELDS 6 SERVINGS.

Blueberry Buttermilk Pudding

½ cup butter
1 cup sugar
3 eggs
½ teaspoon salt
1½ cups flour
2 teaspoons baking powder
1 teaspoon nutmeg
½ cup buttermilk
½ teaspoon baking soda
2 cups blueberries
Hard Sauce (optional; see page 272)

Preheat oven to 350°F. Butter a 5-cup baking dish. In a processor, cream the butter and sugar and add the eggs and salt. Add the flour, baking powder, nutmeg, buttermilk, and soda to the processor and incorporate with on/off turns. Pour into a bowl and fold in the blueberries. Pour into the baking dish and bake for 30 minutes or until a skewer inserted in the center comes out clean. Serve warm, with Hard Sauce if desired. Should be served within 2 to 3 hours of baking. YIELDS 6 SERVINGS.
▪▪▪

Cold Blueberry Pudding Cups

1 quart blueberries
1 cup sugar
1 teaspoon cinnamon
¼ teaspoon salt
1 cup water
5 tablespoons butter
Loaf of bread, crusts removed, sliced
1 cup Hard Sauce flavored with lemon to taste, or Custard Sauce (see pages 272 and 273)

In a 2-quart saucepan, simmer the blueberries, sugar, cinnamon, salt, and water for 10 minutes. Butter the bread slices and cut into ½-inch cubes. Pour 1 tablespoon of hot blueberry mixture into each of 6 custard cups. Fill with bread cubes, press down so cup is half full, then add more blueberry mixture. Fill again with bread cubes, top with more blueberry mixture, and press until each cup is packed full of bread and saturated with the mixture. Chill at least 2 hours. Serve cold with the sauce. Can be prepared 2 days before serving.
▀▙▀   YIELDS 6 SERVINGS.

Blueberry Pudding

1 cup heavy cream
2 tablespoons plus ⅔ cup sugar
½ teaspoon cinnamon
4 slices white bread, crusts removed
¼ pound butter
1 quart blueberries

Whip the cream with 2 tablespoons sugar and the cinnamon until stiff and put in a serving dish. Chill. Cut the bread into cubes and sauté in the butter until golden and crisp. Add the remaining ⅔ cup sugar and stir so the croutons are coated. When ready to serve, reheat the croutons and add the berries. Heat until the juices start to flow. Serve with the chilled whipped cream. Can be prepared several hours ahead to the point of adding the blueberries.   YIELDS 6 SERVINGS.
▀▙▀

Pouding à la Cerise Française

FRENCH CHERRY PUDDING I

1 ¼ cups sugar
½ cup red wine
2 cups pitted cherries
½ cup butter
1 cup dry bread crumbs, plus extra for dusting
1 vanilla bean, split
3 eggs, separated, plus 2 whites
2 tablespoons apricot jam
½ cup kirsch
Whipped cream or ice cream (optional)

Preheat oven to 375°F. In a saucepan, simmer ¾ cup sugar and the wine for 5 minutes. Add the cherries and simmer 15 minutes more. Drain the cherries, reserving the liquid. In a bowl, cream the butter; add the bread crumbs and beat well. Scrape the vanilla bean seeds into the mixture. Beat in the remaining ½ cup sugar and the 3 egg yolks; beat well. Fold in the cherries. Beat the 5 egg whites until stiff, but not dry, and fold into the cherry mixture. Butter a 2-quart pudding mold and dust with bread crumbs. Pour in the pudding mixture and seal the mold (see pages 162–163). Place in a water bath and bake for 30 to 40 minutes or until a knife inserted in the center comes out clean.

Unmold into a deep serving dish. Stir the apricot jam and kirsch into the reserved cherry juices and pour over the pudding. May be accompanied by whipped cream or ice cream if desired. Serve hot. Can be prepared a day ahead and reheated.   YIELDS 6 SERVINGS.
▀▙▀

Clafouti aux Cerises

FRENCH CHERRY PUDDING II

¼ cup plus 3 to 4 tablespoons sugar
12 ounces cherries, pitted
1 cup flour
¼ teaspoon salt
1½ cups milk
1 cup heavy cream
3 eggs
1 teaspoon vanilla

Preheat oven to 375°F. Butter a 10-ounce quiche or gratin pan and sprinkle with 1 tablespoon sugar. Spread the cherries in the dish and sprinkle with another tablespoon sugar. In a bowl, mix the flour, ¼ cup sugar, and salt. Slowly stir in enough milk to form a paste and then beat in the remaining milk, cream, eggs, and vanilla until the mixture is smooth. Strain over the cherries. Bake until puffed and golden, about 35 minutes. Sprinkle the top with remaining 1 to 2 tablespoons sugar and serve warm. Prepare shortly before serving. YIELDS 6 SERVINGS.

Cherry Pudding

1 pound cherries, pitted
¼ cup plus 2½ tablespoons sugar, plus extra for sprinkling
1½ cups milk, scalded
1 cup bread crumbs
2 egg yolks
Grated rind of ½ lemon
2 egg whites
Heavy cream

Preheat oven to 350°F. Cook cherries in 1½ teaspoons sugar over low heat for 2 to 3 minutes. Pour milk over the bread crumbs and let stand 5 minutes. Stir in egg yolks, 2 tablespoons sugar, and lemon rind. Drain cherries and add to the mixture. Pour into a 1½-quart soufflé dish. Bake in a water bath for 30 to 40 minutes or until just set.

Remove from the oven and reduce temperature to 300°F. Beat the egg whites until they hold soft peaks. Beat in 1 teaspoon sugar and when the egg whites are stiff, fold in the remaining ¼ cup sugar. Pile the meringue on top of the pudding, sprinkle with a little extra sugar, and bake for 30 minutes. Serve hot or cold with the cream served separately. Can be prepared the day before.
YIELDS 6 SERVINGS.

Date Pudding with Nut Topping

10 ounces pitted dates
1 cup milk
1 banana
1 tablespoon flour
2 eggs
1 tablespoon vanilla
¼ teaspoon nutmeg
2 cups heavy cream
¼ cup plus 2 tablespoons dark rum
½ cup chopped walnuts
2 tablespoons butter

Preheat oven to 325°F. Lightly butter a 9-inch-square baking pan. Cut 8 dates into ¼-inch dice and reserve for topping. In a processor, purée remaining dates, milk, banana, and flour. Add the eggs, vanilla, and nutmeg. Blend to mix and stir in cream and ¼ cup rum. Pour into prepared pan and bake in a water bath for 1 hour and 15 minutes or until a knife inserted in the center comes out clean. Let cool 15 minutes.

In a skillet, sauté the nuts in the butter until golden. Add the diced dates and sauté 3 minutes more. Pour in the remaining 2 tablespoons rum and boil until the liquid evaporates and sauce is sticky. Spoon over the pudding and let cool. Cut into 3-inch squares and serve at room temperature or chilled. Can be prepared the day before.

❖❖❖   YIELDS 9 SERVINGS.

Date Pudding

1 cup self-rising flour (see Note)
¼ teaspoon cinnamon
¼ teaspoon allspice
Pinch of ground cloves
Pinch of salt
6 tablespoons butter
½ cup bread crumbs
¼ cup firmly packed dark brown sugar
¾ cup dates, pitted and chopped
2 eggs
1 tablespoon honey
3 tablespoons milk
Sauce Mousseline (optional; see
    page 272)

Butter a 1-quart pudding basin. In a processor, mix flour, cinnamon, allspice, cloves, and salt. Add the butter and process until the consistency of coarse meal. Mix in the bread crumbs, brown sugar, and dates. Add the eggs, honey, and milk and process with on/off turns until blended. Pour into the mold, cover with buttered foil, and tie down. Steam for 2 hours (see page 162). Serve hot with sauce. Can be prepared the day before and resteamed.

           YIELDS 6 SERVINGS.

Note: Self-rising flour includes a predetermined blend of salt and leavening. It is available in most supermarkets.

❖❖❖

Fig Compote with Rice

1 cup rice
1 teaspoon salt
4 cups hot water
¼ cup butter
¼ cup sugar
Juice of ½ lemon

12 hot vanilla-poached figs (see
    page 286)
8 tablespoons chopped toasted
    almonds

Put rice in a large saucepan with cold water to cover by 1 inch. Boil, stirring often, for 15 minutes. Drain and rinse under cold water. Add salt and hot water, and cook until the liquid is absorbed and the rice is tender. Add butter, sugar, and lemon juice. Mix well and arrange in a mound on a serving platter. Cut a slit in each fig and stuff with almonds. Arrange on the rice and pour the fig stewing syrup over all. Serve immediately.   YIELDS 6 SERVINGS.

❖❖❖

Steamed Fig Pudding

1 cup dried figs
⅓ cup minced citron
⅓ cup minced candied lemon peel
1 cup chopped walnuts
1¼ cups sifted flour
1 teaspoon baking soda
½ teaspoon salt
¼ cup butter
1 teaspoon cinnamon
½ teaspoon ground cloves
1 cup firmly packed brown sugar
2 eggs
1 cup grated raw carrot
1 cup grated raw potato
Custard Sauce (optional; see page 273)

Butter a 1½-quart mold. In bowl, cover figs with boiling water and let stand for 15 minutes. Drain. Clip off the stems and chop fruit. Mix the fruit with citron, lemon peel, and nuts. In a bowl, sift the 1¼ cups flour, soda, and salt. Add ½ cup of the flour mixture to the dried fruits and nuts and toss well. In another bowl, cream the butter, cinnamon, cloves, and brown sugar until fluffy. Beat in the eggs. Fold in the grated vegetables. Stir in the remaining ¾ cup flour mixture and beat until smooth. Fold in the fruits and nuts.

Pour into the pudding mold and cover with a lid or tie foil on top. Place in a kettle and add 1 inch of boiling water. Cover and steam for 2 hours (see page 162), adding more water as needed. Serve hot, with Custard Sauce if desired. Can be prepared a day or two ahead and resteamed.

▾▾▾ YIELDS 6 SERVINGS.

Ginger-Rum Bread and Butter Pudding

This is a basic recipe for bread pudding. See Note for only a few of the many variations possible.

3 eggs
½ cup sugar
¼ teaspoon salt
¼ teaspoon ginger
¼ teaspoon cinnamon
1 tablespoon dark rum
3 cups milk
4 slices buttered toast

Preheat oven to 375°F. Butter an 8- or 9-inch baking dish. In a bowl, beat the eggs and sugar until blended. Beat in the salt, ginger, cinnamon, rum, and milk. Cut the toast into 1-inch squares and add to the custard mixture. Pour into the baking dish. Let stand for 20 minutes. Bake in a water bath, or without, for about 45 minutes or until set. Serve warm. Can be prepared for baking several hours ahead.

YIELDS 6 SERVINGS.

Note: To vary this bread pudding, you can substitute 1 teaspoon vanilla for the ginger and rum and add ½ cup raisins, if desired. For an orange-flavored pudding, add the grated rind of 1 orange and substitute the juice of 1 orange for the ginger and rum.

▾▾▾

Lemon Sherry Pudding with Caramel Nut Sauce

A rich dessert. If desired, serve with plain cream rather than the caramel sauce.

2 tablespoons cornstarch
½ teaspoon cinnamon
¾ cup sugar
1½ cups milk, scalded
2 tablespoons butter
½ teaspoon salt
Grated rind and juice of 1 lemon, plus juice of 1 more
3 whole eggs, plus 1 yolk
3 tablespoons dry sherry
Caramel Nut Sauce (see recipe following)

Preheat oven to 325°F. In a saucepan, combine the cornstarch, cinnamon, and sugar. Add the milk and stir until the sugar has dissolved. Add the butter, salt, and lemon rind. Cook, stirring, until the butter has melted. Beat the 4 egg yolks. Stir them into the mixture and cook, stirring, until the mixture is thick enough to coat the back of a spoon (180°F.). Remove from the heat and stir in the lemon juice and sherry. Beat the 3 egg whites until stiff and fold into the mixture. Pour the pudding into individual buttered baking cups and set in a water bath. Bake 30 minutes or until a knife inserted in the center comes out clean. Remove from the oven and cool. Serve chilled with Caramel Nut Sauce. Can be prepared the day before.

YIELDS 8 SERVINGS.

Caramel Nut Sauce

4 tablespoons butter
1 cup firmly packed brown sugar
½ cup dry white wine
¼ cup light cream
⅓ cup chopped pecans

In a saucepan, melt the butter. Add the brown sugar and stir until the sugar is dissolved. Add the wine, stirring, and bring to a boil. Remove from the heat and add the cream. Beat until smooth. Fold in the nuts. Serve warm over chilled pudding. YIELDS ABOUT 2 CUPS.

Lemon Dumplings

6 thick slices bread
6 tablespoons butter
2 eggs
Grated rind and juice of 1 lemon
¼ cup sugar, plus additional for
    topping
Lemon Sauce (see page 275)

Butter 12 custard cups. Place the bread in a 250°F. oven and dry until brittle throughout without browning. Crumple the bread into a bowl and cover with boiling water. Let cool and press out as much water as possible. Beat in the butter and eggs while the bread is still warm. Beat in the lemon rind, ¼ cup sugar, and lemon juice. Mix well. Fill the custard cups, put onto a steamer rack, and steam until cooked through, about 40 minutes. Unmold and sprinkle additional sugar on top. Serve warm with Lemon Sauce. Can be prepared ahead and resteamed.   YIELDS 12 SERVINGS.

Note: If you do not have a steamer basket in which to cook these, improvise by putting the custard cups in a baking pan with an inch of hot water. Cover the pan with foil and simmer gently until done. The dumplings are done when a knife inserted in the center comes out clean.

Snowdon Pudding

½ cup raisins
1 cup bread crumbs
1 cup chopped suet
3 tablespoons flour
¾ cup lemon marmalade
¾ cup firmly packed light brown sugar
6 eggs, beaten
Grated rind of 2 lemons
Lemon Sauce (see page 275)

Preheat oven to 325°F. Cut the raisins in half and press against the sides of a 2-quart buttered mold. In a bowl, mix the bread crumbs, suet, flour, marmalade, brown sugar, eggs, and lemon rind together. Pour into the mold and cover with waxed paper and a cloth or foil; tie securely. Place in a water bath. The water should come three-quarters of the way up the mold. Steam for 2 hours in the oven. Serve with Lemon Sauce. Can be prepared ahead and resteamed.   YIELDS 6 SERVINGS.

Pouding aux Noisettes

HAZELNUT PUDDING

Serve this with a fresh fruit sauce such as raspberry or strawberry.

Light brown sugar
⅔ cup ground roasted hazelnuts
½ cup sifted flour
½ cup butter, softened
2 cups hot milk
½ cup granulated sugar
¼ teaspoon salt
4 large eggs, separated
1 teaspoon vanilla
Custard Sauce (see page 273) or
    whipped cream

Preheat oven to 350°F. Butter a 1½-quart casserole and sprinkle with light brown sugar and 2 tablespoons of the nuts. In a saucepan, blend the flour and softened butter. Add the milk, granulated sugar, and salt. Cook, stirring, over moderate heat until the mixture is smooth and thick. Cool 5 minutes. Beat the egg yolks into the mixture, stir in the vanilla, and add the remaining ground nuts. Beat the egg whites until they hold soft peaks and fold into the pudding mixture. Pour into the casserole. Place in a water bath and bake for 1 hour or until the pudding is puffed and firm in the center. Serve warm, immediately, with the Custard Sauce or whipped cream.   YIELDS 6 SERVINGS.

Mincemeat Pudding

2 cups Mincemeat (see recipe
   following)
1 ½ cups flour
6 eggs, separated
Hard Sauce flavored with vanilla and
   nutmeg (see page 272)

Butter a 1-quart mold. In a large bowl, mix the Mincemeat, flour, and egg yolks until well combined. Beat the egg whites until stiff but not dry, and fold into the Mincemeat mixture. Pour into mold, cover, and steam for 4 hours (see page 162). Serve with Hard Sauce. Can be prepared ahead and resteamed.
YIELDS 6 SERVINGS.

Mincemeat

Perhaps everyone has his favorite recipe. This one is mine, taught to me by Leo White, the chef who taught me to cook many years ago.

½ pound cooked beef, chopped
½ pound cooked beef tongue, chopped
1 pound black currants, chopped
1 ½ pounds raisins, chopped
¼ cup chopped candied lemon peel
¼ cup chopped candied orange peel
½ cup chopped candied citron
½ cup chopped candied cherries
½ cup chopped candied pineapple
¾ pound chopped suet
2 cups firmly packed brown sugar
2 cups diced apple
Grated rind of 1 lemon
Grated rind of 1 orange
¼ cup lemon juice
1 teaspoon nutmeg
½ teaspoon ground cloves
½ teaspoon allspice
1 teaspoon cinnamon
2 cups cognac
½ cup dry sherry
½ teaspoon salt

In a large noncorrosible container, combine the beef, tongue, currants, raisins, candied lemon peel, candied orange peel, citron, cherries, pineapple, suet, sugar, apple, lemon rind, orange rind, lemon juice, nutmeg, cloves, allspice, cinnamon, cognac, sherry, and salt. Mix well and keep covered for at least 3 weeks before using. The Mincemeat will keep for months, kept tightly sealed in a cool place. If necessary, add more cognac and sherry to keep the mixture somewhat fluid. If desired, process the ingredients in a processor to a smoother consistency; however, Mincemeat should have a distinctly minced texture.
YIELDS ABOUT 3 QUARTS.

Note: You may, of course, use prepared candied fruits for this Mincemeat. However, if you prefer, see page 284 for my Candied Orange Peel recipes.

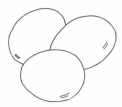

Christmas Pudding

This pudding varies from the more tradi-tional holiday pudding in that it doesn't require long-term curing.

3 cups bread crumbs
6 ounces suet, ground
1¼ cups flour, plus extra for coating
  cloth
1 teaspoon nutmeg
¼ teaspoon salt
½ teaspoon ginger
¼ pound candied fruit, diced
¾ pound raisins
¼ pound currants
¼ cup cognac
3 eggs, lightly beaten
Foamy or Hard Sauce (see page 272)

In a bowl, mix the bread crumbs, suet, 1¼ cups flour, nutmeg, salt, ginger, can-died fruit, raisins, currants, cognac, and eggs. Wring a 14-inch square of un-bleached cotton or muslin in hot water. Spread out and rub in flour to coat well. Pour the pudding into the center of the cloth. Bring up the corners and tie into a ball. Leave room for the pudding to swell. Place in boiling water and cover. Boil for 6 hours. Serve with sauce. Can be prepared several days ahead and re-steamed.   YIELDS 6 TO 8 SERVINGS.

Plum Pudding

Plum pudding, in fact, originally did not have plums. The plums referred to raisins. This particular version does have plums; they give the pudding a full moistness not found in many other recipes.

1½ pounds suet, ground
1 pound brown sugar
1 pound raisins
1 pound prunes, pitted and halved
4 ounces candied mixed fruits
½ teaspoon cinnamon
¼ teaspoon ground cloves
¼ teaspoon nutmeg
2 teaspoons salt
1 pound bread crumbs
4 cups flour
10 eggs
1 cup milk
¾ cup cognac, plus additional for
  soaking
Hard Sauce (see page 272)

In a bowl, mix the suet, brown sugar, raisins, prunes, candied fruits, cinna-mon, cloves, nutmeg, salt, bread crumbs, flour, eggs, milk, and ½ cup cognac until fully blended. Let stand, covered, for 12 hours. Place in large molds (see Note), filling three-quarters full. Cover with buttered paper and tie down with cheesecloth or foil. Tie se-curely. Steam for 5 hours or until a skewer inserted in the center comes out clean. Cool and unmold.

Wrap each pudding in a cloth soaked in additional cognac and store in an air-tight container for at least 3 weeks. When ready to serve, slip the puddings back into their molds and steam for 1 hour or until heated thoroughly. Un-mold onto a platter. Warm remaining ¼ cup cognac and flambé. Serve with Hard Sauce. Can be made several months or more before serving.
YIELDS 3 LARGE PUDDINGS OF
8 TO 12 SERVINGS EACH.

Note: If you do not have several large pudding molds, use coffee cans or more decorative forms such as bundt pans.

Crème Génoise

ALMOND-ORANGE PUDDING

3 tablespoons sugar
4 egg yolks
3 tablespoons flour
¼ teaspoon salt
¼ teaspoon almond extract
¼ teaspoon grated orange rind
4 to 5 tablespoons Grand Marnier
2¼ cups milk, scalded
1 tablespoon butter
2 tablespoons citron, chopped
6 macaroons
½ cup cream, whipped and sweetened

In a saucepan, beat the sugar, egg yolks, flour, salt, almond extract, orange rind, and 3 tablespoons Grand Marnier. Beat well. Gradually pour in the hot milk and cook, stirring, until the mixture just reaches a boil and is thick. Remove from the heat and stir in the butter and citron. Mix well. Crumble each macaroon in the bottom of an individual glass and spoon the custard cream over the top. Chill. Serve garnished with the whipped cream and a few drops of the remaining Grand Marnier. Can be prepared for garnishing the day before.

YIELDS 6 SERVINGS.

Steamed Peach Pudding

¼ cup butter
½ cup sugar
1 egg
1½ cups flour
½ teaspoon salt
4½ teaspoons baking powder
½ cup milk
1 teaspoon almond extract
1 cup dried peaches, diced
Lemon Sauce (see page 275)

Butter a 1½-quart pudding mold. In a processor, cream the butter and sugar. Add the egg and blend. Add the flour, salt, baking powder, and milk. Blend until just mixed. Add the almond extract and the peaches and incorporate with on/off turns. Pour into the mold, cover, and steam for about 1 hour. Unmold and serve with the Lemon Sauce. Can be prepared ahead and resteamed.

YIELDS 6 SERVINGS.

Plum Conde

1½ cups plus 1 tablespoon cold water
7 tablespoons sugar
1 pound fresh plums, pitted
2½ cups milk
6 tablespoons rice
½ teaspoon vanilla
1 tablespoon gelatin
½ cup heavy cream
1 egg white

Lightly oil a 1½-quart bundt pan or ring mold. In a saucepan, bring 1½ cups water and 6 tablespoons sugar to a boil. Poach the plums until tender. Chill. Bring the milk to a boil, add the rice and cook until soft, stirring occasionally to prevent sticking. Test rice after 25 minutes. Remove from the heat and stir in the remaining 1 tablespoon sugar and vanilla. Pour into a bowl and cool. In a saucepan, sprinkle the gelatin over the remaining 1 tablespoon water and stir in 5 tablespoons of syrup from the plums. Let soften and then dissolve over low heat. Stir into the rice and chill.

Whip the cream to the soft-peak stage and fold into the cool rice. Beat the egg white until it holds soft peaks and fold into the rice. Pour into the mold, cover, and chill until set.

Unmold onto a platter; drain the plums (reserving the liquid) and arrange in the center. Any extra plums can be puréed, thinned with the reserved plum syrup, and served as a sauce. Spoon the sauce over the pudding or serve separately. Can be prepared the day before. ❖❖❖   YIELDS 6 SERVINGS.

Pineapple Pudding

2 cups minced fresh pineapple
4 ounces ground almonds
4 egg yolks, lightly beaten
½ to 1 cup sugar as needed
½ cup dry sherry
¼ teaspoon cinnamon
12 ladyfingers (see page 280)
Apricot jam
Sour cream
1 ounce slivered almonds

In a 1-quart saucepan, cook the pineapple, almonds, egg yolks, sugar to taste, and ¼ cup sherry over low heat, stirring constantly, until thickened. Cool and add cinnamon. Spread the ladyfingers with a thin layer of apricot jam. Place half of the ladyfingers in a serving dish. Sprinkle with 2 tablespoons sherry. Spread with half the pineapple mixture. Add a second layer of ladyfingers, the remaining sherry, and the rest of the pineapple mixture. Chill for several hours. Spread with sour cream and stud with the almonds. Can be prepared the day before.   YIELDS 6 SERVINGS.
❖❖❖

Coconut Blancmange with Prune Sauce

Prunes are a delicious fruit, all too often not given their due credit. This sauce shows how wonderful prunes can be.

1½ tablespoons gelatin
¼ cup rum
4 cups milk, scalded

4 tablespoons cornstarch
6 tablespoons sugar
3 cups unsweetened grated coconut
1 teaspoon vanilla
1 pound pitted prunes

Lightly oil a 5- to 6-cup mold and set aside. In a processor, soak the gelatin in the rum until softened. Add the milk, cornstarch, sugar, and coconut. Blend until smooth and pour into a saucepan. Bring just to a boil, stirring constantly. Cool to lukewarm. Add vanilla. Pour into the mold and chill until set, about 4 hours. Soak the prunes in water to cover for 2 hours, then simmer until tender. Purée in a processor; cool. Unmold the blancmange onto a serving platter and surround with the prune sauce. Can be prepared 24 hours before serving.   YIELDS 6 SERVINGS.
❖❖❖

Flaugnarde
FRENCH PRUNE PUDDING

This is a specialty of the Périgord region of France. It is sometimes spelled flagnarde. *Try substituting dried apricots or pears.*

2 ounces raisins
½ pound prunes, pitted and halved
¼ cup cognac
½ cup sugar
4 eggs
Pinch of salt
½ cup flour
1 cup milk
½ teaspoon vanilla
2 tablespoons butter, softened

Cover raisins with cold water and bring to a boil. Then let sit off the heat for 20 minutes. Drain. In a jar, combine the raisins and prunes with the cognac and cover tightly. Macerate for 6 to 7 hours, shaking occasionally until the cognac has been absorbed.

Preheat oven to 375°F. Butter a gratin dish. In a bowl, beat the sugar, eggs, and salt until light in color. Sift in the flour, a little at a time, stirring with a whisk. Stir in the milk, vanilla, prunes, raisins, and any remaining macerating liquid. Stir in the butter and pour mixture into the dish. Bake for 20 minutes. Serve lukewarm from the dish. Can be prepared up to 4 hours before serving.

▼▼▼ YIELDS 4 TO 6 SERVINGS.

Rhubarb-Strawberry Crumble

Apples, blueberries, bananas, peaches, and other fruits can be substituted for the rhubarb in this dessert. Just adjust the sugar to taste.

1 ⅓ cups granulated sugar
1 ¼ cups flour
1 ¾ pounds rhubarb, cut into 1-inch pieces
⅓ cup strawberry preserves
⅓ cup firmly packed dark brown sugar
¼ teaspoon salt
½ cup butter
½ cup chopped pecans
Vanilla ice cream

Preheat oven to 375°F. In a bowl, mix 1 cup granulated sugar and ¼ cup flour with the rhubarb. Put into an unbuttered 9- by 9-inch pan and drop teaspoons of strawberry preserves over the top. In a bowl, mix the remaining 1 cup flour, ⅓ cup granulated sugar, brown sugar, and salt together. Work the butter into the mixture with your fingertips until it resembles coarse meal. Mix in the pecans and spoon over the rhubarb. Bake 35 minutes or until lightly browned and bubbly. Serve warm or cold with vanilla ice cream. Can be prepared up to 4 hours before serving.

▼▼▼ YIELDS 6 TO 8 SERVINGS.

Crème Renversée au Riz et aux Pommes

RICE AND APPLE CARAMEL CUSTARD

Rice pudding is often considered suitable for nurseries and school cafeterias, and as a punishment. This version, however, is truly a reward.

½ cup rice, washed and drained
2 cups milk
¼ teaspoon salt
1 large cooking apple, peeled, cored, and sliced
4 tablespoons butter
¼ cup Calvados
1 cup sugar
3 egg yolks, beaten
2 tablespoons water

In a saucepan, simmer the rice, milk, and salt over low heat for 30 minutes or until the rice is very tender and all but about ½ cup of milk has been absorbed.

Preheat oven to 325°F. In a skillet, sauté the apple slices in 2 tablespoons butter until just tender. Pour on the Calvados and ignite. Let flame subside. In a mixing bowl, cream the remaining 2 tablespoons of butter with ½ cup sugar and blend in the beaten egg yolks. Stir into the rice mixture. In a small saucepan, cook the remaining ½ cup sugar with the 2 tablespoons water until it has caramelized. Pour into a charlotte mold or soufflé dish and tilt and turn the mold to cover the bottom and sides. Add half of the rice mixture to the mold, make a layer of apples, and cover with the remaining rice. Set in a water bath and bake for 30 minutes or until the custard is set.

Remove from the oven and let stand for 15 minutes. Unmold onto a serving dish, letting the caramel drizzle around the rice. Serve warm or cold. Can be prepared the day before.

▼▼▼ YIELDS 6 SERVINGS.

Tyrolean Rice Cream with Apricot Sauce

¼ cup rice
2½ cups milk, or more as needed
4 tablespoons sugar
1 apple, peeled and diced
1 tablespoon gelatin
3 tablespoons orange juice
¾ cup heavy cream
2 tablespoons toasted almonds, shredded
Cold Apricot Sauce (see page 274)

Lightly oil a 1-quart ring mold. In a saucepan, simmer the rice and milk for 35 to 40 minutes or until the rice is very tender, stirring occasionally. Remove from heat, stir in the sugar, and cool. Add more milk if required to make a thick, but not solid, mixture. Fold in the diced apple. In a small pan, soften the gelatin in the orange juice and dissolve over low heat. Stir into the rice. Whip ¼ cup heavy cream until stiff and fold into the rice. Pour into a mold and chill until set. Unmold onto a platter. Whip the remaining ½ cup heavy cream until stiff and decorate the rice with rosettes. Scatter the almonds over the top and spoon the sauce around the base. Can be prepared for garnishing the day before.

▼▼▼   YIELDS 6 SERVINGS.

Pommes au Riz Meringuées

MERINGUE-TOPPED APPLE RICE PUDDING

½ cup rice
2 tablespoons butter
1¼ cups milk, scalded
¼ teaspoon salt
3 tablespoons granulated sugar
2 large eggs, separated
3 apples, peeled, cored, and vanilla-poached (see page 286)

½ cup plus 1 tablespoon sifted confectioners' sugar
Red currant jelly or apricot jam (optional)

Soak the rice for 30 minutes in water to cover. Drain well.

Preheat oven to 325°F. In a 1½-quart saucepan, melt the butter and cook the rice, stirring, until the rice is dry and starts to stick to the pan. Add the milk, salt, and granulated sugar. Cover and simmer until the rice is tender and the milk has been absorbed, about 18 minutes. In a bowl, beat the egg yolks lightly and stir into the rice mixture. Spread on a serving dish. Cut the apples into halves and arrange on the rice. In a bowl, beat the egg whites until they hold soft peaks. Gradually beat in ½ cup confectioners' sugar. Pipe the meringue onto the apples with a pastry bag or swirl on with a spoon. Sprinkle lightly with remaining 1 tablespoon confectioners' sugar. Bake for 12 to 15 minutes or until the meringue has browned lightly. If desired, top each apple with a dot of jelly or jam. Serve warm. Can be prepared several hours ahead to the point before topping with meringue.

YIELDS 6 SERVINGS.

Note: If you prefer, you may put the rice in separate mounds and top each mound with an apple half.

▼▼▼

Pouding de Riz à l'Orange

FRENCH ORANGE RICE PUDDING

½ cup dark raisins
½ cup Cointreau
1 quart milk

¾ cup sugar
½ cup long-grain rice
2 teaspoons grated orange peel
1 teaspoon grated lemon peel
2 teaspoons vanilla
2 tablespoons orange liqueur
1½ cups heavy cream, whipped
6 to 8 orange segments

Macerate the raisins in the Cointreau for at least 30 minutes. In a medium-sized saucepan, simmer the milk, sugar, rice, and orange and lemon peels, covered, stirring occasionally, until most of the milk has been absorbed (45 to 60 minutes). Stir in the raisins with the Cointreau, vanilla, and orange liqueur. Cool. Fold the whipped cream into the cooled pudding and spoon into a serving bowl. Garnish with orange segments just before serving. Can be prepared the day before serving.
 YIELDS 6 SERVINGS.

✓Riz à la Maltaise
ORANGE-FLAVORED RICE PUDDING

⅔ cup long-grain rice
2 cups milk
1½ tablespoons gelatin
⅓ cup cold water
Juice and grated peel of 1 orange
½ cup minced candied orange peel
1 tablespoon orange liqueur
⅔ cup sugar
2 cups heavy cream, whipped
Peeled orange segments
Orange-Apricot Sauce (see page 274)

In a covered saucepan, simmer the rice and milk until the milk is absorbed and the rice is tender. Soften the gelatin in the water and stir into the hot rice. Add the orange juice, fresh and candied peel, orange liqueur, and sugar. Let cool completely and fold in the whipped cream. Transfer to a 6-cup mold and chill for at least 2 hours. Unmold and decorate with the orange segments. Serve the sauce separately. Can be prepared the day before. YIELDS 6 SERVINGS.

Poires à l'Impériale
RICE PUDDING WITH PEARS

½ cup sugar
4 egg yolks
Pinch of salt
1 cup milk
1½ teaspoons vanilla
2 cups cooked white rice
½ cup mixed glacéed fruits
2 teaspoons gelatin softened in ¼ cup
   cold water
1 cup heavy cream
6 vanilla-poached pears (see page 286)
2 tablespoons kirsch
½ cup currant jelly, melted

Lightly oil an 8-inch round cake pan. In a saucepan, cook the sugar, egg yolks, salt, and milk, stirring over moderate heat, until mixture is thick enough to coat the back of a spoon (180°F.). Stir in the vanilla. Add the rice, glacéed fruits, and softened gelatin. Chill until the mixture begins to thicken. Whip ½ cup heavy cream until it holds soft peaks, then fold into the rice. Turn into the cake pan and chill until firm, at least 2 hours.

Unmold onto a platter. Place pears around the top of the rice. Whip the remaining ½ cup heavy cream with the kirsch and pile in the center of the pears. Brush the pears with melted currant jelly. Can be prepared for garnishing the day before. YIELDS 6 SERVINGS.

Ananas à l'Impériale (Pineapple Rice Pudding): Prepare rice mixture as for Poires à l'Impériale and garnish with diced fresh pineapple macerated in kirsch.

1. Use a little more milk to cook rice
2. Left out candied orange peel

Strawberry Rice Romanoff

As almost always, the macaroons should be almond, not coconut.

1 cup rice
1 quart water
Salt to taste
3 cups heavy cream
3 tablespoons kirsch, Grand Marnier, or cognac
3 tablespoons sugar
20 almonds, blanched and sliced
24 macaroons (see page 261) soaked in kirsch, Grand Marnier, or cognac
Whipped cream
Strawberry Sauce (see page 276)

Cook the rice in lightly salted water for 25 minutes or until very tender. Do not stir. Drain the rice and let cool. Whip the cream until stiff and flavor with the liqueur and sugar. Stir in the almonds. Fold the cream-nut mixture into the rice; place a third of the rice mixture in a large glass serving bowl. Arrange half the soaked macaroons on top, cover with another third of rice, and then with the remaining 12 macaroons. Top with remaining third of rice. Chill at least 6 hours.

Garnish with whipped cream. Serve the sauce separately. Can be prepared the day before.   YIELDS 6 SERVINGS.

Creole Pudding

2 cups firmly packed brown sugar
1 cup cake crumbs
1 cup chopped pecans
1 cup raisins
½ cup bourbon whiskey
½ cup water
½ cup diced citron (optional)
1 cup heavy cream, whipped, flavored with bourbon

Preheat oven to 350°F. Butter a 1½-quart soufflé dish. In a bowl, combine the brown sugar, crumbs, pecans, raisins, whiskey, and water. Mix well. Pour into the mold and bake for 15 minutes or until a knife inserted in the center comes out clean. Decorate the top with citron if desired. Serve warm or at room temperature with the whipped cream. Can be prepared up to 6 hours before serving.   YIELDS 6 SERVINGS.

Pouding aux Liqueurs

PUDDING WITH LIQUORS

This pudding is in effect a collapsed soufflé. If you wish to serve it as a soufflé, bake without the water bath for about 18 minutes. See the Soufflés chapter.

4 tablespoons butter
½ cup sugar
½ cup flour
½ cup milk
5 eggs, separated
1 tablespoon liqueur (Ricard, Pernod, framboise, or rum)
Custard Sauce (see page 273) flavored with same liqueur

Preheat oven to 400°F. Generously butter a 6-cup charlotte mold. In a saucepan, melt the 4 tablespoons butter and add the sugar and flour. Cook, stirring, until foamy (about 2 minutes). Stir in the milk, whisking constantly. When the mixture is thickened and smooth, remove from the heat and beat in the egg yolks and the liqueur. Beat the egg whites until stiff, then fold them in. Pour into the mold and bake in a water bath for 30 minutes. Let stand until cool. Run a knife around the rim and unmold onto a serving dish. Serve the sauce separately. Can be prepared the day before.   YIELDS 6 SERVINGS.

DESSERT OMELETS

ALTHOUGH dessert omelets used to be quite popular for a sweet finish to family meals, they have gone out of style. That is really too bad. They are quick and simple to make, light, delicious, and warm — the perfect dessert after a soup and bread supper, or a salad and meatless pasta meal. They can also be served as a light ending to a major dinner.

There are four types of dessert omelets: the traditional folded French omelet; the omelet soufflé, which is puffy and light; the *frittata*, a flat egg cake; and the *omelette en surprise*, or baked Alaska.

THE FRENCH DESSERT OMELET

To prepare a French dessert omelet, break the eggs into a bowl and season with a pinch of salt and sugar to taste. Beat about 40 vigorous strokes with a fork. Place the omelet pan over high heat and preheat until very hot. Add 1 tablespoon of butter and let it melt until it is bubbly and starts to turn golden brown. It should smell nutlike. Pour in the eggs and let set about five seconds. Hold the fork with the tines horizontal to the pan and stir the eggs while shaking the pan back and forth with your hand. The object is to keep the egg mixture moving so that it does not stick. As the omelet begins to set, pull its sides toward the center and lift the edges to let the uncooked egg flow underneath.

When the center is almost set but still moist, place the filling in a line across the center. Tilt the pan up and back toward the handle and use the sloping sides of the pan and a fork to help turn a third of the omelet over the filling. Put the pan on the side of the stovetop and place the palm of your hand under the handle with your thumb pointing away from you. Grasp the handle firmly. In one fluid movement, tilt the pan in the opposite

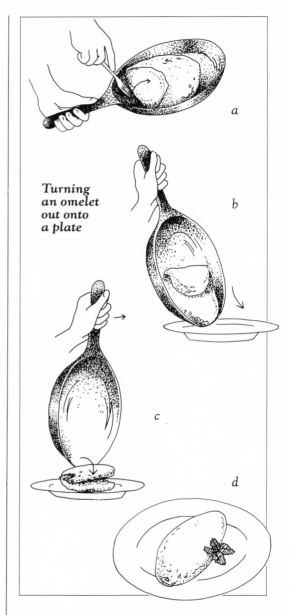

Turning an omelet out onto a plate

a

b

c

d

direction to fold the omelet into thirds (see sketch). Turn the omelet out onto a plate in a neat yellow oval. (Perfectly cooked omelets of this type are not browned because this changes the flavor. Of course, there *are* people who are convinced an omelet is not cooked unless it is brown; you may be required to brown the omelet for them.) Sprinkle the omelet with confectioners' sugar and garnish with some of the filling. Serve at once. These omelets can be prepared in about 30 seconds; therefore, it is possible to prepare omelets for six people in a matter of minutes.

THE SOUFFLÉED OMELET

The second type of omelet is the soufflé omelet. In this instance, the eggs are separated and beaten. The yolks are beaten to a ribbon with sugar; and the whites are beaten until stiff but not dry. The two are folded together with a flavoring and baked in a skillet with a heatproof handle, in a gratin pan, or in a baking dish. The mixture is usually heated on top of the stove before being baked to a puffy lightness. It must be baked and served in the same dish. You cannot transfer the omelet without deflating it. Also, you must serve the omelet immediately. This is not a problem, however. When you serve the salad course of your dinner, fold the whites for the omelet into the beaten egg yolks and let the omelet bake while you are eating the salad. Or, after the salad, prepare the omelet and let your guests relax while waiting for the omelet. Remember that dining should be leisurely, not a race. A few minutes between courses is a pleasure, not a disaster.

FRITTATAS

Frittatas are especially popular in Italy and Spain. The ingredients, including eggs, sugar, and fruit, are mixed together and poured into a hot, buttered skillet. The mixture is allowed to set until the bottom is browned. The frittata is slipped out onto a plate, turned over into the pan, and allowed to brown on the other side. It is often cut into wedges to serve more than one person.

THE OMELET SURPRISE

The fourth type of omelet is really not an omelet at all, but rather one or more flavors of ice cream or fruit topped with meringue that is browned quickly in the oven. Although cooks are often hesitant to prepare these, they ought not to be. The meringue acts as insulation for the ice cream center so that it will not melt.

The classic omelet surprise is a layer of cake, topped with a block of ice cream and decorated with meringue. However, you can fill orange or lemon shells with ice cream, freeze them until firm, and decorate with meringue before browning under the broiler. Or, if desired, you can place a layer of cake in a small, clay flowerpot, pack in the ice cream, and top with meringue; then brown under the broiler and insert a real flower in the center. Remember when making these omelets that you cannot pipe on the meringue and let it stand for more than a few minutes, because the meringue will break down. Ideally, the dessert should be decorated with the meringue and baked just before serving to give a sensation of hot and cold when it is eaten. However, you may not feel up to doing this at the end of the meal. To avoid the last-minute cooking, you can prepare and bake the omelet earlier in the day, or even several days before, and keep it frozen. If frozen, let the omelet mellow in the refrigerator for an hour or two before serving.

Omelette Normande

NORMANDY APPLE OMELET

Although this recipe is written for apples, you can substitute any favorite fruit, such as peaches, pears, or pineapple. Use any liqueur of your choice for the Calvados.

> 2 apples, peeled, cored, and chopped
> 3 tablespoons sugar, plus extra for
>   glazing
> 2½ tablespoons butter
> ½ teaspoon vanilla
> 3 tablespoons Calvados
> 4 eggs
> 2 teaspoons water
> Pinch of salt

Sauté the apples with 1½ tablespoons sugar, 1½ tablespoons butter, and the vanilla until very soft. Add 1 tablespoon Calvados. In a bowl, beat the eggs, the remaining 1½ tablespoons sugar, water, and salt. Heat an omelet pan and melt the remaining 1 tablespoon butter. When the bubbles start to subside, add the eggs. Prepare per French omelet instructions (see pages 184–185). When almost set, place apple mixture in the center, fold, and turn out onto a flameproof platter. Sprinkle the omelet with sugar and glaze under the broiler. Pour remaining 2 tablespoons Calvados, warmed, over the omelet at the table and ignite it. Must be served immediately.

▼·▼   YIELDS 2 OR 3 SERVINGS.

Frittata con le Mele

FLAT OPEN OMELET WITH APPLES

> 2½ tablespoons flour
> Pinch of salt
> ½ cup milk
> 2 eggs, beaten
> 4 teaspoons granulated sugar
> Grated rind of 1 lemon

> 2 apples, peeled and thinly sliced
> 2 to 3 tablespoons butter
> Confectioners' sugar

In a bowl, make a thin, smooth batter with the flour, salt, and milk. Beat in the eggs, granulated sugar, and lemon rind, and mix well. Fold the apples into the batter. In an 8-inch frying pan, melt the butter and heat until hot. Pour in the apple mixture and cook over medium heat until the omelet is golden brown on the underside. Invert onto a hot plate and slide the omelet back into the pan to brown the other side, adding more butter if needed. Slide out onto a platter and sprinkle with the confectioners' sugar. Cut into wedges. Serve immediately.

▼·▼   YIELDS 2 TO 4 SERVINGS.

Apricot and Kümmel Omelet

This omelet is prepared using the French Dessert Omelet instructions (see pages 184–185).

> 2 tablespoons kümmel
> ½ cup apricot preserves
> 6 eggs
> ½ teaspoon salt
> 2 teaspoons granulated sugar
> 2 tablespoons butter
> 1 teaspoon confectioners' sugar

Preheat broiler. In a small bowl, blend the kümmel and apricot preserves; set aside. In another bowl, beat the eggs, salt, and granulated sugar with about 40 vigorous strokes. With 1 tablespoon butter, prepare an omelet, using half of the mixture. Fill with half of the apricot mixture and roll and fold the omelet. Sprinkle with ½ teaspoon confectioners' sugar and glaze under the broiler. Prepare the second omelet in the same fashion. Must be served immediately.

▼·▼   YIELDS 2 TO 4 SERVINGS.

Omelette Soufflée

DESSERT SOUFFLÉED OMELET

8 eggs, separated
1 cup sugar
¼ teaspoon salt
2 tablespoons Clarified Butter (see page 286)
Flavoring (see suggestions below)

Preheat oven to 425°F. In a bowl beat the egg yolks with ½ cup sugar and flavoring until light in color and thickened. In a separate bowl, beat the egg whites with the salt until they form soft peaks. Add the remaining ½ cup sugar, 1 tablespoon at a time, and beat until egg whites are stiff and glossy. Fold the egg yolks into the whites. In a deep 10-inch ovenproof skillet, melt the butter. Spread three-quarters of the batter into the skillet, smoothing the surface with a spatula. Put the remaining mixture into a pastry bag fitted with a no. 6B tip and pipe rosettes or swirls over the soufflé. Or, if desired, you can just swirl the mixture with a spoon. Set over low heat and cook for 3 minutes, or until the bottom starts to set. Transfer to the oven and cook 8 minutes or until the top is firm and golden brown. Serve immediately.

YIELDS 6 TO 8 SERVINGS.

SOUFFLÉED OMELET FLAVORING VARIATIONS

Nutted Omelet Soufflé: Fold in ½ to ¾ cup ground nuts of your choice. Hazelnuts and walnuts are two of the most popular.

Chopped Fruit Omelet Soufflé: Use ½ to ¾ cup chopped fresh fruits, such as strawberries, raspberries, or pears. You can enhance the flavor by macerating the fruit in a complementary liqueur such as framboise, kirsch, or rum for 20 minutes before folding into the omelet.

Vanilla Omelet Soufflé: Fold in 1 teaspoon vanilla extract.

Orange Omelet Soufflé: Fold 1 tablespoon grated orange rind into the mixture with 2 tablespoons orange-flavored liqueur.

Lemon-Flavored Omelet Soufflé: Fold in 1 tablespoon grated lemon rind and 2 tablespoons lemon juice.

Salzburger Nockerln (Salzburg Omelet Soufflé): Fold 1 tablespoon grated lemon rind or 1 tablespoon of rum into the omelet and spoon the mixture into a large oval gratin dish, dropping the mixture in 3 distinct mounds. Bake until puffed and browned and serve with Strawberry Sauce (see page 276).

Omelette en Surprise

BAKED ALASKA

The ice cream for this omelet can be shaped in a round cake or in a log. Use a complementary flavoring for the meringue.

1 quart ice cream
1 (8-inch) Sponge Cake or Génoise layer (see pages 278 and 279)
3 eggs, separated, plus 3 whites
⅔ cup sugar
1 tablespoon kirsch or other flavoring of choice
Pinch of salt

Shape the ice cream in a mold 1 inch smaller than the Génoise layer. Freeze until very hard, at least 4 hours.

Preheat oven to 425°F. In a bowl, beat the 3 egg yolks with ½ cup sugar and the kirsch, or any flavoring appropriate to the ice cream, until thick and lemon-colored. Beat the 6 egg whites with 1 tablespoon sugar and salt until stiff but not dry. Fold the egg whites into the egg yolk mixture. Place the cake layer on an oven-proof serving dish. If desired, sprinkle with some of the liqueur used to flavor the meringue. Unmold the ice cream onto the cake, centering it. Fill a pastry bag fitted with a no. 5 open-star tip with the meringue and pipe it over the ice cream, being sure to cover it completely. Sprinkle top with the remaining sugar.

Bake until golden brown, watching very carefully. Serve immediately or return to the freezer. Can be kept frozen for several days; let temper in the refrigerator for at least 1 hour before serving.
YIELDS 6 TO 8 SERVINGS.

Note: If desired, serve with a strawberry or other fruit sauce. The meringue can be made without the egg yolk enrichment if you prefer. Just beat the egg whites with the 1 tablespoon sugar until they're stiff but not dry.
❖❖❖

Omelette en Surprise Valberge

FRUIT-FILLED BAKED OMELET

1 orange, sliced
1 banana, sliced
5 tablespoons butter
2 teaspoons sugar, plus additional to taste
8 eggs, separated
2 tablespoons Cointreau
4 tablespoons cognac or rum

Preheat broiler. In a skillet, sauté the orange and banana slices in 3 tablespoons butter and 2 teaspoons sugar until warmed. Beat the egg yolks until frothy. Beat the egg whites until very stiff. Fold the yolks into the whites and add sugar to taste. In a large omelet pan,

heat the remaining 2 tablespoons butter and pour in the egg mixture. Spoon the Cointreau over all and cook until the omelet is puffed and set, but still moist. Place the heated fruit slices and their juices in the center and fold over. Place on a hot platter, sprinkle with sugar, and glaze under the broiler. Flame with the cognac and serve immediately.
❖❖❖   YIELDS 6 TO 8 SERVINGS.

Kaiserschmarrn

KAISER'S OMELET

This is reputed to have been the favorite dessert of Emperor Franz Joseph.

6 tablespoons butter
⅔ cup raisins
2 ounces brandy
½ cup granulated sugar
5 eggs, separated
2 cups milk
1 cup flour
Confectioners' sugar

Preheat oven to 350°F. Butter a 9- by 11-inch baking dish. Macerate the raisins in the brandy for at least 20 minutes. In a bowl, stir ¼ cup granulated sugar, egg yolks, and milk until smooth. Gently stir in the flour, stirring until the batter is smooth. Beat egg whites until stiff, then fold into batter. Pour into buttered baking dish and bake for 10 to 15 minutes or until golden.

In a skillet, melt the remaining butter. When the omelet is cooked, tear it into pieces with a fork and put into the skillet with the raisins and remaining ¼ cup sugar. Sauté the omelet pieces until they have a light coating of butter and sugar. Serve immediately with confectioners' sugar over top.
❖❖❖   YIELDS 6 SERVINGS.

CRÊPES

J USTIFIABLY, crêpes captured the imaginations and palates of many people several years ago, and they still hold them. Crêpes are relatively easy to prepare and can even be prepared ahead, ready to be filled at a moment's notice. You can always have a supply in the freezer. Another reason for their popularity may be the elegance and mystery they suggest. They conjure up thoughts of romantic dinners at elegant Parisian restaurants culminating with flaming crêpes. Crêpes also have great versatility. Serve them saturated in liqueurs, aflame or not; rolled and filled with fruits, creams, soufflés, or combinations of these; or stacked into a cake with a filling between each layer.

Although individual crêpes are the thinnest possible pancakes, they can still be rather substantial to eat. Plan to serve one or two filled crêpes and two or three unfilled crêpes for each serving, and serve them after a light meal, rather than after a multicourse dinner. Perhaps they are best served as a mid-evening dessert an hour or two after a dessertless dinner.

Crêpes ought to be very thin, especially dessert crêpes. The batter should be about as thick as heavy cream. Unless you have a pan you use only for crêpes, you may spoil one or two crêpes to get the first successful one. Do not despair; it is just part of making crêpes.

CRÊPE BATTER
Crêpe batter can be made in a processor, in a blender, or by hand. It is simple to prepare. If preparing the batter by hand, combine all of the dry ingredients in a bowl, then add the wet ingredients slowly, working the mixture to a paste and gently turning it into a more liquid form. If the liquid is added all at once, the batter is likely to be lumpy. In a blender or processor, add all of the in-gredients and blend until smooth. For a more tender crêpe, let the batter stand for two to three hours before cooking. Strain the batter and, if necessary, add a little more liquid.

TO SEASON A CRÊPE PAN
Strictly speaking, a crêpe pan is five to seven inches across the base, with straight sides angled away from the bottom (as opposed to an omelet pan, which has curved sides), and a long handle. An omelet pan can be used for crêpes if the classic pan is not available. Crêpe pans are made of aluminum or black steel. Unless the pan has a nonstick finish, it should be seasoned before using the first time and after washing the pan. (Note: Unless you use the pan often, I recommend washing the pan, not scouring it, and reseasoning it when needed, since the oil can go rancid if the pan is just wiped out with salt as is often recommended.) To season the pan, fill it with about half an inch of unflavored vegetable oil and heat until very hot. Let stand until cool and pour off the oil. (Use the oil for deep-frying.) Wipe the pan with paper toweling. If you prepare crêpes fairly often, you may want to retain a pan just for crêpes and omelets. If, however, space is in short supply, use the pan for other cooking. But be sure to reseason it before making crêpes, or they may stick.

TO COOK AND FLIP CRÊPES
There are at least two schools of thought on how to cook crêpes. One is to use a small amount of butter for each crêpe and to flip the crêpe in the air to turn it; the other is to use just enough butter to keep the crêpe from sticking and to use a long, thin metal spatula to turn each crêpe.

Heat about ½ teaspoon butter in a hot pan, swirling to coat the pan fully. Add about ¼ cup batter to the pan and again swirl to spread evenly. Cook over high heat until the edges start to brown. Loosen the sides of the crêpe with a long, flexible metal spatula and shake the pan to loosen the crêpe. Toss it into the air to turn, then cook the second side. (To practice flipping crêpes, place a matchbook in the pan opposite the handle. Give the handle a tug toward you, making a circular upward motion. Once you get the knack, you will be able to toss crêpes, mushrooms, or other foods like a professional.) Cook only until lightly golden. Turn out onto a sheet of waxed paper. Add more butter to the pan and make the next crêpe. Stack the cooked crêpes as you proceed.

The alternative method is to heat a crêpe pan until hot. Add about ½ teaspoon butter to the pan, and swirl to coat the bottom of the pan. Pour in about ¼ cup batter, swirl again to coat the pan evenly, and let cook about 10 seconds. Pour the excess batter into the bowl. Cook until the edges start to brown. With a long, thin, flexible metal spatula, loosen the edges of the crêpe, then slide the spatula under the crêpe and turn it over. Cook until lightly browned. Turn out and make another crêpe, adding butter only when needed.

Which is the right way? There isn't one. The method that works for you is the correct method to use.

Depending on your dexterity, it can be much quicker to prepare crêpes in two's or three's. Set several pans to heat: two, three, or if you are very good, four pans. Add the batter to each pan, return to the first pan, flip the crêpe, and proceed. Go back to the first, turn the crêpe out, refill the pan, and continue along the line. A little practice and you can easily prepare two crêpes at a time, if not more.

Stack the crêpes in groups of 3 to 12 and wrap securely. Freeze until needed.

Do not stack too many crêpes together, but rather make small packages so you can select as many as you need when you need them. The crêpes will keep for at least six months in the freezer if they are well wrapped.

Crêpes Fines Sucrées
SWEET DESSERT CRÊPES

> ¾ cup cold water
> ¾ cup milk
> 3 egg yolks
> 3 tablespoons liqueur
> 1½ cups flour, sifted
> 5 tablespoons butter, melted
> 1 tablespoon sugar

In a blender or processor, blend the water, milk, egg yolks, liqueur, flour, butter, and sugar until smooth. Strain into a bowl. You can use the batter at once, or let it rest for 1 to 2 hours for an even more delicate crêpe. If you wish to prepare the batter by hand, put the flour into a bowl, and work in the egg yolks and liqueur to make a thick, pasty mixture. Then slowly work in the water and milk until the mixture is a smooth, thin liquid. Stir in the butter and sugar. Cook as described above.

▼▼▼ YIELDS ABOUT 24 CRÊPES

Apple Crêpes with Ginger

> 12 dessert crêpes (see preceding recipe)
> 3 tablespoons butter
> 4 apples, peeled, cored, and sliced
> 2 tablespoons sugar
> 2 tablespoons minced crystallized ginger
> 2 tablespoons Calvados or cognac
> ½ to ¾ cup apricot preserves
> Grated nutmeg to taste
> ½ cup dark rum
> 3 tablespoons Calvados

Preheat oven to 300°F. Have crêpes ready. In a skillet, heat the butter and sauté the apples and sugar over moderate to high heat, shaking the pan until the apples are browned and the sugar has caramelized. Add the ginger, 2 tablespoons Calvados or cognac, and apricot preserves. Simmer 2 minutes and sprinkle with the nutmeg. Fill each crêpe with the apples and roll (see sketch).

Place in a buttered ovenproof serving dish and reheat in the oven until hot. In a small saucepan, warm the rum and 3 tablespoons Calvados, pour over the crêpes, and ignite at the table. Can be prepared for reheating several hours before serving.   YIELDS 6 SERVINGS.

Apple Crêpes Brittany

2½ pounds apples, peeled, cored, and diced
½ cup plus 1 tablespoon butter
⅓ cup plus 3 tablespoons sugar
½ cup raisins
½ cup water
Grated rind and juice of 1 orange
1 teaspoon cinnamon
Pinch of nutmeg
¼ cup Grand Marnier
12 dessert crêpes (see page 191)
Juice of ½ lemon, or as needed
⅓ cup dark rum
¼ teaspoon ginger
Blanched rind of 1 orange, cut in julienne strips

Preheat oven to 325°F. In a skillet, sauté the apples in 3 tablespoons butter for 2 minutes. Sprinkle with 3 tablespoons sugar and add the raisins. Cook until the apples are soft and they start to caramelize. Add the water, grated orange rind, cinnamon, and nutmeg. Simmer until the apples are very tender but still hold their shape. Add the Grand Marnier and set aside.

Rolling crêpes

Fill the crêpes with the apples and roll (see sketch). Place in a buttered ovenproof serving dish and set aside. In a small saucepan, melt the remaining 6 tablespoons butter, stir in the ⅓ cup sugar, and cook until light brown. Add the orange and lemon juices and the rum. Simmer 3 minutes, add the ginger, and correct seasoning with more sugar or lemon juice if needed. Spoon over the crêpes and bake until heated, about 20 minutes. Sprinkle with julienned orange rind. Can be prepared for reheating several hours before serving. Apples can be prepared the day before.
              YIELDS 6 SERVINGS.

Gâteau de Crêpes à la Normande

NORMANDY APPLE CAKE

Most crêpes can be layered as a cake as well as rolled or folded.

4 to 5 cups sliced Cortland apples
⅓ cup sugar, plus more to taste
4 tablespoons butter, melted, plus more to taste
12 dessert crêpes (see page 191)
6 to 8 stale macaroons, crushed
Calvados to taste

Preheat oven to 350°F. Spread the apples in a 9- by 13-inch baking pan and sprinkle with ⅓ cup sugar and 4 tablespoons

Stacking crêpes

melted butter. Bake for about 15 minutes or until tender. Place a crêpe in a buttered ovenproof serving dish; spread with a layer of apples; sprinkle with macaroons, a little melted butter, sugar, and Calvados. Continue layering the ingredients (see sketch). About 30 minutes before serving, increase oven heat to 375° and bake until the apple cake is hot. If desired, you can flambé the dessert with Calvados. To test if it is heated through, put a thin knife into the center, leave 30 seconds, then remove and touch the blade. If the cake is done, blade will be hot. If it is cold, bake longer. Can be prepared for baking the day before.　YIELDS 6 SERVINGS.

Palacsintak Barackízzel

APRICOT PANCAKES

These pancakes are practically the national dessert of Hungary.

  12 dessert crêpes (see page 191)
  ¾ cup apricot jam
  1 cup ground walnuts or hazelnuts
  Confectioners' sugar

Preheat oven to 200°F. Spread each crêpe with 2 teaspoons jam and roll into a cylinder; put into a baking dish and sprinkle with the nuts and confectioners' sugar. Heat in the oven until warm,

about 20 minutes. Serve warm. Can be prepared for heating several hours before serving.　YIELDS 6 SERVINGS.

Chestnut Crêpe Torte

This is another of the crêpe recipes calling for stacking the crêpes rather than rolling or folding.

  2 eggs, separated
  8 tablespoons sugar
  ¼ cup cognac
  8 ounces semisweet chocolate
  2 tablespoons coffee
  4 tablespoons cold butter
  1 cup chestnut purée
  12 dessert crêpes (see page 191)
  1 cup heavy cream, whipped

Preheat broiler. In a bowl, beat the egg yolks with 4 tablespoons sugar until they form a ribbon. Add the cognac and set aside. In a saucepan, melt the chocolate in the coffee over low heat, stirring, until the chocolate is smooth. Add to the egg yolk mixture, beating well. Beat in the butter, 1 tablespoon at a time. Fold the chocolate mixture into the chestnut purée and chill. On a serving platter, arrange a crêpe and spread with a thick layer of chestnut mixture; cover with another crêpe and continue to stack the crêpes. Chill for at least 4 hours. Beat the egg whites, adding 4 tablespoons sugar, 1 tablespoon at a time, until the whites are stiff but not dry. With a pastry bag fitted with a no. 4 open-star tip, pipe the meringue over the top, and brown under the broiler. Serve immediately with the cream passed separately. Can be prepared for the meringue the day before.

YIELDS 6 SERVINGS.

Note: Chestnut purée is available in gourmet shops.

Banana Crêpes and Rum Sauce

4 bananas, sliced
9 tablespoons butter
¼ cup firmly packed brown sugar
2 teaspoons grated orange rind
¼ teaspoon ginger
Pinch of nutmeg
12 dessert crêpes (see page 191)
8 tablespoons granulated sugar
½ cup orange juice
⅓ cup dark rum
Vanilla ice cream (optional)

Preheat oven to 325°F. In a skillet, sauté the bananas in 3 tablespoons butter and the brown sugar until well coated. Add 1 teaspoon orange rind, ginger, and nutmeg. Fill the crêpes with the banana mixture and arrange in a buttered ovenproof serving dish. In a saucepan, cook the remaining 6 tablespoons butter and the granulated sugar until the butter turns light brown and the sugar just starts to caramelize. Add the orange juice and bring to a boil. Add the remaining teaspoon orange rind and rum and pour over the crêpes. Bake for 10 to 15 minutes or until heated through. Serve with ice cream if desired. Can be prepared for baking several hours before serving.　　YIELDS 6 SERVINGS.
■.■.■

Crêpes aux Gingembre

CRÊPES WITH GINGER

For these crêpes, the folding technique is employed.

¾ cup orange juice
¼ cup grapefruit juice
¾ cup preserved ginger, minced, plus ½ cup syrup
¼ cup butter
12 dessert crêpes (see page 191)
1 teaspoon sugar

¼ cup dark rum, warmed
1 quart vanilla ice cream

In a skillet, heat the orange and grapefruit juices and stir in the ginger syrup. Add the butter and heat, stirring, until melted. Spread 1 tablespoon of preserved ginger on each crêpe and fold into quarters (see sketch). Place in an ovenproof serving dish, overlapping crêpes slightly. Pour on sauce. Sprinkle with the sugar and flame with the rum. Spoon the flaming rum over the crêpes until flames die out. Serve with the ice cream. Can be prepared for flaming several hours before.　　YIELDS 6 SERVINGS.
■.■.■

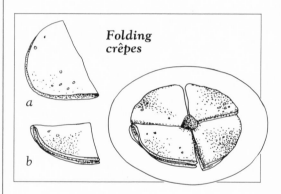

Folding crêpes

a

b

Lemon Crêpes

6 egg yolks
⅔ cup plus ¾ cup sugar
4 tablespoons cornstarch
2 cups milk, scalded
1 teaspoon vanilla
2 tablespoons grated lemon rind
12 dessert crêpes (see page 191)
6 tablespoons butter
⅔ cup lemon juice

In a bowl, beat the egg yolks and ⅔ cup sugar until thick and light in color. Stir in the cornstarch. Beat the milk into the egg yolk mixture and return to the pan. Cook, stirring constantly, over medium heat until thickened and smooth. Strain into a bowl and add the vanilla and 1 tablespoon grated lemon rind. Cover and chill.

Preheat oven to 325°F. When ready to use, spread the crêpes with the filling and arrange in a buttered ovenproof serving dish. In a saucepan, cook the 6 tablespoons butter and ¾ cup sugar over low heat until the butter is melted. Stir in the lemon juice and simmer until the sugar is dissolved. Spoon sauce over the crêpes and sprinkle with remaining 1 tablespoon grated lemon rind. Heat in the oven until hot, 10 to 15 minutes. Can be prepared for saucing and baking the day before.   YIELDS 6 SERVINGS.

Crêpes Gil Blas

How the scoundrel of 17th-century literature gave his name to this dish I do not know, but these crêpes are truly delightful.

6 dessert crêpes made with 1 teaspoon lemon rind added to the batter (see page 191 for basic recipe)
¼ cup butter
1 cup confectioners' sugar
Pinch of salt
½ teaspoon grated lemon rind
¼ cup light cream
1 teaspoon kirsch
Strawberry Sauce (optional; see page 276)

Preheat oven to 350°F. Have crêpes prepared and hot. In a processor, cream the butter, sugar, and salt until very smooth. With the machine running, add the lemon rind and enough cream to make a fluffy mixture. Add the kirsch. Place a tablespoon of the mixture onto each crêpe, then roll it up and heat in the oven for 5 minutes. Serve with the sauce passed separately. The filling and crêpes can be prepared the day before. Heat the crêpes, wrapped in foil, until warm, before filling.
                           YIELDS 3 TO 6 SERVINGS.

Crêpes aux Mandarines
CRÊPES WITH TANGERINE

24 dessert crêpes (see page 191)
Grated zest and juice of 1 tangerine, plus additional teaspoon grated zest
7 tablespoons tangerine liqueur
¾ pound sweet butter

Preheat oven to 375°F. Prepare crêpes, adding the zest of 1 tangerine and 3 tablespoons liqueur to the batter before cooking. In a processor, cream the butter with the tangerine juice and additional teaspoon zest. Add the remaining 4 tablespoons liqueur. Put 1 tablespoon butter mixture in each crêpe and fold into quarters. Place in an ovenproof serving dish and bake until heated thoroughly. Can be prepared for baking several hours ahead.
                           YIELDS 6 TO 12 SERVINGS.

Crêpes aux Poires I
CRÊPES WITH PEARS I

24 to 30 dessert crêpes (see page 191)
1 cup sugar
¼ cup water
10 pears, peeled, cored, and sliced
½ teaspoon vanilla
½ cup chopped crystallized ginger
2 cups Custard Sauce, heated (see page 273)

Prepare crêpes and have ready. In a skillet, cook the sugar and water until caramel-colored. Add the pear slices, vanilla, and ginger. Simmer until the pears are tender and the syrup has thickened. Fill the crêpes with the warm pear mixture, arrange on serving plates, and top with warm custard. The pear mixture can be prepared the day before and reheated.   YIELDS 8 TO 12 SERVINGS.

Crêpes aux Poires II
CRÊPES WITH PEARS II

2 vanilla-poached pears (see page 286)
1 cup Pastry Cream (see page 282)
12 dessert crêpes (see page 191)
6 tablespoons butter
⅓ cup sugar
⅓ cup orange juice
⅓ cup apricot liqueur
¼ cup cognac
2 tablespoons strained apricot
   preserves
Lemon juice to taste
Grated rind of 1 lime

Preheat oven to 325°F. Dice the pears and fold into the Pastry Cream. Fill the crêpes with the mixture and place in an ovenproof baking dish. In a saucepan, cook the butter and sugar, stirring until medium brown. Add the orange juice and beat until smooth. Add the apricot liqueur, cognac, apricot preserves, and lemon juice to taste. Spoon over the crêpes and bake until heated through. Sprinkle with grated lime rind and serve. Can be prepared for baking several hours ahead.   YIELDS 6 SERVINGS.
▀▄▀

Crêpes Soufflé au Cointreau
CRÊPES FILLED WITH COINTREAU-FLAVORED SOUFFLÉ

You can use any flavored soufflé filling for these crêpes. See the chapter on Soufflés for ideas.

24 dessert crêpes (see page 191)
1 recipe Orange Soufflé (see page 205)

Sugar
3 tablespoons Cointreau (optional)
Apricot Sauce (see page 274)

Preheat oven to 400°F. Prepare the crêpes. Prepare the Orange Soufflé. Place a crêpe on a baking sheet, place a generous tablespoon soufflé on top, and fold into quarters. Continue with remaining crêpes and soufflé mixture. Sprinkle the crêpes with sugar. Bake for 10 minutes or until puffed and golden. Remove to a serving platter and, if desired, flame the crêpes with Cointreau. Serve the sauce on the side. The soufflé mixture can be made several hours ahead and kept in a covered bowl.
▀▄▀   YIELDS 8 TO 12 SERVINGS.

Crêpes Suzette

¾ cup butter
¾ cup sugar
¾ cup orange juice
Grated rind of 1 orange
1 teaspoon grated lemon rind
Lemon juice to taste
12 dessert crêpes (see page 191)
¼ cup Grand Marnier
2 tablespoons cognac

In a saucepan, melt the butter and cook the sugar, stirring, until it starts to turn golden. Add the orange juice and bring to a boil. Add the orange and lemon rinds with the lemon juice to taste. Transfer to a skillet. Fold the crêpes into quarters and heat in the sauce, soaking them completely. Add the Grand Marnier and cognac, ignite, and spoon the juices over the crêpes. Serve immediately. The sauce mixture can be prepared ahead and reheated. YIELDS 6 SERVINGS.
▀▄▀

FRITTERS & BEIGNETS

FRITTERS, or beignets, are foods that have been dipped in a batter and deep-fried. They can also be plain pastry, such as cream puff pastry or short pastry, that has been deep-fried and served with a fruit sauce. Generally, fritters have to be cooked just before serving; they do not hold up to being fried and reheated. The exceptions are the fried pastries, as opposed to those with batter coatings. However, like all fried foods, fritters cook quickly and require a very brief time to prepare. The batter can be made well ahead of time and the fruit prepared for dipping. When ready to serve, heat the deep fat and dip the fruits; they will be golden brown in about a minute. Any sauce, of course, should be prepared ahead.

Fritters are usually sprinkled with confectioners' sugar just before serving. If desired, they can be glazed under the broiler. Watch them carefully; the sugar can burn in an instant.

Though fritters are most often coated with a batter, they can also be coated à l'Anglaise, with an egg and bread coating.

DEEP-FRYING FRITTERS

Faultless deep-frying is the result of the right oil heated to the correct temperature. Whenever possible, use a thermometer to check the temperature. In a pinch, you can test the temperature of the oil by dropping in a one-inch cube of bread. It will brown in 50 to 55 seconds at 370°F. — the customary temperature for fritters.

Use an unflavored oil such as cottonseed, soybean, corn, or peanut oil. Fill a heavy pot no more than half full. If you use more oil than that, it may bubble up and over the sides of the pan and catch fire. When deep-frying it is wise to have a large box of salt or baking soda at hand to use on any oil that might catch fire. *Never use water on a grease fire.*

Heat the oil over moderate heat until it is 375°F. Do not add too much food to the pot at one time; the temperature will lower too much and the food will absorb the oil, making it greasy and unpleasant, instead of creating a crisp seal. After you cook the first batch, let the temperature return to 375°F. before cooking more. When the fritters are golden, drain on paper toweling and serve immediately.

The oil can be used several times as long as it is not overheated or heated too often. If the oil is overheated or used too often, it goes through a chemical change that prevents it from browning the food. If you check the last few pieces as they cook, you can tell if they are browning properly. If they are not and the temperature is right, it is time to discard the oil.

When you finish deep-frying, let the oil cool and strain it through a very fine sieve or several thicknesses of fine cheesecloth into a clean container. Store in the refrigerator until needed again. With care, the oil can be used four to six times, which offsets the initial cost.

Pâte à Frire pour Beignets de Fruits

FRITTER BATTER FOR FRUITS

This is the basic batter used for many of the fruit fritter recipes in this section. If beer is not available, you can substitute water or milk; however, the batter will not have the same lightness and delicacy that results from the beer.

½ cup flour
¼ teaspoon salt
1 tablespoon butter, melted

1 whole egg, plus 1 white
½ cup beer

In a bowl, mix the flour and salt together. Add the butter and whole egg and work to a stiff dough. Gradually work in the beer, a tablespoon at a time, until the batter is smooth and the consistency of heavy cream. Let stand in a warm place for 1 to 2 hours. Just before using, beat the egg white until stiff and fold into the batter. Can be prepared the day before. YIELDS BATTER FOR 8 TO 12 SERVINGS.

Note: Occasionally, the batter will not adhere to the fruits because they have been macerated and are too moist. In this case, the fruits can be dried on paper toweling or dipped in flour before dipping into the batter.

Paner à l'Anglaise

ENGLISH OR BREAD CRUMB COATING

This is the egg and bread coating sometimes used for fruit fritters.

Flour, as needed
2 eggs, lightly beaten
2 cups fresh bread crumbs (see Note)

In 3 separate containers, place the flour, eggs, and bread crumbs. Dip the fruits into the flour, roll in the egg, and then roll in the bread crumbs. Let stand on a cake rack until ready to fry. The fruit can be coated up to 6 hours before frying but, if not using right away, keep refrigerated. YIELDS ENOUGH TO COAT 8 TO 12 SERVINGS.

Note: Although the fruit can be coated at the last moment, it is best if the coating has a chance to dry before frying. The bread crumbs should be made from bread that is 2 or 3 days old, but not hard. The crusts should be removed and the bread crumbled in a processor or blender. This gives a light, delicate coating. Bread crumbs made from dried hard bread provide a heavier coating. The crust should be removed because it will darken before the other crumbs and may give your fritters a speckled look.

Chinese Date Rolls

These can be prepared and served as a cookie as well as a dessert on their own.

6 ounces pitted dates
½ cup finely chopped walnuts
2 teaspoons grated orange rind
24 wonton skins
Oil for deep-frying
Confectioners' sugar

Chop the dates into small pieces and mix with the walnuts and orange rind. Place a teaspoon of the filling on the edge of each wonton skin and roll like a jellyroll, pinching along the edge to seal. Leave the ends open. Heat the oil to 350°F. and fry until golden. Cool to room temperature and dust with the sugar. Can be served warm or at room temperature. YIELDS 24 ROLLS.

Note: If the wonton will not stay closed, brush the edge lightly with cold water.

Beignets de Fruits

You can use almost any fruits you choose for these beignets: cherries, strawberries, pineapples, peaches, apricots, pears, apples, etc. Prepare the fruits appropriately. Berries can be left whole, cherries and plums must be pitted, and pineapples can be cut into strips, rings, or chunks. Pears and apples can be cut into wedges or rings.

    2 cups fresh fruits
    Granulated sugar to taste
    Kirsch or orange liqueur
    Fritter Batter for Fruits (see page 198)
    Oil for deep-frying
    Confectioners' sugar

Prepare the fruits and cut into bite-sized pieces. Macerate the fruits in the granulated sugar and kirsch or other liqueur for at least 30 minutes and up to 3 hours. Dip the fruits into the batter and deep-fry at 370°F. until golden and puffed. Drain and sprinkle with confectioners' sugar. Serve plain, or with a favorite fruit sauce (see Sauces chapter).

YIELDS 6 SERVINGS.

Note: The liqueur is not mandatory for these fritters, but it can make a difference. Use just enough to flavor the fruit; do not soak it in the liqueur. Use Cointreau, Grand Marnier, kirsch, rum, framboise, cognac, or other liqueur of your choice. If the batter does not adhere, drain the fruit and roll it lightly in flour before dipping it in the batter.

Fried Bananas and Rum

    6 bananas, peeled and cut into
       1-inch pieces
    3 tablespoons light rum
    1 egg, lightly beaten
    2 cups fresh bread crumbs
    Oil for deep-frying
    Apricot Sauce (see page 274)

In a bowl, macerate bananas in rum for 45 minutes; drain. Dip the bananas into the egg and roll in the bread crumbs. Let dry on a cake rack at least 30 minutes, refrigerated. Fry at 370°F. until golden. Drain and serve with the Apricot Sauce on the side.

YIELDS 6 SERVINGS.

Apricot Rice Croquettes

    ½ cup long-grain rice
    1½ cups milk
    1 vanilla bean, split
    ¼ cup sugar
    Pinch of salt
    2 whole eggs, beaten, plus 3 yolks,
       lightly beaten
    1 cup apricot preserves
    1 cup flour
    2 cups fresh bread crumbs
    Oil for deep-frying
    Apricot Sauce (see page 274)

Preheat the oven to 300°F. In a casserole, bring the rice and cold water to cover to a boil. Drain, rinse, run under warm water, and drain again. Return to the pan. In a saucepan, scald the milk, vanilla, sugar, and salt, and strain over the rice. Discard vanilla bean. Beat the 3 egg yolks into the rice, transfer to a bowl, and cool, covered. Shape the rice mixture into 1½-inch balls and poke a hole in the center of each ball. Fill the hole with apricot jam, forced through a pastry tip. Pinch the opening closed and reshape into a ball. Dip the balls into the flour, eggs, and crumbs. Set aside until ready to fry. Fry at 370°F. until golden. Drain croquettes and serve the Apricot Sauce on the side. Can be prepared for frying the day before.

■▪■   YIELDS 6 SERVINGS.

Beignets de Pruneaux à la Provençale

PROVENÇAL PRUNE FRITTERS

    1 pound pitted prunes
    2 cups hot weak tea
    1 cup light rum
    Fritter Batter for Fruits (see page 198)
    Oil for deep-frying
    ⅓ cup sugar
    ⅓ cup cocoa

Soak the prunes in the tea for several hours. Drain, then soak in the rum for 1 hour or more. Drain the prunes, dip into the batter, and deep-fry at 370°F. until golden brown. Drain on paper toweling. In a bowl, mix the sugar and cocoa and roll the warm fritters in the mixture. Serve immediately.

■▪■   YIELDS 8 TO 10 SERVINGS.

Beignets de Potiron

PUMPKIN FRITTERS

    1 cup cooked pumpkin purée
    2 eggs, separated
    2 tablespoons flour
    ¼ cup granulated sugar

    ½ teaspoon cinnamon
    Pinch of salt
    Oil for deep-frying
    Confectioners' sugar
    ¾ cup honey
    1 teaspoon lemon juice

In a bowl, beat the pumpkin, egg yolks, flour, granulated sugar, cinnamon, and salt together. Beat the egg whites until stiff, but not dry, and fold into the mixture. Heat the oil to 370°F., drop the batter by teaspoonfuls into the oil, and fry until golden. Drain on paper towels and sprinkle with confectioners' sugar.

In a saucepan, heat the honey and lemon juice together and serve separately. The batter can be made several hours before using. Do not add the egg whites until ready to fry.   YIELDS 6 SERVINGS.
■▪■

Beignets d'Ananas

PINEAPPLE FRITTERS

    1 pineapple, peeled, cored, and
       sliced thinly
    ½ cup dark rum
    1 cup apricot jam
    Fritter Batter for Fruits (see page 198)
    Oil for deep-frying
    Sugar to taste
    1 cup raspberry jam

Macerate the pineapple in the rum for several hours. Spread 1 slice of pineapple with apricot jam and sandwich with another slice. Continue pairing until all the slices are used. Dip the sandwiches into the batter and fry at 370°F. until golden. Drain, then sprinkle with sugar. Serve on a warmed platter. Pass the raspberry jam separately.

■▪■   YIELDS 6 SERVINGS.

Soupirs de Nonne

FRIED PUFF BALLS

These airy puffs are politely translated as nun's sighs.

> 1 cup water
> ⅓ cup butter
> ½ tablespoon granulated sugar
> Pinch of salt
> 1 teaspoon grated lemon rind
> 1 cup flour
> 4 eggs
> Oil for deep-frying
> Confectioners' sugar
> Fruit sauce of choice (see Sauces chapter)

In a saucepan, bring the water, butter, granulated sugar, salt, and lemon rind to a full rolling boil. Add the flour all at once and cook, stirring vigorously, until the mixture forms a ball and starts to coat the bottom of the pan. Remove from the heat and allow to cool for 4 to 5 minutes. Beat in the eggs 1 at a time, beating vigorously until the egg mixture is fully incorporated. Or, put the dough into a processor, add all the eggs, and process until blended. Drop teaspoonfuls of the batter into 370°F. oil and cook until puffed and golden. Drain, then sprinkle with confectioners' sugar. Serve the sauce separately. The batter can be prepared several hours before frying.   YIELDS 10 TO 12 SERVINGS.

SOUFFLÉS

THE soufflé is another of those dishes that writers have used to intimidate the novice chef. In fact, though, soufflés are the essence of simplicity. Generally speaking, soufflés consist of three major components: *a thick base* — usually a white sauce that is sweetened for the dessert soufflés, a pastry cream, or possibly a thick fruit purée — *a flavoring*, and *beaten egg whites*. The recipes for whips (see pages 88–98) would produce soufflé-like results.

The most common base for a dessert soufflé is a thick, sweetened cream sauce or pastry cream. Because these creams are made with flour, they must be cooked over high heat and stirred constantly for about two minutes once they reach a boil. This gets rid of any floury taste. Once the cream base is cooked, it should be allowed to cool for about four to five minutes before adding the egg yolks and the flavoring. The flavoring can be a liqueur, grated orange or lemon rind, an extract such as vanilla, or a purée of fruits.

Perhaps the most critical point in making a soufflé is the beating of the egg whites and their subsequent folding into the base and flavorings. The whites should be beaten, preferably with a little sugar, until they have reached their full volume but are not too stiff or dry. When they hold soft, firm peaks, they are ready. Adding sugar helps to prevent overbeating. The goal is to beat the whites until they are fully mounded but not too firm. At the proper stage, they will have the volume to raise the soufflé, but not be so stiff that they will be difficult to fold into the base.

It takes a little practice to learn to fold egg whites or other light ingredients into stiffer ingredients. First, take about a fourth of the beaten egg whites and mix them into the base. Do not be concerned about deflating these whites; the object is to loosen the base mixture. Place the remaining egg whites on top of the base and fold them in as follows: Using a large rubber spatula, cut down through the center of the mixture, then twist the spatula and bring it up along the outside of the bowl and turn it over onto the mixture. Give the bowl a slight turn and repeat the process. Once you have circled the bowl, the mixture should be almost fully blended. If needed, continue around the bowl, folding the egg whites until they are fully incorporated. It is not necessary to fold in all of the white; a few streaks are acceptable and far preferable to overfolding.

SOUFFLÉ DISHES
Soufflé dishes are flat-bottomed, straight-sided molds. They are usually made of porcelain. However, charlotte molds, or for that matter any straight-sided molds, can be used. The only requirement is that the mold be attractive enough to bring to the table.

PREPARING A SOUFFLÉ DISH
Butter a soufflé dish and sprinkle it with sugar. Cut a strip of foil or parchment paper long enough to encircle the dish and overlap with a 2-inch extension above the rim. Pin, crimp, or tie it in place. Butter the paper or foil above the soufflé dish (see sketch on page 132).

BAKING THE SOUFFLÉ
Once made, place the soufflé mixture into the dish, and with your thumb wipe around the inside edge of the dish, about one inch deep. This pushes the soufflé away from the sides of the dish and helps it to rise.

Bake the soufflé on the bottom rack of the oven as close to the heat source as possible. Dessert soufflés generally bake at 375°F. to 400°F. for 18 to 20 minutes.

The interior of the soufflé should be almost runny when served. The runny center provides a sauce and dessert all in one. Some people, however, prefer soufflés that are more fully cooked, almost to the point of being cakelike.

Remember that a cooked soufflé will not wait for your guests; once it is baked, it must be served immediately. This is not as unnerving as it sounds. Soufflés can be prepared for the oven several hours ahead and kept in a draft-free area. If you are concerned about a possible draft, cover the soufflé in its dish with a large bowl. Because the baking is so brief, you can have the base ready and then beat the egg whites, fold them into the mixture, and bake the soufflé after the main course. Serve the salad, and the soufflé should be just done when you are ready for it. More sensible, perhaps, is to put the soufflé dish to bake *after* the salad and cheese. You and your guests can relax and finish the final drams of wine while it bakes. You will all appreciate the chance to rest your palates before dessert.

Soufflé à la Vanille

VANILLA SOUFFLÉ

½ cup milk
1 (1-inch) piece vanilla bean
2 tablespoons butter
1 ½ tablespoons flour
5 eggs, separated, plus 1 white
4 tablespoons sugar

Preheat oven to 400°F. Butter and sugar a 1-quart soufflé dish. Scald the milk and vanilla bean, and let steep. In a 1-quart saucepan, melt the butter, add the flour, and cook until the mixture just starts to turn golden. Stir the milk into the roux and cook, stirring, until thick and smooth. Boil, stirring constantly, for 2 minutes. Remove from the heat,

and remove and discard the vanilla bean. Let cool for 5 minutes. Beat the egg yolks and 3 tablespoons of the sugar into the sauce, beating until well combined. Beat the egg whites with the remaining 1 tablespoon sugar until stiff enough to hold firm peaks. Fold into the sauce mixture and pour into the soufflé dish. Bake on bottom shelf of the oven for 18 to 20 minutes or until puffed and brown.

YIELDS 4 TO 6 SERVINGS.

VARIATIONS

Lemon Soufflé: Omit the vanilla and add the grated rind of 1 lemon and the juice of ½ lemon with the egg yolks.

Orange Soufflé: Omit vanilla and fold the grated rind of 1 orange, 2 tablespoons orange juice, and 1 tablespoon orange liqueur, if desired, into the sauce before folding in egg whites.

Coffee Soufflé: Add 2 tablespoons of double-strength coffee to the base.

Liqueur Soufflé: Omit the vanilla and beat 2 to 4 tablespoons of the liqueur of your choice into the base before folding in the egg whites. For added flavor in a liqueur soufflé, dip 5 or 6 ladyfingers in the liqueur and use to make a layer in the middle of the soufflé.

Soufflé Palmyra (Anisette-Flavored Soufflé): Place one third of the soufflé mixture into a dish. Place 5 ladyfingers on top and sprinkle with 3 tablespoons anisette. Add another third of the soufflé mixture. Place 5 more ladyfingers on top and sprinkle with 3 tablespoons kirsch. Add remaining soufflé mixture.

Ginger Soufflé: Stir ½ tablespoon grated gingerroot into soufflé base, then fold in 2 tablespoons minced candied ginger.

Nutted Soufflé: Fold ¾ cup ground nuts into soufflé base. If desired, serve with rum-flavored whipped cream.

Chocolate Soufflé: Melt 1½ ounces semisweet chocolate in the scalded milk.
◆▾◆

Apple-Macaroon Soufflé

1 cup Apple Purée (see page 283)
½ cup almond macaroon crumbs
2 tablespoons cognac
6 tablespoons butter
6 tablespoons granulated sugar
3 eggs, separated
Confectioners' sugar
1 cup heavy cream, whipped, flavored
   with cognac

Preheat oven to 375°F. Collar, butter, and sprinkle a 1-quart soufflé dish with granulated sugar. In a bowl, combine the purée, macaroon crumbs, and cognac together. In another bowl, cream the butter and granulated sugar and stir in the lightly beaten egg yolks. Fold into the apple mixture. Beat the whites until stiff, then fold into soufflé, pour into the soufflé dish, and bake for 40 minutes. Sprinkle with the confectioners' sugar just before serving. Pass the cream on the side.   YIELDS 4 TO 6 SERVINGS.
◆▾◆

Antonin Carême's Apple Soufflé

Carême was chef to the Prince Regent of England, the Rothschilds, the czar of Russia, and Talleyrand.

3 cups sliced apples
2 cups confectioners' sugar
Grated rind of 1 lemon
1 cup water
9 egg whites

Preheat oven to 350°F. Collar, butter, and sugar a 2-quart soufflé dish. In a large saucepan, cook the apples, 1 cup confectioners' sugar, lemon rind, and water until the apples are tender and dry, but not burned. Beat the egg whites until they hold soft peaks. Gradually beat in the remaining cup confectioners' sugar. Carefully fold the apples into the meringue and pour into the dish. Bake for 40 minutes.
                    YIELDS 8 SERVINGS.

Note: The apples should be somewhat chunky so that the soufflé has texture.
◆▾◆

Apricot Soufflé

1 recipe Lemon Soufflé (see page 205)
½ cup apricot jam

Preheat oven to 375°F. Collar, butter, and sugar a 1-quart soufflé dish. Prepare the Lemon Soufflé base and stir in the apricot jam before adding the egg whites. Pour into the dish. Bake for 18 to 20 minutes.   YIELDS 4 TO 6 SERVINGS.
◆▾◆

Fig Soufflé

This is an especially light soufflé.

6 tablespoons granulated sugar
1½ cups fig purée
3 tablespoons Grand Marnier
5 egg whites
2 tablespoons confectioners' sugar
1 cup heavy cream

Preheat oven to 350°F. Collar, butter, and sugar a 1-quart soufflé dish. In a saucepan, beat the granulated sugar into the fig purée over low heat until the sugar is dissolved. Stir in the Grand Marnier and allow to cool. Beat the egg whites until stiff but not dry. Fold into the fig purée and pour into the prepared dish. Bake for 35 to 40 minutes. Sprinkle with confectioners' sugar. Pass the cream on the side.   YIELDS 4 SERVINGS.
◆▾◆

Hazelnuss Auflauf
HAZELNUT SOUFFLÉ

5 eggs, separated, plus 1 white
¼ cup sugar
¼ cup flour
Pinch of salt
1 cup milk, scalded
1 cup hazelnuts, ground
3 tablespoons butter
2 tablespoons dark rum
1 cup softened coffee ice cream
½ cup heavy cream, whipped,
    sweetened to taste

Preheat oven to 325°F. Collar, butter, and sugar a 1-quart soufflé dish. In a saucepan, beat the egg yolks and sugar until they form a ribbon. Add the flour and salt and beat well. Gradually beat in the hot milk. Cook over low heat, stirring, until mixture thickens and coats a spoon. Remove from the heat and cool. In a skillet, brown the hazelnuts in the butter and add 1 tablespoon rum. Cool. Add the hazelnut mixture to the pastry cream. Beat the egg whites until stiff and fold into the hazelnut mixture. Pour into the soufflé dish and bake in a water bath for 45 minutes or until puffed and golden. Meanwhile, beat the softened ice cream with the remaining tablespoon rum. Fold in the whipped cream and serve with the soufflé.
YIELDS 4 TO 6 SERVINGS.

Soufflé Hilda
LEMON SOUFFLÉ WITH STRAWBERRIES AND RASPBERRIES

1 recipe Lemon Soufflé (see page 205)
1 cup chilled strawberries, sliced
1 cup puréed raspberries

Prepare and bake the soufflé according to the recipe. Serve with strawberries, with the puréed raspberries as a sauce.
YIELDS 4 TO 6 SERVINGS.

Lemon Soufflé with Pernod

1 recipe Lemon Soufflé (see page 205)
1 tablespoon Pernod
¼ teaspoon fennel seeds, crushed

Preheat oven to 400°F. Collar, butter, and sugar a 1-quart soufflé dish. Prepare the soufflé base except for the egg whites; add the Pernod and fennel and mix well. Fold in the egg whites and bake for 18 to 20 minutes.
YIELDS 4 TO 6 SERVINGS.

Hazelnut-Prune Soufflé

3 tablespoons butter, melted
3 tablespoons flour
¾ cup hot prune juice
¼ cup granulated sugar
Pinch of salt
4 eggs, separated, plus 1 white
1 cup cooked prunes, pitted
½ cup ground hazelnuts
1 teaspoon vanilla
Confectioners' sugar
Whipped cream, flavored with cognac
    (optional)

Preheat oven to 375°F. Collar, butter, and sugar a 1-quart soufflé dish. In a saucepan, melt the butter, stir in the flour, and cook just until it starts to turn golden. Stir in the prune juice, granulated sugar, and salt. Cook, stirring, until it is thick and smooth. Simmer 2 minutes. Remove from the heat and beat in the beaten egg yolks. Fold in the prunes, hazelnuts, and vanilla. Beat egg whites stiff and fold into prune mixture. Then pour into the soufflé dish. Bake for 18 to 20 minutes. Sprinkle with confectioners' sugar and pass the whipped cream on the side.
YIELDS 4 TO 6 SERVINGS.

Hot Prune Soufflé

⅔ cup cooked, pitted, and
crushed prunes
6 to 7 tablespoons granulated sugar
6 egg whites
Confectioners' sugar
Sweetened whipped cream, flavored
with rum

Preheat oven to 350°F. Collar, butter, and sugar a 1-quart soufflé dish. In a bowl, combine the prunes and granulated sugar. Beat the egg whites until stiff. Fold into the prune mixture and pour into the soufflé dish. Set in a water bath and bake for 40 minutes. Sprinkle with the confectioners' sugar and pass the cream separately.

YIELDS 6 TO 8 SERVINGS.

Soufflé Grand Marnier in Orange Cases

This is an original soufflé presentation. Arrange the mini-soufflés on green leaves.

6 oranges
½ cup macaroon crumbs
¼ cup Grand Marnier
1 recipe Orange Soufflé (see page 205)

Preheat oven to 400°F. Grate the rind from the top third of each orange and reserve. Cut off the tops and discard. Hollow the oranges, reserving the pulp for another use. If necessary, cut thin slices from the bottom so the shells will stand up. Soak the macaroon crumbs in the Grand Marnier. Fold 2 tablespoons of the grated orange rind and all of the macaroons into the soufflé base before folding in the egg whites. Fill the orange cases and bake for 10 to 12 minutes.

YIELDS 6 SERVINGS.

Soufflé aux Poires

PEAR SOUFFLÉ

3 pears, peeled, cored, quartered, and
vanilla-poached (see page 286)
1½ teaspoons Poire William
2 eggs, separated, plus 4 whites
Pinch of salt
4 tablespoons sugar

Preheat oven to 425°F. Collar, butter, and sugar a 1-quart soufflé dish. Purée the poached pears and the Poire William. Beat in the egg yolks. Beat the egg whites with the salt and sugar. Fold into the pear purée. Pour into the soufflé dish and bake for 18 to 20 minutes.

YIELDS 4 TO 6 SERVINGS.

Soufflé aux Fraises Chambord

STRAWBERRY SOUFFLÉ CHAMBORD

Restaurant Chambord, from which this soufflé gets its name, was once New York's finest restaurant.

1 pound fresh strawberries
½ cup granulated sugar
1½ ounces kirsch
6 egg whites
½ cup confectioners' sugar

Preheat oven to 375°F. Collar, butter, and sugar a 1-quart soufflé dish. Purée the strawberries in a processor, then add the granulated sugar and kirsch. In a bowl, beat the egg whites until stiff, but not dry, with the confectioners' sugar. Fold into the purée. Pour into the prepared dish. Bake for 20 minutes.

YIELDS 4 TO 6 SERVINGS.

Note: If desired, serve with Custard Sauce (see page 273).

TARTS & PIES

FOR many people, pie is the first thought when dessert is mentioned. Whether a two-crust apple pie or a jewel-like open fruit tart, pie is dessert. Cakes, puddings, and the like are okay, but pie is *it*. Although pies are delicious, they can cause trepidation for many otherwise more-than-capable cooks. Some highly experienced cooks and bakers shudder at the thought of pie pastry. I hope the instructions here will dispel much of that fear, or at least provide alternate solutions to making the more difficult kinds of pastry.

If you are the among those who just cannot seem to produce delicate pastry, do not despair. Open tarts can be made with *pâte sablée*, sandtorte pastry, which is virtually indestructible, or with an even simpler cookie-crumb crust. If you feel obligated to make a two-crust pie and are inept at making flaky pastry, you can use one of the frozen versions found in many markets. With a little care, however, most of us can learn to produce acceptable, if not superior, pastry. Just follow the instructions given for making the pastry. Over the years, I have observed that those people who are too meticulous — people who make every cookie exactly the same size and shape — have the greatest problems making pastry. Such machinist perfection in pastry-making is part of the difficulty, if not most of it. Attempting to make the pastry picture-perfect tends to overwork the dough, which develops the gluten and creates a tough result. Always work quickly and lightly.

There are two types of pies: *open tarts* and *two-crust pies*. Open tarts can be filled and baked, or the shells can be partially baked, filled, and baked until done, or fully baked and then filled. The filling can be fruits or creams topped with fruits. The fruits are usual-ly glazed with cooled, melted jam. Apricot and currant are the traditional flavors. The coating not only makes the tarts look inviting, but also protects the fruit from drying out. If you are serving a number of guests, a variety of tarts with different fruits garnishing each will have guests vying with each other for their favorite. Another way to provide variety is to make tiny *barquettes* (boat-shaped pastries) or mini-tarts, so each guest can sample several different flavors.

ROLLING PINS

There are two types of rolling pins. The French pin resembles a log: you roll it over the pastry with the palms of your hands. Many people find this effective and insist that it is the only pin to use. The other type of pin has handles and runs on roller bearings. The handled pin rolls over the dough smoothly without the (to my mind) awkward movement required with the French pin. Whichever pin you select, it should be at least 18 inches long. A smaller pin requires you to do twice as much rolling and can cause you to overwork the dough. The rolling pin should be large enough to roll the dough in one pass without having to roll one side of the pastry and then the other. The pin should be heavy so that it will do much of the work for you.

MOLDS

There are many possibilities for pie molds, including the standard slope-sided pie pan, the traditional tart pan (with or without a removable bottom), and flan rings. Flan rings are generally about one inch high and are round, rectangular, or square. The rings do not have bottoms and are placed on baking sheets without sides. After the shell is baked, the pie is slipped onto a plate and the ring is lifted off, leaving a freestanding tart. Of course, there are also the individual molds such as *barquette*, round, or rectangular tart molds.

TWO-CRUST PIES

Two-crust pies are made without precooking the pastry. To make them, put the fruit into the bottom shell, brush the edges of the shell with cold water or beaten egg to seal the pastry, cover with the top crust, and trim the excess. Crimp the edges together. Cut a steam vent in the top of the crust. You can be as creative or cute as you desire with the vents. They can be a simple V, or more cuts can be used to make a floral design, or perhaps the names of the children can be pricked into the surface. Such extra touches take little time and give people enormous pleasure. Before you bake the pie, brush it with a *dorure*, or gilding. The dorure (egg wash) gives the baked pastry a professional sheen and should not be omitted. Some bakers sprinkle the crust with sugar, plain or mixed with cinnamon or nutmeg, to complement the filling and to give the pie a crystallized finish.

TARTS

There are three principal types of pastry for tarts: *pâte brisée*, flaky pastry; *pâte sablée*, sandtorte pastry; and *pâte feuilletée*, or puff pastry.

Pâte Brisée

Pâte brisée, or flaky pastry, is probably the most common pie pastry. It is necessary for two-crust pies. It can also be used for open tarts when the filling is baked in the shell, but for prebaked shells, *pâte sablée* is more common. The two recipes in this chapter are for the classic method of preparation by hand.

In the classic method for making *pâte brisée*, the butter is worked into the dry ingredients until the mixture resembles coarse meal. You can use your fingertips, but not the palms of your hands. A pair of crossed knives, or a wire pastry blender, works equally well. When the butter is incorporated, make a well in the center of the flour and fat mixture and add most, but not all, of the ice water. With a spoon or fork, pull the sides of the fat-flour mixture just to the center, give the bowl a slight turn, and repeat, pulling the dough together rather than stirring until the dough has been moistened. It will be crumbly and messy. If necessary, add the remaining ice water. Turn the mixture onto a counter and, starting at the edge farthest from you, with the heel of your hand smear the dough in ¼- to ½-cup portions about eight inches across the counter. With a pastry scraper or a knife, push the dough into a flat cake about five inches square, then wrap it in plastic or put it into a plastic bag and chill for about 20 minutes. Do not shape the pastry into a ball. The first step to rolling the dough is to flatten the ball, so if you start flat it will be much easier.

Pâte Sablée or Sandtorte Pastry

Sandtorte pastry is more like a sugar cookie dough than pie dough. It is crisp, rather than flaky. It is also almost impossible to ruin. Sandtorte pastry is prepared by putting all of the ingredients into a bowl and working the mixture with your hand until it is waxy and no longer sticks to your hand. It can be made very quickly in a processor. Shape the dough into a flat cake and chill as above. If you should chill this pastry too long, it will become very hard and you will have trouble rolling it. Let it sit at room temperature until it is soft enough to roll. It is easiest to roll the pastry between sheets of waxed paper. If the pastry is troublesome, you can press it into the tart pan with your fingertips, or repair cracks or holes with patches of pastry. Once the pastry is baked and filled, no one will know the difference.

Pâte Feuilletée or Classic Puff Pastry

This is without question the most difficult pastry to make properly. It is time-consuming and exacting. When done correctly, the results are superb; incorrectly done, it is tough and virtually unpleasant. Do not feel badly if you cannot make this dough; many well-qualified chefs never master the technique. If you *can* produce beautiful puff pastry, then you are justified in patting yourself on the back.

To make the pastry mix the *détrempe*, or dough, of flour, water, and some of the butter. Shape the dough into a flat cake and chill. Shape the remaining butter into a flat cake about 1 inch thick and chill in a plastic bag, if needed, so that the dough and butter are of equal consistency. Roll the pastry large enough so that it can encompass the flat cake of butter. It should be about 1 inch thick. Place the square of butter on top of the pastry, so that the corners of the butter bisect the sides of the pastry square (see sketch). Fold the corners of the pastry envelope fashion over the butter to form a package, letting the pastry edges just meet. Pinch the edges together. With a lightly floured rolling pin, roll the pastry into a 12- by 20-inch rectangle. Fold into thirds, turn the open end toward you, and roll again into a 12- by 20-inch rectangle. Fold again, thus completing 2 turns, and put back into the plastic bag. Refrigerate for 40 minutes.

Remove the pastry from the refrigerator. If the pastry is firm, bang it with the side of the rolling pin until the pastry starts to move on itself. Roll into a 12- by 20-inch rectangle and fold into thirds. Repeat the process. Chill for 40 minutes. Repeat folding and rolling process 2 more times. Chill for 2 hours.

Do not try to roll and fold the pastry more than twice without letting it rest for at least 40 minutes in the refrigera-

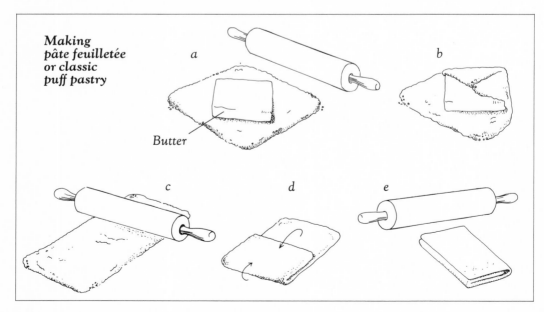

Making pâte feuilletée or classic puff pastry

a

b

Butter

c

d

e

tor. If you do all of the rolling and folding at one time, the pastry will develop too much gluten and will be extremely tough. The pastry can be used for open or closed tarts. If you have trouble preparing puff pastry don't despair: there are several brands that can be purchased in the market.

TO ROLL PASTRY

One major mistake in making pastry is to attempt to roll the pastry into a circle. Think of the pastry as a fabric with a warp and woof. Roll the pastry from the center out and from the center back toward you to make a rectangle. Turn the pastry a quarter-turn and roll again, forming a square. Turn the pastry and continue rolling until it is as thin as you desire. It does not matter what shape the baked shell is going to be; rolling the dough into a square or rectangle prevents you from trying to pull the dough in several different directions at once, and it gives the dough the layers needed to create a flaky result. When the dough is as thin as required, lift it into the mold. You can roll it around the rolling pin, lift it over to the mold and unroll it, or fold the pastry in half and slide it in one fluid movement over half of the pan and unfold it. Once there, lift the edges and place the pastry into position. Do not try to press the dough into place because it will stretch, and when it bakes will shrink again. Trim pastry to fit the pan.

DORURE OR GILDING

A *dorure* is a gilding for the pie. It can be as simple (in bread-making) as salted water. For pies, it is best if based on egg, either whole or the yolk. Beat the egg with a pinch of salt or a tablespoon of water, milk, or cream. Egg yolk and heavy cream will give the darkest, richest sheen to the finished pie.

TO BAKE THE PIE SHELL

Pie shells are filled before or after baking, depending on the desired results. If the recipe calls for an uncooked shell, fill it and bake as directed.

For a partially or completely baked pie shell, prick the pastry with a fork, line the shell with foil, and fill it with beans, rice, or pie weights. Preheat oven to 400°F. Keep the prepared shell in the freezer until the oven is ready, then bake the shell until set. Carefully lift out the foil and weights and bake the shell again until it just starts to turn golden for a partially baked shell or until completely browned for a fully baked one.

TO MAKE A PASTRY MOLD

Both flaky pastry and classic puff pastry can be shaped without the aid of a mold. Roll the pastry about 1/4-inch thick and cut into the desired shape. Rinse a baking sheet under cold water but do not dry it: the steam will help the pastry to rise. Turn the pastry over onto the dampened baking sheet and brush on a one-inch border of water. Cut strips of pastry about one inch wide, and arrange

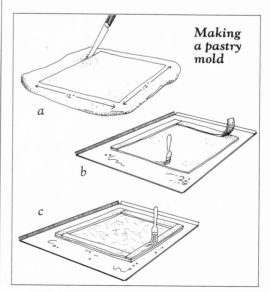

Making a pastry mold

a

b

c

over the edge of the pastry to make a boxlike case (see sketch). Brush the edge with a dorure. Be sure the dorure does not dribble down the sides of the pastry: if it does, it will act as an anchor and hold the pastry to the baking sheet, preventing it from rising. If desired, use a sharp knife to slash a crosshatch design on the edging. Prick the bottom of the pastry with a fork. The pastry can be filled with fruit and baked as an open tart, or baked empty and then filled.

TINY TARTS OR BARQUETTES

Use two- to three-inch molds. Arrange the molds together on a flat surface. Roll the pastry ⅛-inch thick and large enough to cover the group of molds. Lift the pastry onto the molds and let it "rest" into position for a few minutes. With a small ball of dough, press the pastry into each mold. Roll a rolling pin over the top of the pastry, letting the edges of the molds cut the pastry to fit (see sketch).

Stack two pastry-lined molds with one empty mold on top and arrange on a baking sheet. When all of the molds are

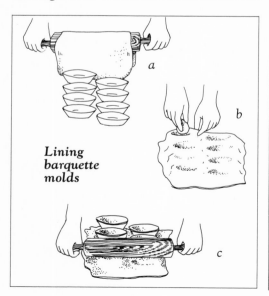

Lining barquette molds

a

b

c

arranged on the sheet, cover with another baking sheet and weight with half a brick or a heavy ovenproof pot. Bake at 375°F. until set and golden, about 25 minutes.

TURNOVERS

Roll the pastry ⅛- to ¼-inch thick and cut into three- to seven-inch circles. Place one teaspoon to two tablespoons of filling in the center of each circle. Moisten the edges and fold one side over the filling to form a half-circle. Press the edges to seal with the fingertips or with the tines of a fork. Crimp the edges with the point of a knife or the tines of a fork. Prick the tops of the pastries to allow the steam to escape. You can also cut the pastry into squares and fold into triangles. Brush with a dorure. Bake about 20 minutes or until golden at 400°F.

Pâte Brisée I

FLAKY PASTRY

This flaky pastry is used both for tarts and for two-crust pies.

> 3½ cups flour
> 2 teaspoons salt
> ¼ teaspoon sugar
> 1¼ cups butter
> 5 tablespoons lard
> 1 cup ice water (approximately)

Put the flour, salt, and sugar into a bowl and mix with your fingers. Cut the butter and lard into 1-inch pieces and add to the flour using your fingertips, a pastry blender, or two knives. Crumble the mixture to the consistency of coarse meal, working quickly and lightly. Add ¾ cup ice water and mix to combine. Add more water if required until the mixture is crumbly and just about holds together. Do not add too much water and do not stir into a neat package.

Turn the pastry onto a board in a pile. It will look messy. With the heel of your hand, starting at the far edge of the dough, smear about 3 tablespoons of dough at a time 8 inches across the surface. Repeat until all of the pastry has been smeared. Form the mixture into a flat cake and wrap in waxed paper, plastic wrap, or a plastic bag. Chill at least 20 minutes. Can be frozen before or after shaping and baking.

YIELDS ENOUGH FOR 4 TO 6 OPEN TARTS
OR 2 TO 3 TWO-CRUST PIES
OR ABOUT 36 TO 72 TURNOVERS.

Pâte Brisée II

FLAKY PASTRY, PROCESSOR METHOD

1 ½ cups flour
1 teaspoon salt
8 tablespoons cold butter
4 tablespoons cold lard
3 ½ tablespoons cold water

In the bowl of a food processor, combine flour and salt. Process 10 seconds. Cut butter and lard into tablespoon-sized pieces and process with on/off turns until mixture is the consistency of coarse meal, about 30 seconds. With machine running, add water. Process until mixture is moistened and starts to form clumps. Remove and put into a plastic bag. Shape into a flat cake about 5 inches square. Chill 20 minutes.

YIELDS ENOUGH FOR
ONE 10-INCH OPEN TART SHELL
OR AN 8-INCH TWO-CRUST PIE.

Note: The lard gives the pastry flakiness. If necessary, you can substitute vegetable shortening, but it will not be the same, just as using margarine for the butter is not the same.

Pâte Sablée

SANDTORTE PASTRY

¼ pound butter
¼ cup sugar
2 egg yolks or 1 whole egg
1 ½ cups flour
1 teaspoon baking powder

In a bowl, combine the butter, sugar, egg, flour, and baking powder. Work until the pastry feels waxy and holds together. Shape into a flat cake and chill for about 20 minutes before rolling. Can be shaped and frozen.

YIELDS ONE 9- TO 10-INCH
OPEN TART SHELL.

Note: This recipe can be made in a processor. Put butter, sugar, egg yolks, flour, and baking powder into a bowl and process until mixture forms a clump. Remove and press into a flat cake about 1 inch thick.

Pâte Feuilletée

PUFF PASTRY

4 cups flour
2 teaspoons salt
1 pound cold unsalted butter
1 cup ice water, or as needed

In a bowl, mix the flour and salt with your fingertips. Cut ¼ pound butter into thin slices and work in with your fingertips until mixture resembles coarse meal. Add just enough water to make a medium-firm pliable dough. With a fork, pull the dough together. *Do not mix or beat.* Work quickly and lightly.

Turn the dough onto a board. It should be a crumbly mess. With a pastry scraper or broad-bladed putty knife, pick up the dough from the bottom and press it onto itself about 8 to 10 times, going around the edges. Use the blade of the scraper to cut through the dough repeatedly to incorporate the ingredients. The process should take no more than 2 minutes. It will still be crumbly. With a pastry scraper, pick up the dough and put it into a plastic bag. Press gently into a flat cake about 5 inches square and refrigerate for 20 minutes.

Put the remaining ¾ pound butter in a plastic bag and work to form a pliable waxy mass. Work quickly and do not let the butter get too warm. Shape it into a 5-inch square. Refrigerate until ready to work the pastry.

Place the pastry on a lightly floured board and roll into a 12- by 12-inch square. It will look messy. Place the square of butter on top of the pastry, so that the corners of the butter bisect the sides of the pastry squares. Fold the corners of the pastry envelope-fashion over the butter to form a package, letting the pastry edges just meet. Pinch the edges together. With a lightly floured rolling pin, roll the pastry into a 12- by 20-inch rectangle. Fold into thirds, turn the open end toward you, and roll again into a 12- by 20-inch rectangle. Fold again, thus completing 2 turns, and put back into the plastic bag. Refrigerate for 40 minutes.

Remove the pastry from the refrigerator. If the pastry is firm, bang it with the side of the rolling pin until it starts to move on itself. Roll into a 12- by 20-inch rectangle and fold into thirds. Repeat the process. Chill 40 minutes. Repeat folding and rolling process 2 more times. Chill 2 hours. The pastry is now ready to roll and shape.

YIELDS ABOUT 2½ POUNDS PASTRY.

Fruit Tarts

Of all the possible fillings for fruit tarts, I think this is the best.

¼ pound butter
½ cup sugar
¼ cup orange liqueur
⅛ teaspoon almond extract
1 cup ground almonds
1 cup heavy cream
1 (10-inch) *Pâte Sablée* shell, baked
  (see page 215)
2 cups fruit or berries
¼ cup sieved Apricot or Currant Glaze
  (see page 283)
Chopped almonds or pistachios
  (optional)

In a processor, cream the butter and sugar until pale and light. Beat in the orange liqueur and almond extract and process until the sugar is dissolved. Add the almonds and process until well mixed. Remove to a bowl. Beat the cream until stiff and fold into the butter mixture. Spread the mixture in the shell and arrange the fruit on top. Brush fruit with glaze. If desired, sprinkle outside edge with chopped nuts. Serve within 6 hours for the best results.

YIELDS 6 TO 8 SERVINGS.

Viennese Fruit Tart

You can substitute fruits of the season for those suggested here.

1 (9-inch) tart shell, baked
2 cups Pastry Cream (see page 282)
Peach halves
Greengage plums, halved
Cherries, strawberries, or raspberries
1 cup heavy cream, whipped
1 tablespoon Currant Glaze (see
  page 283)

Fill the shell with the Pastry Cream and chill until cold. Arrange the peach halves around the outer edge of the tart, make an inner circle of plums, and fill the center with the cherries or berries. In a bowl, mix ½ cup of whipped cream with the Currant Glaze and use it and the plain whipped cream to garnish the tart. Serve within 6 hours.

YIELDS 6 TO 8 SERVINGS.

Tourtière de Quercy

APPLE, PRUNE, AND ARMAGNAC TART

The original version of this recipe calls for hand-stretched strudel dough. Substituting phyllo dough makes the job simpler.

2 pounds apples, peeled and thinly sliced
1½ cups granulated sugar
¼ cup water
½ pound prunes, pitted and quartered
½ cup Armagnac or rum
1 tablespoon peanut oil
½ pound phyllo dough
2 tablespoons confectioners' sugar

Preheat oven to 350°F. In a medium saucepan over medium heat, cook the apples, ½ cup granulated sugar, and water until quite dry, about 20 minutes. Set aside. Macerate the prunes in the Armagnac or rum while the apples cook. Drain the prunes, reserving the Armagnac, and combine them with the apples. With a pastry brush, lightly oil the bottom and sides of a 16-inch paella pan or cake pan. Center 1 sheet of phyllo in the baking pan and sprinkle generously with granulated sugar and reserved Armagnac. Repeat 3 more times, using 4 sheets of phyllo in all. Spoon the apple-prune mixture on top of the pastry, covering bottom and up side. Top with the remaining sheets of phyllo, sprinkling with more granulated sugar and Armagnac until they are used. Trim any rough edges of pastry and scatter trimmings on top of the pastry. Bake

for 30 minutes, lower heat to 300° and bake 1 hour longer. Dust with confectioners' sugar. Serve hot or at room temperature. YIELDS 10 TO 12 SERVINGS.

Tarte aux Pommes I

APPLE TART I

¼ recipe Puff Pastry (see page 215)
1 cup strained apricot jam
3 to 5 apples, peeled, cored, and sliced
¼ cup plus 1 tablespoon sugar
Dorure (see page 213)
1 cup heavy cream, whipped and flavored to taste (optional)

Preheat oven to 450°F. Run a pastry sheet under cold water, but do not dry it. Roll the pastry into a large rectangle. Cut out an 8- by 16-inch section and turn over onto a pastry sheet. Brush a 1-inch border of cold water around pastry. Cut 1-inch-wide strips from the remainder of the pastry and lay them neatly around the edges to make a boxlike case. Pierce the bottom of the dough with a fork. Brush the pastry shell with some of the jam and line the fruit slices in even rows. Sprinkle the ¼ cup sugar over the fruit. Paint the edges of the pastry with the dorure. Crosshatch the border of the tart. Set into the oven and bake for 20 minutes or until the sides have puffed and begun to brown. Lower the heat to 400° and bake another 20 minutes or until the sides of the tart feel crispy and firm. If the pastry is browning too much, cover loosely with a sheet of foil.

Remove to a rack to cool. In a saucepan, simmer the remaining apricot jam and 1 tablespoon sugar until mixture is sticky. Brush the hot jam over the apples. Serve the tart warm with the cream on the side if desired.

YIELDS 6 TO 8 SERVINGS.

Tarte aux Pommes II

APPLE TART II

1 (9-inch) tart shell, unbaked
Juice of 2 lemons, plus grated rind of 1
1 teaspoon vanilla
3 pounds apples, peeled, cored, and
thinly sliced
½ cup water
½ cup yellow raisins
½ to 1 cup sugar to taste
½ cup Apricot Glaze (see page 283)

Chill the tart shell for 1 hour. Preheat oven to 350°F. In a bowl, combine with the juice of 1 lemon and the vanilla enough apple slices to cover the tart. Add water to cover. In a medium-sized saucepan, cook the remaining apples, remaining lemon juice, grated rind, and ½ cup water, covered, until the apples begin to steam. Stir gently. Cook uncovered until tender, mashing with a fork. They do not have to be smooth. Stir in the raisins and sugar to taste. Cool. Fill the tart shell with the applesauce. Drain the reserved apples and arrange in concentric circles on the top. Bake for 1 hour on the lowest rack. Cool to room temperature. Brush with the Apricot Glaze.   YIELDS 6 TO 8 SERVINGS.

Marlborough Pie

2 cups finely shredded apples
½ cup dark raisins or currants
½ cup heavy cream
3 eggs, well beaten
⅓ cup firmly packed brown sugar
2 tablespoons dark rum
¼ teaspoon nutmeg
Pinch of salt
1 (10-inch) pie shell, unbaked

Preheat oven to 450°F. In a bowl, mix the apples, raisins, cream, eggs, sugar, rum, nutmeg, and salt. Pour into the prepared shell. Bake 15 minutes; reduce heat to 325°. Bake until the filling is set, about 30 minutes. Cool on a wire rack for 15 minutes. Serve warm or at room temperature.   YIELDS 6 TO 8 SERVINGS.

Tarte Tatin

CARAMELIZED APPLE TART
See photograph on page 70.

Named for several sisters who ran a small restaurant in the Loire Valley.

4 pounds apples, peeled, cored, and
sliced (see Note)
⅓ cup plus ½ cup granulated sugar
1 teaspoon cinnamon (optional)
2 tablespoons butter, softened
6 tablespoons butter, melted
1 (9-inch) circle Flaky Pastry (see
pages 214–215)
Confectioners' sugar
2 cups heavy cream
Rum (optional)

Preheat oven to 375°F. In a bowl, toss the apples, ⅓ cup granulated sugar, and cinnamon together. In a 9-inch black cast-iron skillet, spread 2 tablespoons softened butter and sprinkle with ¼ cup of granulated sugar. Arrange a third of the apples on the sugar; sprinkle with 2 tablespoons melted butter; repeat with the apples and butter twice more. Sprinkle remaining ¼ cup granulated sugar on top. Roll the pastry ¼-inch thick and cut large enough to fit the pan. Place it over the pan, allowing the edges to fall inside the edge of the pan. Cut 4 to 5 vents. Bake in the bottom of the oven for 45 minutes to an hour or until the liquid is a thick, brown syrup. If the top starts to darken too much, cover with a sheet of foil.

When the syrup is dark, remove from the oven. Let set for 10 minutes, then invert onto an ovenproof serving dish. The apples should be a light caramel brown. If they are not, sprinkle heavily with confectioners' sugar and run under a broiler to caramelize the surface. Watch them carefully. Serve warm accompanied by the heavy cream. You can whip the cream and flavor it with rum, if desired.   YIELDS 6 TO 8 SERVINGS.

Note: If desired, for a different finish you can use peeled, cored, and halved apples, standing on end instead of sliced.

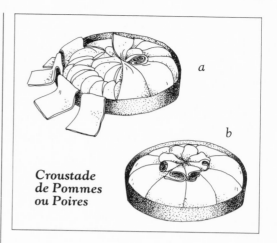

Croustade de Pommes ou Poires

Croustade de Pommes ou Poires

APPLES OR PEARS IN PHYLLO DOUGH
See photograph on page 70.

You can substitute peaches or apricots for the apples or pears if you like.

> 2½ pounds apples or pears, peeled and
>   thinly sliced
> ½ cup granulated sugar
> ¼ cup Armagnac, plus more for
>   topping
> 1 tablespoon orange flower water
> 9 to 10 phyllo dough leaves
> Butter
> Confectioners' sugar

Brush a 10-inch cake pan with some butter. In a bowl, mix the fruit, granulated sugar, Armagnac, and orange flower water together and let stand for 2 to 12 hours.

Place a baking sheet on the lowest rack of the oven. Preheat oven to 400°F. Drain fruit, reserving the liquid. Spread a sheet of phyllo with butter, fold lengthwise, and place 1 end in the center of the pan. Continue with remaining sheets, encircling the pan. Sprinkle lightly with reserved liquid. Pile the fruit in the center of the pastry. Bring

the phyllo up over the fruit, and at the center of the fruit, give the phyllo sheet a twist, then open it and pinch it at the base so it looks like a flower. Continue with the remaining leaves. Sprinkle with reserved liquid. Bake 12 minutes, lower heat to 350°, and bake 20 to 25 minutes longer. Slide onto a wire rack, and sprinkle with confectioners' sugar and additional Armagnac. Serve warm or cold.   YIELDS 8 TO 10 SERVINGS.

Note: Orange flower water is available in pharmacies and gourmet shops.

Apricot Sour Cream Meringue Pie

> 1 cup dried apricots
> 1 cup sour cream
> 1 cup plus 3 tablespoons sugar
> 1 tablespoon cornstarch
> 1 tablespoon butter, melted
> 4 eggs, separated
> 1 teaspoon vanilla
> 1 (9-inch) pie shell, unbaked

Soak the apricots in water to cover for 1 hour. Drain and chop finely.

Preheat oven to 400°F. In a bowl, mix the sour cream, 1 cup sugar, cornstarch, butter, beaten egg yolks, chopped apricots, and vanilla. Pour into the pie shell and bake for 10 minutes. Reduce the heat to 325° and bake for 20 minutes more. Cool the pie. Beat the egg whites and 3 remaining tablespoons sugar until stiff. Spread over the pie, being sure to seal the edges. Swirl decoratively with the back of a spoon. Bake at 375° for 8 to 10 minutes. YIELDS 6 SERVINGS.

Apricot Marzipan Tart

½ cup butter
8 ounces almond paste
2 eggs
1 tablespoon flour
4 tablespoons brandy
1 (9-inch) Flaky Pastry shell, partially baked (see pages 214–215)
1 can (28 ounces) apricot halves
¾ cup Apricot Glaze (see page 283)

Preheat oven to 350°F. In a processor, cream the butter and almond paste together. Add eggs and blend until mixed. Add the flour and 2 tablespoons brandy. Mix well. Spread in partly baked crust and bake on lowest rack for 45 minutes. Drain apricot halves and arrange over almond filling. Heat glaze and remaining 2 tablespoons brandy until syrupy. Brush over the apricots. Serve at room temperature. Can be made a day before and served at room temperature.
YIELDS 6 TO 8 SERVINGS.

Blueberry Cloud Pie

4 large egg whites
¾ cup sugar
½ teaspoon vanilla
Pinch of salt
Pinch of cream of tartar
1½ cups blueberries
1 (9-inch) pie shell, baked

Preheat oven to 375°F. Beat the egg whites to the soft-peak stage. Still beating, slowly add the sugar, vanilla, salt, and cream of tartar until stiff. When stiff, fold in the blueberries and pour into the pie shell. Starting from the outside and working toward the center, make a spiral groove with the back of a wet spoon, about ¾-inch deep in the meringue. Bake for 15 minutes or until the top browns. Serve warm or cold.
YIELDS 6 SERVINGS.

Blueberry Cassis Pie

The crème de cassis accents the flavor of the blueberries in this tasty pie.

3 eggs, separated, plus 1 white
½ teaspoon salt
1 teaspoon vanilla
2 cups granulated sugar
1 teaspoon baking powder
1 cup graham cracker crumbs
½ cup shredded coconut
½ cup chopped hazelnuts
3 cups blueberries
3 tablespoons flour
1 tablespoon lemon juice
3 tablespoons crème de cassis
1 cup heavy cream
3 tablespoons confectioners' sugar

Preheat oven to 350°F. Butter and flour a 9-inch pie pan. Beat the 4 egg whites with ¼ teaspoon salt and the vanilla until foamy. Beat in 1 cup granulated sugar in a slow, steady stream. Continue beating until the egg whites form shiny peaks. Combine the baking powder, graham cracker crumbs, coconut, and nuts and fold into the egg whites. Spread in the pie pan, making the rim slightly higher than the center. Bake for 30 minutes and cool.

In a medium-sized saucepan, cook the berries, 1 cup granulated sugar, flour, remaining ¼ teaspoon salt, lemon juice, 2 tablespoons crème de cassis, and beaten egg yolks over medium heat until the mixture thickens, stirring constantly. Pour the berry mixture into the pie shell and chill. Whip the cream with the confectioners' sugar until the mixture forms stiff peaks. Flavor with remaining 1 tablespoon crème de cassis. Mound the cream on top of the pie, or pipe through a pastry bag fitted with a no. 6A tip. Can be prepared the day before.

❖ YIELDS 6 TO 8 SERVINGS.

Cherry Tart

    1 (9-inch) Sandtorte Pastry shell,
        unbaked (see page 215)
    2 cups cherries, pitted
    3 tablespoons currant jelly, melted

Preheat oven to 400°F. Fill the pie shell with the cherries. Bake for 15 minutes. Reduce heat to 375° and bake 30 minutes longer. Remove from oven and spread with currant jelly.

❖ YIELDS 6 TO 8 SERVINGS.

Tarte aux Cerises

FRENCH CHERRY TART

In France, this tart is often made with unpitted cherries. In theory, the flavor is better, if inconvenient to eat.

    1 pound cherries, pitted
    1 (9-inch) Sandtorte Pastry shell,
        unbaked (see page 215)
    ½ cup sugar
    ¾ cup heavy cream
    1 egg yolk

Preheat oven to 425°F. Arrange the cherries in the pastry in 1 layer. Sprinkle with the sugar. In a bowl, beat the cream and egg yolk until blended. Pour over the cherries and place on the middle rack of the oven. Bake for 20 minutes, lower the heat to 350°, and bake for 15 to 20 minutes or until the pastry is cooked and the custard tests done. Allow to cool partially and serve warm.

❖ YIELDS 6 TO 8 SERVINGS.

Date and Honey Tartlets

After the shell is made, these little tartlets require no cooking.

    1 cup chopped dates
    ½ cup rum
    ½ cup honey
    ½ cup water
    2 teaspoons lemon juice
    ¼ cup toasted slivered almonds
    14 to 16 (2-inch) tart shells, baked
    ½ cup whipped cream

Macerate the dates in the rum for at least 24 hours. In a saucepan, boil the honey and water for 10 minutes. Let cool. Stir in lemon juice. Pour over the dates and stir in the almonds. Fill the tarts. Top each tart with a dollop of whipped cream. The filling can be made the day before. Do not fill more than 2 hours before serving.

❖ YIELDS 14 TO 16 SERVINGS.

Brandied Date Pie

1 cup dates, pitted and chopped
½ cup brandy
1 tablespoon gelatin
¼ cup water
1¼ cups milk
2 eggs, separated
¼ cup sugar
⅛ teaspoon salt
¾ cup heavy cream
1 (9-inch) pie shell, baked
1 cup heavy cream, whipped

Soak the dates in the brandy overnight. In a bowl, soften the gelatin in the water. In a medium-sized saucepan over low heat, cook the milk, egg yolks, sugar, and salt until thick enough to coat the back of a spoon, stirring constantly. Stir in the softened gelatin. Cool and chill until it is nearly ready to set. Whip the ¾ cup heavy cream. Beat the egg whites until stiff. Fold the whipped cream, dates, and egg whites into the gelatin mixture. Pour into the pie shell and chill thoroughly. Garnish the pie with rosettes of remaining whipped cream. Can be prepared the day before serving.   YIELDS 6 TO 8 SERVINGS.
▼▪▼

Grape Tarts

3 cups green grapes
9 tablespoons sugar
6 (3-inch) tart shells, unbaked
3 egg whites
½ cup ground almonds

Preheat oven to 350°F. Toss the grapes in 3 tablespoons sugar and fill the tart shells. Bake for 15 minutes. Beat the egg whites until stiff, beating in the remaining 6 tablespoons sugar. Fold in the almonds. Spread over grapes. Bake for 8 to 10 minutes longer or until the tops are golden. Serve warm or at room temperature.   YIELDS 6 TARTS.
▼▪▼

Lemon Chess Pie

2 cups sugar
Pinch of salt
2 tablespoons grated lemon rind
1 tablespoon flour
1 tablespoon cornmeal
4 eggs
¼ cup butter, melted
¼ cup lemon juice
¼ cup milk
1 (9-inch) pie shell, unbaked

Preheat oven to 350°F. In a bowl, mix the sugar, salt, lemon rind, flour, and cornmeal. Beat in the eggs, butter, lemon juice, and milk. Pour into the pie shell and bake for 50 to 60 minutes or until pie is set and a wooden skewer inserted in the center comes out clean. Serve warm or at room temperature.
▼▪▼   YIELDS 6 SERVINGS.

Mace Lemon Soufflé Pie

4 eggs, separated
¾ cup sugar
½ teaspoon mace
¼ cup lemon juice
1 teaspoon grated lemon rind
1 teaspoon vanilla
Dash of salt
1 (9-inch) pie shell, partially baked

Preheat oven to 325°F. In a heavy saucepan, cook the egg yolks, ¼ cup sugar, mace, and lemon juice, stirring over low heat until the mixture thickens. Remove from the heat, and mix in the lemon rind and vanilla. Add the salt to the egg whites and beat to the soft-peak stage. Beat in the remaining ½ cup of sugar, a tablespoon at a time, until stiff. Fold into the hot lemon mixture. Turn into the shell and bake until golden, about 30 minutes. Cool. Serve at room temperature.   YIELDS 6 TO 8 SERVINGS.
▼▪▼

Fresh Lemon Tartlets

This can be made as one large pie. However, use only one candied violet for each tart no matter what the tart size.

1 cup sugar
1 lemon, thinly sliced, seeded, and cut into quarters
3 eggs
2 tablespoons butter
8 (2-inch) tart shells, baked
Candied violets (optional)

In a bowl, combine the sugar and lemon and toss until the sugar is moistened. Let stand for 2 hours, stirring occasionally. In a saucepan, beat the eggs until thick and pale in color. Stir in the butter and the sugar-lemon mixture. Cook over medium heat, stirring until thickened. Cool. Spoon into the tart shells and garnish with the candied violets if desired. Serve within 6 hours.

▼▼▼   YIELDS 8 TARTS.

Lemon Curd Tarts

1 cup sugar
6 egg yolks
½ cup lemon juice
½ cup unsalted butter
1 tablespoon grated lemon peel
12 (3-inch) Sandtorte Pastry tart shells, baked (see page 215)
1 cup heavy cream, whipped, flavored, and sweetened to taste
Candied violets

In a saucepan, cook the sugar, egg yolks, and lemon juice over low heat, stirring constantly, until the mixture coats the back of a spoon (180°F.). Remove from the heat and whisk until cooled slightly. Stir in the butter and grated lemon peel. Cool completely. Spoon into the tart shells. Pipe a rosette of whipped cream

on each tart and garnish with a candied violet. Serve within 6 hours.

▼▼▼   YIELDS 6 TARTS.

Lemon-Macaroon Tart

2½ tablespoons cornstarch
1½ cups cold water
1½ tablespoons gelatin
⅔ cup lemon juice
⅓ cup sugar
7 egg yolks, beaten well
Grated rind of 2 lemons
1½ tablespoons butter
1 to 1½ cups heavy cream
6 almond macaroons, crushed (see page 261)
1 (10-inch) tart shell, baked
⅔ cup Apricot Glaze (see page 283)
3 lemons, very thinly sliced and seeded

In a small bowl, combine the cornstarch with ¼ cup cold water. In a small saucepan, soften the gelatin in ¼ cup cold water and dissolve over low heat. In another saucepan, boil the remaining 1 cup water, lemon juice, and sugar, stirring until the sugar has dissolved. Carefully stir in the cornstarch and the gelatin. Mix well and bring to a boil. Add a small amount of hot liquid to the beaten egg yolks. Slowly pour the egg yolks into the lemon mixture, mixing well, and bring just to a boil. Remove from the heat and stir in the lemon rind and the butter. Strain into a mixing bowl and cool.

Whip the cream until stiff. Fold into the cooled lemon mixture with the macaroons. Turn into the tart shell. Heat the Apricot Glaze until fluid but not hot. Carefully dip each lemon slice into the glaze and arrange the slices on the top of the tart. Chill until the glaze has set. Serve within 6 hours.

▼▼▼   YIELDS 8 TO 10 SERVINGS.

Lime Meringue Pie

3 tablespoons cornstarch
1 ¼ cups plus 6 tablespoons sugar
¼ cup lime juice
1 tablespoon grated lime rind
3 eggs, separated
1 ½ cups boiling water
1 (9-inch) pie shell, baked

Preheat oven to 425°F. In a saucepan, combine the cornstarch, 1 ¼ cups sugar, lime juice, and rind. Beat in the egg yolks and gradually mix in the boiling water. Simmer, stirring constantly, for 4 minutes. Pour into the pie shell. Beat the egg whites until stiff but not dry, and gradually beat in the remaining 6 tablespoons sugar. Spread over the lime filling, being sure to seal completely. Bake for 5 to 8 minutes or until golden. Serve at room temperature or cold.

▼▼▼   YIELDS 6 TO 8 SERVINGS.

Sour Cream Lime Pie

1 cup granulated sugar
3 tablespoons cornstarch
¼ cup butter
2 tablespoons grated lime rind, plus
    extra for sprinkling
⅓ cup lime juice
1 cup light cream
2 cups sour cream
1 (9-inch) pie shell, baked
1 cup heavy cream
1 tablespoon confectioners' sugar

In a saucepan, simmer the granulated sugar, cornstarch, butter, 1 tablespoon grated lime rind, lime juice, and light cream, stirring constantly, until thickened and smooth. Remove from the heat and let cool. Stir in 1 cup sour cream. Pour into the pie shell. Whip the heavy cream and fold in the confectioners' sugar and remaining 1 cup sour cream. Spread over the pie and sprinkle with the remaining grated lime rind. Can be made the day before.

▼▼▼   YIELDS 6 TO 8 SERVINGS.

Tarte aux Oranges I

ORANGE TART I
See photograph on page 65.

¾ cup water
⅔ cup sugar, plus extra for dusting
2 oranges, thinly sliced, unpeeled
1 ½ cups Pastry Cream (see page 282)
Juice of 1 orange
⅔ cup whipped cream
1 (10-inch) Sandtorte Pastry shell,
    sugar-baked (see page 215)

Preheat broiler. In a saucepan, bring the water and ⅔ cup sugar to a boil, then simmer the oranges for 15 minutes. Remove from the heat and let cool. Chop slightly fewer than a quarter of the orange slices into small pieces. Fold into the Pastry Cream with orange juice, and then fold into the whipped cream. Spread on the baked pie shell and decorate with the remaining orange slices. Dust with sugar. Put under broiler and cook until sugar caramelizes. Watch carefully lest it burn. Protect pastry with foil if required.

▼▼▼   YIELDS 6 TO 8 SERVINGS.

Tarte aux Oranges II

ORANGE TART II

3 cups fresh orange segments
⅔ cup sugar
2 tablespoons cornstarch
Pinch of salt
½ teaspoon vanilla
1 (9-inch) pastry shell, baked
Candied Orange Slices (see page 267)
Glacéed cherries

In a bowl, macerate the orange segments in sugar for 30 minutes. Drain in a sieve for 15 minutes, reserving the juice. Measure the juice and add enough water, if needed, to make 1 cup. In a small saucepan, blend the cornstarch and salt and stir in the orange juice until smooth. Cook over moderate heat, stirring until thickened and clear. Remove from the heat and stir in the vanilla. Arrange the macerated orange segments in the pastry shell. Pour the sauce over the top and chill for 2 hours. Garnish with Candied Orange Slices and glacéed cherries. Can be prepared 6 hours before serving.
❖❖❖ YIELDS 6 TO 8 SERVINGS.

Tarte Meringue à l'Orange

ORANGE MERINGUE TART

3 navel oranges
1 cup sugar
3 eggs
¼ cup orange liqueur
2 teaspoons lemon juice
Grated rind of 1 lemon
⅔ cup butter, melted and cooled
1 (10-inch) pie shell, baked
4 egg whites
Pinch of salt

Preheat oven to 375°F. Remove the zest from the oranges with a sharp knife. Cut off and discard the pith and chop the oranges. In a processor, purée the oranges and rind. Stir in ½ cup sugar, eggs, orange liqueur, lemon juice, grated lemon rind, and butter. Pour into the pastry shell and bake for 35 to 40 minutes or until the filling is set. Increase oven temperature to 400°. Beat the 4 egg whites with a pinch of salt until they hold soft peaks. Add the remaining ½ cup sugar 2 tablespoons at a time, beat-

ing constantly. Beat the meringue until it holds stiff peaks. Transfer the tart to a baking sheet and spread the meringue over the filling. Bake in the upper third of the oven for 8 minutes or until the meringue is golden. Transfer to a rack and let cool. Serve at room temperature.
❖❖❖ YIELDS 6 TO 8 SERVINGS.

Deep-Dish Peach Pie with Almonds

If you like, you can use pears, apples, plums, or bananas for this pie. For the pastry, you can use either flaky pastry or puff pastry.

8 peaches, sliced
1 cup chopped and toasted almonds
½ cup butter, melted
2 tablespoons tapioca
½ to 1 cup sugar
2 tablespoons rum
1 (8-inch) square Flaky Pastry, ¼-inch thick (see pages 214–215)
Dorure (see page 213)
Heavy cream or sour cream

Preheat oven to 450°F. Place the peaches in an 8-inch square ovenproof serving dish. In a bowl, mix the almonds, butter, tapioca, sugar to taste, and rum together. Pour over peaches. Place the 8-inch square of pastry on top and press the edges firmly to the sides of the dish. Brush with the dorure. Bake for 10 minutes. Lower the heat to 350° and bake for 30 to 40 minutes or until golden. Serve warm with the heavy cream or sour cream on the side.
YIELDS 6 SERVINGS.

Note: If desired, decorate the top of the pastry with cutouts. For a simple decoration, use the tip of a sharp knife to draw designs on the pastry.
❖❖❖

Peach Cream Pie

This is another dessert that can be changed to suit your needs. Use about four cups of puréed fruit — strawberries, pears, raspberries, apples, or blackberries — and substitute a suitably flavored liqueur.

    4 cups puréed peaches
    2 tablespoons lemon juice
    2 tablespoons gelatin
    2 tablespoons orange liqueur
    4 tablespoons sugar
    2 cups heavy cream
    1 (10-inch) flan shell, baked
    7 to 8 peach halves, peeled and sliced

In a bowl, mix the peach purée with lemon juice, then turn into a fine sieve and set the sieve over the bowl to drain for 20 minutes. In a saucepan, soften the gelatin with ½ cup of the juice from the peaches and dissolve over low heat. Mix into the peach purée with the orange liqueur and sugar. Beat the cream to the soft-firm stage and fold into the purée. Spoon into the flan shell and refrigerate for 4 to 6 hours. Just before serving, arrange the sliced peach halves on top. Can be prepared to the point of garnishing about 6 hours before.
▼▼▼   YIELDS 6 TO 8 SERVINGS.

Quiche aux Pêches

PEACH CUSTARD TART

Apples or pears may be substituted for the peaches if you like.

    ½ cup chopped almonds (optional)
    1 (9-inch) pie shell, baked
    5 vanilla-poached peaches, halved (see
       page 286)
    3 eggs
    1 cup heavy cream
    ½ cup sugar

    ½ teaspoon vanilla
    2 tablespoons bourbon

Preheat oven to 350°F. Sprinkle the almonds, if desired, over the bottom of the pie shell. Drain the peaches and arrange on top, cut side down. In a mixing bowl, beat the eggs to blend. Stir in the cream, along with the sugar, vanilla, and bourbon. Pour over peaches. Bake until the custard is set, about 25 minutes. Cool to room temperature before serving.   YIELDS 6 TO 8 SERVINGS.
▼▼▼

Pear Tart with Hot Chocolate Sauce

Peaches, apples, raspberries, or strawberries can be substituted for the pears in this tart. To make individual servings, use pastry shells cut from puff pastry in the shape of pears.

    1½ cups Custard Sauce (see page 273)
    3 tablespoons almond or
       orange liqueur
    1 (9-inch) tart shell, baked
    4 to 5 vanilla-poached pears (see
       page 286)
    2 cups chocolate sauce, warmed

In a bowl, mix the Custard Sauce and liqueur. Spread evenly inside the tart shell. Slice the pears thinly and arrange on top of the custard. Serve the warmed chocolate sauce separately. The pears, custard, and tart shell can all be prepared the day before. Do not fill until shortly before serving.
▼▼▼   YIELDS 6 TO 8 SERVINGS.

Pear and Ginger Tart

    8 pears, peeled, cored, and sliced
    ⅔ cup sugar
    ¾ teaspoon ginger

½ cup water
1 (9-inch) Sandtorte Pastry shell,
   partially baked (see page 215)
6 tablespoons apricot preserves
Whipped cream (optional)

In a saucepan, simmer the pears, sugar, ginger, and water until the pears are tender but still firm. Chill.

Preheat oven to 400°F. Drain pears, reserving 4 tablespoons liquid. Arrange pears in the pastry shell. In a saucepan, boil the apricot preserves and reserved poaching liquid for 1 minute. Strain. Brush the tart with the apricot glaze and bake for 30 minutes. Remove from the oven and brush with the remaining sauce. Serve warm, with the whipped cream if desired.

▼▼▼   YIELDS 6 TO 8 SERVINGS.

Douillons à la Paysanne

PASTRY-WRAPPED PEARS

Apples or peaches can be substituted for the pears in this pastry.

⅓ cup white wine
7 ounces butter
2 tablespoons sugar
2½ cups flour
¼ teaspoon cinnamon
4 pears, peeled and cored from
   the bottom
1 egg
1 cup Crème Fraîche (see page 286)

In a saucepan, reduce the wine by half. Remove from the heat and whisk in butter, bit by bit, to form a creamy mixture. Add 1 tablespoon sugar. Mix well. Add the flour and make into a dough. Shape into a flat cake and let rest in the refrigerator for 2 hours.

Preheat oven to 425°F. In a small bowl, combine the remaining 1 tablespoon sugar and the cinnamon. Roll the

pears in the mixture. Roll out the pastry ¼-inch thick and cut into squares. Wrap each pear in the pastry, leaving the stem exposed. Pinch dough together. Beat the egg with a little water and brush each pear. Bake in the oven for 25 minutes or until the pears are tender and the pastry is golden. Serve warm with the Crème Fraîche.   YIELDS 4 SERVINGS.
▼▼▼

Tarte de Cambrai

PEAR TART

Apples, peaches, or plums may be substituted for the pears in this tart.

4 to 5 pears, peeled, cored, and sliced
1 tablespoon lemon juice
10 tablespoons self-rising flour
   (see Note)
6 tablespoons vanilla sugar (see Note)
4 tablespoons oil
8 tablespoons milk
2 eggs
Pinch of salt
2 tablespoons butter
Sugar

Preheat oven to 400°F. Butter a 10-inch flan pan or cake tin and line with buttered parchment. Sprinkle the pears with lemon juice and toss to coat. In a bowl, mix the flour, vanilla sugar, oil, milk, eggs, and salt together. Pour the batter into the pan and arrange the pears on top. Dot with butter and sprinkle with extra sugar. Bake until golden and risen, about 40 minutes. Serve warm.   YIELDS 6 SERVINGS.

Note: Self-rising flour contains a premeasured amount of the salt and leavening needed for baking. Vanilla sugar can be made by storing 1 to 2 vanilla beans with 2 cups sugar in a tightly closed container.
▼▼▼

Piquenchâgne

PEAR CAKE

This "cake" is really a turnover.

6 pears, peeled and thinly sliced
3 tablespoons sugar
1 (1-inch) piece vanilla bean, split
Pinch of white pepper
2 tablespoons dark rum
½ cup heavy cream
⅓ recipe Flaky Pastry or Puff Pastry
    (see pages 214 and 215)
1 egg yolk

In a bowl, macerate the pears, sugar, vanilla, pepper, rum, and cream for 3 hours.

Preheat oven to 375°F. Roll the pastry into a thin oval. Drain the pears, reserving the liquid. Place pears in the center of the pastry. Fold over the sides to make a turnover. Crimp the edges and seal. Brush the top with the egg yolk. Bake for 45 minutes. In a saucepan, reduce the macerating liquid until it is syrupy. Remove and discard the vanilla bean. Brush the syrup on the baked turnover. Serve warm or at room temperature.   YIELDS 6 TO 8 SERVINGS.

Upside-Down Pear Tart

Upside-Down Pear Tart

7 pears, peeled, halved, and cored
½ cup sugar
½ teaspoon cinnamon
2½ cups red wine
1 recipe Flaky Pastry, Processor
    Method (see page 215)

In a 12-inch enamel or stainless steel skillet, arrange the pears, cut side up. In a small bowl, combine the sugar and cinnamon and sprinkle over the pears. Pour on the wine and bring to a boil. Simmer, covered, just until the pears are tender, about 30 to 45 minutes. Remove the pears with a slotted spoon and arrange them in a 10-inch glass or ceramic pie plate.

Preheat oven to 375°F. Boil the wine and juices until reduced to ½ cup. Pour over the pears.

Roll the pastry into a 12-inch circle. Place over the pears, fold back ½ inch around the edge, and then fold back another ½ inch. Make several slits in the pastry. Bake for 45 minutes or until golden and crisp. Let cool for 10 to 15 minutes before inverting onto a serving platter. Serve warm or at room temperature.   YIELDS 6 TO 8 SERVINGS.

Almond Pear Pie

See photograph on page 66.

⅓ cup butter
⅓ cup sugar, plus extra for topping
1 egg, beaten lightly, plus 1 yolk
½ cup blanched almonds, ground
2 tablespoons flour

2 teaspoons kirsch
1 (10-inch) pie shell, unbaked
4 pears, peeled, cored, and sliced
½ cup Apricot Glaze (see page 283)

Preheat oven to 400°F. In a processor, cream the butter and sugar until fluffy. Add the egg and extra yolk, and stir in the almonds, flour, and kirsch. Pour into the pastry shell. Arrange the pears on the top and press into the filling. Bake for 15 minutes or until the dough starts to brown. Lower the heat to 350° and bake 20 minutes longer. Sprinkle the pie with sugar and bake until the sugar melts and starts to caramelize, about 10 minutes. Cool and brush with the apricot jam. Serve at room temperature. Can be frozen, and then reheated in a 300°F. oven until at least room temperature.   YIELDS 10 TO 12 SERVINGS.

Pear Flan

4 eggs, plus 1 yolk
1½ cups milk, scalded
⅓ cup sugar
3 vanilla-poached pears (see page 286)
2 tablespoons Poire William, amaretto, or Grand Marnier
1 (9-inch) pie shell, partially baked
5 tablespoons apricot jam, strained (optional)

Preheat oven to 350°F. In a bowl, beat the eggs and yolk together. Add milk and sugar; stir in ⅓ cup of the poaching liquid from the pears and the liqueur. Place the pear halves, cut side down, in the pastry shell and pour on the custard mixture. Bake for 35 to 40 minutes or until the custard is set, puffed, and spotted with brown. Serve warm, glazed with the jam if desired.
     YIELDS 6 TO 8 SERVINGS.

La Tarte Chaude aux Poires

HOT PEAR TART

⅓ recipe Puff Pastry (see page 215)
4 to 5 pears, peeled, cored, and sliced
6 tablespoons sugar
5 tablespoons butter

Preheat oven to 400°F. Line a 10-inch flan with the pastry and prick the bottom with a fork. Arrange the pear slices on the pastry and sprinkle with the sugar. Dot with butter. Bake for 30 minutes or until pastry is golden and crisp. Serve at room temperature.
     YIELDS 6 SERVINGS.

Pineapple Tart I

1 pineapple, cut into ½-inch-thick slices
⅓ cup kirsch
1 recipe Flaky Pastry, Processor Method (see page 215)
¼ cup confectioners' sugar

Macerate the pineapple in the kirsch for 20 minutes. Roll the pastry into a 4- by 12-inch rectangle. Place on a baking sheet and crimp the edges as you would for a pie crust.

Preheat oven to 425°F. Chill pastry 20 minutes. Prick the bottom with a fork and bake for 15 minutes or until lightly browned. Drain the pineapple, reserving the marinade. Pat the pineapple dry and arrange on pastry. Sprinkle with sugar and brown under the broiler. Cool. Just before serving, sprinkle with the reserved marinade. Can be prepared for serving 6 hours ahead.
     YIELDS 6 SERVINGS.

Tarte Feuilletée à l'Ananas

PINEAPPLE TART II

½ recipe Puff Pastry (see page 215)
Dorure (see page 213)
1 cup Rum Pastry Cream (see page 282)
1 pineapple, peeled, cored, and sliced
Candied cherries
⅓ cup Apricot Glaze (see page 283)

Preheat oven to 425°F. Roll the pastry ¼-inch thick and trim to a 12-inch square. Cut off 1-inch borders around the tart. Dampen the main portion of the pastry with cold water and place the trimmed strips on top to form the sides of the tart. Place on a dampened baking sheet and prick the interior with a fork. Brush the edges with dorure. Bake 20 minutes, or until puffed and golden. Cool. Spread the pastry with Pastry Cream. Arrange the pineapple slices on the cream and garnish with cherries. Brush with the Apricot Glaze. Serve within 3 hours of filling.

▀▀▀   YIELDS 10 TO 12 SERVINGS.

Plum Tart

Just about any fruit can be substituted for the plums in this tart. Accompany with whipped cream or with cold heavy cream if desired.

¾ cup blanched almonds
⅓ cup sugar
1 egg
2 tablespoons butter
1 teaspoon vanilla
¼ teaspoon almond extract
1 teaspoon grated lemon rind
1 (9-inch) tart shell, unbaked
24 plums, pitted
1 cup currant jelly
2 tablespoons port

Preheat oven to 350°F. In a processor, grind the almonds and sugar to a fine powder. *Do not let them turn into a paste.* Add the egg, butter, vanilla, almond extract, and lemon rind. Process until well mixed. Spread the mixture in the pie shell. Arrange the plums on top, cut side down, and bake for 1 hour. Remove from the oven and cool. In a small saucepan, melt the currant jelly and port until smooth. Brush over the plums. Serve warm or at room temperature.

▀▀▀   YIELDS 6 TO 8 SERVINGS.

Plum Cobbler

¾ pound plums, pitted
½ cup water
2 tablespoons firmly packed brown sugar
1 teaspoon grated orange peel
2 teaspoons cinnamon
1 teaspoon arrowroot
2 teaspoons cognac
3 tablespoons butter
¼ cup granulated sugar
½ cup flour
1 teaspoon baking powder
Pinch of salt
¼ cup milk
Whipped cream, flavored with cinnamon, or vanilla ice cream (optional)

Preheat oven to 425°F. Butter a 1-quart baking dish. In a saucepan, simmer the plums, water, brown sugar, orange peel, and 1 teaspoon cinnamon for 5 minutes. In a small bowl, blend the arrowroot and cognac and stir into the mixture, cooking 2 minutes. Pour into the baking dish. Cream 2 tablespoons butter with the granulated sugar until smooth. In a bowl, sift the flour, baking powder, and salt; add the creamed butter and milk and beat until well mixed. Spread over the plums. Dot with remaining 1 tablespoon butter and sprinkle with additional 1 teaspoon cinnamon. Bake until golden, about 30 minutes. Serve with the whipped cream or vanilla ice cream if desired.　　YIELDS 4 TO 6 SERVINGS.

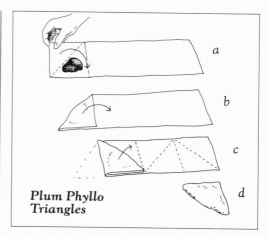

Plum Phyllo
Triangles

Plum Phyllo Triangles

A word of warning: until you get the knack of folding these triangles, keep unused phyllo sheets covered with a damp cloth. Phyllo dough crumbles if it gets too dry.

½ cup honey
⅓ cup water
2 slices lemon peel
1 cinnamon stick
2 pounds plums, pitted and quartered
½ teaspoon ground cinnamon
¼ teaspoon ground cloves
1 tablespoon arrowroot, dissolved in
　3 tablespoons cold water
12 sheets phyllo dough
1 cup butter, melted
1 cup heavy cream, whipped with
　1 tablespoon honey

In a saucepan, simmer the honey, water, lemon peel, and cinnamon stick for 5 minutes. Add the plums, ground cinnamon, and cloves and simmer 30 minutes or until thickened.

Preheat oven to 375°F. Stir the arrowroot into the honey mixture and simmer until thick and clear. Remove from the heat and cool. Place the phyllo on a counter. Brush one sheet of phyllo with butter and cut into strips 3 inches wide. Place a generous teaspoon of filling at one end of the pastry. Pick up one corner and fold it over the filling, aligning the short edge with one of the long edges to form a triangle. Pick up the uppermost point and fold it, as if folding a flag, straight down to form a triangle again. Continue these folding steps until you reach the end of the strip. Place seam side down on a baking sheet and brush with butter. Repeat process for each strip. Bake 25 to 30 minutes or until puffed and golden. Cool for at least 5 minutes. Serve warm with whipped cream. Can be prepared ahead and frozen before or after baking.
　　YIELDS ABOUT 36 TURNOVERS.

Note: The following Prune Filling can also be used to fill the Phyllo Triangles.

Prune Filling

This filling could be used for tarts as well as for these triangles.

1½ pounds pitted prunes
1½ cups cool tea
¼ cup sugar
3 tablespoons Armagnac

Soak the prunes in the tea overnight, drain, chop coarsely, and mix in the sugar and Armagnac.

Note: Raspberries and strawberries as well as blueberries can be used but they should be sprinkled with 2 tablespoons cornstarch before putting into the pastry. They need to be macerated for only 20 minutes.

Prune Tart with Walnut Dough

Two common ingredients combine to make a superior dessert. The walnut dough can be used for other fruit tarts as well.

    2 cups prunes
    1 recipe Walnut Dough (see recipe
      following)
    Juice of 1 orange
    ½ cup sugar
    Grated lemon rind
    1 tablespoon flour
    4 tablespoons prune juice
    Butter

In a saucepan, soak the prunes in water to cover for 1 hour and simmer for 10 minutes.

Preheat oven to 400°F. Drain the prunes. Pit and cut into quarters. Line a 9-inch tart pan with Walnut Dough. Add the prunes; sprinkle with the orange juice, sugar, lemon rind, flour, and prune juice. Dot with butter. Bake for 10 minutes, lower the heat to 325°F. and bake 15 minutes longer. Can be prepared the day before. Serve at room temperature.   YIELDS 6 TO 8 SERVINGS.

Walnut Dough

    1½ cups flour
    Pinch of salt
    ½ cup ground walnuts
    ½ cup butter
    3 tablespoons ice water

In a bowl, mix the flour, salt, and walnuts together. Cut in the butter with your fingertips, two knives, or a pastry blender until mixture resembles coarse meal. Add the water; mix into a dough. Shape into a flat cake and refrigerate for 20 minutes before rolling.
▀▝▀   YIELDS ONE 9-INCH TART SHELL.

Pumpkin Pie

    1½ cups cooked or canned
      pumpkin purée
    3 tablespoons butter, melted
    ½ cup sugar
    ¼ cup maple syrup
    Pinch of salt
    ¾ teaspoon cinnamon
    ½ teaspoon nutmeg or mace
    ¼ teaspoon ground cloves
    3 eggs, separated
    ¾ cup milk
    1 (10-inch) pie shell, unbaked

Preheat oven to 350°F. In a bowl, beat the pumpkin purée, butter, sugar, maple syrup, salt, cinnamon, nutmeg, cloves, egg yolks, and milk together. Beat the egg whites until stiff, then fold them into the mixture.

Pour into the pie shell and bake for 55 minutes, or until it tests done. Serve warm or at room temperature.
          YIELDS 6 TO 8 SERVINGS.

Note: For a more traditional pumpkin pie, substitute molasses for the maple syrup and beat the whole eggs into the pumpkin mixture.

Pumpkin and Orange Pie

1 cup firmly packed light brown sugar
1 teaspoon cinnamon
1 teaspoon ginger
½ teaspoon nutmeg
¼ teaspoon salt
1½ cups cooked or canned
    pumpkin purée
1 tablespoon molasses
2 cups heavy cream
2 eggs, lightly beaten
¼ cup orange marmalade
2 tablespoons Grand Marnier
1 (9-inch) pie shell, partially baked
2 tablespoons confectioners' sugar

Preheat oven to 350°F. In a bowl, mix the light brown sugar, cinnamon, ginger, nutmeg, salt, pumpkin, molasses, 1 cup heavy cream, and eggs together. Stir in the marmalade and liqueur. Pour into the pie shell and bake until just barely set, about 55 to 60 minutes. Cool. Whip the remaining 1 cup heavy cream with confectioners' sugar until stiff and use to garnish the pie. Can be prepared the day before.   YIELDS 6 TO 8 SERVINGS.

Rhubarb Custard Pie

1½ pounds rhubarb
1 cup plus 3 tablespoons
    granulated sugar
1 egg, plus 1 yolk
½ cup milk
½ cup heavy cream
¼ teaspoon ground cardamom
1 (10-inch) pie shell, unbaked
Confectioners' sugar

Preheat oven to 400°F. Scrape the rhubarb stalks and cut into 1-inch lengths. In a saucepan, cook the rhubarb and all the granulated sugar, covered, for 8 minutes until tender. Cool and chill. In a bowl, mix the egg, egg yolk, milk, cream, and cardamom and stir in the rhubarb. Pour into the pie shell. Place the pan on a baking sheet and bake for 30 minutes. Lower the heat to 350° and bake 20 minutes longer or until the custard tests done. Serve warm or at room temperature sprinkled with the confectioners' sugar. YIELDS 6 TO 8 SERVINGS.

Raspberry Cream Tart

One of the best desserts ever.

2 cups fresh raspberries
4 tablespoons granulated sugar
1 (9-inch) Sandtorte Pastry shell,
    partially baked (see page 215)
2 eggs
½ cup ground almonds
¾ cup confectioners' sugar
2 cups heavy cream
1 tablespoon framboise

Preheat oven to 350°F. In a bowl, mix the raspberries with 2 tablespoons granulated sugar and place in the tart shell. In the same bowl, beat the eggs, almonds, confectioners' sugar, and 1 cup cream and mix well. Pour over the raspberries. Bake for 30 minutes until set and lightly browned. Cool. Whip the remaining cup cream with the remaining 2 tablespoons granulated sugar and framboise. Serve separately. Serve the tart at room temperature. Can be prepared the day before.
YIELDS 6 TO 8 SERVINGS.

Note: Fresh raspberries are a must. If desired, substitute blueberries, strawberries, kiwifruit, or pears for the raspberries and use kirsch or Poire William instead of framboise.

Raspberry Chiffon Pie

Strawberries and peaches also work well for this pie.

1 tablespoon gelatin
¼ cup sherry
3 eggs, separated
⅔ cup sugar
Pinch of salt
1½ tablespoons lemon juice
½ cup raspberry pulp and juice
1 cup heavy cream, whipped
1 (9-inch) Sandtorte Pastry shell, baked (see page 215)
Whipped cream
1½ cups fresh raspberries

In a saucepan, soften the gelatin in the sherry and dissolve over low heat. In a bowl, beat the egg yolks with the sugar and salt until light in color. Beat in the lemon juice. Strain the raspberry purée to remove the seeds and add it to the egg mixture. Cook over low heat, stirring, until mixture thickens slightly. Stir in the gelatin-sherry mixture and cool until almost ready to set. Fold the whipped heavy cream into the raspberry purée. Beat the egg whites until they reach the soft-firm stage and fold into the raspberry mixture. Pour into the pie shell, mounding as high as possible. Chill until set. Garnish with the whipped cream and decorate with the whole raspberries. Can be prepared the day before and may be frozen. YIELDS 6 TO 8 SERVINGS. ▪▫▪

Strawberry Tart

2 cups Pastry Cream (see page 282)
1 (9-inch) Sandtorte Pastry shell, baked (see page 215)
1 pint strawberries
Currant Glaze (see page 283)

Place the Pastry Cream in the pie shell and arrange the strawberries in concentric circles over the top. Brush with currant glaze. Serve cold. Can be prepared the day before serving.
                    YIELDS 6 TO 8 SERVINGS.

Note: The pastry can also be filled with whipped cream. Flavor the cream with cognac, rum, orange liqueur, or vanilla. ▪▫▪

Barquettes aux Fraises
STRAWBERRY PASTRY BOATS

See page 214 for instructions on how to make barquettes.

12 barquettes of Puff Pastry (see page 215)
Egg yolk dorure (see page 213)
1 cup heavy cream, whipped, sweetened, and flavored with kirsch
1 pint strawberries
Confectioners' sugar

Preheat oven to 425°F. To make the barquettes, cut the pastry into ovals and place on a baking sheet dampened with cold water. Brush the tops only with the egg yolk dorure. Bake until puffed, golden, and crisp. Cool about 1 hour.

When ready to serve, cut in half horizontally. Pipe whipped cream from a no. 5 star tip on the bottom of the pastry. Arrange the strawberries on top. Gently rest the top of the pastry on the strawberries and sprinkle with the confectioners' sugar. Serve immediately.
▪▫▪   YIELDS 12 SERVINGS.

GÂTEAUX, TORTEN & FANCY CAKES

WHATEVER you call these desserts, they are luscious, eye-appealing, and exciting. These are the show-stoppers that have guests raving. Many are easily and quickly prepared, but others require more time and several distinct steps. Very often, however, the components of even the most complicated can be prepared ahead and frozen for several weeks, or at the very least kept refrigerated for two or three days so that the final assembly can be done quickly and easily. With just a little careful planning, you can prepare these marvelous desserts on a moment's notice.

There is no true definition of what a gâteau, torte, or fancy cake is — these desserts can be composed of many things. They can be as simple as a frosted sponge layer, or can be combinations of génoise, meringue, nutted layers, cream puffs, etc. They can be assembled with fruit or liqueur syrups, butter creams, pastry creams, whipped creams, or a combination of these. They can be garnished with fruits, nuts, chocolate, or various glazes. The common point for the recipes in this book is that they all include fruit; many wonderful desserts made with chocolate alone are not included.

These are often big desserts. Plan your meal and make the dessert the star. Better still, invite guests for dessert and coffee and let one or two of these shine. Accompany them with a Bavarian cream or a mélange of fruit to give variety. To accompany the desserts with something other than coffee or tea, provide a not-too-dry champagne.

Because many of the basic preparations used in this section are also used in other chapters, you will find them in the chapter on Basic Recipes. You should quickly realize that although I have provided many suggestions for suitable combinations, you can easily create your own

desserts. You can almost always change one fruit for another or substitute a different-flavored frosting, filling, or glaze. You may prefer the addition or substitution of a nutted cake layer or a meringue layer. As an example, Black Forest Cherry Cake is composed of chocolate génoise layers, moistened with kirsch syrup and covered with whipped cream and cherries. Try this variation: use 2 layers of chocolate génoise and one layer of meringue (nutted if desired). Sprinkle the cake layers with kirsch syrup. Spread one cake layer with a thick coating of apricot-flavored butter cream, cover with the meringue layer, and coat that thickly with whipped cream mixed with chopped fresh apricots. It will no longer be a Black Forest Cherry Cake, but it will be delicious.

Vacherin

SPANISH WIND TORTE

This is one of the most impressive-looking desserts. However, making the shell is time-consuming. Also, it must be kept in an airtight container or it will become sticky from the humidity.

MERINGUE SHELL:

    5 egg whites
    ¾ cup superfine sugar
    ¾ cup superfine sugar
    5 egg whites
    ¾ cup superfine sugar
    ¾ cup superfine sugar

Preheat oven to 225°F. In an electric mixer, beat 5 egg whites to the soft-peak stage. Slowly add ¾ cup sugar, beating constantly until the meringue is very stiff. Fold in another ¾ cup sugar and put mixture into a pastry bag fitted with a no. 6 plain tip.

On large baking sheets lined with parchment paper, draw five 8-inch cir-

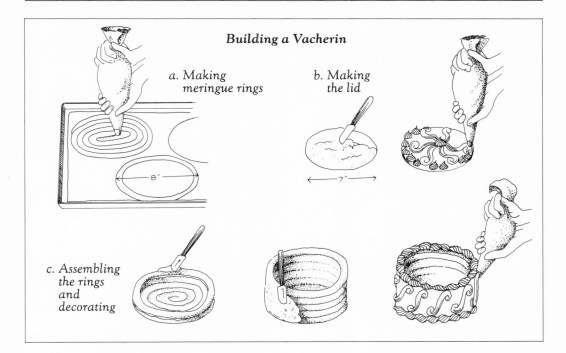

Building a Vacherin

a. Making meringue rings

b. Making the lid

c. Assembling the rings and decorating

cles. Pipe the meringue in a spiral on one of the circles, filling it in completely. On the remaining circles, pipe a ring of meringue about 1 inch thick.

On a smaller sheet, draw a 7-inch circle. Spread a thin layer of meringue evenly within the circle. Put the remaining meringue into a pastry bag fitted with a no. 5 star tip. Pipe arabesques of meringue on top of the thin layer. Bake the meringues for about 45 minutes to an hour, or until crisp. Keep the oven door propped open with a pot holder.

Loosen the meringues from the parchment paper and leave in the turned-off oven until dried. This can take 4 hours or longer, depending on your oven and the humidity.

Repeat the recipe for the meringue with egg whites and sugar. Place the large spiral of cooked meringue on a baking sheet, frost around the edge, and place a ring on top. Frost that, and continue building the rings, using the fresh meringue as a glue. Set the 7-inch ring

aside; you will use it later. Frost the pile of rings with a thin layer of meringue. With the remaining meringue in a pastry bag fitted with a no. 5 star tip, pipe a base of rosettes around the meringue shell, then use the remaining meringue to make arabesques around the sides (see sketch).

Bake at 200° for about 1 hour or until dry. Leave in a turned-off oven for 4 hours or overnight until dry and crispy. Fill the shell, then set the 7-inch piece of meringue on top before serving. The individual rings or the entire shell can be made several days before serving, then kept in an airtight container or a carefully sealed plastic bag. Handle the shell gently or it will break.

FILLING:

1½ cups heavy cream
2 tablespoons kirsch
Sugar to taste
2 cups fruits of choice (strawberries, peaches, raspberries, etc.)

Beat the cream to the soft-peak stage, beat in the kirsch and sugar, and beat until stiff. Fold in the fruit and fill the meringue shell. Serve within 1 hour of filling.   YIELDS 6 TO 10 SERVINGS.

◆▪◆

Pavlova

This dessert is a favorite in Australia. The customary fruits used are bananas, peaches, papayas, pineapples, or mangoes. You may, of course, use whatever fruits are in season.

> 4 egg whites
> 1 cup sugar, plus extra for sweetening
>   whipped cream
> 4 teaspoons cornstarch
> 2 teaspoons vinegar
> 1 teaspoon vanilla
> 2 cups cut-up fruit in season
> 1 cup heavy cream

Preheat oven to 275°F. Butter a shallow 9- by 11-inch ovenproof serving dish and set aside. In an electric mixer, whip the egg whites until they hold soft peaks. Add the sugar, 1 tablespoon at a time, beating until the mixture is stiff and glossy. Beat in the cornstarch, vinegar, and vanilla. Fill the baking dish, hollowing the center slightly. Bake for 1¼ to 1½ hours or until lightly browned. Cool. Just before serving, prepare the fruit. Whip the cream to the soft-peak stage, adding sugar to taste. Pile in the meringue shell and garnish with the fruit. Can be prepared the day before filling.

◆▪◆   YIELDS 6 TO 8 SERVINGS.

Dark Fruitcake

> 2½ cups butter
> 3¾ cups firmly packed brown sugar
> 3¾ cups raisins
> 3¾ cups currants
> 2½ cups citron
> 10 cups flour
> 10 eggs
> 2½ cups molasses
> 2½ cups milk
> 2½ teaspoons cinnamon
> 2½ teaspoons mace
> 2½ teaspoons allspice
> 2½ teaspoons ground cloves
> 2½ teaspoons lemon extract

Preheat oven to 300°F. Butter five 9- by 5- by 3-inch loaf pans; line with parchment paper and butter the paper. In a large bowl, cream the butter and brown sugar until light and fluffy. In another bowl, combine the raisins, currants, and citron and mix well. Add 1 cup flour and toss to coat evenly. Beat the eggs gradually into the creamed butter, beating well after each addition. Fold in the raisin mixture, molasses, milk, spices, lemon extract, and remaining 9 cups flour. Mix well. Pour into the loaf pans and bake for 1½ hours or until a cake tester comes out clean. Unmold and wrap in cloths soaked in liqueur. Can be prepared up to a year before serving.   YIELDS 5 LOAVES.

◆▪◆

Fruit Terrine with Almond Cream

If you prefer, the Almond Cream for this Fruit Terrine can be replaced with the Walnut Cream following.

> 1 (9-inch) square Génoise layer (see
>   page 279)
> Almond Filling for Fruit Tarts (see
>   page 216)
> 3 cups small strawberries
> Custard Sauce (see page 273)
> 2 kiwifruits, peeled

4 vanilla-poached peaches (see
page 286)
Raspberry Sauce (see page 276)

Make the Génoise a day or two before using. This will allow it to firm up. Line a
2½- by 4½- by 8½-inch loaf pan with plastic wrap, leaving ends of wrap extended
beyond ends of pan. Cut the cake into
thin slices and line the cake pan on bottom and both long sides, but not the
ends. Spread a layer of almond filling in
the pan, arrange a row of strawberries on
top, and cover with layer of custard sauce.
Make a layer of kiwi, another layer of almond, a layer of peaches, another layer of
almond, and a layer of strawberries.
Spread on the remaining layer of almond
filling. Smooth the top. Cover with a layer of Génoise and the ends of plastic
wrap. Chill until set, about 6 hours.
When ready to serve, unmold onto a platter and peel off the plastic. Cut into ½-
inch slices and serve with the 2 sauces.
Can be prepared ahead and frozen. Let
defrost in the refrigerator.
YIELDS 12 TO 16 SERVINGS.

Walnut Cream

½ cup hot milk
1 ½ cups ground walnuts
1 cup heavy cream
½ cup butter
⅔ cup confectioners' sugar, sifted
2 tablespoons Armagnac or cognac

Pour the hot milk over the walnuts and
let stand for 30 minutes. Purée in a processor. Beat the cream until stiff. Cream
the butter until light and fluffy. Beat the
confectioners' sugar into the butter until
almost white in color. Beat creamed butter into the walnut purée with the Armagnac, then fold in the whipped cream.

Note: This Walnut Cream is a good filling for tarts as well.

Zuccotto alla Michelangelo

MICHELANGELO'S PUMPKIN
See photograph on page 69.

*A favorite of Northern Italy, this unmolded
dessert should resemble a pumpkin.*

2 (10-inch) round layers Sponge Cake
(see page 278)
1 ¼ cups sugar
⅔ cup water
1 cup Cointreau
7 cups heavy cream
¾ cup chopped candied fruit
⅔ cup chopped pecans
1 ½ cups grated semisweet chocolate
⅔ cup cocoa
Spun Sugar (optional; see page 285)

Cut 1 Sponge Cake layer into 16 wedges
and the other layer in half horizontally.
Line an approximately 5-quart round-
bottomed mixing bowl with plastic wrap
and then arrange the wedges, slightly
overlapping, around the bowl. In another bowl, dissolve ½ cup sugar in the
water, add the Cointreau, and brush generously over the cake. Whip the cream
until almost stiff, add remaining ¾ cup
sugar, and beat until stiff. Fold in the candied fruit, pecans, and 1 cup grated
chocolate. Spoon half of the cream mixture into the mold, arrange a layer of cake
on top, and brush with the syrup. Stir the
cocoa into the remaining cream mixture
and spoon on top of the cake layer. Save
any remaining cream. Cover with the final Sponge Cake layer. Brush with the
remaining syrup. Chill until set.
When ready to serve, unmold onto a
platter, spread with remaining cream,
and sprinkle with remaining ½ cup grated chocolate. Surround with Spun Sugar
if desired. Can be prepared up to 2 days
before serving. Can be frozen.
YIELDS 8 TO 10 SERVINGS.

Gâteau de Fruits
FRUIT SHORTCAKE

> 1 (10-inch) layer Nutted Sponge Cake, using almonds (see page 279)
> 1½ cups heavy cream, whipped, sweetened, and flavored with orange liqueur to taste
> 2 cups fruits (bananas, strawberries, cherries, pineapples, oranges, etc.)
> ½ cup Apricot Glaze (see page 283)

Place the cake on a serving platter and cut in half horizontally. Spread a layer of whipped cream on the bottom layer, cover with the second layer, and spread with remaining whipped cream. Arrange the fruits in an attractive design on the top and glaze. Can be prepared up to 4 hours before serving. YIELDS 8 TO 10 SERVINGS.

Panforte
SIENESE CHRISTMAS FRUITCAKE

> ½ cup finely ground almonds
> 4 cups blanched almonds
> 2 cups candied lemon peel, chopped
> 2 cups candied orange peel, chopped
> 1 cup blanched hazelnuts
> Grated peel of 1 orange
> Grated peel of 1 lemon
> ¼ teaspoon ground cloves
> ¼ teaspoon cinnamon
> ¼ teaspoon coriander
> ¼ teaspoon nutmeg
> 1 cup ground almonds or hazelnuts
> ¼ cup flour
> 2 cups granulated sugar
> 1 cup honey
> ¼ cup butter
> 1 teaspoon salt
> Confectioners' sugar

Preheat oven to 300°F. Butter two 9-inch round cake pans with removable bottoms. Line bottom and sides with parchment paper and butter well. (If you are using pans with fluted sides, do not line, but butter generously.) Dust the pans with the ½ cup finely ground almonds. In a large bowl, mix the blanched almonds, candied lemon and orange peels, blanched hazelnuts, grated orange and lemon peels, cloves, cinnamon, coriander, nutmeg, additional ground nuts, and flour. Mix well to coat evenly.

In a large saucepan, heat granulated sugar, honey, butter, and salt over low heat until the sugar is melted. Increase the heat to medium and cook, stirring, until it registers 260°. Remove from the heat and pour over the nut mixture. Mix well. Divide between the pans and bake about 35 minutes or until bubbles appear in the pan. Cool in the pan.

Sift a thick layer of confectioners' sugar onto a piece of waxed paper, invert the cakes onto the sugar and remove the bottoms. Sift more sugar on top. Store in an airtight container for at least a week before serving. Can be kept for up to 6 months. YIELDS 16 TO 24 SERVINGS.

Fruitcake with Candied Grapefruit Shells

Wrap individually to give as extra-special Christmas gifts. If you don't want to use the grapefruit shells, you can use loaf pans or substitute 12 oranges.

> 6 grapefruits, halved
> 2 cups granulated sugar, plus extra for rolling
> 1 cup light corn syrup
> 1 cup water
> 2½ pounds seedless raisins
> 1 pound golden raisins
> 1 pound currants
> ½ pound candied cherries
> ½ pound slivered almonds
> ¼ pound citron, chopped

⅛ pound candied orange peel, chopped
⅛ pound candied lemon peel, chopped
6 cups sifted flour
2 cups butter, softened
2 cups firmly packed brown sugar
6 eggs, beaten
¼ cup sherry
¼ cup molasses
¼ cup orange juice
2 tablespoons vanilla
1 ½ teaspoons cinnamon
1 teaspoon baking powder
½ teaspoon ground cloves
½ teaspoon nutmeg
½ teaspoon baking soda
½ teaspoon allspice
Cognac (optional)

Remove the pulp and membrane from the grapefruit halves. In a large pan, boil the shells for 10 minutes in water to cover. In a large saucepan, cook the 2 cups granulated sugar, corn syrup, water, and drained grapefruit shells for 10 minutes or until syrup registers 230°F. Drain the shells on a cookie rack until cool, then roll in additional granulated sugar. The shells can be prepared a month before serving.

Preheat oven to 250°F. Simmer raisins and currants in water to cover for 5 minutes; drain. In a large bowl, toss drained raisins and currants, cherries, almonds, citron, orange and lemon peels, and 1 cup flour together. In another large bowl, cream the butter and brown sugar until light and fluffy. Beat in the eggs, sherry, molasses, orange juice, and vanilla. Stir in the remaining 5 cups flour, cinnamon, baking powder, cloves, nutmeg, baking soda, and allspice. Fold in the floured fruits and nuts. Pack into the grapefruit shells and bake for 1 hour or until the cakes test done. (Or put into four 2- by 4- by 8-inch loaf pans lined with buttered parchment paper, and bake 2½ hours.)

When cakes are cooled, pour on cognac to moisten and store in tightly covered tins. Store at least 1 week before serving. Cut the grapefruits into wedges to serve. Serve grapefruit cakes within a month of making. The loaves can be sprinkled with cognac and stored for up to a year wrapped in cognac-soaked cloths and kept in an airtight container.

YIELDS 12 GRAPEFRUIT CAKES
OR FOUR 1-POUND LOAVES.

Pine Nut, Almond, and Berry Torte

As almost always, you can substitute other fruits of your choice for the strawberries and blackberries.

6 eggs, separated
1 ¼ cups blanched almonds, ground
1 cup granulated sugar
⅓ cup flour
½ teaspoon baking powder
Pinch of salt
Pinch of cream of tartar
½ cup lightly toasted pine nuts
1 cup heavy cream
1 tablespoon confectioners' sugar
1 teaspoon vanilla
1 pint strawberries
½ pint blackberries
½ cup currant jelly, melted
Slivered, blanched almonds (optional)

Preheat oven to 350°F. Butter a 10-inch spring-form pan. In a bowl, beat the egg yolks until thick and lemon-colored. Beat the ground almonds and ½ cup granulated sugar into the yolks. Mix the flour and baking powder together and stir into the almond mixture. Beat the egg whites with salt and cream of tartar until they form soft peaks. Gradually add remaining ½ cup granulated sugar, beating until stiff peaks form. Fold a third of the beaten whites into the almond mixture, then fold in the remaining whites and pine nuts. Pour into the prepared pan and bake for 40 minutes or until it tests done. Cool on a wire rack, then remove from pan.

Whip the cream, confectioners' sugar, and vanilla until stiff. Spread a fourth of the whipped cream on the top of the cooled cake. Put the remaining cream into a pastry bag fitted with a no. 4 star tip and pipe a border around the top of the cake. Garnish the center with the strawberries and blackberries. Brush the fruits with jelly and garnish with the almonds if desired. Can be prepared for garnishing up to 2 days ahead. Garnish no more than 4 hours before serving.

❖❖❖   YIELDS 8 TO 10 SERVINGS.

Torta di Mele

APPLE TORTE

> 1½ cups sifted flour
> 6 tablespoons sugar
> 1½ teaspoons salt
> 1 package (scant tablespoon) yeast
> 1½ cups milk
> ¼ cup butter, melted and cooled
> ¼ cup Grand Marnier
> 4 apples, peeled, cored, and sliced
> Cold heavy cream (optional)

Butter a 12- by 18-inch ovenproof serving dish and dust with flour. In a bowl, mix the flour, 3 tablespoons sugar, salt, and yeast together. Add milk and beat until smooth. Beat in the butter and Grand Marnier. Let batter rise for 30 minutes.

Preheat oven to 400°F. Arrange the apples in the baking pan; beat the batter again and pour it over the apples. Sprinkle with remaining 3 tablespoons sugar. Bake 1 hour or until the top is golden and the crust starts to pull away from the sides of the pan. Serve warm or cold. If desired, serve with cold heavy cream.

❖❖❖   YIELDS 6 TO 8 SERVINGS.

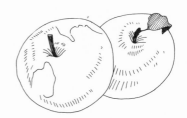

Hot Apple Cake with Caramel Sauce

> 1 cup butter
> 1 cup sugar
> 2 eggs
> 1½ cups flour
> 1 teaspoon nutmeg
> 1 teaspoon cinnamon
> 1 teaspoon baking soda
> ½ teaspoon salt
> 3 apples, peeled, cored, and chopped
> ¾ cup chopped walnuts
> 1 teaspoon vanilla
> Caramel Sauce II (see page 271)

Preheat oven to 350°F. Butter a 10-inch pie plate and set aside. In a bowl, cream the butter and sugar until light and fluffy. Beat in the eggs, 1 at a time. Sift the flour, nutmeg, cinnamon, baking soda, and salt together. Stir into the butter mixture with the apples, nuts, and vanilla. Pour into the pie plate and bake until lightly browned, about 45 minutes. Serve the cake warm or at room temperature with the Caramel Sauce.

❖❖❖   YIELDS 6 TO 8 SERVINGS.

Gâteau Campagnard

FRENCH APPLE CAKE

> 1½ pounds apples, peeled, cored, and
>   thickly sliced
> ¾ cup confectioners' sugar
> ¼ teaspoon nutmeg
> 2 cups flour
> ½ pound butter, softened
> ¼ cup heavy cream

Preheat oven to 400°F. Butter a 9- by 13-inch baking dish. Put the apples in the bottom of the dish. Sprinkle with confectioners' sugar and nutmeg and bake for 15 minutes. In a bowl, mix the flour, butter, and cream to make a soft dough. Pour over the apples and bake 45 minutes or until golden. Serve hot, warm, or cool.

❖❖❖ YIELDS 6 TO 8 SERVINGS.

Gâteau aux Pommes Lyonnais

APPLE CAKE FROM LYON

1 ½ cups sugar
5 eggs
Pinch of salt
Grated rind of 1 lemon
½ teaspoon almond extract
2 ½ tablespoons oil
⅔ cup milk
2 ½ cups cake flour
2 teaspoons baking powder
1 pound apples, peeled, cored, and
    sliced
⅓ cup sliced almonds
½ cup Praline Powder (see page 284)
½ cup butter, melted
Heavy cream or Crème Fraîche (see
    page 286)

Preheat oven to 375°F. Butter and flour a 9-inch spring-form pan. In a bowl, beat ¾ cup sugar and 3 eggs until they form a ribbon. Add the salt, lemon rind, and almond extract. Mix well. Beat in the oil and milk. Sift together the flour and baking powder. Add to the batter and blend well. Pour into the prepared pan. Arrange half of the apples neatly over the batter leaving a ½-inch border. Sprinkle the almonds over the apples and then sprinkle on 2 tablespoons Praline Powder. Cover with the remaining apples and sprinkle on 2 more tablespoons of praline. Bake for 30 minutes or until the cen-ter tests done when pierced with a cake tester.

While the cake is baking, cool the melted butter and beat it with the remaining 2 eggs and ¾ cup sugar. Set aside. When the cake is done, remove it from the oven and prick it with a small knife. Pour the butter-sugar topping over the cake and let soak in. Sprinkle with the remaining ¼ cup praline. Return to the oven and bake for 15 minutes. Remove from the oven, cool, and let stand for a day before serving. Unmold the cake from the pan and serve with heavy cream or Crème Fraîche. Can be frozen.

❖❖❖ YIELDS 8 TO 10 SERVINGS.

Banana Shortcake

Knead the dough only enough to bring it together; overkneading will produce tough shortcake.

3 cups sifted flour
½ teaspoon salt
4 teaspoons baking powder
2 tablespoons sugar
½ cup butter
1 cup milk
2 tablespoons butter, melted
1 ½ cups marmalade
3 bananas, sliced
1 cup heavy cream, whipped

Preheat oven to 425°F. Sift the flour, salt, baking powder, and sugar together. Cut in the ½ cup butter until the mixture resembles coarse meal. Add the milk and stir to make a soft dough. Turn onto a floured board and knead about 10 times. Press half the dough into an 8-inch buttered pan. Brush with 2 tablespoons melted butter and press the remaining dough on top. Bake until browned, about 20 minutes.

Unmold and separate the layers. Place the bottom layer on a serving plate and spread with the marmalade, then cover with the banana slices, a layer of whipped cream, and the top of the cake. Garnish with the remaining whipped cream. The cake can be made ahead of time and kept frozen. If it is to be served on the same day, do not make the cake more than 4 hours before serving.   YIELDS 6 TO 8 SERVINGS.

Blueberry Grunt

You may substitute other berries of choice for the blueberries.

- 4 cups blueberries
- 1 cup sugar
- 1 (11- by 15-inch) Sponge Cake sheet (see page 278)
- 4 tablespoons butter
- 1 cup heavy cream, whipped, sweetened to taste

Preheat oven to 350°F. Butter a 6- by 10-inch baking dish. In a saucepan, cook the blueberries and sugar over low heat for 10 minutes, stirring occasionally. Cut the Sponge Cake into two 11- by 7½-inch sheets and split each sheet in half horizontally. Place a cake layer in the baking dish and spoon on some of the blueberries. Dot with butter and cover with another slice of cake, more blueberries, butter, and so on, ending with the butter. Bake for 20 minutes. Let cool and then chill for 3 to 4 hours. Serve with sweetened whipped cream on the side. Can be made the day before.

YIELDS 6 TO 8 SERVINGS.

Blueberry Pound Cake

- 1 pound butter, softened
- 2 cups sugar
- 8 large eggs
- 4 cups flour
- 4 cups blueberries
- 4 tablespoons minced lemon rind

Preheat oven to 300°F. Lightly butter a 6-cup loaf pan or tube pan. In a large bowl, cream the butter and sugar until light and fluffy. Beat in the eggs, 1 at a time. Gently fold in all but 3 tablespoons of the flour, ¼ cup at a time. Toss the blueberries with the lemon rind and the remaining flour. Fold into the batter and pour into the pan. Bake for 1 hour and 20 minutes or until cake tests done. Cool completely and unmold. Let stand overnight before serving. Can be prepared several days ahead and can be frozen.

YIELDS 18 HALF-INCH SLICES.

Chocolate Cake with Blueberries

An unusual combination of ingredients that is unusually delicious.

- 4 cups blueberries
- ¾ cup sugar
- 3 tablespoons lemon juice
- 3 tablespoons dark rum
- 1 pound semisweet chocolate, chopped
- 2 cups heavy cream
- 2 (8-inch) layers Chocolate Génoise (see page 280)

In a saucepan, cook 3 cups blueberries, sugar and lemon juice over medium heat, stirring until the sugar dissolves. Simmer 10 minutes, mashing the blueberries. Cool for 5 minutes and stir in 1½ tablespoons rum. In a saucepan, bring the chocolate and cream to a boil, stirring. Remove from the heat and cool, stirring occasionally. When cool to the touch, put in an electric mixer and beat with the remaining 1½ tablespoons rum until the mixture thickens and lightens in color. Split each cake layer horizontally and spread both with the blueberry filling and some of the chocolate mixture. Stack the layers and coat with the remaining chocolate. Garnish with the remaining 1 cup blueberries. Can be prepared two days before serving.

YIELDS 8 TO 10 SERVINGS.

Note: The chocolate mixture must be used very quickly after beating or it will become too firm to spread. If that should happen, reheat until fluid; let come to room temperature, then beat again.

❖❖❖

Blueberry Streusel Küchen

1½ cups plus ⅓ cup sifted flour
2½ teaspoons baking powder
½ teaspoon salt
¼ cup milk
1 egg, beaten
4 tablespoons butter, melted
1 cup sugar
2½ cups blueberries
4 tablespoons butter, softened
½ teaspoon cinnamon
Cold heavy cream or whipped cream
   (optional)

Preheat oven to 375°F. Butter and flour a 9-inch layer-cake pan. Sift the 1½ cups flour, baking powder, and salt together. In a bowl, beat the milk, egg, melted butter, and ½ cup sugar together. Add the dry ingredients and pour into the pan. Cover with blueberries. In a bowl, mix the remaining ⅓ cup flour, remaining ½ cup sugar, and softened butter with the cinnamon to a coarse meal. Sprinkle over

the berries. Bake for 40 to 50 minutes or until streusel tests done. Serve warm with chilled cream or whipped cream if desired. Can be prepared the day before, but is best if served warm.

❖❖❖   YIELDS 6 TO 8 SERVINGS.

Gâteau Bigarreau

CHERRY CAKE

3 eggs
½ cup sugar
¾ cup flour, sifted
1 teaspoon baking powder
Pinch of salt
½ cup heavy cream
2 tablespoons plus ¾ cup Praline
   Powder (see page 284)
3 tablespoons apricot jam
3 tablespoons currant jelly
1 to 2 tablespoons water
1½ pounds cherries, pitted

Preheat oven to 350°F. Butter an 8-inch pan, line with parchment paper, butter the paper, and sprinkle with flour and sugar. In a bowl, beat the eggs and sugar until thick and light in color. In another bowl, mix the flour, baking powder, and salt together. Fold the flour into the eggs, pour into the prepared pan, and bake for 25 minutes or until cake tests done.

Whip the cream until stiff and fold in the 2 tablespoons praline. When the cake is cool, split in half horizontally and sandwich with the praline cream. In a saucepan, simmer the jam, jelly, and water until melted. Strain and cool. Brush the cake top with the jam mixture, arrange the cherries on top, and brush with jam again. Press ¾ cup praline around the sides of the cake. Can be prepared the day before.   YIELDS 6 SERVINGS.

❖❖❖

Schwarzwalder Kirsch Torte

BLACK FOREST CHERRY CAKE

Long a favorite dessert. Try this simple authentic version.

¾ cup granulated sugar
1 cup cold water
⅓ cup plus ¼ cup kirsch
3 (7-inch) Chocolate Génoise layers
　(see page 280)
½ cup confectioners' sugar
3 cups heavy cream
1 cup cherries, pitted
Maraschino cherries
Chocolate curls

In a saucepan, boil the granulated sugar and water until dissolved, then boil for 4 minutes more. Cool and stir in ⅓ cup kirsch. Prick the cake layers with a fork and sprinkle with the syrup. Beat the cream until it thickens. Beat the confectioners' sugar into the cream until stiff; add the remaining ¼ cup kirsch and beat until liqueur is absorbed. Place a cake layer on a serving dish and spread with a ½-inch-thick layer of whipped cream. Strew with the pitted cherries, set a second layer on top, and spread with a ½-inch-thick layer of cream. Set the third layer on top and spread the cream on the top and sides of the cake. Garnish the top of the cake with maraschino cherries and press the grated chocolate into the sides. Chill. Can be prepared the day before.
▾▾▾　　　　　　　YIELDS 8 SERVINGS.

Date Nut Cake

1½ cups butter
1½ cups firmly packed dark
　brown sugar
1 pound dates, chopped
1 cup flour
1 cup walnuts, chopped
2 eggs, beaten
½ teaspoon salt
1 cup boiling water
1 teaspoon baking soda
4½ tablespoons dark rum
1½ cups confectioners' sugar

Preheat oven to 350°F. Line the bottom of a 10-inch tube pan with parchment paper, and butter the paper. In a bowl, cream ¾ cup butter and the brown sugar until light and fluffy. Blend in the dates, flour, walnuts, eggs, and salt. In a bowl, combine the water and baking soda and pour into the batter. Blend well. Turn into the prepared pan. Bake for 1 hour or until cake tests done. Pour 2 tablespoons rum over the top of warm cake. Let stand until the outside of the pan is cool. Unmold and finish cooling. In a bowl, combine the confectioners' sugar, remaining ¾ cup butter, and remaining 2½ tablespoons rum, and mix well. Spread over the cake. Can be prepared up to 2 days before serving, or can be frozen.
▾▾▾　　　　YIELDS 8 TO 10 SERVINGS.

Ginger Cheesecake

½ cup crushed gingersnaps
½ cup crushed chocolate wafers
⅓ cup butter, melted
2 pounds cream cheese
½ cup heavy cream
4 eggs
1½ cups sugar
1 teaspoon vanilla
2 tablespoons grated gingerroot
1 cup minced candied ginger

Preheat oven to 300°F. Butter the inside of a metal 8-inch cheesecake pan. In a bowl, mix the gingersnaps, chocolate crumbs, and butter. Press into the bottom and halfway up the sides of the pan. With an electric mixer, beat the cream cheese, heavy cream, eggs, sugar, vanilla, and grated ginger. Beat until blended and smooth. Fold in the candied ginger. Pour into the pan and shake gently to level the mixture. Place in a water bath. Bake for 1 hour and 40 minutes. Shut off the oven and let cake stand for 1 hour longer. Lift the cake from the bath and let cool 2 hours before unmolding. Can be prepared 2 days before serving.

❖❖❖   YIELDS 8 SERVINGS.

Sticky Ginger Cake

An old-fashioned favorite that is equally delicious served with warm applesauce, cold vanilla sauce, whipped cream, or ice cream.

> ½ cup butter, plus extra for spreading
> ½ cup firmly packed brown sugar
> 2 eggs
> 1 cup molasses
> 2 cups flour
> Pinch of salt
> 1 teaspoon ginger
> ¾ cup golden raisins
> ½ teaspoon baking soda
> 2 tablespoons warm milk
> Gouda or Swiss cheese (optional)
> Apple slices (optional)

Preheat oven to 325°F. Butter and flour an 8-inch spring-form pan. In a bowl, cream the ½ cup butter and the brown sugar until light and fluffy. Beat in the eggs, 1 at a time, then the molasses. In a bowl, sift the flour, salt, and ginger together and fold into the egg mixture with the raisins. Dissolve the baking soda in the milk and stir into the batter. Pour into the pan and bake 1 hour or until cake tests done. Cool in the pan.

Unmold and cut into wedges. Spread generously with the extra butter and serve with a slice of cheese and crisp apple slices if desired. Can be prepared the day before.   YIELDS 6 TO 8 SERVINGS.

❖❖❖

Lemon Supreme

A lovely marriage of lemon and blueberry.

> ⅔ cup lemon juice
> 1¼ cups granulated sugar
> Peel of 1 orange
> ¾ cup milk
> 9 tablespoons butter
> ⅔ cup cake flour
> 6 eggs, separated
> Pinch of cream of tartar
> Pinch of salt
> Blueberry Sauce (see page 275)

Preheat oven to 325°F. Butter a 12-cup bundt pan and sprinkle with confectioners' sugar; shake out the excess. In a saucepan, reduce the lemon juice to ¼ cup. In a processor, process ½ cup granulated sugar and the orange peel until fine. Transfer to a 2-quart saucepan. Add the milk and butter and heat until the butter is melted. Add the cake flour and mix until incorporated (mixture will be lumpy). Put into a processor and mix for 20 seconds. Add the egg yolks and lemon juice and process until smooth. Turn into a bowl. Beat the egg whites with the cream of tartar and salt until stiff but not dry. Gradually beat in the remaining ¾ cup granulated sugar, 2 tablespoons at a time, until glossy. Fold a fourth of the beaten egg whites into the lemon mixture to loosen, then fold in the remainder. Pour into the bundt pan. Bake in a water bath about 55 to 60 minutes or until the top is golden and cracks develop. Cool on a rack for 15 minutes; unmold. Serve warm or at room temperature with Blueberry Sauce. Can be frozen.

❖❖❖   YIELDS 10 TO 12 SERVINGS.

Gâteau au Citron

FRENCH LEMON CAKE

    1 lemon
    ½ cup granulated sugar
    ½ cup butter
    2 eggs
    1 cup less 2 tablespoons flour
    1 teaspoon baking powder
    ½ cup confectioners' sugar

Preheat oven to 350°F. Butter and flour an 8-inch cake tin. Grate the rind from the lemon and cream with the granulated sugar and butter until light and fluffy. Beat in the eggs, 1 at a time. Beat in the flour and baking powder. Pour into the cake pan and bake for 25 minutes. Let rest for 10 minutes, then unmold. Squeeze the juice from the lemon and mix with the confectioners' sugar. Spoon over the cake. Repeat until the liquid is absorbed. Can be prepared the day before serving. Can be frozen.   YIELDS 6 TO 8 SERVINGS.

Cottage Pudding with Lemon Sauce

The cake is delicious on its own. Although it is not added traditionally, a few drops of yellow food coloring will improve the grayish color of the sauce.

    2 cups sifted flour
    1 tablespoon baking powder
    ⅓ cup plus 2 tablespoons butter
    1 teaspoon vanilla
    ⅔ cup plus 1 ½ cups sugar
    2 eggs, separated
    1 cup milk
    ¼ teaspoon salt
    ¼ teaspoon cream of tartar
    1 ½ tablespoons cornstarch
    1 cup boiling water
    3 tablespoons lemon juice
    1 tablespoon grated lemon rind

Preheat oven to 350°F. Butter a 9- by 13-inch pan. In a bowl, sift the flour and baking powder. In a processor, cream the ⅓ cup butter, the vanilla, and ⅔ cup sugar until light and fluffy. Beat in the egg yolks 1 at a time. Stir in the flour and milk with on/off turns. (If mixing by hand, alternate the flour and milk.) Beat the egg whites with the salt and cream of tartar until stiff. Fold into the batter and pour into the pan. Sprinkle with 1 to 2 tablespoons sugar and bake for 25 minutes. Let cool to lukewarm. Cut into squares.

In a saucepan, combine the remaining sugar and cornstarch. Stir in the boiling water and cook, stirring, over low heat until thickened and clear. Remove from the heat and stir in the lemon juice, 2 tablespoons butter, and lemon rind. Stir until the butter is melted and sauce is smooth. Place cake squares in individual serving dishes and pour sauce over all. Both the cake and sauce can be made ahead and reheated.

YIELDS 6 TO 8 SERVINGS.

Tarte Citron

LEMON TART

    3 eggs, separated, plus 2 whites
    1 cup sugar
    Grated rind of 1 lemon
    1 ¾ cups finely ground almonds
    1 tablespoon flour
    2 lemons, peeled and thinly sliced

Preheat oven to 350°F. Butter a 9-inch spring-form pan. Beat the egg yolks and ¾ cup sugar until very pale. Beat in the lemon rind and mix well. Blend in 1 cup almonds and the flour. Beat 3 egg whites until stiff. Stir a fourth of the beaten whites into the yolks to loosen the mixture. Carefully fold in the remaining beaten whites. Pour into the pan and bake for 30 minutes or until the cake is lightly browned. Remove from the oven and cover the top with overlapping lemon slices. Beat the remaining 2 egg whites until soft peaks form. Gradually beat in the remaining ¼ cup sugar and fold in the remaining ¾ cup almonds. With a spatula dipped in cold water, carefully spread egg white mixture evenly over the lemon slices, covering them completely. Bake for 15 minutes or until the meringue is golden. Can be prepared the day before. ❖❖❖   YIELDS 6 TO 8 SERVINGS.

Lemon Cream Roll

1 (11- by 16-inch) Sponge Cake sheet,
    freshly baked (see page 278)
2 tablespoons confectioners' sugar, or
    more as needed
1 ½ cups heavy cream
⅔ cup granulated sugar
Grated rind of 2 lemons

Turn the sponge sheet out of the baking pan onto a sheet of waxed paper sprinkled with confectioners' sugar. Roll tightly and keep wrapped in a damp towel for at least 20 minutes. Recipe can be prepared to this point the day before.

Up to 6 hours before serving, unroll the cake; remove the waxed paper and discard. Beat the cream with the granulated sugar and lemon rind, and spread over the cake. Reroll and cut off the ragged ends. Sprinkle with additional confectioners' sugar and put on a serving dish.   YIELDS 8 TO 10 SERVINGS.
❖❖❖

Lemon Tea Cake

1 cup butter, softened
1 ⅓ cups sugar
2 eggs
1 ¼ cups flour

1 teaspoon baking powder
½ teaspoon salt
½ cup milk
¼ cup lemon juice
2 tablespoons grated lemon rind

Preheat oven to 350°F. Butter a 3- by 5- by 9-inch loaf pan. In a processor, cream the butter and 1 cup sugar; add the eggs, 1 at a time, beating well. Add the flour, baking powder, salt, and milk with on/off turns. Pour into the pan and bake for 45 minutes or until cake tests done. In a small saucepan, heat the remaining ⅓ cup sugar, the lemon juice, and the lemon rind just to boiling. Pour over the cake as soon as it comes from the oven. Cool in the pan. Can be made the day before serving. ❖❖❖   YIELDS 18 HALF-INCH SERVINGS.

Lemon Cake with Yogurt

1 cup butter
1 ½ cups sugar
4 eggs
1 tablespoon grated lemon rind
1 teaspoon vanilla
2 ½ cups flour
1 teaspoon baking powder
1 teaspoon baking soda
½ teaspoon salt
1 cup yogurt
¾ cup ground blanched almonds
½ cup lemon juice

Preheat oven to 350°F. Butter a 9-inch tube pan. In a processor, cream the butter and 1 cup sugar. With the machine running, add the eggs, 1 at a time. Add the lemon rind and vanilla and process with on/off turns. Add the flour, baking powder, baking soda, and salt, and process. With the machine running, add the yogurt and the almonds. When mixed, pour into the pan and bake for 1 hour, or until cake tests done. Cool in the pan for 4 minutes.

In a small saucepan, simmer the lemon juice and remaining ½ cup sugar for 5 minutes. Brush over the cake, allowing the syrup to soak in. Cool in the pan. Can be made a day or two before serving.

■.■.■   YIELDS 12 TO 16 SERVINGS.

Mandarin Slices

See photograph on pages 68–69.

These slices can be made using other fruits, jams, and butter creams. Create your own versions.

> 1 (11- by 16-inch) Sponge Cake roll (see page 278)
> 4 cups mandarin orange segments
> 1 jar (12 ounces) orange marmalade, strained
> 2 tablespoons orange liqueur
> 3 cups orange-flavored Butter Cream Frosting (see page 282)
> 2 ounces grated semisweet chocolate or chocolate shot

Cut the sponge roll into 3 long strips. On a work surface, carefully arrange 2 cups orange segments over one of the strips. In a small saucepan, boil the strained marmalade and orange liqueur for 3 minutes. Glaze the orange slices and allow to cool. Cover with another strip of sponge roll. Spread generously with the Butter Cream Frosting and cover with the remaining strip of cake. Frost the sides of the cake with the Orange Butter Cream and press chocolate into the sides. Arrange remaining 2 cups orange segments on the top and glaze with the remaining marmalade-liqueur mixture. Chill for at least 3 hours. Cut into 1-inch-thick slices to serve.   YIELDS 14 TO 15 SLICES.

■.■.■

Orange Cake

> ¾ cup butter, softened
> 1½ cups sugar
> 3 eggs
> 1 tablespoon grated orange rind
> 3 cups sifted cake flour
> 1 tablespoon baking powder
> ½ teaspoon salt
> ½ cup orange juice
> ⅔ cup milk
> Orange-flavored Butter Cream Frosting (see page 282)

Preheat oven to 350°F. Butter two 9-inch layer pans and dust with flour. In a processor, cream the butter, sugar, eggs, and orange rind until light and fluffy. Add the flour, baking powder, and salt, processing with on/off turns. Add the orange juice and milk and process with on/off turns until smooth. Pour into the pans. Bake 30 minutes or until centers spring back when lightly pressed with a fingertip. Cool in pans on wire racks for 20 minutes. Turn out and cool completely. Frost with orange-flavored Butter Cream Frosting. Can be prepared the day before serving.

■.■.■   YIELDS 8 TO 10 SERVINGS.

Macedonian Orange Cake

The plain chocolate coating belies the delightful flavor of this cake.

> 9 eggs, separated, plus 2 whole eggs
> 2 cups confectioners' sugar
> 1 cup ground almonds
> Juice and grated rind of 1 orange
> Pinch of salt
> Pinch of cream of tartar
> ⅔ cup butter
> 4 ounces unsweetened chocolate, melted

Preheat oven to 350°F. Line the bottom and sides of a 10-inch spring-form pan with parchment paper. In a bowl, beat the 9 egg yolks and 1 cup confectioners' sugar until light in color. Beat in the almonds, orange rind, and juice. Beat the 9 egg whites to the soft-peak stage, then beat in the salt and cream of tartar until stiff but not dry. Fold into the orange mixture. Turn into the pan and bake 1 hour. Cool in the pan.

In a processor, cream the butter and remaining cup confectioners' sugar; blend in the chocolate and remaining 2 eggs. Frost the top and sides of the cake. Can be prepared the day before serving.

♥♥♥   YIELDS 8 SERVINGS.

Orange Torte

1 tablespoon gelatin
2 tablespoons water
6 tablespoons orange juice
Grated rind of 1 orange
2 cups heavy cream
4 tablespoons confectioners' sugar
1 (10-inch) Chocolate Génoise layer (see page 280)
2 tablespoons orange marmalade
12 to 16 orange segments

In a small saucepan, soften the gelatin in the water and dissolve over low heat. Stir in the orange juice and grated rind and allow to cool. Whip the cream until almost stiff and stir in the gelatin and confectioners' sugar. Beat until stiff. Cut the cake into thirds horizontally. Spread the bottom layer with orange marmalade and about a third of the whipped cream. Spread the middle layer with less than half of the remaining cream. Put on the top layer and frost the top and sides of the cake with some of the remaining cream.

Score the top into 12 to 16 slices. With a no. 3 star tip, decorate each slice with a rosette of whipped cream and garnish with an orange segment. Can be prepared the day before.

♥♥♥   YIELDS 12 TO 16 SERVINGS.

Victorian Orange Cake

Peel of 3 large oranges
1 cup raisins
1½ cups sugar
½ cup butter
2 eggs
¾ cup buttermilk
2 cups flour
1 teaspoon baking soda
½ teaspoon salt
½ cup chopped walnuts
1 cup orange juice
2 tablespoons dark rum

Preheat oven to 325°F. Butter a 9-inch spring-form or tube pan. In a processor, grind the orange peel and raisins until fine. Remove and set aside. In processor, cream 1 cup sugar and the butter until light and fluffy. Add the eggs and buttermilk and mix completely. Incorporate the flour, baking soda, and salt with on/off turns. Turn into the bowl with the orange-raisin mixture and fold together with the walnuts. Pour into the baking pan and bake for 45 to 50 minutes or until cake tests done.

In a saucepan, heat the orange juice, remaining ½ cup sugar, and rum until sugar is completely dissolved. Let the cake stand 10 minutes, then remove from the pan. Turn the cake upside down and slowly pour the flavored orange juice, 1 tablespoon at a time, over the cake. Allow to stand overnight or several days. Can be kept for several days if refrigerated.

♥♥♥   YIELDS 8 TO 10 SERVINGS.

Orange Poppyseed Cake

½ cup butter
¾ cup granulated sugar
2 eggs
½ cup sour cream
⅓ cup poppyseeds, plus extra
    for dusting
¼ cup orange juice
1 tablespoon grated orange rind
1 teaspoon vanilla
1 ¼ cups flour
½ teaspoon baking powder
¼ teaspoon baking soda
Pinch of salt
Sifted confectioners' sugar

Preheat oven to 350°F. Butter and flour a 1-quart ring mold. In a processor, cream the butter and granulated sugar until light and fluffy. Beat in the eggs, 1 at a time. Beat in the sour cream, poppyseeds, orange juice, orange rind, and vanilla. Mix the flour with the baking powder, soda, and salt, and add to mixture. Incorporate with on/off turns. Pour into the mold and bake for 40 minutes or until cake tests done. Unmold and cool on a rack. When cool, dust with confectioners' sugar and poppyseeds. Can be made a day or two before serving. Freezes well.

▼▼▼   YIELDS 8 SERVINGS.

Meringue Cake
with Peaches

The cake can be prepared without the meringue topping. As always, feel free to use other fruits or berries.

½ cup butter
1 ½ cups granulated sugar
4 eggs, separated
¼ cup milk
½ teaspoon vanilla
1 cup flour
1 ½ teaspoons baking powder

Pinch of salt
¼ cup chopped walnuts or pecans
1 cup heavy cream
2 tablespoons confectioners' sugar
2 peaches, peeled and diced

Preheat oven to 350°F. Butter two 8-inch cake pans and line with waxed paper. In a bowl, cream the butter and ½ cup granulated sugar until light and fluffy. Beat in the yolks, 1 at a time, then add the milk and vanilla. Sift the flour and baking powder together and add to the egg mixture, beating just until mixed. Divide between the pans and smooth the tops.

In a separate bowl, beat the egg whites with the salt to the soft-peak stage. With the mixer running, add the remaining 1 cup granulated sugar, 1 tablespoon at a time, beating constantly until the mixture is very stiff and glossy, and the sugar has dissolved. Rub the meringue between your fingertips; it should feel smooth. Spread the meringue over the cake batter in both pans and sprinkle 1 layer with the chopped nuts. Bake for 30 minutes. Cool on a rack for 10 minutes and carefully unmold. Continue cooling with the meringue side up.

Whip the cream and sweeten with the confectioners' sugar. Fold in the peaches. Place the nutless meringue layer, meringue side down, on a plate. Spread with the peaches and cream and cover with the nutted layer, meringue side up. Chill for 2 hours before serving. Can be prepared the day before serving.

▼▼▼   YIELDS 6 TO 8 SERVINGS.

Pear Küchen

1 ¼ cups flour
½ cup butter
3 tablespoons plus ½ cup heavy cream,
    plus extra for accompaniment
3 tablespoons firmly packed
    brown sugar

½ teaspoon ginger
¼ teaspoon nutmeg
¼ teaspoon salt
¾ cup granulated sugar
¼ cup flour
3 egg yolks
1 teaspoon lemon juice
1 teaspoon vanilla
3 pears, peeled, cored, and sliced

Preheat oven to 375°F. Butter a 9-inch tart pan. In a processor, blend flour, butter, 3 tablespoons cream, 1 teaspoon brown sugar, ginger, nutmeg, and salt with on/off turns until the mixture resembles coarse meal. Transfer ½ cup of the mixture to a small bowl and stir in the remaining brown sugar. Set aside.

Press the remaining mixture into the bottom and sides of the tart pan. Bake until lightly browned, about 20 minutes. Let cool.

Lower the heat to 350°. In a processor, blend the granulated sugar, ½ cup cream, flour, egg yolks, lemon juice, and vanilla for 30 seconds. Pour into the tart shell and arrange the pears on top. Sprinkle with the crumb mixture. Bake for about 45 minutes or until set. Let stand for 20 minutes before removing the sides. Serve warm or at room temperature with the heavy cream passed separately.
❖❖❖   YIELDS 6 TO 8 SERVINGS.

Gâteau Poire William

PEAR AND CHOCOLATE CAKE

A perfect dessert for your finest dinner party.

1 (9-inch) Chocolate Sponge Cake layer
   (see page 279)
3½ tablespoons Poire William
4 vanilla-poached pears, halved (see
   page 286)
1 tablespoon gelatin
7 tablespoons water
5½ ounces semisweet chocolate, melted
2 cups heavy cream, whipped

Chocolate sprinkles
Cocoa
½ cup heavy cream, whipped

Lightly oil a 9-inch spring-form pan. Place the cake in the pan and brush with the Poire William. Arrange the pears, rounded sides down, with stem ends toward the center of the cake. In a saucepan, soften the gelatin in the water and dissolve over low heat. Add the melted chocolate and blend well. Cool in a bowl.

Fold in the whipped cream and spread over the pears. Smooth the top. Chill until set, at least 3 hours.

Remove the sides of the pan, and pat the chocolate sprinkles about 1 inch high around the bottom of the cake. Cut a 3-inch circle of cardboard and place in the center of the cake. Sieve the cocoa over the top of the cake. Carefully remove the cardboard circle. With a no. 5 star tip, pipe rosettes of the whipped cream around the edge of the cake. Can be prepared the day before serving.
❖❖❖   YIELDS 8 TO 10 SERVINGS.

Pineapple Cream Cake

1 pineapple, peeled, cored, and cut in
   8 slices, saving the juice
2 tablespoons cornstarch
1 tablespoon granulated sugar
1 tablespoon gelatin
2 tablespoons cold water
2 cups heavy cream
¼ cup confectioners' sugar
1 (9-inch) Sponge Cake layer, split in
   half horizontally (see page 278)
Apricot Glaze (see page 283)

Cut 5 pineapple slices into small pieces and 3 slices into quarters, reserving the juice. In a saucepan, measure 1 cup juice and blend in the cornstarch and granulated sugar. Bring to a boil and add the chopped pineapple, reserving the quartered slices. Bring to a boil again and set aside to cool.

In a small saucepan, soften the gelatin in the water and dissolve over low heat. Set aside. Whip the cream until almost stiff, and whisk in the gelatin and the confectioners' sugar. Whip until stiff. Fold the pineapple mixture into half of the whipped cream. Spread the bottom layer of the cake with the pineapple cream filling. Cut the top layer into 12 wedges and place over the pineapple cream, pressing lightly. Spread the top and the sides of the cake with half of the remaining whipped cream. Place a reserved pineapple quarter on each slice and garnish with the remaining whipped cream. Glaze the pineapple with the Apricot Glaze. Chill for at least 2 hours before serving. Can be prepared ahead and even frozen.   YIELDS 12 SERVINGS.

Note: Cutting the upper layer of cake before assembling makes serving much simpler. You can use this technique with most oven cakes.
❖❖❖

Purple Plum Torte

See photograph on pages 68–69.

> 1 cup plus 1 tablespoon sugar
> ½ cup butter, softened
> 1 cup flour
> 1 teaspoon baking powder
> Salt to taste
> 2 eggs
> 12 plums, pitted and halved
> 2 teaspoons lemon juice
> 1 tablespoon cinnamon
> Whipped cream (optional)

Preheat oven to 350°F. Butter a 9-inch spring-form pan. In a processor, cream 1 cup sugar and the butter until light and fluffy. Add the flour, baking powder, and salt, and process with on/off turns. Add

the eggs and process with on/off turns. Spoon into the pan. Place the plum halves skin side up on the cake, and sprinkle with the tablespoon sugar, lemon juice, and cinnamon. Bake for 1 hour. Cool to lukewarm. Serve with whipped cream if desired. Can be made the day before.   YIELDS 6 TO 8 SERVINGS.
❖❖❖

Prune Torte

A perfect winter dessert when fresh fruits are not at their best.

> 1 cup firmly packed brown sugar
> ½ cup granulated sugar
> ¾ cup butter
> 3 eggs
> ⅓ cup milk
> 2½ cups sifted flour
> 2 teaspoons baking powder
> ¼ teaspoon salt
> ½ teaspoon baking soda
> 1 teaspoon cinnamon
> 1½ cups cooked prunes, pitted
>   and chopped
> 1 cup chopped walnuts
> 2 cups heavy cream, whipped
> Grand Marnier or rum (optional)

Preheat oven to 375°F. Butter two 9-inch layer pans. In a processor, cream the brown sugar, granulated sugar, and butter until light and fluffy. Add the eggs and milk and process until well mixed. Add the flour, baking powder, salt, soda, and cinnamon and process with on/off turns until just mixed. Fold in the prunes and walnuts. Spread evenly in the cake pan and bake for 30 minutes or until cake tests done. Cool in the pans for 10 minutes, then unmold and continue cooling.

To serve, assemble the cake with the whipped cream as filling and frosting. If desired, the cream may be flavored with rum or Grand Marnier. Can be prepared the day before.   YIELDS 6 TO 8 SERVINGS.
❖❖❖

Paris-Brest aux Framboises

RASPBERRY CREAM CAKE

Strawberries, peaches, and other fruit can be used in place of the raspberries. Instead of whipped cream, pastry cream can be used to fill the dessert. The pastry can be shaped as a large rectangle, as a completely filled circle like a 9-inch cake, or in a large fat ring.

- 1 recipe Pâte à Choux (see page 280)
- 2 cups heavy cream
- 3 tablespoons granulated sugar
- 1 ½ tablespoons plus 1 teaspoon framboise
- 1 pint raspberries
- 1 cup confectioners' sugar
- 1 teaspoon water

Preheat oven to 425°F. With a pastry bag fitted with a no. 5 large open-star pastry tip, pipe the pastry into a long 5- by 12-inch rectangle, filling in with coils of the

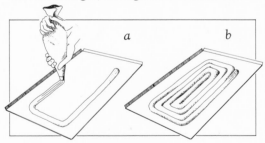

dough. Bake for 40 minutes or until puffed and golden. Remove to the edge of the rack and pierce the outside edges in many places around the shell. Return to the oven and lower the heat to 350°. Bake for 15 minutes longer. Remove from the oven and cool.

With a large serrated knife, split the pastry in half horizontally. Set the top aside. Whip the cream, sweeten to taste with the granulated sugar, and flavor with 1½ tablespoons framboise. Place half of the whipped cream on the bottom of the pastry and scatter raspberries generously over the top. Cover with the remaining whipped cream. Place the top of the pastry on the cream.

In a small bowl, combine the confectioners' sugar with the remaining teaspoon framboise and just enough water to make a runny icing. Drizzle the icing over the top of the cake in irregular patterns. Can be prepared up to 6 hours before serving.   YIELDS 6 TO 9 SERVINGS.

Note: If desired, the pastry can be brushed with a dorure (see page 213) and sprinkled with sliced almonds before baking.
▟▗▖

Montmartre

RASPBERRY-STRAWBERRY CREAM TORTE

Although this dessert takes time to prepare, it is well worth it.

- 1 (8-inch) Génoise layer, split in half horizontally (see page 279)
- Framboise
- 1 tablespoon gelatin
- 3 tablespoons orange juice
- 4 egg yolks
- ¾ cup plus 6 tablespoons sugar
- 1 ½ cups sour cream
- 3 tablespoons Grand Marnier
- 3 ½ cups heavy cream
- 10 ounces raspberry jelly, melted
- 1 quart strawberries
- 10 ounces frozen raspberries, thawed
- 6 mint leaves

Place a cake layer in the bottom of an 8-inch spring-form pan. Brush with framboise and set aside. In a saucepan, soften the gelatin in the orange juice. Beat in the egg yolks and ¾ cup plus 2 tablespoons sugar, and cook over low heat until thickened. Remove from the heat and stir in the sour cream and Grand Marnier. Beat 1½ cups heavy cream and 2 tablespoons sugar until soft peaks form. Fold into the sour cream mixture and spread the filling on the Génoise layer. Cover with second

Génoise layer and brush with more framboise. Chill overnight.

When ready to serve, or up to 3 hours beforehand, wipe a hot towel around the edges of the spring-form pan and remove the sides. Place the cake on a large, round serving platter. For the prettiest effect, the platter should be 14 or 16 inches in diameter. Brush the top of the cake with half of the melted raspberry jelly and arrange the strawberries, stem sides down, over the top of the Génoise. Glaze the strawberries with the remaining jelly.

Set aside ⅓ cup of the remaining heavy cream. Whip the remaining 1⅔ cups heavy cream with the remaining 2 tablespoons sugar until stiff. Put the whipped cream into a pastry bag fitted with a no. 5 plain tip and pipe vertical columns just joining around the cake.

In a processor, purée the frozen raspberries and mint, then force through a sieve. Pour the sauce around the base of the cake. Put the reserved ⅓ cup heavy cream into a pitcher. Pour it around the cake in 3 rings. With the tip of a knife, draw it away from the cake to the edge of the plate every 3 inches. Then draw lines from the edge of the plate toward the cake between the original lines to make a flower effect. Can be prepared for garnishing with the sauce up to 2 days before.

❖❖❖   YIELDS 12 SERVINGS.

Galette aux Fraises

STRAWBERRY CAKE

- ¼ cup granulated sugar
- 5 tablespoons water
- 2 tablespoons maraschino liqueur or Cointreau
- 1 pint strawberries, thinly sliced
- 1 (7-inch) Sponge Cake layer (see page 278)
- 3 cups sifted confectioners' sugar
- Juice of ½ orange

In a saucepan, dissolve the granulated sugar in the 5 tablespoons water and boil until it spins a thread (230°F.). Cool. Stir in the maraschino or Cointreau and pour over the strawberries. Let stand 10 minutes. Drain strawberries, reserving syrup. Split the cake in half horizontally and arrange drained strawberries on the bottom layer. Spoon on some of the sugar syrup, cover with the second layer, and spoon on the remaining syrup. In a saucepan, combine the confectioners' sugar and orange juice with just enough water to make a thick paste. Heat over low heat until mixture is of a spreading consistency and shiny. Spread over the top of the cake about 30 minutes before serving. Do not assemble more than 4 hours before serving.   YIELDS 6 SERVINGS.

❖❖❖

Raspberry Butter Cream Cake

- 1 (9-inch) Sponge Cake layer (see page 278)
- ¼ cup Dessert Syrup flavored with framboise (see page 284)
- 1¼ cups Butter Cream Frosting flavored with framboise (see page 282)
- 2 cups fresh raspberries
- 1½ cups heavy cream
- 2 tablespoons confectioners' sugar
- 1 tablespoon framboise

Cut the cake in half horizontally. Brush each layer with the Dessert Syrup. Spread the bottom half with the Butter Cream and scatter 1 cup of raspberries on top, pressing lightly. Arrange the top layer on the cake. Beat the cream until thickened and flavor with confectioners' sugar and framboise. Frost the cake with the cream, reserving some cream for garnish. With a pastry bag fitted with a no. 5 open-star tip, pipe rosettes on top of the cake and garnish with the remaining 1 cup raspberries. Can be prepared the day before serving.

❖ YIELDS 6 TO 8 SERVINGS.

Strawberry-Walnut Cream Cake

4 eggs
½ cup sugar
1 tablespoon instant coffee
¾ cup flour
½ cup chopped walnuts
1 pint strawberries
1 cup heavy cream

Preheat oven to 350°F. Butter an 8-inch cake pan and sprinkle with sugar and flour. In an electric mixer, beat the eggs, sugar, and instant coffee until the mixture is tripled in bulk and the consistency of mayonnaise. Gently fold in the flour and walnuts. Turn into the pan and bake for 30 to 35 minutes or until cake springs back when touched. Unmold onto a wire rack and cool.

Set aside 6 to 8 whole strawberries and slice the remainder. Whip the cream to the soft-peak stage and fold the sliced strawberries into two-thirds of the cream. Split the cake in half horizontally and fill lavishly with the whipped cream, then cover with top layer, spread with the reserved strawberry-flavored whipped cream and garnish with the remaining berries. Can be prepared up to 6 hours before serving. YIELDS 6 TO 8 SERVINGS.

❖

Strawberry Sponge Roll

This is a standard recipe for a sponge roll. If desired, 1 cup heavy cream, whipped and sweetened and flavored to taste, can be substituted for the cheese. Kirsch may be used instead of Grand Marnier. For a raspberry roll, substitute raspberries for strawberries. Other fruits such as peaches, pears, blueberries, or the like can be used in place of the strawberries as well.

1 (11- by 15-inch) Sponge Cake layer (see page 278)
Confectioners' sugar
9 ounces cream cheese, softened
3 tablespoons Grand Marnier
1 quart strawberries, sliced

Turn the sponge sheet onto a towel dusted with confectioners' sugar, roll tightly, and chill. In a processor, cream the cheese until fluffy and sweeten to taste with more confectioners' sugar and the Grand Marnier. Unroll the cake, spread with the cheese mixture, and sprinkle on at least half of the berries. Roll again and chill. Serve the roll with remaining berries, crushed and sweetened to taste.

❖ YIELDS 6 TO 10 SERVINGS.

Strawberry Sponge Layers

1 (11- by 15-inch) Sponge Cake layer (see page 278)
1 quart strawberries
Sugar and kirsch to taste
3 cups heavy cream
Currant Glaze (see page 283)

Cut the sponge sheet into strips approximately 3½ inches wide and 15 inches long. Hull the strawberries. Cut three-quarters of the berries in half and save the remainder whole. Add the sugar and kirsch to taste to the halved strawberries. Whip the cream until stiff. Spread a thin layer of whipped cream on a sponge strip, arrange halved strawberries over the top, cover with a layer of sponge cake, spread with more whipped cream, and arrange another layer of halved strawberries. Cover with final layer of sponge cake and spread with whipped cream. With a pastry bag fitted with a no. 5 star tip, pipe rosettes on the cake and garnish with the whole strawberries. Brush the berries with the Currant Glaze. Can be prepared the day before serving.

❖ YIELDS 15 ONE-INCH SERVINGS.

Génoise aux Fraises Lucullus

GÉNOISE AND STRAWBERRIES LUCULLUS

> 2 cups raspberries
> ½ cup superfine sugar
> 1 quart small strawberries
> 2 cups Royal Icing (see page 283)
> 2 (9-inch) Génoise layers (see page 279)

In a processor, purée the raspberries; then strain through a fine sieve. Place the purée in a saucepan with the sugar and two-thirds of the strawberries. Simmer 3 minutes. The strawberries should retain their shape. Drain the fruits, reserving the juice, and cool.

Prepare the Royal Icing. Fill the layers of the cake with the cooked strawberries. Pour the Royal Icing over the top and allow to dribble down the sides of the cake. Decorate with the uncooked strawberries and drizzle the reserved fruit juice over the cake. Serve within 2 hours of assembling. The components can be made the day before.

❖❖❖   YIELDS 6 TO 8 SERVINGS.

Torta alla Crema di Fragole

STRAWBERRY CREAM CAKE

> 1 ½ pints strawberries
> 6 ounces strawberry preserves
> ½ cup sweet sherry
> 1 (9-inch) Sponge Cake layer (see page 278)
> 2 cups heavy cream
> ⅓ cup superfine sugar

In a bowl, mash 1 pint of the berries and combine with half of the preserves and the sherry. Let macerate for 30 minutes. Purée in a processor.

Split the sponge layer in thirds. Douse each layer with the purée. Place 1 layer on a platter. Whip the cream with the sugar until stiff, and fold in the remaining strawberry preserves. Spread a third of the cream mixture over the layer, top with another cake layer, and coat with more cream. Cover with the top layer. Put remaining cream into a pastry bag fitted with a no. 4 tip and pipe a lattice of cream over the top. Fill the spaces with remaining 1 cup whole strawberries. Chill for at least 2 hours before serving. Can be prepared up to 8 hours before serving.

❖❖❖   YIELDS 6 TO 8 SERVINGS.

Strawberry Cheesecake

See photograph on page 68.

> ½ cup graham cracker crumbs
> 2 pounds cream cheese
> 4 eggs
> 1 ¾ cups sugar
> Grated rind and juice of 1 lemon
> 1 teaspoon vanilla
> 1 ½ cups strawberries or other fruit
> Apricot Glaze (see page 283)

Preheat oven to 325°F. Butter the inside of an 8-inch cheesecake pan and set aside; do not use a spring-form pan. Sprinkle the inside of the pan with cracker crumbs and dump out the excess. In a bowl, beat the cream cheese, eggs, sugar, lemon rind, lemon juice, and vanilla until blended. Beat until smooth. Turn the batter into the pan and level. Place in a water bath and bake for 1½ hours. Turn off the oven and let stand for 30 minutes.

Remove the cake from the water bath and let stand until it reaches room temperature. Unmold so that it is right side up. Arrange the fruit on the top of the cake. Brush the fruit with the Apricot Glaze. Chill until ready to serve. Can be made a day or two before serving.

❖❖❖   YIELDS 6 TO 8 SERVINGS.

COOKIES, PLAIN CAKES
& CONFECTIONS

FRUIT desserts, especially those found in the first couple of chapters, are not only enhanced but also completed with a suitable cookie or slice of plain but flavorful cake. These simple pastries provide the balance required to make the dessert whole. Coupes and bombes are occasionally garnished with cookies. The cookie that serves best on these occasions is plain, crisp, and buttery; elaborate confections intrude on the fruit flavors. The one exception for which I allow is jelly-filled cookies. The cakes are served unadorned without frosting, except for a sprinkle of confectioners' sugar. These are not the cakes for the gâteaux in the previous chapter, although they sometimes are used as the base for such gâteaux. Plain sponge cake or génoise, especially if baked in an interesting mold, can serve very well as a plain cake. In fact, many of the cakes are baked in elaborate molds to make them more eye-appealing.

Without question, the flavor of these cookies and cakes depends on the finest of ingredients, all of which are available in your local market: fresh eggs, unsweetened butter, flour, sugar, and real vanilla extract. If you use powdered eggs, margarine or some other fat, and imitation vanilla, you will get a dreadful result.

Whenever possible, the recipes in this section are made with a food processor, as it is quicker and the results are superb. However, as always, it is important to follow the instructions carefully. Do not overprocess.

If you do not have a processor, all of the recipes can be made by hand or with an electric mixer. The only tedious part is creaming the butter and sugar. If you are doing this by hand, leave the butter at room temperature to soften. When adding the dry and liquid ingredients, add one-third of the dry ingredients, one-half of the liquid ingredients, another one-third of the dry ingredients, the remaining liquid, and then the remaining dry ingredients. Beat until the ingredients are well combined, but again, do not overbeat.

These cookies and cakes can usually be made ahead, and they freeze perfectly for longer storage. Freeze the cookies in metal or plastic boxes to protect them from being broken. Arrange them so you can remove as many as you need without disturbing the rest. The cookies thaw quickly, usually in less than 20 minutes. Even whole cakes can be ready to eat in an hour. If you wish to hasten the process, slice the cakes, separate the slices, and let them stand for about 20 minutes. You can then reassemble the slices to the original shape.

Confections can be used to garnish fruit desserts or can be served on their own. In fact, a collection of different fruit confections can be the perfect dessert at the end of a large meal. Guests can choose to have a sliver of orange peel or apricot dipped in chocolate, or to sample as many as you have prepared.

In addition, many confections are used as parts of other desserts. Apricots dipped in chocolate are recommended for garnishing a gâteau. Candied citrus peel can be used to garnish desserts such as fruit cups or can be chopped to add to bombes, mousses, and fruitcakes. In most cases, the confections can be prepared well ahead and kept in airtight containers. Some, however, such as chocolate- or caramel-dipped strawberries, should be served within a few hours of making so that the strawberry or other fruit retains its peak of perfection.

Crispy Almond Cookies

1 cup butter
1¼ cups sugar
1 egg, plus 1 white
1 tablespoon grated lemon rind
2 tablespoons rum
3 cups sifted flour
½ teaspoon baking powder
¼ teaspoon cinnamon
½ cup chopped blanched almonds
Whole almonds (optional)

In a processor, cream the butter with 1 cup sugar until light and fluffy. Add the whole egg, lemon rind, and rum, and process until well combined. Add the flour and baking powder and incorporate with on/off turns. Turn onto a board and shape into a flat cake. Wrap in waxed paper or plastic wrap and chill for about 1 hour.

Preheat oven to 325°F. In a small bowl, combine the remaining ¼ cup sugar, cinnamon, and chopped almonds. On a floured board, roll the pastry about ⅛-inch thick. With cookie cutters, cut out shapes; then arrange on an unbuttered baking sheet. Brush lightly with the beaten egg white and sprinkle with the cinnamon-almond mixture. If desired, press a whole almond into the center of each cookie. Bake 10 to 12 minutes or until lightly browned around the edges. Remove and cool on a wire rack. Can be frozen.   YIELDS ABOUT 5 DOZEN COOKIES, DEPENDING ON SIZE.

Almond Macaroons

Multiply this recipe to have plenty on hand. Freeze immediately so they stay soft and chewy. To use in desserts, let macaroons dry and keep them in an airtight container for use whole or crumbled.

1 cup unblanched almonds, ground
   finely

1 cup sugar
2 to 3 egg whites
½ teaspoon almond extract
½ teaspoon vanilla
Blanched almond halves (optional)

Preheat oven to 400°F. Butter and flour a baking sheet. In a bowl, mix the ground almonds with ⅔ cup sugar. Gradually add the egg whites, a little at a time, to make the mixture about the same consistency as mashed potatoes. Beat hard for 3 minutes with a wooden spoon. Beat in the almond extract and vanilla. Fit a pastry bag with a no. 5 star tip and pipe 1½-inch rounds on the cookie sheet about 1 inch apart. Sprinkle each cookie with some of the remaining ⅓ cup sugar. If desired, press an almond half into each cookie. Bake 15 minutes or until the tops are crackled and lightly browned. Can be frozen.   YIELDS ABOUT 24 COOKIES.

Macarons de Monte Carlo

CHOCOLATE MACAROONS

5 ounces blanched almonds,
   finely ground
1 cup plus 1 teaspoon sugar
⅓ cup egg whites
½ teaspoon vanilla
¼ teaspoon almond extract
2½ ounces unsweetened
   chocolate, melted

Preheat oven to 325°F. Line a baking sheet with parchment paper. In a bowl, combine the almonds and 1 cup sugar and mix well. Stir in the egg whites, vanilla, almond extract, and chocolate, and stir thoroughly. The mixture should be firm enough to hold a soft shape. If it is too sticky, let stand for 15 minutes. Wet your hands and form 24 mounds, using a rounded teaspoonful for each macaroon. Shape into balls. Place on the parchment paper at least 1 inch apart. Sprinkle the top with the remaining 1 teaspoon sugar. Bake 18 to 20 minutes. Reverse the sheets, if using more than one, from top to bottom and from front to back once during the baking.

Slide the papers off the cookie sheets and let stand 1 minute. Turn each piece of paper over and brush the back with water. Let stand about 3 minutes; the paper should dry out. Brush again with water, turn over, and lift the macaroons from the paper. Cool on racks.

❖❖❖   YIELDS ABOUT 24 COOKIES.

Carquinyolis

BARCELONA ALMOND COOKIES

  2⅓ cups flour
  1 cup plus 1 tablespoon sugar
  1 teaspoon baking soda
  ½ teaspoon salt
  2 eggs
  2 tablespoons grated lemon rind
  ¼ teaspoon almond extract
  ½ pound blanched almonds

Preheat oven to 350°F. Butter a baking sheet. In a processor, mix the flour, sugar, baking soda, salt, eggs, lemon rind, and almond extract until the dough almost forms a ball on top of the blades. Remove to a board and knead in the almonds. The dough will be sticky. Divide the dough in half and transfer one half to a baking sheet. Pat it into a rectangular loaf 1½-inches wide and ¾-inch high. Repeat with remaining dough. Bake loaves until golden, about 25 minutes. Immediately cut into ¾-inch slices.

Raise oven temperature to 450°. Arrange the cookies, cut side down, on a baking sheet and bake until centers are just golden (about 5 minutes), watching carefully. Cool. Can be frozen. Keep several days at room temperature. These

cookies turn very hard and are then delicious if dipped into a cup of coffee to soften them.   YIELDS ABOUT 60 COOKIES. ❖❖❖

Shortcake Cookies

These are the perfect accompaniment to macédoines, mélanges, and compotes of fruit.

  1 cup flour
  ¾ cup butter
  ½ cup cornstarch
  ½ cup confectioners' sugar

In a processor, combine the flour, butter, cornstarch, and sugar with on/off turns until well blended. Turn onto a board and shape into a log about 2 inches thick. Wrap in waxed paper. Chill for about 30 minutes.

Preheat oven to 300°F. Cut cookies into ⅛-inch-thick slices and place on unbuttered cookie sheets. Bake about 10 minutes or until they just start to turn golden. Can be frozen.

❖❖❖   MAKES ABOUT 40 COOKIES.

Nut Butter Cookies

See photograph on page 67.

  ½ cup butter
  ¾ cup plus 2 tablespoons
    confectioners' sugar
  1 cup flour
  Juice of 1 lemon
  1 cup finely ground almonds, walnuts,
    or pecans

Preheat oven to 350°F. Prepare 1 or 2 buttered baking sheets. In a processor, cream the butter and ¾ cup confectioners' sugar until light and fluffy. Add the flour and process until smooth. Add the lemon juice and nuts and process with on/off turns. Drop by teaspoonfuls onto the buttered baking sheets, or put into a pastry bag and pipe out small mounds with a no. 4 plain tip. Bake 6 or 7 minutes or until pale golden. Remove from baking sheet and put on a cooling rack. Sift remaining 2 tablespoons confectioners' sugar over the top. Can be frozen.

YIELDS SIXTY TO EIGHTY
1½- TO 2-INCH COOKIES.

Nut Butter Balls

1 cup butter
¼ cup superfine sugar
1 teaspoon vanilla
1 teaspoon almond extract
2 cups flour, sifted
2 cups pecans or walnuts, grated
Confectioners' sugar

Preheat oven to 350°F. In a processor, cream the butter and superfine sugar until light and fluffy. Add the vanilla and almond extracts and process until incorporated. Add the flour and nuts and process until the mixture is creamy and almost forms a ball on top of the blades. Shape into ½-inch balls. Place on an unbuttered baking sheet. Bake for 10 to 12 minutes. The cookies need to dry but not brown. Remove from the oven and let stand for 3 minutes. Transfer to a wire rack. Let cool for 15 minutes, then roll in the confectioners' sugar. Store in a cool dry place.   MAKES ABOUT 48 COOKIES.

Jelly Cookies

1 cup unsalted butter
⅔ cup sugar
2 large egg yolks
2 teaspoons vanilla
2 cups sifted flour
Currant jelly

Preheat oven to 375°F. Butter cookie sheet. In a processor, cream the butter and sugar until light and fluffy. Add the egg yolks and vanilla and process with on/off turns. Add the flour and process until the dough begins to form a ball on top of the blades. Roll the dough into walnut-sized balls and place on the cookie sheet about 2 inches apart. With the tip of your finger, make an indentation in each cookie. Fill with jelly. Bake about 8 minutes or until the edges turn pale golden. Cool on a rack. Can be frozen.
YIELDS ABOUT 4 DOZEN COOKIES.

Jumbals

An early American recipe that is still wonderful today.

⅓ cup butter
⅓ cup sugar
1 egg
¾ cup sifted flour
¼ teaspoon salt
1 teaspoon mace

Preheat oven to 350°F. Butter a baking sheet. In a processor, cream the butter and sugar until light and fluffy. Add the egg and incorporate. Add the flour, salt, and mace and process until combined. Drop by teaspoonfuls onto a baking sheet about 4 inches apart. Dip a spatula into cold water and spread cookies about ⅛-inch thick with spatula. Bake 10 minutes or until the edges are light brown. Cool on a rack. Can be frozen.
YIELDS ABOUT 24 COOKIES.

Sables

SAND COOKIES

2 cups sifted flour
¾ cup butter
½ cup sugar
6 hard-boiled egg yolks
½ teaspoon salt
½ teaspoon cinnamon

Butter and flour a baking sheet. In a processor, combine the flour, butter, and sugar and mix with on/off turns. Force the egg yolks through a sieve and add to the processor with the salt and cinnamon. Process into a dough. Roll the pastry between sheets of waxed paper until ¼-inch thick. Chill until firm, about 1 hour.

Preheat oven to 400°F. Remove the waxed paper and cut cookies into shapes. Bake for 10 to 12 minutes or until pale golden. Can be frozen.

YIELDS ABOUT 20 COOKIES.

Langues de Chat

CATS' TONGUES

½ cup butter
½ cup sugar
3 egg whites
1 cup sifted flour
Pinch of salt
½ teaspoon vanilla

Preheat oven to 400°F. Butter and flour baking sheets. In a bowl, cream the butter and sugar together until light and fluffy. Beat in the unbeaten egg whites a little at a time. Fold in the flour, salt, and vanilla. Fit a pastry bag with a no. 3 plain tip. Pipe out pencils of the batter about 2 inches long and 1 inch apart. They will spread during baking. Bake about 7 minutes or until the edges are golden. Remove to a wire rack immediately. Can be frozen.

YIELDS ABOUT 50 COOKIES.

Shortbread

1 cup butter
½ teaspoon vanilla
½ cup plus 1 tablespoon sugar
3 cups flour

Preheat oven to 350°F. Lightly butter a baking sheet. In a processor, cream the butter, vanilla, and sugar until light and smooth. The sugar should be completely dissolved. With the machine running, add the flour ¼ cup at a time. When incorporated, remove to a board and knead into a smooth ball. Roll between sheets of waxed paper into a 10-inch circle. Remove the top sheet of paper and invert onto the baking sheet. With a fork, prick into 6 wedges. Bake for 30 to 40 minutes or until an even golden. Remove from the oven and cut into wedges while still warm. Can be frozen; however, this is best when served within a day of baking.

YIELDS 6 WEDGES.

Walnut Butter Crisps

6 tablespoons butter
¼ cup sugar
½ cup ground walnuts
½ teaspoon vanilla
1 cup flour
Pinch of salt

Preheat oven to 350°F. Butter a baking sheet. In a processor, cream the butter and sugar until light and fluffy. Add the walnuts, vanilla, flour, and salt and process until blended. Shape into ¾-inch balls and place on the baking sheet at least 1 inch apart. With the bottom of a glass wrapped in a damp cloth, press each cookie to flatten. Bake until lightly browned. YIELDS ABOUT 24 COOKIES.

Madeleines

See photograph on page 67.

These are among the most delicious of small cakes. They are extraordinarily delicate when first baked, but they lose some of their delicious fresh quality quickly. If you cannot serve them within two or three hours of baking, freeze immediately.

10 tablespoons butter
⅔ cup plus 1 tablespoon flour
4 eggs
⅔ cup granulated sugar
2 teaspoons vanilla
Grated rind of 1 lemon
⅓ cup cake flour
Confectioners' sugar (optional)

Preheat oven to 375°F. In a saucepan, melt the butter over medium heat until it is lightly browned and smells nutlike. Let cool to room temperature. In a bowl, combine 2 tablespoons of the butter and 1 tablespoon flour. With a pastry brush, brush the butter-flour mixture into four 12-shell madeleine molds and set aside.

In a mixing bowl, beat the eggs over hot but not boiling water until warm to the touch. Put the bowl in an electric mixer and start beating at slow speed, adding the granulated sugar 1 tablespoon at a time. Add the vanilla and lemon rind and increase the speed to high. Beat constantly until the batter is doubled in bulk and the consistency of heavy mayonnaise. Combine the remaining flours, sift the flours over the batter, and start to fold. When half the flour is incorporated, gently fold in the browned butter. Put about 1 tablespoon batter into each shell and bake for 12 minutes or until golden and cakes start to shrink from the sides of the mold. Unmold immediately. If desired, sprinkle with sifted confectioners' sugar before serving. Can be frozen.
▚▚▚ YIELDS ABOUT 48 MADELEINES.

Palmiers

See photograph on page 67.

¼ recipe Puff Pastry (see page 215)
Sugar

Preheat oven to 400°F. Run a baking sheet under cold water, let excess water drain off, and set aside. Rolling the pastry in sugar instead of flour to prevent sticking, form it into a large rectangle about ¼ inch thick, 12 inches wide, and 18 inches

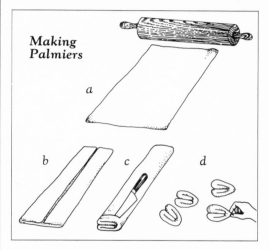

Making Palmiers

long. Be sure to use plenty of sugar to prevent sticking. Fold each long side over twice so that the folds almost meet in the center. Fold once again so that the pastry is in one long strip.

Cut each strip crosswise into ½-inch slices. Place slices cut side down on the baking sheet about 2 inches apart. If desired, pinch the bottom of each palmier to make it heart shaped.

Bake about 20 minutes, or until the bottoms just start to turn golden. With a spatula, turn the palmiers over and return to the oven. Bake until golden on the second side, about 10 minutes. Remove from the oven and cool on a pastry rack. Can be frozen. YIELDS ABOUT 36.

Note: Take care when handling the just-baked pastries. The sugar will have caramelized and will be extremely hot and sticky. If you should get any on you, plunge that portion of you under cold water to prevent it from burning you.

❖❖❖

Madeira Cake

This old-fashioned cake is named Madeira Cake because it was originally served with Madeira. There is no Madeira in the recipe, however, and it is usually served plain. It can be garnished with a dusting of confectioners' sugar if you like, though, or you can glaze it with a thin icing of confectioners' sugar and Madeira.

> 1 cup butter
> Grated rind of ½ lemon
> 1¼ cups sugar
> 5 eggs
> 3¼ cups flour
> Pinch of salt
> 2 teaspoons baking powder
> 1 cup milk

Preheat oven to 350°F. Butter and flour an 8-inch cake pan. In a processor, cream the butter, lemon rind, and sugar until light and fluffy. Add the eggs and process until blended. Add the flour, salt, and baking powder; process with 2 turns; add the milk and process until just combined. Pour into the pan and bake for 45 minutes or until cake tests done. When done, a wooden skewer should come out clean, and the surface will spring back when touched lightly. The cake will also have pulled away from the sides of the pan. Cool 5 minutes in the pan and then unmold and let cool. Can be frozen.

YIELDS 1 CAKE.

Note: This can also be baked in a ring mold, a small bundt pan, or a spring-form pan.

❖❖❖

Almond Cake

> ½ pound butter
> ⅓ cup sugar
> 6 ounces almond paste
> 3 eggs
> ¼ teaspoon orange flower water
> ¼ cup flour
> ⅓ teaspoon baking powder
> Apricot Glaze (see page 283)

Preheat oven to 350°F. Butter and flour a 3- to 4-cup fancy mold. In a processor, cream the butter, sugar, and almond paste until light and fluffy. Add the eggs and orange flower water until fully incorporated. Add the flour and baking powder and process until just blended. Pour into the mold and bake for 30 to 40 minutes or until a cake tester comes out clean. Cool for 20 minutes and unmold. When cool, brush with Apricot Glaze.

❖❖❖   YIELDS 1 CAKE.

Pamelas

CANDIED GRAPEFRUIT RIND
See photograph on page 71.

This same method can be used with orange or lemon rind. If desired, the peel can be dipped into melted semisweet chocolate. Let cool on waxed paper until chocolate is set.

> 4 to 6 grapefruits
> 3¼ cups granulated sugar
> ¼ pound crystallized rock sugar, crushed

Cut off the ends of the grapefruits, then cut the grapefruits into quarters. Pry the skin from the grapefruits and cut the skin into ½-inch-thick strips. Use the flesh for another purpose.

In a large kettle, combine the grapefruit rind and enough cold water to cover. Bring to a boil and simmer for 5 minutes. Drain and repeat 3 more times, starting with cold water each time. After the last time, return the drained peel to the pot and add the granulated sugar. Cook over low heat, uncovered, turning often, for 1½ hours or until the peel is glazed. Arrange the peel on a cooling rack set over a baking sheet and drain until cool enough to handle. Roll the peel in the crushed sugar. Keeps for several weeks, stored in an airtight container.

YIELDS 100 TO 150 PIECES.

Chocolate-Coated Orange Peel

See photograph on page 71.

These are perfect as an accompaniment to a dessert, as a dessert on their own, or in place of or in addition to candied peels in other recipes.

> 2 large oranges
> 2 cups water
> 2¾ cups sugar
> 5 ounces semisweet chocolate, melted
> 4 tablespoons cocoa

With a sharp knife, peel the rind from the oranges, removing the color only with none of the white pith. If necessary, cut off the pith. Cut rind into 1-inch strips, and cut the strips into 1-inch squares. Blanch the orange squares in boiling water for 3 minutes; drain and repeat 2 more times. Drain. Place the 2 cups water and the sugar in a saucepan and bring to a boil. Simmer the peel in the syrup for 2 hours over very low heat. Separate the peels and drain on a rack for 3 hours. Dip each piece of orange in melted chocolate and return to the rack. Place the cocoa in a pie plate. When the chocolate starts to lose its gloss, toss the coated rind in the cocoa. Leave in the cocoa until cooled. Store in an airtight container. Keeps for at least 1 month. YIELDS 60 TO 100 PIECES.

Candied Orange Slices

This also works well with lemon slices.

> 4 oranges, thinly sliced
> 2 cups water
> 1½ cups sugar

Discard the ends of the oranges and any seeds. Place the water and sugar in a saucepan and bring to a boil. Add the orange slices and simmer very gently for 1½ hours. Cover the saucepan and macerate at room temperature for 24 hours, then store in a covered jar in the refrigerator. Keeps at least 2 weeks and as long as 6 weeks. When ready to use, drain on a wire rack. Use to garnish desserts.

Chocolate-Coated Fruits

See photograph on page 71.

> ½ pound semisweet chocolate, melted
> Fruits of choice (strawberries, apricots, blueberries, etc.)

Keep the chocolate over hot, but not boiling, water. Ideally, use strawberries with stems. Dip each strawberry halfway into the chocolate, lift and shake to remove excess chocolate, and place on a waxed paper–lined baking sheet. When they are all coated, refrigerate for about 5 minutes or just until the chocolate is set. Serve within a few hours. YIELDS ENOUGH FOR 1 QUART OF FRUIT.

Apricots: Use dried apricots. Dip halfway into the chocolate and let set on a sheet of waxed paper.

Blueberries: Obviously it is difficult, and messy, to dip individual blueberries. Use small paper candy cups, put 2 or 3 blueberries in each cup, and pour on about ½ teaspoon chocolate. Let set in the refrigerator. Serve within a few hours.

Caramel-Coated Fruits

2 cups sugar
½ cup water
Strawberries or other fruit

In a medium-sized heavy saucepan, combine the sugar and water, stirring gently until the mixture just comes to a boil. Boil without stirring until the caramel forms bubbles and starts to turn golden. Remove from the heat and set in a pan of hot water.

Using strawberries with stems, dip into the syrup to coat, remove, drain, and place on a buttered baking sheet. Let cool until set. Tangerine segments or small clusters of grapes can also be dipped in the caramel. It is most important that the fruit not be pierced; any openings out of which juices can flow will soften the caramel quickly. Caramel-dipped fruits must always be served within an hour or two of dipping.

YIELDS ENOUGH FOR 1 QUART OF FRUIT.

Note: Be extremely careful in dipping the fruits. If you get any of the caramel on you while dipping, it will stick to your skin and cause a severe burn. Immediately plunge the affected area under cold running water and keep it there. (See warning on caramel on page 41.)

❖❖❖

Meringue Mushrooms

See photograph on page 71.

1 recipe Pâte à Meringue (see page 281)
2 tablespoons cocoa
½ cup melted semisweet chocolate

Preheat oven to 225°F. Line a baking sheet with foil or parchment paper. Fill a

pastry bag, fitted with a no. 5 or no. 6 plain tip, with the meringue and pipe out round mounds of meringue for the caps. Then, holding the bag straight up, pipe up a column about 1 to 1½ inches high. Ideally, there should be an equal number of rounds and columns, or the "mushroom" caps and stems. Put the cocoa into a sieve and tap it lightly over the mounds and stems to give them a light dusting. Bake until the meringues are light and crisp, about 1 hour. To test if they are done, remove 1 piece and let it stand out of the oven for a minute or two. It should become dry and crisp.

When baked, remove from the oven and let cool. With the point of a small knife, cut a small hole in the bottom side of each mound. Spread the bottom with the chocolate and stick a stem through the chocolate into the hole. Let rest upside down until the chocolate has set. Store in an airtight container. Can be made up to 2 weeks before serving.

YIELDS 50 TO 75 MUSHROOMS,
DEPENDING ON THE SIZE.

Note: I prefer to have the mushrooms look as natural as possible. Consequently, I prepare the mushrooms in different sizes and let the stems list to one side as well as standing upright. Many bakers go to great effort to smooth off the caps and to make each one the same size. In addition, they bake the meringue without letting it color at all. Again, I prefer a light coloring to the meringue so that the confections look more like real mushrooms. Serve the mushrooms piled in baskets, or as part of a centerpiece placed on leaves directly on the table.

❖❖❖

SAUCES

FRUIT desserts often provide their own sauces, such as the juices from a macédoine, but others are complemented by the addition of a suitable sauce. In fact, a sauce can change the quality of a dessert almost *ad infinitum*. For example, a single fruit or a combination of fresh fruits can be served alone; sprinkled with sugar; mixed with liqueurs; sauced with whipped cream, sour cream, yogurt, raspberry, apricot, chocolate, strawberry, or other fruit sauces; coated with *crème à l'anglaise* (English custard) or sabayon sauce flavored with a number of different liqueurs; or accompanied with a pastry cream.

The sauce you choose to serve with a dessert will depend on your mood and what is available. Many of the desserts in this book call for specific sauces. Usually these are traditional to the dessert and are, or were when the dessert was created, considered to be the most complementary for the particular dessert. You may feel a preference for another flavor or texture, however, and you need not be bound by the recipes' suggestions. Feel free to play fast and loose, interchanging sauces to your liking. Some of these sauces are not that well known, but do not be put off because of a general lack of familiarity with the recipes or a dislike of certain flavors. For instance, *Sauce Riche* is flavored with sloe gin, a flavor I generally do not like; however, when used in this sauce it is no less than mouth-watering. On the other hand, I have known people whose thinking limits them to the same boring combinations. For many people, the fruit flavor to include with chocolate is orange. It *is* a very good combination, but not the only one.

Use sauces not only as a flavor complement to desserts, but also as garnishes. Use the sauce as a visual excitement. Change the look of a dessert by applying the sauce in different ways. Pour the sauce over the top to form a thin glaze of color, or if the dessert has been prepared in a fancy mold, pour the sauce so that it sets off the shape of the mold. Pour the sauce in a line across the dessert, or in a series of lines or crosshatchings. Place the sauce on the plate and add the dessert so that it floats like an island, or use two or three sauces in concentric circles or dividing the plate into halves or thirds.

For a fabulous flowerlike appearance, pour one sauce on the plate around the dessert. With another sauce of a contrasting color, pour a spiral around the dessert. Using the point of a knife, draw through the spiral into and away from the center to create a flower (see sketch on page 22). If you wish, draw the spiral on one side of the plate and drizzle a stem. Use the point of a knife to draw through the sauces to create a flower and draw points away from the stem to create leaflike effects.

Yogurt Dressing for Fruits

⅓ cup sugar
Grated peel of 1 orange
¾ cup yogurt
¼ cup vegetable oil
2 tablespoons raspberry vinegar
1 tablespoon orange juice
1 tablespoon Grand Marnier
1 tablespoon poppyseeds

In a bowl mix the sugar, orange peel, yogurt, oil, vinegar, orange juice, Grand Marnier, and poppyseeds together. Serve over cut-up fruits. Can be prepared the day before serving.   YIELDS 1½ CUPS.

Brown Sugar Rum Fruit Sauce

1 ½ cups sour cream
¼ cup firmly packed brown sugar
1 tablespoon light rum
1 tablespoon Irish whiskey or Scotch
¼ cup raisins

In a bowl, mix the sour cream, brown sugar, rum, and whiskey together. Fold in the raisins and chill, covered, for 2 hours. Serve with fresh fruit. Can be prepared the day before serving.

 YIELDS ABOUT 2 CUPS.

Caramel Sauce I

¼ cup water
½ cup sugar
1 ½ cups heavy cream, heated

In a heavy saucepan, cook the water and sugar over moderate heat until the sugar is dissolved. Raise the heat and cook until mixture is a deep golden brown. Remove from the heat and add the hot heavy cream, stirring constantly. Allow to cool. Use with fruits, cakes, or puddings. Can be prepared the day before and reheated if serving warm. YIELDS ABOUT 2 CUPS.

Caramel Sauce II

½ cup granulated sugar
½ cup firmly packed brown sugar
½ cup heavy cream
½ cup butter
¼ cup rum

In a double boiler over gently simmering water, cook the granulated sugar, brown sugar, and cream for 1 ½ hours, replenishing the water in the bottom of the double boiler as needed. Stir in the butter and cook 30 minutes longer. Remove from the heat and beat briskly. Stir in the rum.

Serve warm. Can be prepared ahead and reheated. YIELDS 1 ½ CUPS.

Dark Caramel Sauce

1 cup sugar
¾ cup cold water
¼ teaspoon cream of tartar

In a skillet, stir the sugar, ½ cup cold water, and cream of tartar over low heat until the sugar is dissolved. Raise the heat to moderate and boil the sauce, without stirring, until it is a dark caramel. Remove from the heat, stir in the remaining ¼ cup water, and let cool. Serve with cakes or puddings. YIELDS ABOUT 1 CUP.

Note: Be extremely careful not to let the caramel get too dark or it will taste burnt. Also be sure to remove it from the heat and let it stop cooking before adding the water. If the sauce should "seize," stir in another ¼ cup water and stir mixture over low heat until it dissolves and turns into a sauce.

Hot Fudge Sauce

½ cup cocoa
½ cup firmly packed light brown sugar
½ cup granulated sugar
1 cup light corn syrup
½ cup light cream
½ teaspoon salt
3 tablespoons butter
1 teaspoon vanilla
2 tablespoons rum

In a saucepan, simmer the cocoa, brown sugar, granulated sugar, corn syrup, cream, salt, and butter, stirring for 3 minutes. Remove from the heat and stir in the vanilla and rum. Serve warm. Can be prepared a week before serving and reheated. YIELDS ABOUT 2 ½ CUPS.

Creamed Fudge Sauce

1 cup sugar
¼ cup light corn syrup
⅓ cup cocoa
½ teaspoon salt
½ cup water
1 teaspoon vanilla
2 tablespoons butter
½ cup heavy cream, whipped

In a saucepan, simmer the sugar, corn syrup, cocoa, salt, and water until mixture reaches 228°F. on a candy thermometer. Stir in the vanilla and butter. Cool to room temperature. Fold in the whipped cream. Can be partially prepared a day or two ahead, but fold in the cream shortly before serving.   YIELDS 1½ CUPS.

Foamy Sauce

½ cup butter
1 cup confectioners' sugar
1 egg
1 teaspoon vanilla

In a double boiler, cream the butter and sugar until light and fluffy. Over hot but not boiling water, beat in the egg and vanilla and heat, beating until the sauce is foamy. Serve with puddings.
          YIELDS ABOUT 2 CUPS.

Hard Sauce

½ cup butter
1½ cups confectioners' sugar
2 tablespoons liqueur (see Note)

In a processor, cream the butter and sugar until light and fluffy. Beat in the liqueur of your choice. Can be kept refrigerated for a week or longer.
          YIELDS 1½ CUPS.

Note: The sauce can be flavored with cognac, rum, vanilla, or orange liqueur. Other liqueurs, such as kirsch or framboise, may also be used.

Sabayon Sauce (Zabaglione)

6 egg yolks
1 cup sugar
⅛ teaspoon vanilla
¼ cup Marsala, sherry, or other wine or liqueur
2 tablespoons cold water

In a heavy saucepan, beat the egg yolks with 2 tablespoons sugar and the vanilla until thick and light in color. Beat in the remaining sugar. Cook over low heat, beating constantly, while adding the wine or liqueur and the water, 1 tablespoon at a time. Continue beating until the mixture is the consistency of mayonnaise. Serve immediately over fruits or puddings. The sauce can be allowed to cool and served cold.
          YIELDS ABOUT 3 CUPS.

Note: The flavor can be varied to suit your specific taste. Use kirsch, Grand Marnier, sauterne, cognac, etc.

Sauce Mousseline

1 recipe Sabayon Sauce (see preceding recipe)
1 cup heavy cream, whipped

Let the Sabayon Sauce cool and fold in the whipped cream. Can be prepared the day before.   YIELDS ABOUT 3 CUPS.

Grand Marnier Sauce

5 egg yolks
½ cup sugar
4 tablespoons Grand Marnier
1 cup heavy cream

In a double boiler, beat the egg yolks, 2 tablespoons sugar, and 2 tablespoons Grand Marnier over hot, not boiling, water until very thick, about 20 minutes. Mixture will double in bulk. Chill. Beat the cream to the soft-peak stage, and sweeten with remaining 6 tablespoons sugar and the remaining 2 tablespoons Grand Marnier. Fold into the egg mixture and serve cold over fruit.

YIELDS ABOUT 3 CUPS.

Note: Because of the amount of beating, it is often easier to place a steel bowl over the pan of hot, not boiling, water and to use a very large wire whisk or a hand-held electric mixer. This is a slightly different version of the Sauce Mousseline.

Sauce Vanille or Crème à l'Anglaise

VANILLA CUSTARD SAUCE OR ENGLISH CUSTARD SAUCE

This can be made in a double boiler; be sure that the water is hot but never boils. It is important to strain the sauce immediately to stop the cooking. To prevent a skin from forming on the surface, stir often while it cools, cover tightly with plastic wrap, place waxed paper directly on the surface, or daub a stick of butter over the surface. If vanilla bean is not available, prepare the sauce without it, then strain it and add 1 teaspoon vanilla extract. If you are using the vanilla bean, rinse it off and let dry. It can be used twice.

1 cup milk
1 cup heavy cream
1 (3-inch) piece vanilla bean
5 egg yolks
½ cup sugar

In a heavy saucepan, scald the milk and cream with the vanilla bean. In a saucepan, beat the egg yolks and sugar until they are thick and light in color. Stir in the hot milk with a wire whisk. Cook over low heat, stirring constantly with a wire whisk, until the sauce is thick enough to coat the back of a spoon (180°F.). Strain through a fine sieve into a bowl and let cool. Can be prepared the day before using.

YIELDS ABOUT 2½ CUPS.

Note: Custard Sauce can be flavored however you desire. Add rum, cognac, or any other liqueur to taste.

Sauce à la Ritz

½ cup Custard Sauce (see preceding recipe)
¼ cup Grand Marnier
½ cup heavy cream, whipped
Few drops of food coloring (optional)

In a bowl, stir the Custard Sauce and Grand Marnier together. Fold in the whipped cream and the coloring if desired. Use over fruits and bombes.

YIELDS ABOUT 1¾ CUPS.

Sauce Parisienne

½ cup Custard Sauce (see this page)
½ cup puréed strawberries
¼ cup maraschino liqueur
¾ cup heavy cream, whipped

In a bowl, mix the Custard Sauce, strawberry purée, and liqueur together. Fold in the whipped cream. Use with fruits or bombes.

YIELDS 2 CUPS.

Sauce Riche

½ cup Custard Sauce (see page 273)
¼ cup prunelle or sloe gin
½ cup heavy cream, whipped

In a bowl, fold Custard Sauce, liqueur, and cream together. Serve with fruits or bombes.   YIELDS ABOUT 1¼ CUPS.

Note: Other liqueurs of choice can be substituted for the prunelle or sloe gin.
▀▄▀

Apricot Sauce I

2 cups apricot jam
2 tablespoons orange liqueur

Sieve the jam into a saucepan and add the liqueur. Simmer 3 minutes; let cool to room temperature. Can be prepared weeks before using and stored in the refrigerator. Use to glaze tarts and other pastries or as a sauce for fruits.
▀▄▀   YIELDS 2 CUPS.

Apricot Sauce II

1½ cups apricot jam
½ cup water
2 tablespoons sugar
2 tablespoons kirsch or cognac

In a saucepan, simmer the jam, water, and sugar for 4 minutes, stirring. Sieve mixture and stir in the liqueur. Serve warm or cold. Can be prepared several days before using.   YIELDS 2 CUPS.
▀▄▀

Apricot-Lemon Sauce

1 cup apricot preserves
2 tablespoons lemon juice
2 tablespoons confectioners' sugar
1 teaspoon grated lemon peel
⅓ cup apricot brandy

In a saucepan, melt the preserves with the lemon juice, sugar, and lemon peel. Simmer until the sugar is dissolved. Add the apricot brandy. Sieve and chill until ready to serve. Can be prepared a day or two before serving.   YIELDS 1½ CUPS.
▀▄▀

Orange-Apricot Sauce

¾ cup sieved apricot jam
1½ cups orange juice
3 tablespoons grated orange rind
3 tablespoons orange liqueur

In a medium-sized bowl, mix the jam, orange juice, orange rind, and liqueur together until smooth. Serve with ice cream, puffs, or puddings. Can be prepared up to 3 days before using.
▀▄▀   YIELDS ABOUT 2½ CUPS.

Apricot-Walnut Sauce

1½ cups apricot jam
½ cup water
1 tablespoon sugar
1 teaspoon grated orange rind
2 tablespoons rum
½ cup chopped walnuts

In a saucepan, simmer the apricot jam, water, sugar, and orange rind for 5 minutes, stirring constantly. Remove from the heat and stir in the rum. If desired, force through a sieve for a smoother sauce. Stir in the walnuts. Serve warm over ice cream, or cold with fruits or puddings.   YIELDS 2½ CUPS.
▀▄▀

Blueberry Sauce

1 pint blueberries
½ cup sugar
Grated rind of 1 lemon

In a saucepan, simmer the blueberries, sugar, and lemon rind for 5 minutes. Cool. Serve with lemon mousse, over cakes, or on ice cream. For a smoother sauce, force through a sieve. Can be prepared 2 or 3 days before using and stored in refrigerator. YIELDS ABOUT 2½ CUPS.
◼◽◼

Blueberry Cassis Sauce

1 tablespoon butter
1 tablespoon cornstarch
¼ cup crème de cassis
¾ cup dry white wine
1 tablespoon lemon juice
1½ cups blueberries

In a saucepan, melt the butter. In a small bowl, stir the cornstarch and cassis together and gradually stir into the butter. Add the wine and lemon juice and cook, stirring, until the mixture thickens. Stir in the berries and cook until they begin to burst. Cool. Serve with ice cream, puddings, or cakes. Can be prepared a day or two before using.
YIELDS ABOUT 2½ CUPS.

Note: Either fresh or frozen blueberries can be used.
◼◽◼

Cherry Sauce

1 pound tart cherries, pitted
2 to 3 tablespoons sugar
Pinch of cinnamon
½ cup plus 1 tablespoon cold water
Lemon juice to taste
2 teaspoons arrowroot

In a saucepan, simmer the cherries, sugar, and cinnamon, covered, over low heat until the juices run freely. Remove the cherries with a slotted spoon. Add ½ cup water to the juices and simmer 4 minutes. Correct the sweetness with more sugar or with lemon juice. In a small bowl, mix the arrowroot with remaining 1 tablespoon cold water. Stir into the hot cherry syrup and simmer until the liquid is the consistency of heavy cream. Return the cherries to the sauce. Cool. Can be prepared 2 to 3 days before using.
◼◽◼ YIELDS ABOUT 3 CUPS.

Lemon Sauce

½ cup sugar
1 tablespoon cornstarch
1 cup boiling water
2 tablespoons butter
1½ tablespoons lemon juice
½ teaspoon grated lemon rind

In a saucepan, mix the sugar and cornstarch together. With a wire whisk, beat in the boiling water, and cook until the sauce thickens and clears. Remove from the heat and whisk in the butter, lemon juice, and lemon rind. Serve warm. Can be reheated.   YIELDS ABOUT 1½ CUPS.
◼◽◼

Eunice's Walnut-Orange Sauce

3 oranges
¾ cup sugar
½ cup light corn syrup
1 tablespoon lemon juice
Pinch of salt
¼ cup chopped walnuts

Remove the orange-colored rind, leaving the pith on the orange, and cut the rind into fine julienne. Squeeze the oranges to make 1 cup juice. In a saucepan, simmer the juice and the julienned peel for 4 minutes. Stir in the sugar, corn syrup, lemon juice, and salt; cook, stirring, until the sugar is dissolved. Simmer until syrupy, about 20 minutes. Cool and stir in the nuts. Serve with ice cream, crêpes, or soufflés.　YIELDS 1½ CUPS.

Raspberry Sauce

20 ounces frozen raspberries, thawed
⅓ cup currant jelly

In a blender or processor, purée the berries with their juices. Strain through a fine sieve, discarding the seeds. In a small saucepan, melt the currant jelly over moderate heat and stir into the raspberry purée. Chill. Can be prepared 2 to 3 days before serving. YIELDS ABOUT 2½ CUPS.

Raspberry-Almond Sauce

10 ounces frozen raspberries, thawed
2 tablespoons almond liqueur

In a processor or blender, purée the raspberries with their juices and the almond liqueur. Strain, discarding the seeds. Serve cold over mousses, cakes, or ice cream. Can be prepared a day or two before serving.　YIELDS ABOUT 1 CUP.

Melba Sauce

1 cup puréed raspberries
¼ cup sugar

In a saucepan, simmer the raspberry purée and sugar for 3 minutes. Cool. Can be prepared several days before serving.
YIELDS 1 CUP.

Sauce Cardinale
RASPBERRY-STRAWBERRY SAUCE

1 cup mashed raspberries
1 cup mashed strawberries
1 cup sugar
1 teaspoon cornstarch

In a small saucepan, combine the raspberries, strawberries, sugar, and cornstarch. Bring to a boil, stirring, and cook until slightly thickened. Purée in a processor or blender, and strain through a fine sieve. Can be prepared 2 to 3 days before using.　YIELDS ABOUT 2½ CUPS.

Strawberry Sauce

1 pint strawberries, sliced
¼ cup sugar
2 to 3 tablespoons orange liqueur
or kirsch

In a bowl, mix the strawberries, sugar, and liqueur. Cover and let macerate at room temperature for 1 hour, stirring occasionally. Can be prepared up to 6 hours before serving. Use with cakes, mousses, or crêpes.　YIELDS ABOUT 2 CUPS.

Hot Strawberry Sauce

6 tablespoons butter
½ cup sugar
¼ cup kirsch or framboise
1 quart strawberries

In a skillet, melt butter. Stir in sugar, liqueur, and strawberries. Shake, over high heat, for 3 to 5 minutes. The object is to heat the strawberries but not to cook them. Serve with crêpes or over ice cream or cold fruits. Serve immediately.
YIELDS ABOUT 3 CUPS.

BASIC RECIPES

MANY of the desserts in this book call for a base recipe. Rather than repeat these recipes every time they are required, I have combined them in this chapter. You will find the recipes here for Meringue, Sponge Cake, Génoise, Vanilla-Poached Fruits, Pastry Cream, Praline Powder, etc.

None of the recipes is difficult, but as in all fine cooking, care and attention are required. There is a list of hints and suggestions following each basic recipe to help you produce superior results. Many of these can be prepared ahead by at least a day or two and in many cases up to months in advance. The busy cook may find it wise to have several of these preparations in the freezer or on the shelf ready to be transformed into an almost-instant dessert. I have indicated how to store them until you are ready to use them.

Note: Many of these recipes call for eggs — as do others in this book. The recipes were tested using large eggs. If you use medium, you may need to add an extra egg for every 5 large eggs. Extra-large eggs work in these recipes without any adjustment.

Biscuit de Savoie

SPONGE CAKE

This is a lovely light sponge with several flavor variations.

　6 eggs, separated
　Pinch of salt
　1 cup sugar
　1 tablespoon lemon juice
　1 teaspoon grated lemon rind
　1 teaspoon vanilla
　1 cup sifted flour

Butter the bottom(s), but not the sides, of one of the following mold alternatives. Dust with flour.

1 (9-inch) layer pan
3 (7-inch) layer pans
1 (11- by 16-inch) jellyroll pan
2 (10-inch) shallow layer pans
2 (3- by 9-inch) loaf pans

Preheat oven to 350°F. In a large bowl, beat the egg whites with the salt until frothy. Beat in the sugar, 1 tablespoon at a time, and continue beating until the egg whites are very stiff. In a bowl, stir the egg yolks with the lemon juice, lemon rind, and vanilla until just mixed. Fold one-fourth of the egg whites into the yolks. Add the remaining egg whites, sprinkle the flour gently on the top, and fold together using a large rubber spatula, your hand, or an electric mixer set on low speed. Fold until no traces of white show. Do not overmix. Pour into the prepared pan. Hit the pan sharply on a counter once to remove air pockets. Bake 20 to 40 minutes, depending on the pan size. To test for doneness, touch the cake with your finger. It should spring back, and the cake should have started to pull away from the sides of the pan. Cool in the pan and unmold.

Notes: The sugar beaten into the egg whites makes a very heavy mixture. Although it is possible to beat the eggs by hand in a copper bowl (a copper bowl helps the whites to mound higher and hold the mound longer), many people find the effort required is more than they can give. A large electric mixer will produce just as good a result much more comfortably.

It is often easier to put the egg yolks into the large egg white bowl. If you do this, push the egg whites to one side of the bowl and pour the egg yolk mixture onto the cleared side of the bowl.

To make folding the flour easier, sift it over the eggs in one or two additions.

Although the cakes should cool in the pan(s), there is no reason to turn them upside down.

FLAVOR VARIATIONS

Nutted Sponge Cake: Fold ½ cup finely grated toasted nuts in with the flour. Walnuts, almonds, and hazelnuts are customary.

Praline/Nougat Sponge Cake: Fold ⅔ cup Praline Powder (see page 284) in with the flour.

Chocolate Sponge Cake: Omit the lemon juice and lemon rind and substitute ½ cup dark unsweetened cocoa for ½ cup of the flour.

Génoise

Another classic cake — again, with flavor variations.

> **6 large eggs**
> **1 cup sugar**
> **1 cup sifted flour**
> **1 teaspoon vanilla**
> **½ cup Clarified Butter, melted (see page 286)**

Preheat oven to 350°F. Lightly butter and flour one of the following: 1 (8- or 9-inch) layer pan; 3 (7-inch) layer pans; 1 (11- by 16-inch) jellyroll pan; 2 (10-inch) shallow layer pans. In the large bowl of an electric mixer set over a saucepan of hot, not boiling, water, beat the eggs and sugar until they are combined. The water must not touch the bottom of the bowl. Heat over low heat until the eggs are warm to the touch, stirring often so that they do not cook. When the eggs are warm and look bright yellow, remove from heat and set on the electric mixer. Turn on the machine and beat at high speed until the eggs become light, fluffy, and almost tripled in bulk. They should look like softly whipped cream.

Sprinkle the flour, half a cup at a time, over the eggs and fold gently into the eggs with a large rubber spatula, your hand, or an electric mixer on slow speed. Gently fold in the vanilla and butter, folding up from the bottom to make sure they are incorporated. Do not overfold.

Pour into the prepared tin(s) and bake for 15 to 30 minutes or until the cakes pull away from the sides of the pans and are golden and springy when lightly touched. Remove from the oven, let cool 5 minutes, then run a knife around the edge and unmold onto wire racks to cool.

ALTERNATE METHOD OF PREPARING GÉNOISE

If you do not have an electric mixer, this is an easier way to make the génoise by hand. Separate the eggs and add the vanilla to the yolks. Beat the whites until they hold soft peaks. Beat in the sugar, 1 tablespoon at a time, until the whites are very stiff. Fold one-fourth of the whites into the yolks. Push the remaining whites to one side of the bowl and pour the yolk mixture into the empty space. Sprinkle the flour gently over the top and start to fold, adding the butter slowly until no traces of white show.

Note: The Clarified Butter should be the same temperature as the eggs after beating. If it is too hot, it will sink to the bottom of the bowl instead of folding in evenly. If it is too cold, it will clump.

FLAVOR VARIATIONS

Lemon or Orange Génoise: Add 1 tablespoon orange or lemon rind and 2 tablespoons of juice with the butter.

Nutted Génoise: Add ½ cup toasted nuts with the flour. Walnuts, almonds, hazelnuts, or pecans are customary.

Praline/Nougat Génoise: Fold ⅔ cup Praline Powder (see page 284) with the flour.

Chocolate Génoise: Substitute ½ cup cocoa for ½ cup flour.

⹁⹁⹁

Ladyfingers

Ladyfingers can be served as a cookie to accompany a dessert or used to make any one of the charlottes. Do not panic when it comes to turning the strips over onto the confectioners' sugar. Do it in one fluid movement. The ladyfingers will stick to the paper. If this really does frighten you, you can sift a thick layer of confectioners' sugar over the top of the ladyfingers and then bake them.

> 3 eggs, separated
> Pinch of salt
> 2 tablespoons granulated sugar
> 1 cup sifted confectioners' sugar, plus more as needed
> ¾ teaspoon vanilla
> ¾ cup sifted flour

Preheat oven to 350°F. Cut strips of parchment paper or aluminum foil about 2 inches wider than the length of the ladyfingers you plan to pipe.

Fit a large pastry bag with a no. 5 or no. 6 plain tip. In a bowl, beat the egg whites with the salt until soft peaks form. Beat, adding the granulated sugar, until the whites are stiff. In another bowl, beat the egg yolks and 1 cup confectioners' sugar with the vanilla until the eggs are thick and light in color. Fold in the egg whites and flour until all traces of white are gone.

Pipe the ladyfingers, each about 4 inches long, onto the strips of paper or foil. Space them at least 1 inch apart. On a sheet of waxed paper, sift a thick layer of confectioners' sugar as wide as the ladyfingers are long. Lift each strip of lady-fingers and turn it over onto the adjacent sugar. Let sit for 30 seconds, pick up strip, and place on the baking sheet. Bake for 12 to 15 minutes or until lightly browned. Let cool on the paper.

Run the strip along the edge of the baking sheet, paper side down, to remove the ladyfingers, or pick them off. Can be prepared months ahead and frozen.

YIELDS ABOUT 30 LADYFINGERS.

Note: Ladyfingers can be bought at supermarkets, but are usually soft and spongy. If you need to buy them, find a good bakery that has well-flavored crisp ladyfingers.

⹁⹁⹁

Pâte à Choux

CREAM PUFFS

> 1 cup water
> ½ teaspoon salt
> 1 teaspoon sugar
> ½ cup butter
> 1 cup flour
> 4 eggs

Preheat oven to 400°F. In a medium-sized saucepan, bring the water, salt, sugar, and butter to a full rolling boil. Dump in the flour all at once and beat it briskly over moderate heat until the ingredients are thoroughly combined. The mixture will form a ball around the sides and start to film the bottom of the pan. Remove from the heat and let cool for 2 to 3 minutes.

Put the dough into a processor, add all of the eggs, and process until smooth. Put the dough into a pastry bag with a plain tip and pipe out mounds, logs, spirals, etc. Or, make two 9-inch spiral cakes. If there is extra batter after you have made the shape required, pipe out small mounds to have on hand as cream puffs. Bake until puffed, golden brown, and dried. There should be no drops of moisture on the puffs. Let cool, then split and fill according to the recipe. Freezes very well.

YIELDS FROM 24 LARGE PUFFS
UP TO 100 SMALL PUFFS,
DEPENDING ON THE SIZE.

Notes: This is one of the simplest pastries to prepare, especially if you have a processor at hand. If you do not have a processor, beat the eggs, 1 at a time, into the slightly cooled mixture. Be sure each egg is fully incorporated before adding the next egg.

If you do not have a pastry bag, you can drop the mixture from a teaspoon to make cream puffs, or from the edge of a knife for éclairs. The pastry can also be spread about ½-inch thick into a circle or rectangle.

If the puffs are small, they are generally fully cooked when there is no moisture on the outside. However, with larger puffs and whole cakes, the inside often needs further baking. Slide the baking sheet to the edge of the oven and prick the sides of the pastry in several places to let the steam escape, and take one of the puffs out of the oven and let it sit for a minute or two. If it is not cooked, it will collapse. If it does stand, then split it open. The inside should be slightly moist-looking, but not uncooked.
▼.▼

Pâte à Meringue

4 egg whites
1 cup sugar
1 teaspoon vanilla

Preheat oven to 225°F. Butter and flour a baking sheet or line it with parchment paper. Let the egg whites come to room temperature. In a copper bowl, or the bowl of an electric mixer, beat the egg whites to the soft-peak stage. Beat in sugar, 1 tablespoon at a time, and continue beating until the whites stand in very

stiff peaks and are shiny and moist. Beat in the vanilla.

MERINGUE SHELLS

With a pastry bag fitted with a no. 6 plain tip or star tip, pipe out mounds or shell shapes. Sprinkle with granulated sugar. Bake for 30 minutes. They should feel crisp on the outside. If not, prop the oven door open about ¼ inch and bake another 30 minutes. While the shells are warm, place the rounded side of each down in the palm of your hand and press the underside to make a shell. Return to the oven, turn off, and leave until shells are dry.

MERINGUE NESTS

With a pastry bag fitted with a no. 4 or no. 5 plain or star tip, pipe out 2- to 3-inch circles, then pipe a rim 1 to 2 inches high around each base. Sprinkle with granulated sugar and bake for 40 minutes, then turn off the oven and leave until dry.

MERINGUE LAYERS

With a pastry bag fitted with a no. 5 or no. 6 plain tip, pipe out 9- or 10-inch circles. Bake for about 40 minutes, then turn off the oven and leave until dry.

Notes: Meringues are tricky. They are not really baked, but rather dried out in the oven. Be sure to beat the egg whites and sugar until they hold stiff unwavering peaks. If they are not stiff enough, the meringue will not dry out properly.

Humidity makes it difficult to prepare meringues. If it is humid, expect it to take longer for the meringues to dry. Gas ovens with pilot lights work very well. Electric ovens often seal too tightly and it is necessary to prop the oven door open slightly so that the moisture can escape. A potholder or the handle of a wooden spoon is enough.

Meringues should be used fairly quickly after preparing. If you must keep them, place them in an airtight container. If there is extra meringue, pipe out arabesques, S-curves, or curlicues to use as a garnish for gâteaux, or in place of cookies. They can, of course, be sandwiched with whipped cream or ice cream and served with one of the fruit sauces in the previous chapter.

Nutted Meringue Layers: Fold ¾ cup toasted ground almonds into the meringue mixture before piping. Walnuts or hazelnuts can be used in place of the almonds.

▀▀▀

Crème Pâtissière

PASTRY CREAM OR VANILLA PUDDING

> 2 cups milk
> 1 (1-inch) piece vanilla bean
> 5 egg yolks
> ¾ cup sugar
> ⅓ cup flour
> Pinch of salt

In a saucepan, scald the milk and vanilla bean; cover and let steep for 10 minutes. In another saucepan, beat the egg yolks and sugar until thick and light in color. Beat in the flour and salt until the mixture is smooth. Beat in the hot milk and vanilla bean mixture and cook over medium heat, stirring constantly, until the mixture comes to a boil and is thick and smooth. Simmer for 3 minutes, stirring constantly. Strain into a bowl and let cool, stirring occasionally. Press a sheet of waxed paper on the surface, cover tightly with plastic wrap, or daub the top of the cream with a stick of butter to prevent a skin from forming. Can be prepared 2 to 3 days before using.

YIELDS ABOUT 3½ CUPS.

Note: Pastry cream is the basis for many desserts. It can be eaten on its own as vanilla, chocolate, or other pudding. It is also used to fill tarts, cakes, or cream puffs. The cream is simple to prepare, but it must be stirred vigorously and constantly. Use a wire whisk and be sure to push it into the corners of the pan. Strain it after it is cooked to remove the vanilla bean, to stop the cooking, and to ensure that the sauce is smooth.

FLAVOR VARIATIONS

Crème au Chocolat (Chocolate Pastry Cream): Melt 2 ounces unsweetened chocolate with the milk. Increase the sugar to 1 cup.

Crème au Moka (Mocha Pastry Cream): Flavor 1 cup of Chocolate Pastry Cream with 1 tablespoon boiling water mixed with 1 teaspoon instant coffee.

Crème au Café (Coffee Pastry Cream): Flavor 1 cup of Vanilla Pastry Cream with 1 tablespoon boiling water mixed with 1 teaspoon instant coffee.

Rum or Other Liqueur-Flavored Pastry Cream: Add rum or other liqueur to taste.

▀▀▀

Butter Cream Frosting

> ⅔ cup sugar
> Pinch of cream of tartar
> ⅓ cup water
> 5 egg yolks
> 1 cup butter, softened

In a heavy saucepan, boil the sugar, cream of tartar, and water until mixture reaches 238°F. on a candy thermometer. In an electric mixer, beat the egg yolks until fluffy. With the machine running, beat the syrup into the egg yolks in a thin, steady stream, beating constantly. As the mixture cools, it will become thick and light. If it has not cooled during the beating process, set aside until cooled to room temperature. Beat in the softened butter and flavor as desired (see Note below). Can be prepared several days ahead. Can be frozen. YIELDS ABOUT 2 CUPS.

Note: To flavor the Butter Cream, add one of the following: 1 ounce melted unsweetened chocolate, cooled; 1 tablespoon extra-strong coffee; 1 tablespoon liqueur such as Grand Marnier, kirsch, or framboise; 2 tablespoons Praline Powder (see page 284); 2 tablespoons grated lemon rind and 1 teaspoon lemon juice; 1 tablespoon grated orange rind and 1 tablespoon orange juice; or 1 tablespoon vanilla extract.

Quick Butter Cream

3 egg yolks
3 tablespoons sugar
1 teaspoon vanilla
1 cup butter

In a processor, beat the egg yolks, sugar, and vanilla for about 2 minutes. Add the butter, bit by bit, until fully incorporated. Flavor as indicated for Butter Cream Frosting (preceding recipe).
YIELDS APPROXIMATELY 1½ CUPS.

Royal Icing

3 egg whites
½ teaspoon cream of tartar
1 pound sifted confectioners' sugar

Beat the egg whites until foamy and beat in the cream of tartar. Beat in the sugar, ½ cup at a time, until smooth. Beat continually until soft peaks form. Store at room temperature in an airtight container. Can be prepared several weeks before using if securely sealed. YIELDS 3½ CUPS.

Apricot or Currant Glaze

1 cup apricot preserves or currant jam, sieved
4 tablespoons water or liqueur

In a small saucepan, boil the preserves or jam and water or liqueur for 1 minute. Let cool. Use to glaze fruits or tarts and cakes. Can be prepared weeks ahead of time. YIELDS ABOUT 1 CUP.

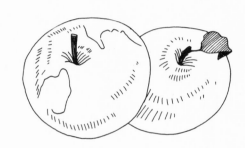

Apple Purée

This might be more familiar if we called it applesauce. The preparation is the same.

Peel, core, and slice or chop the apples. Put into a saucepan, cover, and simmer for 15 minutes. Stir well and add sugar to taste if desired. If the apples are very watery, cook over medium-high heat, stirring often, until reduced to the desired thickness.

Note: Use the same technique to create purées of other fruits.

Raspberry Purée

Purée raspberries in a processor, then strain through a fine sieve to remove the seeds. Or, force fruit pulp through a fine sieve.

Dessert Syrup

⅔ cup water
½ cup sugar
3 tablespoons liqueur, vanilla, or
    coffee

In a saucepan, heat the water and sugar, stirring, until the sugar is dissolved. Remove from the heat and add the flavoring. Can be prepared weeks ahead.

YIELDS ABOUT 1¼ CUPS.

Note: This syrup is used to moisten cake layers and to give them flavor. Use the liqueur of your choice. It should complement the cake, such as kirsch for Black Forest Cherry Cake.

Praline/Nougat Powder

1 cup sugar
1 cup blanched almonds or other nuts
    (see Note)
¼ cup water
½ teaspoon vanilla

Butter a baking sheet. In a heavy skillet, cook the sugar, almonds, water, and vanilla over moderate heat, stirring until the mixture comes to a boil. When it reaches the boil, cook without stirring until the syrup turns a deep golden brown. Turn onto the baking sheet and let flow into a large blob. Cool.

When it is completely cooled, break it into chunks and pulverize in a processor or blender in batches. Sift each batch and reprocess the larger pieces. Can be prepared months ahead and kept in a tightly covered container.

YIELDS ABOUT 1 CUP.

Notes: Although almonds are traditional, hazelnuts and walnuts are also used. Hazelnuts and almonds are often used together.

Take care when pouring the praline syrup onto the baking sheet. It is ex-tremely hot and sticky. If any of it should get on you, immediately plunge that portion of you under cold running water and keep it there for at least 5 minutes. Do not try to peel off the caramel; let the water rinse it away.

When breaking the praline to put into the processor or blender, use caution. The caramel breaks into shards that are literally as sharp as glass.

If the nuts are fresh, the praline keeps for months on the pantry shelf. However, it can go rancid. If you are concerned, keep it in the freezer or refrigerator. If the powder should stick together, it can be reprocessed into a powder.

Candied Orange Peel I

2 oranges
1 cup water
½ cup sugar

With a zester, remove tiny strips of peel from the oranges, or, using a vegetable peeler, remove the colored rind only. Cut the rind into the thinnest possible strips. Blanch the strips in boiling water for 5 minutes, drain, refresh under cold water, and drain again. In a saucepan, combine the cup of water and the sugar, and simmer 5 minutes. Add the orange peel and cook, turning often, for about 10 minutes or until peel is translucent. When done, the orange peel can be stored in a covered container on a pantry shelf for months. To use, drain the peel and sprinkle on desserts, or in some cases use both the peel and orange syrup.

YIELDS ABOUT ½ CUP OF CANDIED PEEL.

Candied Orange Peel II

4 thick-skinned oranges
2 cups water
1½ cups sugar

Cut off the ends of the oranges and cut oranges into quarters. With a spoon or your fingers, pry the skin away from the flesh. Save the flesh for another use. Cut the peel into ½-inch-wide strips. Place in a saucepan with cold water and boil for 10 minutes. Drain.

In a saucepan, bring the 2 cups water and sugar to a boil, stirring until the sugar is melted. As soon as the syrup boils, add the orange peels; lower the heat and simmer, uncovered, for 2 hours. Cover the pot and let stand at room temperature for 12 hours. Store the peels in their syrup in a jar in the refrigerator. Drain before using. They will keep at least a month. To use, drain and perhaps roll in sugar as a confection, or add to drinks such as an old-fashioned, or chop to use in various desserts. YIELDS ABOUT 75 STRIPS.

Note: Although this can be used in recipes that call for candied peel, you can also buy candied peel in many markets to save yourself the work.

Candied Orange, Lemon, and Lime Rinds in Syrup

3 oranges
3 lemons
2 limes
5 cups sugar
3½ cups water
1 teaspoon cream of tartar

Cut the rinds from the fruits and slice into the thinnest possible julienne strips. The fruit can be cut up and used in the fruit bowl itself. In a saucepan, combine the sugar, water, and cream of tartar. Heat over low heat until the sugar has dissolved. Add the fruit rinds and simmer until they are translucent, about 1 hour. Cool and store in a screw-top jar in the cupboard, *not in the refrigerator.* The syrup will keep for months on the shelf and

can be used to garnish any combination of fresh fruits. The rinds can be used to garnish other desserts.

YIELDS ABOUT 1 CUP RINDS
AND 4 CUPS SYRUP.

Spun Sugar

4 cups sugar
2 cups water
Pinch of cream of tartar
1 teaspoon white corn syrup
Food coloring (optional)

In a heavy saucepan, heat the sugar and water to the soft-crack stage, 270°F. Add the cream of tartar and corn syrup and heat to the hard-crack stage, 310°F. Remove from the heat and set the pan in cold water to stop the cooking. Add food coloring if desired. Then place it in a pan of warm water.

Oil several rolling pins, broom handles, wooden spoons, and so on. Arrange on the edge of a counter so that they overhang. Line the floor with newspapers. Dip a fork into the hot syrup and whisk it back and forth over the rods vigorously, forming thin threads. When you have collected a cluster of threads, gather them together and wrap gently around the dessert. Must be prepared and served immediately. YIELDS ENOUGH TO COVER A LARGE DESSERT.

Note: This is one of the most impractical recipes in this book. If you choose to prepare the spun sugar, realize that it has to be done within an hour or so of serving. Humidity will cause the sugar to wilt and literally dissolve. I recommend that you plan this when you are having guests for dessert and coffee. Have everything ready, and just before the guests arrive, go into the kitchen and spin the sugar. Remember, if it doesn't work, no one will be the wiser.

Clarified Butter

In a heavy saucepan, melt 1 pound of butter over low heat until it just reaches a boil. Let stand off the heat for 5 minutes. With a spoon, carefully skim the froth from the top of the butter. Then carefully pour the yellow oil through several thicknesses of cheesecloth wrung out in cold water, leaving the sediment in the bottom of the pan. Keeps refrigerated for up to 6 months. YIELDS ABOUT 1¾ CUPS.

Note: It is easiest to prepare this in large quantities. Making a few tablespoons is time-consuming and awkward. Once prepared the butter can be left at room temperature if all of the milk solids have been removed.

Crème Fraîche

  1 cup heavy cream
  1 tablespoon buttermilk

In a saucepan, warm the cream to 90°F. Remove from the heat and whisk in the buttermilk. Let stand for up to 24 hours or until the cream has thickened to the consistency of sour cream. After thickening, can be refrigerated up to 3 weeks. YIELDS 1 CUP.

Note: The cream can be made several weeks in advance. In fact, it is a way of preserving cream. The cream should be made from pasteurized heavy or extra-heavy cream. Ultra-pasteurized cream is not suitable. Ultra-pasteurized cream is also unsuitable for whipping, since the process often creates problems.

Vanilla-Poached Fruits

  6 pears, peaches, apples, etc.
  1 cup sugar
  Pinch of salt
  2 teaspoons lemon juice
  1 cup water
  1 (2-inch) piece vanilla bean, split

Peel the fruit and core as directed in the recipe. In a saucepan, simmer the sugar, salt, lemon juice, water, and vanilla for 3 minutes. Add the fruits and simmer gently until tender, turning often. Cool the fruit in the syrup. Can be done at least 1 day before serving. YIELDS 6 SERVINGS.

Notes: This syrup can be doubled or tripled according to needs. With this quantity, it will be necessary to poach pears, apples, or peaches in batches. Poach half the fruits, remove with a slotted spoon, poach the remaining half, and then let all of them cool in the syrup.

Pears have a tendency to darken on the inside if prepared more than a day in advance. Unfortunately, you cannot see this condition until you cut into the pears. Therefore, it is best to poach the pears no more than 1 day before serving. To prevent the pears from darkening, place in the syrup and cover with a piece of cheesecloth to keep the tops moist.

Wine-Poached Fruits: To poach fruits in wine, substitute red wine for the water in the recipe and add a stick of cinnamon if desired.

INDEX

Abricots au Cognac, 30
Abricots Fines Bouches, 30
Abricots Hélène, 30
Almond(s)
  cookies, 261, 262
  cream, 238
  gâteaux, torten, and fancy cakes,
    241, 250, 266
  génoise, 279
  meringue, 282
  pudding, 177
  sauce, 276
  simple desserts, 27, 53
  sponge cake, 279
  tarts and pies, 216, 225, 228
Almond-Baked Pears, 54
Almond, and Berry Torte, Pine Nut,
  241
Almond Cake, 266
Almond Cookies, Barcelona, 262
Almond-Filled Pears with Raspberry
  Sauce, 53
Almond Macaroons, 261
Almond-Orange Pudding, 177
Almond Pear Pie, 228
Almond Sauce, Raspberry-, 276
Ananas Brûlés, 58
Ananas Frais Crème Chantilly, 84
Ananas et Fraises Créoles, 85
Ananas Georgette, 114
Ananas Glacé à la Bourbonnaise,
  156
Ananas à l'Orange, 58
Ananas au Rhum, 58
Ananas Romanoff, 57
Ananas Surprise, 85
Angel Cream, 90
Angela Pia, 90
Anisette-Flavored Soufflé, 205
Antonin Carême's Apple Soufflé,
  206
Apple(s)
  charlottes, 129
  cider, with pears, 46
  compotes, 83, 86
  crêpes, 191–92
  dessert omelets, 186
  flambé, 83
  gâteaux, torten, and fancy cakes,
    242–43
  mélange, 85
  mousses, 133–35
  preparation of, 12

puddings, 165–67, 179, 180
purée, 283
sauce
  with lemon and orange, 24
  in Veiled Country Lass III, 168
simple desserts, 24–29
snow, 90
soufflés, 206
tarts and pies, 217–19
whip, 91
with Zabaglione, 74
Apple Cake with Caramel Sauce,
  Hot, 242
Apple Cake, French, 242
Apple Cake from Lyon, 243
Apple Cake, Normandy, 192
Apple Caramel Custard, Rice and,
  179
Apple Charlotte, 129
Apple Charlotte Comtoise, 129
Apple Compote, Pear and, 83
Apple Compote, Prune and, 86
Apple Crêpes Brittany, 192
Apple Crêpes with Ginger, 191
Apple Crisp, 28
Apple Halves with Almond
  Topping, French Baked, 27
Apple Hedgehog, 28
Apple Layer Pudding, 165
Apple Loaf, Grated, 167
Apple Mousse, 133
Apple Mousse with Bénédictine, 135
Apple Mousse Brittany-Style, 134
Apple Mousse with Calvados, 134
Apple Omelet, Normandy, 186
Apple, Pineapple, and Papaya
  Mélange, 85
Apple, Prune, and Armagnac Tart,
  217
Apple Pudding I, II, 166
Apple Pudding, Spiced, 167
Apple Purée, 283
Apple Rice Pudding, Meringue-
  Topped, 180
Apple Slices, Caramelized, 25
Apple Snow, 90
Apple Soufflé, Antonin Carême's,
  206
Apple Tart I, II, 217, 218
Apple Tart, Caramelized, 218
Apple Torte, 242
Apple Whip, 91

Apples Baked in White Wine, 26
Apples Bourgeois I, II, 29
Apples, Brandied, 26
Apples, Cantonese Baked, 28
Apples, Cold Baked, 25
Apples, Flat Open Omelet with, 186
Apples, Gingered, 24
Apples, Minted Baked 26
Apples and Pears Flambé, 83
Apples or Pears in Phyllo Dough,
  219
Apples and Praline-Flavored Cream,
  24
Apples with Red Wine, Baked, 27
Apples, Scrambled Baked, 25
Applesauce with Lemon and
  Orange, 24
Apricot(s)
  chantilly, 82
  charlotte, 120
  compote, 80
  cream, 91
  croquettes, 200
  glaze, 283
  omelet, 186
  pancakes, 193
  preparation of, 13
  sauces, 274
  simple desserts, 30
  soufflé, 206
  tarts and pies, 219–20
Apricot Chantilly, Orange-, 82
Apricot Charlotte, 120
Apricot Compote, 80
Apricot or Currant Glaze, 283
Apricot Cream, 91
Apricot and Kümmel Omelet, 186
Apricot-Lemon Sauce, 274
Apricot Marzipan Tart, 220
Apricot Pancakes, 193
Apricot Rice Croquettes, 200
Apricot Sauce I, II, 274
Apricot Sauce, Orange-, 274
Apricot Soufflé, 206
Apricot Sour Cream Meringue Pie,
  219
Apricot-Walnut Sauce, 274
Apricots, Bananas and, 31
Apricots with Cognac, 30
Apricots Helen, 30
Apricots with Kirsch Butter Sauce,
  30
Arance Caramellate, 41

Armagnac Tart, Apple, Prune, and, 217
Avocado(s)
    dessert, 30
    preparation of, 13
Avocado Chartreuse Dessert, 30

Baby's Dream Bombe, 157
Baked Alaska, 187
Baked Apples, Cold, 26
Baked Apples with Red Wine, 27
Baked Oranges with Sabayon Sauce, 42
Baked Papayas, 43
Baked Pears, 54
Baked Pears with Brandy, 55
Baked Pears with Maple Nut Sauce, 56
Baked Pears Savoyard, 56
Baked Pineapple, 59
Baked Quince, 60
Banana(s)
    bombe, 149
    in caramel syrup, 80
    charlotte, 130
    crêpes, 194
    custard, 108
    fried, 200
    mousses, 135–36
    omelet, 188
    preparation of, 13
    pudding, 168
    shortcake, 243
    simple desserts, 31–34
    whip, 92
Banana Boats, 31
Banana Charlotte, 130
Banana Crêpes and Rum Sauce, 194
Banana Mousse I, II, 135, 136
Banana Pudding, 168
Banana Shortcake, 243
Banana Whip with Orange Sabayon Sauce, 92
Bananas with Apricots, 31
Bananas a Brasiliera, 33
Bananas Brazilian-Style I, II, 33
Bananas in Caramel Cream, 32
Bananas with Coconut and Cardamom, 34
Bananas Foster, 32
Bananas and Grapes in Caramel Syrup, 80
Bananas, Kirsch-Flamed, 32
Bananas Maltese-Style, 33
Bananas, Meringue-Topped, 31
Bananas, Orange-Glazed, 34
Bananas and Rum, Fried, 200
Bananas, Sautéed, 32
Bananes aux Abricots, 31
Bananes Caribe, 33
Bananes Flambées, 32
Bananes Maltaise, 33
Bananes Meringuées, 31
Bananes au Rhum, 33
Bananes Sautées, 32
Barcelona Almond Cookies, 262
Barquette(s), preparation of, 214

Barquettes de Bananes, 31
Barquettes aux Fraises, 234
Bavarian(s), preparation of, 111
Bavarian Cream with Kirsch and Strawberries, 116
Bavarois à l'Ananas, 113
Bavarois de Cassis, 112
Bavarois aux Fraises, 116
Bavarois au Kirsch et Fraises, 116
Bavarois à l'Orange, 113
Bavarois Praliné, 114
Bavarois Rubané aux Framboises, 115
Beignets d'Ananas, 201
Beignets de Fruits, 200
Beignets de Potiron, 201
Beignets de Pruneaux à la Provençale, 201
Bénédictine, Apple Mousse with, 135
Biscuit de Savoie, 278
Black Currant Bavarian Cream, 112
Black Forest Cherry Cake, 246
Blackberry(ies)
    Bavarian cream, 112
    preparation of, 13
    pudding, 164
    torte, 241
Blackberry Bavarian Cream, 112
Blueberry(ies)
    bombe, 149
    charlotte, 121
    fool, 92
    gâteaux, torten, and fancy cakes, 244–45
    mélange, 82
    minted, 82
    mousse, 141
    preparation of, 13
    puddings, 169–70
    sauces, 275
    simple desserts, 34, 61
    tarts and pies, 220
Blueberries, Chocolate Cake with, 244
Blueberries, Minted Cantaloupe and, 82
Blueberry Bombe, Lemon-, 149
Blueberry Buttermilk Pudding, 169
Blueberry Cassis Pie, 220
Blueberry Cassis Sauce, 275
Blueberry Charlotte, Lemon-, 121
Blueberry Cloud Pie, 220
Blueberry Compote, Gingered, 34
Blueberry Conde, 169
Blueberry Crumble, 34
Blueberry Fool, 92
Blueberry Grunt, 244
Blueberry Mélange, Melon, Orange, and, 82
Blueberry Mousse, Peach and, 141
Blueberry Pound Cake, 244
Blueberry Pudding, 170
Blueberry Pudding Cups, Cold, 170
Blueberry Sauce, 275
Blueberry Streusel Küchen, 245
Bombe Alhambra, 160

Bombe Edna May, 150
Bombe Esperanza, 148
Bombe Eunice, 153
Bombe Germaine, 150
Bombe Grimaldi, 152
Bombe Lilian, 148
Bombe Mascotte, 155
Bombe Mayerling, 156
Bombe aux Myrtilles, 149
Bombe Palm Springs, 151
Bombe de Rêve de Bébé, 157
Bombe Teixeira, 160
Bondepige med Slør I–III, 167–68
Bourbon, in crème brûlée, 105
Braised Pears Bresse-Style, 83
Brandied Apples, 26
Brandied Date Pie, 222
Brandy. See also Cognac
    in date pie, 222
    in omelet, 188
    with pears, 55
Bread Crumb Coating, 199
Bread pudding, 164, 173
Broiled Fruit with Pastry Cream Brûlé, 79
Broiled Fruits with Sabayon Sauce, 79
Broiled Pineapple, 58
Brouillade aux Pommes, 25
Brown Sugar Rum Fruit Sauce, 271
Butter, Clarified, 286
Butter Cream Frosting, 282
Butter Cream, Quick, 283
Buttered Oranges, 42

Cactus pear(s), preparation of, 13
Calvados
    in crêpes, 192
    in mousse, 134
Candied Fruit Charlotte, 120
Candied Grapefruit Rind, 266
Candied Orange, Lemon, and Lime Rinds, 285
Candied Orange Peel I, II, 284
Candied Orange Slices, 267
Cantaloupe and Blueberries, Minted, 82. See also Melon(s)
Cantonese Baked Apples, 28
Carambola, preparation of, 13
Caramel
    coating
        fruits, 41, 268
        molds, 101
    sauces, 173, 271
    in simple desserts, 32, 41
Caramel-Coated Fruits, 268
Caramel Nut Sauce, 173
Caramel Sauce, Dark, 271
Caramel Sauce I, II, 271
Caramelized Apple Slices, 25
Caramelized Apple Tart, 218
Cardamom-Flavored Pears, 55
Carquinyolis, 262
Cats' Tongues, 264
Cerises au Cognac, 35
Cerises des Gourmets, 150
Cerises Montmorency, 35

Cerises Pompadour, 149
Champagne, Mango Slices with, 39
Charlotte aux Abricots, 120
Charlotte à la Chambourienne, 122
Charlotte Comtoise, 129
Charlotte aux Fraises, 127
Charlotte à l'Indienne, 130
Charlotte Makrauer, 128
Charlotte Malakoff aux Fraises, 126
Charlotte Malakoff aux Framboises,
    124
Charlotte Nesselrode, 120
Charlotte aux Poires, 130
Charlotte aux Poires avec Coulis de
    Framboise, 122
Charlotte aux Pommes, 129
Charlotte de Potiron, 123
Charlotte Russe, 124
Charlotte with Tangerines, 128
Chartreuse, in simple desserts, 30,
    38
Cheesecake(s)
    ginger, 246
    strawberry, 258
Cherry(ies)
    frozen desserts, 149–50
    gâteaux, torten, and fancy cakes,
        245–46
    preparation of, 13
    puddings, 170–71
    sauce, 275
    simple desserts, 35–36
    spiced, 80
    tarts and pies, 221
Cherries in Brandy, 35
Cherries in Cream, 36
Cherries Jubilee, 36
Cherries Laurette, 150
Cherries with Liqueurs, 35
Cherries Los Angeles, 149
Cherries Monte Carlo, 149
Cherries with Orange, Macaroons,
    and Cream, 35
Cherries with Pineapple, Spiced, 80
Cherry Bombe with Raspberry
    Sauce, 150
Cherry Cake, 245
Cherry Cake, Black Forest, 246
Cherry and Chestnut Bombe, 150
Cherry and Chestnut Sundae, 150
Cherry Compote, 35
Cherry and Pineapple Sundaes, 150
Cherry Pudding, 171
Cherry Pudding I, II, French,
    170–71
Cherry Sauce, 275
Cherry Tart, 221
Cherry Tart, French, 221
Chestnut(s)
    bombe, 150
    compote, 82
    coupe, 148
    crêpes, 193
    fool, 92
    with pears, 50
    preparation of, 13
    sundae, 150

Chestnut Bombe, Cherry and, 150
Chestnut Crêpe Torte, 193
Chestnut Fool, 92
Chestnut and Orange Compote, 82
Chestnut Sundae, Cherry and, 150
Chilled Glazed Pears, 47
Chinese Date Rolls, 199
Chippolata, 127
Chistera aux Fruits, 86
Chocolate. See also Fudge
    bombe, 149
    coating, 267
    gâteaux, torten, and fancy cakes,
        244, 253
    génoise, 280
    macaroons, 261
    pastry cream, 282
    sauce, 56
    shaved, 108
    simple desserts, 38, 56
    soufflé, 206
    sponge cake, 279
    wedges, 142
Chocolate Cake with Blueberries,
    244
Chocolate Cake, Pear and, 253
Chocolate Caraque, 108
Chocolate-Coated Fruits, 267
Chocolate-Coated Orange Peel, 267
Chocolate Fruit Bombe, Rum and,
    149
Chocolate Génoise, 280
Chocolate Macaroons, 261
Chocolate Pastry Cream, 282
Chocolate Soufflé, 206
Chocolate soufflé shell, 133
Chocolate Sponge Cake, 279
Chocolate Wedges, 142
Chopped Fruit Omelet Soufflé, 187
Christmas Pudding, 176
Citronfromage, 138
Clafouti aux Cerises, 171
Clarified Butter, 286
Coconut(s)
    with bananas, 34
    blancmange, 178
    preparation of, 13
Coconut Blancmange with Prune
    Sauce, 178
Coconut and Cardamom, Bananas
    with, 34
Coeur à la Crème, 89
Coffee Ice Cream with Pineapple,
    157
Coffee Ice Cream, Raspberry Sauce,
    and Strawberries, 160
Coffee Pastry Cream, 282
Coffee Soufflé, 205
Cognac
    in bombe, 151
    in simple desserts, 26, 30, 35, 39,
        40
Cointreau
    in Fujiyama I, 153
    in Michelangelo's Pumpkin, 239
    in mousse, 140
    with pears, 45

in soufflé, 196
Cold Baked Apples, 26
Cold Blueberry Pudding Cups, 170
Cold Lemon Soufflé, 138
Cold Lime Soufflé I, II, 139
Cold Rum Soufflé, 142
Compote de Pruneaux et Pommes,
    86
Cookies, cakes, and confections,
    preparation of, 260
Coppa Primavera, 107
Coppette alle Nocciole, 137
Cottage Pudding with Lemon Sauce,
    248
Country Cheese with Berries, 61
Coupe Clo-Clo, 148
Coupe Germaine, 150
Coupe Jamaïque, 157
Coupe Nectarine Sultane, 152
Coupe à l'Orange au Chocolat, 153
Coupe St. André, 148
Cranberry Cassis Mousse, Frozen,
    151
Cream(s)
    draining of, 88
    preparation of, 88
Cream Heart, 89
Cream Puffs, 280
Creamed Fudge Sauce, 272
Crème aux Abricots, 91
Crème à l'Anglaise
    preparation of, 110
    recipe for, 273
Crème Brûlée, 104
Crème Brûlée au Potiron et
    Bourbon, 105
Crème de cacao, with figs, 37
Crème au Café, 282
Crème de cassis
    in mousse, 151
    in pie, 220
    in sauce, 275
Crème au Chocolat, 282
Crème Fraîche, 286
Crème Génoise, 177
Crème Josephine Baker, 108
Crème Louisa, 88
Crème Margot, 115
Crème au Moka, 282
Crème Pâtissière, 282
Crème aux Pêches, 94
Crème Renversée au Citron, 102
Crème Renversée au Riz et aux
    Pommes, 179
Crème à la Vanille Caramelisée, 102
Cremets d'Angers, 90
Creole Pudding, 182
Crêpe(s)
    batter, 190
    cooking, 190
    pan, seasoning, 190
Crêpes Filled with Cointreau-
    Flavored Soufflé, 196
Crêpes Fines Sucrées, 191
Crêpes Gil Blas, 195
Crêpes aux Gingembre, 194
Crêpes with Ginger, 194

Crêpes aux Mandarines, 195
Crêpes with Pears I, II, 195, 196
Crêpes aux Poires I, II, 195, 196
Crêpes Soufflé au Cointreau, 196
Crêpes Suzette, 196
Crêpes with Tangerine, 195
Crispy Almond Cookies, 261
Croustade de Pommes ou Poires, 219
Croûtes aux Prunes, 60
Curaçao, with figs, 37
Currant(s)
    Bavarian cream, 112
    glaze, 283
    mousses, 141
Currant Glaze, Apricot or, 283
Currant Mousses, Pear and, 141
Custard(s)
    cooking on stove, 100
    testing, 100
    water baths for, 100
Custard sauce, preparation of, 110
Custard with Strawberries, 107

Dark Caramel Sauce, 271
Dark Fruitcake, 238
Date(s)
    bombe, 151
    cake, 246
    preparation of, 14
    puddings, 171–72
    rolls, 199
    tarts and pies, 221–22
    in whipped cream, 81
Date and Honey Tartlets, 221
Date Nut Cake, 246
Date Pie, Brandied, 222
Date Pudding, 172
Date Pudding with Nut Topping, 171
Date Rolls, Chinese, 199
Dates, and Walnuts in Sherried Whipped Cream, Figs, 81
Deep-Dish Peach Pie with Almonds, 225
Dessert Souffléed Omelet, 187
Dessert Syrup, 284
Diplomate aux Bananes, 168
Douillons à la Paysanne, 227

English Coating, 199
English custard, preparation of, 110
English Custard Sauce, 273
Eunice's Walnut-Orange Sauce, 275

Fichi alla Cioccolata, 38
Fichi alla Gritti, 36
Fig(s)
    mousse, 136
    preparation of, 14
    puddings, 172
    simple desserts, 36–38
    soufflé, 206
    in whipped cream, 81
Fig Compote with Rice, 172
Fig Mousse, Fresh, 136

Fig Pudding, Steamed, 172
Fig Soufflé, 206
Figs with Chartreuse-Flavored Cheese, Poached, 38
Figs with Chocolate, 38
Figs in Crème de Cacao, 37
Figs in Curaçao, 37
Figs, Dates, and Walnuts in Sherried Whipped Cream, 81
Figs, Gingered, 38
Figs alla Gritti Palace, 36
Figs with Port and Honey Sabayon Sauce, 37
Figs with Raspberry Cream, 36
Figs with Thyme, 37
Figues au Thym, 37
Flaky Pastry, 214
Flaky Pastry, Processor Method, 215
Flan de Naranja, 103
Flan de Potiron, 104
Flat Open Omelet with Apples, 186
Flaugnarde, 178
Flower technique, for presenting sauces, 22
Foamy Sauce, 272
Fool(s), preparation of, 88
Fragole al Aceto, 63
Fragole al Limone, 61
Fraises à la Cardinale, 62
Fraises Cordon Bleu I, II, 62
Fraises Eugénie, 97
Fraises de Jeanne Granier, 159
Fraises à la Nino, 86
Fraises au Rhum, 62
Fransk Äppelkaka, 27
French Apple Cake, 242
French Baked Apple Halves with Almond Topping, 27
French Cherry Pudding I, II, 170, 171
French Cherry Tart, 221
French dessert omelet, preparation of, 184
French Lemon Cake, 248
French Orange Rice Pudding, 180
French Prune Pudding, 178
Fresh Fig Mousse, 136
Fresh Fruits with Almond Jelly, 78
Fresh Fruits with Kirsch, 77
Fresh Lemon Tartlets, 223
Fresh Pineapple Cream, 84
Fried Bananas and Rum, 200
Fried Puff Balls, 202
Frittata(s), preparation of, 185
Frittata con le Mele, 186
Fritter(s), deep-frying, 198
Fritter Batter for Fruits, 198
Frosted Fruits, 20
Frozen Cranberry Cassis Mousse, 151
Frozen Grand Marnier Mousse, 154
Frozen Lemon Cream in Lemon Shells, 152
Frozen Lemon Soufflé, 151
Frozen Orange Meringues, 154
Frozen Pumpkin Mousse, 157
Frozen Raspberry Dessert, 158

Frozen Raspberry-Macaroon Mousse, 143
Frozen Raspberry Torte, 158
Frozen Strawberry Soufflé, 159
Fruit(s), handling of, 12
Fruit cornucopia, making, 20
Fruit-Filled Baked Omelet, 188
Fruit Loaf with Raspberry Sauce, 77
Fruit mixtures, preparation of, 74
Fruit Shortcake, 240
Fruit-Stuffed Melon, 81
Fruit Tarts, 216
Fruit Terrine with Almond Cream, 238
Fruitcake(s)
    with candied grapefruit shells, 240
    dark, 238
    Sienese, 240
Fruitcake with Candied Grapefruit Shells, 240
Fruits Beatrice, 147
Fruits Frais à la Gelée d'Amande, 78
Fruits Rafraîchis au Kirsch, 77
Fruits in Red Wine, 76
Fruits au Vin Rouge, 76
Fruits with Zabaglione, 74
Fudge, sauces, 271-72
Fujiyama I, II, 153

Galette aux Fraises, 256
Gâteau Bigarreau, 245
Gâteau Campagnard, 242
Gâteau au Citron, 248
Gâteau de Crêpes à la Normande, 192
Gâteau aux Fruits, 164
Gâteau de Fruits, 240
Gâteau Poire William, 253
Gâteau aux Pommes Lyonnais, 243
Gâteau des Pommes Reinettes, 166
Gelatin, preparation of, 110
Génoise, 279
Génoise aux Fraises Lucullus, 258
Génoise and Strawberries Lucullus, 258
Ginger
    Bavarian cream, 112
    charlottes, 127–28
    crêpes, 191, 194
    flan, 102
    gâteaux, torten, and fancy cakes, 246–47
    mousse, 136
    pudding, 173
    simple desserts, 24, 38, 40, 48, 57
    soufflé, 205
    tart, 226
Ginger Bavarian Cream, 112
Ginger Cake, Sticky, 247
Ginger Charlotte, Tangerine and, 127
Ginger Cheesecake, 246
Ginger Mousse, 136
Ginger and Orange Flan, 102
Ginger-Rum Bread and Butter Pudding, 173
Ginger Soufflé, 205

Gingered Apples, 24
Gingered Blueberry Compote, 34
Gingered Figs, 38
Gingered Pears, 48
Glazed Baked Peaches, 45
Glazed Oranges with Grand
  Marnier, 42
Gooseberry Fool, 92
Grand Marnier
  in crêpes, 192
  in frozen desserts, 153, 154
  with oranges, 42
  in sauces, 273
  in soufflé, 208
Grand Marnier Sauce, 273
Grape(s)
  in caramel syrup, 80
  preparation of, 14
  simple desserts, 39
  tarts, 222
Grape Tarts, 222
Grapefruit
  candied rind, 266
  preparation of. See Lemons
Grapes in Brandy, 39
Grapes in Caramel Syrup, Bananas
  and, 80
Grapes and Sour Cream, White, 39
Grated Apple Loaf, 167
Gratin de Fruits, 79

Hard Sauce, 272
Hazelnuss Auflauf, 207
Hazelnut(s)
  génoise, 279
  meringue, 282
  mousse, 137
  omelet soufflé, 187
  pudding, 174
  soufflés, 207
  sponge cake, 279
Hazelnut Mousse, 137
Hazelnut-Prune Soufflé, 207
Hazelnut Pudding, 174
Hazelnut Soufflé, 207
Honey
  simple desserts, 43, 47, 55, 61
  tartlets, 221
Honey-Baked Pears, 55
Hot Apple Cake with Caramel
  Sauce, 242
Hot Fudge Sauce, 271
Hot Pear Charlotte, 130
Hot Pear Tart, 229
Hot Prune Soufflé, 208
Hot Strawberry Sauce, 276

Individual Strawberry Charlottes,
  126

Jelly Cookies, 263
Jumbals, 263

Kaiser's Omelet, 188
Kaiserschmarrn, 188
Kirsch
  in Bavarian cream, 116

in bombe, 155
  with fruits, 77
  in simple desserts, 30, 32, 36, 64
Kirsch-Flamed Bananas, 32
Kiwi Fool, 93
Kiwi Mousse, 137
Kiwifruit
  fool, 93
  in fruit terrine, 238
  mousse, 137
  preparation of, 14
Kümmel, omelet, 186

Ladyfingers, 280
Langues de Chat, 264
Lemon(s)
  candied rind, 285
  charlottes, 121
  cream, 94
  crêpes, 194–95
  custards, 102, 108
  frozen desserts, 149, 151–52
  gâteaux, torten, and fancy cakes,
    247–49
  génoise, 279
  mousses, 137–38
  omelet soufflé, 187
  posset, 39
  preparation of, 14
  puddings, 173–74
  sauces, 274, 275
  snow, 93
  soufflés, 205, 207
  tarts and pies, 222–23
Lemon-Blueberry Bombe, 149
Lemon-Blueberry Charlotte, 121
Lemon Cake, French, 248
Lemon Cake with Yogurt, 249
Lemon Charlotte, 121
Lemon "Cheese," 138
Lemon Chess Pie, 222
Lemon Cream, 94
Lemon Cream in Lemon Shells,
  Frozen, 152
Lemon Cream Roll, 249
Lemon Crêpes, 194
Lemon Curd Tarts, 223
Lemon Dumplings, 174
Lemon-Flavored Caramel Custard,
  102
Lemon-Flavored Omelet Soufflé,
  187
Lemon Génoise, 279
Lemon, and Lime Rinds, Candied
  Orange, 285
Lemon-Macaroon Tart, 223
Lemon Mousse I, II, 137, 138
Lemon Posset, 39
Lemon Sauce, 275
Lemon Sauce, Apricot-, 274
Lemon Sherry Pudding with
  Caramel Nut Sauce, 173
Lemon Snow, 93
Lemon Soufflé, 205
Lemon Soufflé, Cold, 138
Lemon Soufflé, Frozen, 151
Lemon Soufflé with Pernod, 207

Lemon Soufflé Pie, Mace, 222
Lemon Soufflé with Strawberries
  and Raspberries, 207
Lemon Sponge Custard, 108
Lemon Supreme, 247
Lemon Tart, 248
Lemon Tartlets, Fresh, 223
Lemon Tea Cake, 249
Lime(s)
  candied rind, 285
  mousses, 138–39
  preparation of. See Lemons
  sauce, 43
  tarts and pies, 224
Lime Meringue Pie, 224
Lime Pie, Sour Cream, 224
Lime Rinds, Candied Orange,
  Lemon, and, 285
Lime Soufflé, 138
Lime Soufflé I, II, Cold, 139
Liqueur(s). See also individual
  liqueurs
  in hard sauce, 272
  in pastry cream, 282
  in pudding, 182
  in simple desserts, 35, 62
  in soufflé, 205
Liqueur-Flavored Pastry Cream, 282
Liqueur Soufflé, 205
Loganberry(ies), pudding, 164

Macarons de Monte Carlo, 261
Macaroons, 261
Mace Lemon Soufflé Pie, 222
Macédoine of Fruit I–IV, 75–76
Macédoine de Fruits I–III, 75–76
Macedonia di Frutta, 75
Macedonian Orange Cake, 250
Madeira Cake, 266
Madeleines, 265
Mandarin orange(s)
  bombe, 160
  charlotte, 128
  slices, 250
Mandarin Orange Bombe,
  Strawberry-, 160
Mandarin Orange and Ginger
  Charlotte, 128
Mandarin Slices, 250
Mango(es)
  with champagne, 39
  preparation of, 15
Mango Slices with Champagne, 39
Marlborough Pie, 218
Mélange de Fruits, 76
Melba Sauce, 276
Melon(s). See also Cantaloupe
  balls
    making, 16
    with raspberry sauce, 40
  as container, 16
  flowers, 16
  fruit-stuffed, 81
  mélange, 82
  mousse, 140
  preparation of, 15
  wedges, 15

Melon Balls with Raspberry Sauce, 40
Melon, Fruit-Stuffed, 81
Melon Mousse, 140
Melon, Orange, and Blueberry Mélange, 82
Melon de Scheherazade, 81
Meringue, 281
Meringue Cake with Peaches, 252
Meringue Mushrooms, 268
Meringue-Topped Apple Rice Pudding, 180
Meringue-Topped Bananas, 31
Michelangelo's Pumpkin, 239
Mincemeat, 175
Mincemeat Pudding, 175
Minted Baked Apples, 26
Minted Cantaloupe and Blueberries, 82
Mirabelle-Flavored Bavarian Cream, 114
Miveh Makhlout, 76
Mixed Fruit Bread Pudding, 164
Mixed Fruit Sundae, 148
Mixture of Fruits, 76
Mocha Pastry Cream, 282
Mold(s)
    lining
        with bread slices, 119
        with ice cream, 147
        with ladyfingers, 118
        with sponge rolls, 119
    pastry, preparation of, 213
    pie, 210
    pudding, 162
Molded Cream, 90
Molded Fruit Pudding I, II, 78
Montmartre, 255
Mousse(s), preparation of, 132–33
Mousse de Bananes, 136
Mousse au Cointreau, 140
Mousse aux Fraises, 143
Mousse aux Framboises, 143
Mousse Glacée Grand Marnier, 154
Mousse de Kiwi, 137
Mousse à l'Orange, 140
Mousse de Pommes à la Bénédictine, 135
Mousse aux Pommes Calvados, 134

Nectarine(s)
    coupe, 152
    preparation of, 17
    simple desserts, 40, 45
Nectarines and Brandy, 40
Nectarines Flambé, 40
Nectarines, Nut-Stuffed Peaches, Pears, or, 45
Neruppu Vazhai, 34
Nesselrode, 120
Normandy Apple Cake, 192
Normandy Apple Omelet, 186
Norwegian Cream, 108
Nut Butter Balls, 263
Nut Butter Cookies, 262
Nut-Stuffed Peaches, Pears, or Nectarines, 45

Nutted Génoise, 279
Nutted Meringue Layers, 282
Nutted Omelet Soufflé, 187
Nutted Soufflé, 205
Nutted Sponge Cake, 279

Omelet
    dessert, preparation of, 184
    souffléed, preparation of, 185
Omelet surprise, preparation of, 185
Omelette Normande, 186
Omelette Soufflée, 187
Omelette en Surprise, 187
Omelette en Surprise Valberge, 188
Orange(s). See also Mandarin orange(s)
    Bavarian cream, 113
    candied rind, 267, 284–85
    chantillies, 82, 94
    chocolate-coated, 267
    compote, 82
    custards, 103, 105
    dessert omelets, 187, 188
    flan, 102
    frozen desserts, 148, 153–54
    gâteaux, torten, and fancy cakes, 250–52
    génoise, 279
    mélange, 82
    mousses, 140
    preparation of. See Lemons
    puddings, 177, 180, 181
    sauces, 274, 275
    simple desserts, 40–42
    slices, 17
    soufflés, 205, 208
    tarts and pies, 224–25, 233
    wedges, 17
Orange-Apricot Chantilly, 82
Orange-Apricot Sauce, 274
Orange Bavarian Cream, 113
Orange, and Blueberry Mélange, Melon, 82
Orange Cake, 250
Orange Cake, Macedonian, 250
Orange Cake, Victorian, 251
Orange Caramel Custard, 103
Orange Chantilly, 94
Orange Compote, Chestnut and, 82
Orange Custard, 105
Orange Flan, Ginger and, 102
Orange-Flavored Rice Pudding, 181
Orange Génoise, 279
Orange-Glazed Bananas, 34
Orange, Lemon, and Lime Rinds, Candied, 285
Orange Meringue Tart, 225
Orange Meringues, Frozen, 154
Orange Mousse, 140
Orange Mousse with Cointreau, 140
Orange Omelet Soufflé, 187
Orange Peel I, II, Candied, 284
Orange Peel, Chocolate-Coated, 267
Orange Pie, Pumpkin and, 233
Orange and Pistachio Ice Cream Mold, 148
Orange Poppyseed Cake, 252

Orange Pots de Crème, 105
Orange Pudding, Almond-, 177
Orange Rice Pudding, French, 180
Orange Sauce, Eunice's Walnut-, 275
Orange Shells Glacé, 154
Orange Sherbet with Oranges and Chocolate Sauce, 153
Orange Slices, Candied, 267
Orange Slices with Rosemary Syrup, 42
Orange Soufflé, 205
Orange Tart I, II, 224
Orange Torte, 251
Orange-Walnut Bombe, 153
Oranges, Buttered, 42
Oranges in Caramel, 41
Oranges and Chocolate Sauce, Orange Sherbet with, 153
Oranges with Ginger and White Wine, 40
Oranges Glacées au Grand Marnier, 42
Oranges with Grand Marnier, Glazed, 42
Oranges in Red Wine, 41
Oranges with Sabayon Sauce, Baked, 42

Pain de Pommes Râpées, 167
Palacsintak Barackízzel, 193
Palmiers, 265
Pamelas, 266
Paner à l'Anglaise, 199
Panforte, 240
Papaya(s)
    baked, 43
    custard, 106
    mélange, 85
    preparation of, 17
Papaya Custard, 106
Papaya Mélange, Apple, Pineapple, and, 85
Paris-Brest aux Framboises, 255
Pastry
    dorure, 213
    flaky
        preparation of, 211
        recipes for, 214–15
    puff
        preparation of, 212
        recipe for, 215
        rolling, 213
    sandtorte
        preparation of, 211
        recipe for, 215
Pastry Cream, 282
Pastry-Wrapped Pears, 227
Pâte Brisée I, II, 214, 215
Pâte à Choux, 280
Pâte Feuilletée, 215
Pâte à Frire pour Beignets de Fruits, 198
Pâte à Meringue, 281
Pâte Sablée, 215
Pavé aux Framboises, Le, 158
Pavlova, 238

Peach(es)
  charlotte, 122
  cream, 94
  frozen desserts, 155
  gâteaux, torten, and fancy cakes, 238, 252
  mousse, 141
  preparation of. See Nectarines
  puddings, 164, 177
  simple desserts, 43–45
  tarts and pies, 225–26
  with Zabaglione, 74
Peach and Blueberry Mousse, 141
Peach Charlotte, 122
Peach Cream, 94
Peach Cream Pie, 226
Peach Custard Tart, 226
Peach and Kirsch Bombe, 155
Peach Melba, 155
Peach Pie with Almonds, Deep-Dish, 225
Peach Pudding, Steamed, 177
Peach-Raspberry Bombe, 155
Peaches Farmer-Style, 43
Peaches with Fluffy Sabayon Sauce, 44
Peaches, Glazed Baked, 45
Peaches with Honey-Lime Sauce, 43
Peaches, Meringue Cake with, 252
Peaches I, II, Stuffed, 44
Peaches in Orange Liqueur, 45
Peaches, Pears, or Nectarines, Nut-Stuffed, 45
Peaches in White or Red Wine, 43
Pear(s). See also Cactus pear(s), Prickly pears
  braised, 83
  charlottes, 122, 130
  compote, 83
  crêpes, 195–96
  flambé, 83
  frozen desserts, 156
  gâteaux, torten, and fancy cakes, 252–53
  mousses, 141
  poached, 106
  preparation of, 17
  pudding, 181
  purée, 95
  Rosamond, 84
  simple desserts, 45–56
  snow, 94
  soufflé, 208
  tarts and pies, 219, 226–29
  in wine, 84
  with Zabaglione, 47, 74
Pear and Apple Compote, 83
Pear Bombe, Raspberry and, 156
Pear Cake, 228
Pear Charlotte, Hot, 130
Pear Charlotte with Raspberry Sauce I, II, 122
Pear and Chocolate Cake, 253
Pear and Currant Mousses, 141
Pear Flan, 229
Pear and Fudge Sauce Sundaes, 156
Pear and Ginger Tart, 226

Pear Küchen, 252
Pear and Orange Sherbet Sundae, 156
Pear Pie, Almond, 228
Pear Purée, 95
Pear Snow, 94
Pear Soufflé, 208
Pear Tart, 227
Pear Tart, Hot, 229
Pear Tart with Hot Chocolate Sauce, 226
Pear Tart, Upside-Down, 228
Pears, Almond-Baked, 54
Pears, Baked, 54
Pears Bordeaux-Style, 46
Pears with Brandy, Baked, 55
Pears Bresse-Style, Braised, 83
Pears Burgundy-Style, 46
Pears in Caramel Syrup, 48
Pears, Cardamom-Flavored, 55
Pears with Chestnuts, Poached, 50
Pears, Chilled Glazed, 47
Pears in Cider, 46
Pears in Cointreau, 45
Pears I, II, Crêpes with, 195, 196
Pears with Currant Jelly, 46
Pears with Custard, Poached, 106
Pears Flambé, Apples and, 83
Pears Flambé, Poached, 52
Pears with Ginger, 48
Pears, Gingered, 48
Pears Grand Vefour, Poached, 51
Pears, Honey-Baked, 55
Pears Little Flower, 53
Pears with Maple Nut Sauce, Baked, 56
Pears Mary Garden, Poached, 50
Pears with Meringue and Chocolate Sauce, 56
Pears Milan-Style, Stuffed, 54
Pears, or Nectarines, Nut-Stuffed Peaches, 45
Pears in Orange Sabayon Sauce, 49
Pears, Pastry-Wrapped, 227
Pears in Pepper and Honey Syrup, 47
Pears in Phyllo Dough, Apples or, 219
Pears and Plums in Wine, 84
Pears Poached in Port with Praline, 51
Pears in Port, 46
Pears with Raspberry Sauce, 49
Pear with Raspberry Sauce, Almond-Filled, 53
Pears with Raspberry Sauce, Sautéed, 48
Pears in Red Wine, 46
Pears, Rice Pudding with, 181
Pears Rosamond, 84
Pears Savoyard, Baked, 56
Pears Stuffed with Amaretti, 54
Pears Stuffed with Gorgonzola I–III, 52
Pears Susanna, 50
Pears, Vermouth-Glazed, 56
Pears with Wine, 46

Pears with Wine and Basil, Poached, 46
Pears Wine Growers–Style, 49
Pears in Zabaglione, 47
Pecan(s)
  cookies, 262, 263
  génoise, 279
  sauce, 173
  stuffing, 45
Pêches à la Fermière, 43
Pêches Melba, 155
Pêches au Sabayon Mousseline, 44
Pere alla Gelatina di Frutta, 46
Pere Ripiene alla Gorgonzola I–III, 52
Pere Ripiene alla Milanese, 54
Pere al Vino, 46
Pernod
  with lemon soufflé, 207
  with pineapple, 57
Persian Fruit Mélange, 76
Pesche Ripiene I, II, 44
Phyllo dough
  with apples or pears, 219
  triangles, 231
Pickled Strawberries, 63
Pie(s)
  shells, baking, 213
  two-crust, preparation of, 211
Piñas Natillas, 59
Pine Nut, Almond, and Berry Torte, 241
Pineapple(s)
  baskets, 86
  Bavarian creams, 113–14
  cake, 253
  charlotte, 124
  as container, 19
  cream, 84
  Creole-style, 85
  flan, 103
  fool, 95
  fritters, 201
  frozen desserts, 150, 152, 156–57
  mélange, 85
  peeling, 17–18
  pudding, 178
  simple desserts, 57–59
  slices, 19
  surprise, 85
  tarts and pies, 229–30
  wedges, 17
Pineapple, Baked, 59
Pineapple Baskets, 86
Pineapple Bavarian Cream, 113
Pineapple Bavarian Cream Georgette, 114
Pineapple Bombe, Tangerine and, 152
Pineapple, Broiled, 58
Pineapple Charlotte, Raspberry and, 124
Pineapple, Coffee Ice Cream with, 157
Pineapple Cream Cake, 253
Pineapple Cream, Fresh, 84
Pineapple Flambé, 58

Pineapple Flan, Puerto Rican, 103
Pineapple Fool, 95
Pineapple Fritters, 201
Pineapple with Gingered Yogurt
   Sauce, 57
Pineapple Ice Cream Mold, 156
Pineapple in Orange Syrup, 58
Pineapple, and Papaya Mélange,
   Apple, 85
Pineapple in Pernod, 57
Pineapple Pudding, 178
Pineapple with Rum, 58
Pineapple with Rum Cream, 57
Pineapple in Rum Custard, 57
Pineapple, Spiced Cherries with, 80
Pineapple and Strawberries Creole-
   Style, 85
Pineapple Sundaes, Cherry and, 150
Pineapple Surprise, 85
Pineapple Tart I, II, 229, 230
Pineapple and Vanilla Bombe, 156
Piquenchâgne, 228
Pistachio(s)
   custard, 106
   ice cream mold, 148
   with strawberries, 63
Pistachio Cream Custard with
   Custard and Strawberry Sauce,
   106
Platters, fruit and cheese, 22
Plum(s)
   preparation of, 19
   puddings, 167, 177
   simple desserts, 59–60
   tarts and pies, 230–31
   torte, 254
   in wine, 84
Plum Cobbler, 230
Plum Conde, 177
Plum Phyllo Triangles, 231
Plum Pudding, 176
Plum Tart, 230
Plum Toast, 60
Plum Torte, Purple, 254
Plums and Port, 59
Plums Swedish-Style, 59
Plums in Wine, Pears and, 84
Poached Figs with Chartreuse-
   Flavored Cheese, 38
Poached Pears with Chestnuts, 50
Poached Pears with Custard, 106
Poached Pears Flambé, 52
Poached Pears Grand Vefour, 51
Poached Pears Mary Garden, 50
Poached Pears with Wine and Basil,
   46
Poaching
   with vanilla, 286
   with wine, 286
Poires Belle Angevine, 46
Poires Belle Hélène, 156
Poires Belles Dijonnaises, 156
Poires à la Bordelaise, 46
Poires Bourguignon, 46
Poires Braisée à la Bressane, 83
Poires à la Cardinale, 49
Poires en Cointreau, 45

Poires Cuites à la Savoyarde, 56
Poires Fioretta, 53
Poires Geraldine Farrar, 156
Poires Glacées, 47
Poires à l'Impériale, 181
Poires à la Joinville, 106
Poires Pralinées au Porto Blanc, 51
Poires Rosemond, 84
Poires au Sirop, 47
Poires Susanne, 50
Poires Vefour, 51
Poires à la Vigneronne, 49
Pommes Bourgeoises I, II, 29
Pommes à la Neige, 90
Pommes et Poires Flambées, 83
Pommes au Riz Meringuées, 180
Port
   with prune fool, 96
   in simple desserts, 37, 51, 59
Pots de Crème aux Fraises, 107
Pouding à la Cerise Française, 170
Pouding aux Liqueurs, 182
Pouding aux Noisettes, 174
Pouding de Riz à l'Orange, 180
Praline
   Bavarian cream, 114
   génoise, 280
   powder, 284
   simple desserts, 24, 51
   sponge cake, 279
Praline Bavarian Cream, 114
Praline/Nougat Génoise, 280
Praline/Nougat Powder, 284
Praline/Nougat Sponge Cake, 279
Prickly pears, preparation of, 19
Provençal Prune Fritters, 201
Prune(s)
   compote, 86
   fool, 96
   fritters, 201
   preparation of, 19
   pudding, 178
   sauce, 178
   soufflés, 207–8
   tarts and pies, 217, 231–32
   torte, 254
   whip, 95
Prune and Apple Compote, 86
Prune, and Armagnac Tart, Apple,
   217
Prune Filling, 231
Prune Fool with Port Wine, 96
Prune Fritters, Provençal, 201
Prune Pudding, French, 178
Prune Soufflé, Hazelnut-, 207
Prune Soufflé, Hot, 208
Prune Tart with Walnut Dough, 232
Prune Torte, 254
Prune Whip, 95
Prunelle, in Sauce Riche, 274
Prunes Suédoise, 59
Pudding(s)
   curing, 163
   steaming, 162–63
   vanilla and chocolate, 163
Pudding with Liquors, 182
Puerto Rican Pineapple Flan, 103

Puff Pastry, 215
Pumpkin
   charlotte, 123
   crème brûlée, 105
   flans, 104
   fritters, 201
   mousses, 142, 157
   tarts and pies, 232–33
Pumpkin and Bourbon-Flavored
   Crème Brûlée, 105
Pumpkin Charlotte, 123
Pumpkin Flan, 104
Pumpkin Flan, Rum-Flavored, 104
Pumpkin Fritters, 201
Pumpkin Mousse, Frozen, 157
Pumpkin Mousse, Rum, 142
Pumpkin and Orange Pie, 233
Pumpkin Pie, 232
Purée de Pommes au Citron, 24
Purple Plum Torte, 254

Quiche aux Pêches, 226
Quick Butter Cream, 283
Quince(s)
   preparation of. See Apples
   simple desserts, 60
Quince, Baked, 60
Quince Compote, 60

Raisin(s)
   omelet, 188
   preparation of, 19
Raspberry(ies)
   Bavarian cream, 115
   charlottes, 124
   Coeur à la Crème, 96
   cream, 36, 63, 126
   frozen desserts, 155, 156, 158
   gâteaux, torten, and fancy cakes,
      255–56
   mousses, 143
   parfait, 96
   preparation of, 19
   pudding, 164
   purée, 283
   sauces, 40, 48, 53, 62, 122, 150, 276
   simple desserts, 36, 60–61, 63
   soufflé, 207
   tarts and pies, 233–34
   whip, 95
Raspberries Hamilton, 61
Raspberries in Sherry Cream, 60
Raspberries, Striped Bavarian
   Cream with, 115
Raspberry-Almond Sauce, 276
Raspberry Bombe, 158
Raspberry Bombe, Peach-, 155
Raspberry Butter Cream Cake, 256
Raspberry Chiffon Pie, 234
Raspberry Coeur à la Crème, 96
Raspberry Cream, 126
Raspberry Cream Cake, 255
Raspberry Cream Tart, 233
Raspberry Dessert, Frozen, 158
Raspberry-Macaroon Mousse,
   Frozen, 143
Raspberry Malakoff, 124

Raspberry Mousse, 143
Raspberry Parfait, 96
Raspberry and Pear Bombe, 156
Raspberry and Pineapple Charlotte, 124
Raspberry Purée, 283
Raspberry Sauce, 276
Raspberry-Strawberry Cream Torte, 255
Raspberry-Strawberry Sauce, 276
Raspberry Torte, Frozen, 158
Raspberry Whip, 95
Rhubarb
  charlotte, 125
  fool, 97
  pie, 233
  preparation of, 19
  puddings, 168, 179
Rhubarb Charlotte, 125
Rhubarb Custard Pie, 233
Rhubarb Fool, 97
Rhubarb-Strawberry Crumble, 179
Rice
  croquettes, 200
  puddings, 162, 172, 179–82
Rice and Apple Caramel Custard, 179
Rice Pudding with Pears, 181
Riz à la Maltaise, 181
Rolling pins, 210
Rote Grütze I, II, 78
Royal Icing, 283
Rum
  in bombe, 149
  in coupe, 157
  in flan, 104
  with fried bananas, 200
  in mousses, 142
  in omelet soufflé, 187
  in pastry cream, 282
  with pineapple, 156
  in pudding, 173
  in sauces, 194, 271
  in simple desserts, 26, 33, 57, 58, 62
  in Viennese Food for the Gods, 98
Rum and Chocolate Fruit Bombe, 149
Rum-Flavored Pastry Cream, 282
Rum-Flavored Pumpkin Flan, 104
Rum Pumpkin Mousse, 142

Sabayon Sauce, 272
Sables, 264
Salzburg Omelet Soufflé, 187
Salzburger Nockerln, 187
Sand Cookies, 264
Sandtorte Pastry, 215
Sauce Cardinale, 276
Sauce Mousseline, 272
Sauce Parisienne, 273
Sauce Riche, 274
Sauce à la Ritz, 273
Sauce Vanille, 273
Sautéed Bananas, 32
Sautéed Pears with Raspberry Sauce, 48

Schwarzwalder Kirsch Torte, 246
Scrambled Baked Apples, 25
Sformata Dolce Fantasia, 149
Shaved Chocolate, 108
Sherried Watermelon, 64
Sherry
  in cream, 60
  in pudding, 173
  with watermelon, 64
  in whipped cream, 81
Shortbread, 264
Shortcake Cookies, 262
Sienese Christmas Fruitcake, 240
Sloe gin, in Sauce Riche, 274
Snow(s), preparation of, 88
Snowdon Pudding, 174
Soufflé(s), preparation of, 204–5
Soufflé dishes
  collaring, 132
  pastry, 132
  preparation of, 204
Soufflé aux Fraises Chambord, 208
Soufflé Grand Marnier in Orange Cases, 208
Soufflé Hilda, 207
Soufflé Palmyra, 205
Soufflé aux Poires, 208
Soufflé shell, chocolate, 133
Soufflé à la Vanille, 205
Souffléed omelet, preparation of, 185
Soupirs de Nonne, 202
Sour Cream Lime Pie, 224
Spanish Wind Torte, 236
Spiced Apple Pudding, 167
Spiced Cherries with Pineapple, 80
Sponge Cake, 278
Spring Cup, 107
Spun Sugar, 285
Starfruit, preparation of. See Carambola
Steamed Fig Pudding, 172
Steamed Peach Pudding, 177
Sticky Ginger Cake, 247
Strawberry(ies)
  Bavarian creams, 115–16
  charlottes, 126–27
  cream, 97
  Creole-style, 85
  custard, 107
  frozen desserts, 148, 159–60
  gâteaux, torten, and fancy cakes, 238, 241, 255–58
  mélange, 86
  mousses, 143–44
  preparation of, 19
  puddings, 164, 179, 182
  Romanoff I, II, 98
  sauces, 273, 276
  simple desserts, 61–64
  soufflés, 207, 208
  Spring Cup, 107
  tarts and pies, 234
  Viennese Food for the Gods, 98
  whip, 97
Strawberries, Bavarian Cream with Kirsch and, 116

Strawberries, Coffee Ice Cream, Raspberry Sauce, and, 160
Strawberries Cordon Bleu I, II, 62
Strawberries Creole-Style, Pineapple and, 85
Strawberries, Custard with, 107
Strawberries Jubilee, 64
Strawberries with Lemon, 61
Strawberries in Liqueur, 62
Strawberries Lucullus, Génoise and, 258
Strawberries, Pickled, 63
Strawberries and Pistachios, 63
Strawberries in Raspberry Cream, 63
Strawberries with Raspberry Sauce, 62
Strawberries Romanoff I, II, 98
Strawberries in Rum Custard, 62
Strawberries with Vinegar, 63
Strawberry Bavarian Cream I, II, 115, 116
Strawberry Cake, 256
Strawberry Charlotte, 127
Strawberry Charlotte Malakoff, 126
Strawberry Charlottes, Individual, 126
Strawberry Cheesecake, 258
Strawberry Cream, 97
Strawberry Cream Cake, 258
Strawberry Cream Torte, Raspberry-, 255
Strawberry Crumble, Rhubarb-, 179
Strawberry–Mandarin Orange Bombe, 160
Strawberry Mousse I–III, 143–44
Strawberry and Orange Sherbet Sundaes, 159
Strawberry Pastry Boats, 234
Strawberry Rice Romanoff, 182
Strawberry Sauce, 276
Strawberry Sauce, Hot, 276
Strawberry Sauce, Raspberry-, 276
Strawberry Soufflé Chambord, 208
Strawberry Soufflé, Frozen, 159
Strawberry Sponge Layers, 257
Strawberry Sponge Roll, 257
Strawberry Tart, 234
Strawberry-Walnut Cream Cake, 257
Strawberry Whip, 97
Striped Bavarian Cream with Raspberries, 115
Stuffed Peaches I, II, 44
Stuffed Pears Milan-Style, 54
Sugar, Spun, 285
Summer Pudding I, II, 164
Sweet Dessert Crêpes, 191
Swiss Pudding, 165

Tangerine(s)
  bombe, 152
  charlottes, 127, 128
  crêpes, 195
  in kirsch, 64
  preparation of, 19
Tangerine, Crêpes with, 195

Tangerine and Ginger Charlotte, 127
Tangerine and Pineapple Bombe, 152
Tangerines, Charlotte with, 128
Tangerines in Kirsch, 64
Tarte de Cambrai, 227
Tarte aux Cerises, 221
Tarte Chaude aux Poires, La, 229
Tarte Citron, 248
Tarte Feuilletée à l'Ananas, 230
Tarte Meringue à l'Orange, 225
Tarte aux Oranges I, II, 224
Tarte aux Pommes I, II, 217, 218
Tarte Tatin, 218
Tarts, open, preparation of, 210
Torta alla Crema di Fragole, 258
Torta di Mele, 242
Tourtière de Quercy, 217
Turnovers, preparation of, 214
Tyrolean Rice Cream with Apricot Sauce, 180

Upside-Down Pear Tart, 228

Vacherin, 236
Vanilla Bavarian Cream, 111

Vanilla Custard Sauce, 273
Vanilla Omelet Soufflé, 187
Vanilla-Poached Fruits, 286
Vanilla Pudding, 282
Vanilla Soufflé, 205
Veiled Country Lass I–III, 167–68
Vermouth-Glazed Pears, 56
Victorian Orange Cake, 251
Viennese Food for the Gods, 98
Viennese Fruit Tart, 216

Walnut(s)
  cake, 257
  cookies, 262, 263, 264
  cream, 239
  dough, 232
  génoise, 279
  meringue, 282
  omelet soufflé, 187
  sauces, 274, 275
  sponge cake, 279
  in whipped cream, 81
Walnut Bombe, Orange-, 153
Walnut Butter Crisps, 264
Walnut Cream, 239
Walnut Cream Cake, Strawberry-, 257

Walnut Dough, 232
Walnut-Orange Sauce, Eunice's, 275
Walnut Sauce, Apricot-, 274
Walnuts in Sherried Whipped Cream, Figs, Dates, and, 81
Warm Fruit Compote, 79
Water baths, 100
Watermelon, Sherried, 64
Whip(s), preparation of, 88
Whipped cream, preparation of, 111
White Grapes and Sour Cream, 39
Wiener Götterspeise, 98
Wine-Poached Fruits, 286
Wined Watermelon, 64

Yogurt
  dressing, 270
  with lemon cake, 249
  sauce, 57
Yogurt Dressing for Fruits, 270

Zabaglione
  with fruits, 74
  with pears, 47
  sauce, 272
Zuccotto alla Michelangelo, 239